IMPLEMENTING YOUR STRATEGIC PLAN

IMPLEMENTING YOUR STRATEGIC PLAN

How to Turn "Intent" Into Effective Action for Sustainable Change

C. Davis Fogg

Contents

List of Exhibits

PART I

Understanding Strategic Change

The Strategic Change Process

It's almost trite to observe that we are assaulted by change every day.

But it's true. Yesterday's generation of leaders would blanch at what we accept as a way of life: accelerating change in our markets and customer needs, increasing competitive pressure, shortened product life cycles, increasing foreign competition, and new innovative technologies. The time between the introduction of new personal computer models, for example, has fallen from two years in the early 1980s to months now, while computation speeds and new features increase at a dizzying rate.

Such a pace demands that organizations quickly detect and respond to shifting needs in the outside world. Just plain keeping your head above water requires fast, imaginative anticipation of market changes before the competition has a chance to respond first.

Truly innovative organizations go way beyond merely fulfilling customer demands or countering the actions of the competition. They create demand by offering the customer something new and highly inventive, setting the pace for their industries. They are the big winners, the companies that control their markets, like Intel and Hewlett-Packard.

Using its formidable experience in computers, scientific instruments, and recorders, Hewlett-Packard set out to dominate the personal computer printer business from the beginning. To do that, HP developed technologies to produce printers in virtually every price/performance bracket. It forced prices down with a cost-driven strategy fueled by the volume of the mass markets it developed. The company's strategies effectively kept the Japanese, masters of using price to gain market share, at bay.

The list of such innovative companies is, fortunately for America, long—including Intel, Microsoft, 3M, Dell, Compaq, Netscape, MCI, GE, Coca Cola, Merck, Pfizer, Procter & Gamble, Disney, and Corning. The list of those that stumbled is, unfortunately, equally long—among them, GM, Kodak, Apple Computer, IBM, Digital Equipment, and Wang.

What's the difference between the winners and the losers? The winners are constantly scanning the outside world and their markets. They have strong leadership, core competencies with high leverage in the market, talented people in depth, high performance standards, a will to dominate their markets, and the flexibility and mentality to deal with change.

In addition, I have found that long-term strategic winners faithfully and artfully practice 18 keys to strategy implementation. The bulk of this book is a guide to applying those keys.

In this chapter, I will:

- Set the stage for strategy implementation by first reviewing the role of strategic planning in change
- Define and provide a brief overview of the 18 keys to strategy implementation
- Describe the four-phase strategic change process

The Strategic Plan: A Precondition for Change

The strategic plan is the road map for impelling continuous change in your organization and ensuring your future. It guides your change effort and your business. It is also the wedge that you drive between believers in change and the infidels in your organization who oppose it. The plan is not a one-shot effort to "change direction and get us going." It is an entire system that is geared toward *continuously* detecting changes in the outside world, deciding how to deal with them, and translating these needed changes into programs that produce desired results. The system goes on day in and day out, year in and year out.[1]

This book assumes that you have or will develop a realistic strategic plan and a process for continuously reshaping it. Your plan must have the following three critical components:

1. A direction statement
2. Strategic objectives
3. Strategic priority issues

The Direction Statement

The organization's direction should be established by a thoughtful, fact-based strategic planning process. That process yields planning's seminal document, the direction statement. It is your constitution.

The metaphor is appropriate. The direction statement, like the Constitution, guides the institution's actions and thinking. Crafted with care

[1] See C. Davis Fogg, *Team-Based Strategic Planning* (New York: AMACOM, 1994).

by management, it is so fundamentally sound that changes (amendments) are made only with considerable debate and thought.

The direction statement is a short one- or two-page document that, combined with your strategic objectives, contains all you need to direct the organization's strategic change actions for the foreseeable future. The direction statement, shown in the accompanying exhibit, contains:

- *Mission:* Your purpose in life; your reason for being
- *Vision:* Where you want to be in the future—what kind of business you want to become
- *Business definition:* Definition of the current and future business on important dimensions such as products, services, geography, distribution, technology, customers, and markets
- *Competitive advantages:* Those customer needs that you will meet better than the competition
- *Core competencies:* Those competencies, tangible and intangible, that you will leverage to gain a competitive advantage and fulfill your vision
- *Values/beliefs:* The driving values and beliefs that define your culture—which, in turn, is the culture that you believe will produce the market performance that you desire

Over time, it is the duty of the top management team to turn each word, concept, and phrase in the statement into action through pro-

Direction Statement Contents

▼ **Mission:** Your fundamental purpose in life. Why you exist.

▼ **Vision:** Your view for the future. Where you want to be, what you want to become in the future.

▼ **Business definition:** How you define the boundaries of your business. Usually expressed in terms of markets, customers, products, services, geography, technology, and distribution. Anyone should be able to read your definition and know exactly where you're headed.

▼ **Competitive advantages:** The key customer needs that you will meet better than the competition.

▼ **Core competencies:** The competencies—the key systems, targeted assets, intellectual prowess, programs, or skills—that will allow you to continue to enhance your competitive advantage.

▼ **Values/beliefs:** The handful of values and beliefs that will govern your behaviors inside as you build the company, select directors, and train people and that support your competitive advantage and the needs of your employees and shareholders.

grams and strategic moves such as acquisitions, divestitures, delegated departmental objectives, policies, and procedures.

The Direction Statement and the Change Process

For it to drive the change process, the organization's direction must be initially and frequently communicated to employees to help them align their efforts with it. The direction statement guides such actions as:

- *Decision making*—ensuring that decisions covering the allocation of resources, alternative investments, and arbitration of investment, directional, or spending disputes conform with corporate direction
- *Staffing*—so that hiring, firing, and succession planning result in an organization that reflects the needed skills and values
- *Task alignment*—so that departmental and lower-level tasks are in sync with corporate intent
- *Public relations*—ensuring that communications with stockholders, the investment community, the industry, potential employees, and the general public inform accurately, help increase the stock price and shareholder value, and attract the best employees
- *Maintaining strategic focus*—keeping the organization on track by regularly reviewing the direction statement word by word, concept by concept, and by taking corrective action when necessary

Strategic Objectives

Strategic objectives allow you to measure how you are performing on the key dimensions of the direction statement. They are the scorecard that measures your success in fulfilling your intent on items such as profitability, shareholder value, market position, quality, service, and innovation.

Strategic Priority Issues

If the direction statement is the seminal instrument of direction, strategic priority issues are your primary instruments of action. They decree your urgent marching orders, your absolute "must-dos." When fleshed out, heavily resourced, and turned into actions, this handful of broad issues will lead you toward your envisioned future. They are usually competitive issues but often include "fix-the-ship" and internal changes needed to support competitive strategy. Common issues are cost, service, new markets and products, geographic expansion, organization, and information systems.

Successful strategic plan implementation hinges on turning priority issues into action plans and delegating them effectively to teams or functional departments. How to do this is covered in depth in Part II (see Key 2, "Turn Strategic Priority Issues Into Assigned, Measurable Actions").

Desire

Any plan—no matter how good, how in tune with market direction, and how penetrating its nascent strategy—is worthless unless the CEO and the rest of the top management team have a burning desire to make it happen at all reasonable and ethical costs. They must be willing to bear the pain of implementation. They must be willing to put an organization under stress and sometimes make tough decisions that will cause others pain. They need to go into the process recognizing that there will be several years of some degree of organizational turmoil. They must take risks.

As they become adept at driving the strategic change process, the top team's work habits will change. They will focus less on day-to-day matters and much more on helping people and teams accomplish strategic programs. They will concentrate on getting the organization "right" and especially reviewing and judging the plans delegated throughout the organization. They may have to retrain themselves in new techniques such as team management and process redesign. They may have to transform themselves through tough, introspective team building.

In short, the price of strategic progress is a different job description and a different managerial pattern for the top team.

If desire doesn't burn in the hearts of the top-team members, don't start down the path of implementation. Stay where you are until you can change the team. A partially or badly implemented plan changes a lot of things in the organization—but only temporarily. It also creates chaos and cynicism in the organization that will make a second change effort doubly difficult.

The 18 Keys to Plan Implementation

Although necessary, a strategic plan and top management desire are not sufficient to make change happen. Success lies in implementation.

There are 18 keys to implementation that, if well executed, almost guarantee that you will make significant progress in realizing a well-crafted plan. If ignored, you leave success to chance. These keys, which guide the development and execution of the strategic plan tasks, fall into five broad categories:

1. Setting accountability
2. Enabling and aligning action
3. Fixing the organization
4. Providing an environment in which people can excel
5. Judging and rewarding

The keys (shown schematically in the accompanying exhibit) are summarized below and explored in depth in Part II.

---

1. *Setting Accountability*

Key 1: Develop an accountability system. Design an accountability system that aligns action throughout the organization with the corporate plan and develops interlocking scorecards that hold the top team, functional departments, teams addressing strategic priority issues (program teams), and individuals accountable for measurable objectives. Such a system identifies, coordinates, and "interlocks" interfunctional tasks needed to execute the plan. It includes both strategic and operational tasks and ties in to budgeting, compensation, and strategic and operating plan review systems.

Key 2: Turn strategic priority issues into assigned, measurable action plans. Translate your major plan strategic priority issues, those broad major issues such as geographic expansion or new-product development, into detailed action plans. Set objectives for each strategy and decide who must do what, when to accomplish them. Note in detail the gain and cost for each action and estimate critical skills needed. This key sets the stage for resource allocation and accountability setting.

Key 3: Embed departmental planning. The functional departments are unquestionably a critical key to strategic success. They alone have the dollars, skills, and managerial resources to execute the plan. They balance strategic with operating efforts. It is important that they develop an interlocking scorecard that embraces (1) corporate strategic issues delegated to the department for execution, (2) departmental strategic, operating and infrastructure issues, (3) strategic team responsibilities, and (4) work the department owes others and the work others owe the department.

Key 4: Negotiate individual accountabilities. Develop an individual performance management system that embraces all of an

(continues)

The 18 Keys to Strategy Implementation

An Implementation Plan

18

1 Setting accountability

Key 1: Develop an accountability system.
Key 2: Turn strategic priority issues into assigned, measurable action plans.
Key 3: Embed departmental planning.
Key 4: Negotiate individual account-abilities.

2 Fixing the organization

Key 5: Change the organization structure—fast.
Key 6: Change the people—fast.
Key 7: Foster creative leadership and mental toughness.
Key 8: Remove resistance.
Key 9: Use teams (appropriately).

3 Enabling and aligning

Key 10: Define the future culture.
Key 11: Allocate resources effectively, putting your money and people where your future is.
Key 12: Align your organization's work with the plan—from top to bottom.

4 Providing an environment in which people can excel

Key 13: Empower execution.
Key 14: Select, train, and develop for the future—now.
Key 15: Fix broken core processes.
Key 16: Communicate to everyone, all the time.

5 Judging and rewarding

Key 17: Review performance.
Key 18: Reward strategic results.

individual's objectives in the areas of (1) the day-to-day job, (2) strategic team participation, (3) delegated department-level issues, (4) personal development, and (5) personal values, behaviors, and competencies.

2. *Fixing the Organization*

Key 5: Change the organization structure—fast. Make sure that your organization's structure follows strategy. If it doesn't, change it. Whatever the change—be it simple like adding a marketing department or complex like breaking the organization into multiple business units—do it quickly. Define the people competencies and skills that you'll need in the future.

Key 6: Change the people—fast. Put people with the skills you really need in the tough jobs. If you don't have such people, get them. Remove people who can't do the job from the line of fire or the company. People are one of the most important keys to successful implementation. Make needed changes quickly, without wasting any time.

Key 7: Foster creative leadership and mental toughness. Without leaders, forget implementing anything. Strategic change is risky, costly, and resisted by most organizations. Only strong leadership can pull it off.

Leadership means setting strategic direction throughout the organization and motivating the organization to follow. It means continuously reinforcing and resetting direction. Toughness means making quick, timely, and often risky calls on the difficult tasks—assigning and replacing people, cleansing or writing off businesses or products, cutting costs, making acquisitions and organization changes, and undertaking external ventures.

Key 8: Remove resistance. Identify and quickly remove the inevitable resisters, those people who just won't get with the program as well as those who openly fight it. They can be up to one-third of your workforce and have the power to derail expected progress. Seek out and streamline or remove internal policies, procedures, systems, and processes that inhibit quick plan action.

Key 9: Use teams (appropriately). Only teams manage complex tasks well. Use cross-functional teams to execute complex cross-functional projects. But don't get "teamitis," the unfortunate propensity to see teams as the solution to every execution problem. Manage teams well, from the top down. They require a lot of training and nurturing.

Make sure that the top team has its teamwork act together first.

Its members are often the first to preach teamwork and the last to practice it.

3. *Enabling and Aligning Action*

Key 10: Define the future culture. Define both the cultural values and norms you have now and those you want in the future. Use the new norms to guide actions that will develop the culture, including promotions, compensation, hiring, organization structure and changes, decision-making methods, training, and personal development programs.

Key 11: Allocate resources effectively, putting your money and people where your future is. Allocate your strategic dollars, investable cash after funding the existing business, and scarce "leverage people" to the most important strategic programs and priorities. Pay particular attention to your leverage people—the handful of highly talented, specially skilled, always-seem-to-get-the-job-done people who will drive the plan. Ensure that plenty of stretch, but not an inordinate amount, is put in the organization's objectives and workload. Make sure that the balance between ongoing work and strategic work is reasonable, particularly for leverage managers.

Key 12: Align your organization's work with the plan—from top to bottom. Each of the 18 implementation keys is a means of aligning the organization's work with the plan. If alignment is in doubt, use an alignment meeting to stack up corporate priorities against departmental and strategic team plans and ensure alignment and needed cross-functional, cross-layer cooperation.

Key 13: Empower execution. Empower teams and individuals to accomplish their objectives. Give them the personal skills, wide but well delineated latitude in decision making, the resources needed to do their jobs, and management systems that quickly surface and address critical issues and provide decisions beyond their empowered limits.

Providing an Environment in Which People Can Excel

Key 14: Select, train, and develop for the future—now. You get "past" performance from old skills. Training and personal development of people is an inexpensive way to give your organization the new skills needed to execute your plan now and in the future.

You need both process and content training programs to develop and effectively implement strategy. Process and management skills programs often include the strategic and departmental planning process; team management; facilitation; change management; management, leadership, and supervisory skills; and performance appraisal.

Content training develops the skills needed to implement the plan, such as marketing, systems, or manufacturing techniques. It should focus on weak functional areas where change is required.

Select internal and external candidates for jobs and leadership development using proven tests of values, behavior, and skills. Testing will increase the competence and capacity of your organization significantly over time.

Key 15: Fix broken core processes. Core business processes are the arteries of your business. They must deliver your competitive advantage—what the customer wants—better than the competition. The handful of critical processes may include product fulfillment, new-product development, and shop-floor management. If these are broken, customers and profits suffer and the organization loses share to the competition. Ignore core processes at your peril.

Key 16: Communicate to everyone, all the time. It's a basic human condition: People need to know what's going on in order to be motivated and to align their tasks with the priorities of the plan. You must ensure that everyone understands the plan, believes in it, accepts his or her part in making it happen, and is continuously advised of the plan's essence and progress. Otherwise, people will underperform their strategic tasks or, more damaging, undermine your desired direction.

Judging and Rewarding

Key 17: Review performance. Develop an integrated review system that includes the review and revision of the overall plan and departmental, team, and individual objectives. Forget the hands-off theory. Stay on top of your plan. Schedule regular reviews to detect changes in the outside world or internal task implementation that is off track. Reviews result in judgments of the competency of teams and individuals and subsequent changes to improve the organization's ability to execute its plans. They can lead to redirection of strategy, reformulation of projects and jobs, and most of all, reallocation of scarce resources.

Key 18: Reward strategic results. Design a balanced compensation and reward package that rewards long-term strategic accomplishment as well as ongoing results from each of the contributing organization units—functional departments, cross-functional teams, and of course, individuals. Make sure that the reward system reflects the conditions of your business, whether you are turning a business around, stabilizing a troubled company, undertaking planned growth, or experiencing rapid entrepreneurial growth.

Putting It Together: How the Strategic Change Process Plays Out Over Time

The strategic plan and the 18 implementation keys don't happen in a vacuum. Nor are they one-time events. They play out over time, often four to six years, in the context of a strategic change process. During this process, the psychology of the organization, its ability to change, the change barriers, leadership styles required, and strategic results are relatively predictable. Knowing what to expect may help you expedite the change process in the face of an organization's natural resistance to change.[2]

Pressures For and Against Change

Pressures for change are often obscured in the heat of the day-to-day business battles. But any astute executive has an eye out for the pressures both for and against change coming from within or outside the organization. If valid pressure for change is there, the perceptive executive takes action when it's relatively easy and without high organizational and financial cost. Similarly, if resistances to change are building, the executive cuts them down before the cost of dealing with them escalates.

The pressures that singly or collectively goad an organization to change and the internal factors that resist change are shown in the accompanying exhibit.

Pressures for Change

All companies should deal constantly with competitive threats and ever-changing competitive markets. Lucky companies have visionary leaders, who, like Alfred Sloan of General Motors in the twenties or Jack Welch of current-day GE, push change before other pressures force the issue. They become the change agents for their company and often their industry. Unlucky companies, like Studebaker Automotive in the fifties or current-day Eastman Kodak, wait until they are battered by finan-

---

[2] Note that what follows is a summary of more extensive coverage of the change process in *Team-Based Strategic Planning*.

Strategic Change Model

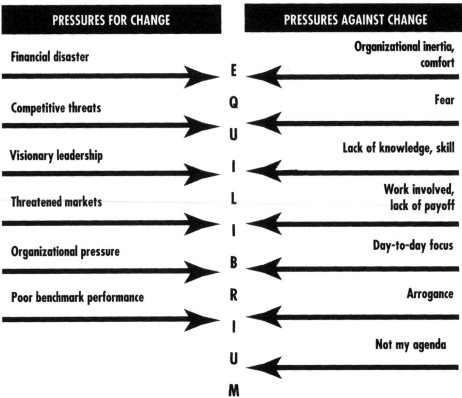

cial disaster, severe marketplace losses, or competitive carnage before acting.

Pressure to change can come from inside the organization, too. Lower levels are often more in touch with the market and competition than top management. They may not only see the need for change but have specific suggestions about what changes should be made.

Finally, companies are often shaken out of their lethargy and motivated to change only when confronted with plummeting performance in the market. Those that wait suffer financial and market share losses. And in this era of board and stockholder activism, their top officers frequently and rightfully pay for inaction with their heads.

Pressures Against Change

Myopic leadership at the top likes the status quo and doesn't develop and aggressively implement needed strategic change. Often comfortable and sometimes arrogant, with a strong sense of entitlement when it comes to their jobs, pay, and trappings of office, these executives are usually coddled by a workforce that is similarly entitled. Leaders at American Express, General Motors, Montgomery Ward, Bausch and Lomb, IBM, Genesco, and a host of other banner yet tarnished-marquee names fell because of their comfortable myopia. As we will see later, often the only solution is to surgically remove such leaders and their court of key board members and officers so that the rest of the corporate organism can survive.

Even after a change program is well under way, there are people who are comfortable with the way things have always been done and have a natural tendency to keep executing the job that way, regardless of new marching orders from management. Fear plays a big role—fear of failure in implementing the new order, fear of losing one's job, or fear of losing one's traditional power in the organization. Lack of skill frequently plays a part. Progress is slowed, for example, when people lack important content skills, such as cutting-edge computer literacy, or process skills, such as functioning on teams. The theme song of change resistance—"I already have too much to do on this job. How can I possibly do more?"—is usually a disguise for one of these fundamental reasons for resisting change.

As discussed in Part II (see Key 8, "Remove Resistance"), the change agent has a double-edged role: to remove barriers to change, encouraging individual change to take place, and to cause sufficient personal pain to dislodge those mired in the status quo, prodding those who can't or won't change right out of the organization.

Individuals have to know what will happen to them if they don't succeed: At best, they will stagnate; more likely, they will be demoted or out of a job. They also need to know what to expect if they do succeed: vital jobs, more money, promotions. Top leaders must continuously communicate the realities of the outside world, the necessity of changing if the business is to survive in it, and the implications for the organization and its people if it doesn't.

Talk is cheap, though. Tangible evidence—such as downsizing, elimination of unprofitable products and businesses, and firing of marginal personnel at all levels—is often the only force that wakes up an organization. Sacrificial lambs still serve their symbolic purpose. Such moves imbue the organization with a needed sense of urgency, recognition of the consequences of not changing, and sufficient stress, anxiety, and fear to get moving. Sad but true.

The Four-Phase Strategic Change Process

When embarking on a change process, the organization and individuals within it will go through the four-phase process summarized below. My observations of what happens at each stage are typical for most companies. Although all companies must go through the four phases, atypical companies that commit needed time and resources can accelerate the process and significantly increase the impact of their efforts.

The first of the three accompanying exhibits shows for each phase the organization psychology that both drives and limits the process and the appropriate leadership style. The second exhibit shows when each of the 18 implementation keys is used during each phase of the change process. And the third exhibit shows the role of strategic planning in each phase and the types of tangible strategic accomplishments that result.

Phase 1: Recognition/Elation/Shock

Hallmarks

The hallmarks that distinguish an organization in phase 1 are a sober recognition spreading through the organization that the company has to change and the beginning of efforts to define and grapple with needed changes.

Strategic Planning

A traditional strategic planning process produces the company's plan, moving from expedient external analysis through programs to address priority strategic issues. The process is usually rushed because,

Phases of Strategic Change

▼ *Organization psychology*

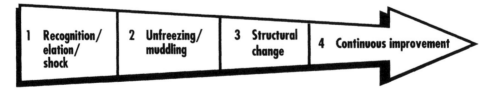

▼ *Phases of leadership*

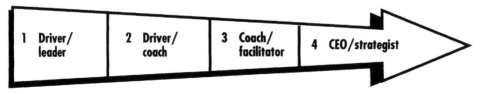

(Text continues on page 26.)

Use of Implementation Keys in Each Change Phase

Key	Phase 1	Phase 2	Phase 3	Phase 4
1 Develop an accountability system.	Design and introduce an interlocking scorecard and accountability system that covers operating and strategic plans, individual departments, and teams and coordinates cross-functional and cross-boundary tasks.	Struggle through making the system work; fine-tune.	System relatively routine.	Routine.
2 Turn strategic priority issues into assigned, measurable action plans.	Assign annual strategic priority action plans to cross-functional teams or individual departments.	Ensure that most priority issues are move-forward, not fix-the-ship.	Continue.	Continue.
3 Embed departmental planning.	Departments establish their own priority issues, recommend corporate priority issues.	Introduce comprehensive departmental planning for strategic, operating, infrastructure, and coordination issues.	Struggle through making the system work; fine-tune.	Running in steady state as standard operating procedure.

(continued)

Use of Implementation Keys in Each Change Phase (*continued*)

	Key	Phase 1	Phase 2	Phase 3	Phase 4
4	Negotiate individual accountabilities.	Install or revive an individual performance management system. Train and coach people in its use.	Struggle and push hard to enforce understanding and use. Use effectiveness audits and compensation to drive importance home.	System taking hold.	System running relatively smoothly.
5	Change the organization structure—fast.	Restructure the organization to fit new strategy if needed.	Fine-tune.	Continue as needed.	Continue as needed.
6	Change the people—fast.	Get the right people in the right place quickly.	Make second round of people changes.	Continue as needed.	Continue as needed.

Key	Phase 1	Phase 2	Phase 3	Phase 4
7 Foster creative leadership and mental toughness.	"ABCD" managers and supervisors. Select "leverage" leaders for leverage jobs. Remove Ds. Judge future of Cs. Develop program for As and Bs. Hire leadership from outside to fill voids. Place As in charge of critical positions.	Continue. Introduce formal leadership development program.	Routine. Continue formal leadership development.	Routine. Continue formal leadership development.
8 Remove resistance.	Remove from harm's way people resisting your change efforts—early retirement, voluntary and involuntary severance, moves to jobs where competencies match need. Remove policy, procedure, system, and process barriers to plan.	Continue first wave of changes.	Continue as new resistance and barriers arise.	Continue as new resistance and barriers arise.

(continued)

Use of Implementation Keys in Each Change Phase (*continued*)

Key	Phase 1	Phase 2	Phase 3	Phase 4
9 Use teams (appropriately).	Use cross-functional teams for addressing corporate priority issues. Give them team training and facilitation help.	Conduct team building for top teams. Use teams beyond priority issue programs.	Conduct team building for other teams. Establish teams as a major management tool.	Continue teams as part of culture.
10 Define the future culture.	Define the values, beliefs, and competencies that you want the organization to have. Build these into hiring practices, performance reviews, the reward structure, communication, organization structure, and physical surroundings.	Intensively communicate culture.	Intensively communicate culture.	Intensively communicate culture.

Key	Phase 1	Phase 2	Phase 3	Phase 4
11 Allocate resources effectively, putting your money and people where your future is.	Institute system for formally allocating strategic and operating resources, simultaneously shortening budget cycle.	Debug system.	Routine.	Routine.
12 Align your organization's work with the plan—from top to bottom.	Use the implementation keys to get and keep alignment. If in doubt, use alignment meetings to ensure. Use alignment audits to check how well the system is working.	Routine.	Routine.	Routine.

(continued)

Use of Implementation Keys in Each Change Phase (*continued*)

Key	Phase 1	Phase 2	Phase 3	Phase 4
13 Empower execution.	Audit barriers to empowerment and progress. Remove most egregious. Remove policies and procedures that block lower-level action. Empower individuals, teams, and departments with as much authority, resources, and responsibility as they can handle.	Widen scope of empowerment as people's experience and competence grow. Survey barriers to be removed or changed (organization, people, systems, or procedures).	Continue.	Reach steady state—appropriate and systematic empowerment of new people and teams; maximum empowerment of experienced people.
14 Select, train, and develop for the future—now.	Institute basic training course in company philosophies and critical team, behavioral, planning, performance management, objective-setting, supervisory, and "content" skills immediately required by the plan.	Add training to include management, leadership, supervision, and the broad range of technical, behavioral, and management skills required in the future.	Provide broad formal training and development programs.	Provide broad formal training and development programs.

Key	Phase 1	Phase 2	Phase 3	Phase 4
15 Fix broken core processes.	Begin work on re-engineering business processes delivering your competitive advantage.	Complete work on broken processes. Embed process redesign as a basic management skill. Start secondary process improvement.	Ensure continuous improvement. Ensure continuous improvement.	Ensure continuous improvement. Ensure continuous improvement.
16 Communicate to everyone, all the time.	Establish communication network focusing on supervisor-employee interface. Weave in role of CEO, "all hands" meetings, small-group discussions, newsletters, Internet, and E-mail.	Continue. Stress impact of outside world, company culture, "wins" from plan.	Continue. Stress impact of outside world, company culture, "wins" from plan.	Continue. Stress impact of outside world, company culture, "wins" from plan.

(continued)

Use of Implementation Keys in Each Change Phase (*continued*)

Key	Phase 1	Phase 2	Phase 3	Phase 4
17 Review performance.	Establish rigorous system to review results of the overall plan, project teams, departments, individuals. Judge each team's and individual's competence, worth to the organization. Prepare individual development plans.	Press hard at all levels to sharpen people's thinking, clarify objectives, pass realistic judgment on results.	Routine.	Steady-state system except for "educating" newcomers.
18 Reward strategic results.	Design strategic pay for performance, reward system balancing reward for strategic and operating contribution of all organizational elements.	Modify as objectives are met and business situation changes. Drive down into the organization.	Modify as objectives are met and business situation changes.	Modify as objectives are met and business situation changes.

Strategic Planning and Tangible Accomplishments by Phase

	Phase 1	Phase 2	Phase 3	Phase 4

Strategic planning	• Complete strategic plan developed
	• Planning process becomes the spine for:
	  – Changing direction
	  – Deciding when to use the 18 keys to implementation
		• Priority issues revised
		• First objective survey of markets, customers, and competition completed
		• First survey of internal culture and climate completed
			• Priority issues revised
			• Continuing measures of market performance established
				• "Ground-up" strategic plan repeated

Accomplishments	• Fix-the-ship priority issues identified
	• Some crucial strategic issues identified
	• Little tangible progress except:
	  – Budget and people cuts
	  – Organization structure and some managerial changes
		• Many fix-the-ship issues completed
		• Work started on true strategic issues
		• Profitability improvements seen
		• Some improvement achieved in strategic objectives such as service
			• Beginning fruits of strategic change, such as new products and penetration of new markets, seen
			• Financial performance and performance versus strategic objectives significantly improved
				• Substantial strategic change and ability to continue it achieved
				• Strategic objectives constantly hit and the bar frequently raised

once the leaders make up their minds to develop the plan, they want the basic plan completed quickly. Time pressure prevents much external analysis, market research, or development of fact-based competitive strategies. The analysis that is done relies on polling of internal opinion combined with top-team assessment. From this, the planning team develops its market and competitive data and conclusions. The internal organization's attitudes toward change and the barriers to such change are not surveyed.

The resulting plan contains a direction statement that, without good external analysis, may be subject to later fine-tuning. There is good focus on a valid mixture of fix-the-ship (for example, cut cost) and move-forward (for example, new-product development) strategic priority issues to be addressed by cross-functional and departmental teams. It will take the company two to three years to resolve most of these initial issues to the point where responsibility for their management can be delegated to the appropriate functional departments.

What People Are Asked to Do

People are asked to achieve operating and strategic performance standards that are significantly higher than in the past. They are asked to accept the new strategic direction and plan their activities accordingly. They are told that they will be held accountable for their results, perhaps for the first time. They will be asked to accept new values such as an outward customer orientation. They may be required to learn new behaviors: how to work effectively as members of a team, for example, and to coordinate efforts with other functional departments as the organization becomes less hierarchical. These are major changes producing major stress, particularly if the old ways of doing things have had decades to solidify.

Organization Psychology

During phase 1 of change, which lasts from a few months to a year and a half, management typically decides to embark on a strategic plan and change effort. Many employees are both relieved and happy that the company is developing a sense of direction. They are ready to participate. These are the "seed corn" and "leverage" managers of change. Some are skeptical. Others, particularly in seriously troubled companies, may be shocked, depressed, or angry to the point of being ineffective, and bewildered and fearful for the company and their jobs. It is among these latter employees that significant resistance to change will arise.

Leadership

The chief executive officer/chief operating officer and those members of the top team who buy into the process at this point are hard drivers of the change process. They push preparation of the plan, are strong and directive when necessary, and are quick to make decisions, particularly those involving dollar and people allocations. They show people why the plan and changes are necessary and instill a sense of urgency in the organization. They resist with a vengeance the organization's attempts to change the plan and go back to business as usual.

Implementation Keys

Ideally, during the initial strategic planning process, plans are developed for executing the 18 implementation keys. The keys are then installed during phase 1.

In this scenario, an interlocking accountability system, combined with a new compensation and incentive system and a rigorously enforced review system, is installed at the beginning. Needed organization changes are made as soon as practical during the early months of the plan. The obvious resisters are dealt with quickly. Leverage leaders are placed in the most important jobs and cross-functional teams established to deal with priority strategic issues, some of which will be to fix broken core processes. Systematic communication programs are implemented to embed the plan direction, report on progress, and continuously communicate the new organizational values throughout the organization.

Typically, management installs a strategic planning system but waits until the second year to initiate departmental planning, resulting in marginal alignment of lower-level tasks with the strategic direction. Strategic priority issue programs are reviewed at the top level. Specific dollar and people resources are set aside for strategic programs.

The compensation system is not changed to reflect the new strategic direction or the use of teams, so a major means of motivating strategic performance is missing.

In addition, the existing individual performance review system, if any, continues to be used to set and review individual goals. Since these goals are only loosely tied to the plan, the system is not likely to be very effective in increasing organization performance. Plan execution is behind schedule due to overcommitment, the press of day-to-day business, the confusion of dealing with new cross-functional tasks and teams, the lack of knowledge needed to deal with strategic priorities, and resistance from the organization.

The company probably deals with some resisters and makes obvious organization changes. There is an initial flurry of communication about the plan and its priorities, but it quickly dwindles to an ineffective and perfunctory level.

Tangible Results

In a typical situation, the company makes some progress in resolving the initial list of priority strategic issues. It may, for example, fix some core business processes, cut surplus overhead and people, repair a sales organization, and make urgent product line changes. Costs are down due to cuts, and some resisters are gone.

Why So Slow?

There are, of course, time, money, and people resource limits on how quickly a company can change and how many of the 18 keys you can implement immediately. Practically, you take what you can get based on the condition of the business, the capacity of the organization for change, and the fully informed judgment of the chief executive officer/chief operating officer and the top team on what is practical. Realistically, most organizations can't do all that's ideal during the first year or so of the change program.

Every CEO we surveyed told us that implementing their plan took *twice* as long as they originally anticipated. Organizations lag the ideal in implementing the 18 implementation keys for the following reasons and rationalizations:

- *Failure to see the need:* Leaders don't understand the immediate need for sometimes expensive and complicated implementation tools such as performance management systems and training. They neglect critical organizational issues because they think the business elements of the strategic plan—new products, markets, and cost reduction, for example—are all that are necessary to drive change and achieve success.

- *Business demands:* Time demands of running the current business get in the way of performing all the steps of ideal planning, such as up-front market research, and installing the implementation keys.

- *Resistance:* The organization and staff resist change, usually by citing their need to deal with the business at hand or by arguing that planned new directions are not right.

- *Inadequate staffing:* The organization does not have the key people needed to carry out the change work. These holes are usually in marketing and human resources and some members of the top team.

- *Dislike for making tough choices:* Senior managers shy away from making unpopular decisions, such as downsizing, firing top people, or cutting out businesses or products that are no longer vital.

Confronted with the preceding obstacles, management's top priorities have to focus narrowly on executing strategic priority issues, fixing the organization, and installing an accountability and review system. The accompanying exhibit shows management's top five priorities during phase 1.

Phase 2: Unfreezing/Muddling

Hallmark

The hallmark of phase 2 is reality. The hard truths that change is needed and is happening are accepted. The people resisting change are removed, new people are brought in where needed, and the hard work of figuring out how to change begins in earnest. Management puts mind and muscle behind the 18 keys.

Strategic Planning

The planning process in phase 2 is simple. It emphasizes the review and modification of existing plans. Market, competitive, new-product, and internal cultural research, bypassed in phase 1, is often accomplished in phase 2. Management stresses quarterly and sometimes more frequent reviews of priority issue projects and departmental plans. The company's planning system—which flows from the overall strategic plan development to departmental strategic and operating plans, budgets, and reviews—is integrated relatively smoothly into an annual, predictable rhythm on which the organization can count.

The company rarely takes on new priority strategic issues at this stage. Instead, it takes the previous years' priority issue programs, which are usually incomplete, and updates them for the next level of performance. The annual review of the overall strategic plan asks:

Management's Top Five Priorities: Phase 1

1 Develop the strategic plan to focus the organization on its strategic priority issues.
2 Establish accountability and review for the entire organization.
3 Put in place the appropriate compensation and incentive program to back up the accountabilities.
4 Put leverage managers in place.
5 Make needed organization and people changes.

- How well did the company carry out its programs last year?
- What has changed in the outside and inside world, and how might these changes affect the company?
- Should the company add or subtract any priority issues?
- What programs will the company undertake this year to address its old priority issues and any new ones it has selected?
- Where does installation of the 18 implementation keys stand? How effective are they? What are the company's next steps?

What People Are Asked to Do

Knuckle down and get the change job done. Accomplish corporate strategic priorities and team and departmental plans. Hit significantly increased performance objectives.

Organization Psychology

During phase 2, which lasts from one to two years, the tough work, both emotional and tangible, starts. Unfreezing—questioning old attitudes, behaviors, and work methods—begins. People seek new methods and solutions to problems, a process that will lead to cultural change and plan achievement. There is considerable stress on the organization as people handle more than their usual workload, deal with new key players, and learn to use new work methods to boot.

At the same time, resistance reaches its height during this phase, and there is danger of sabotage to the plan by people wedded to the old order and their comfortable place in it. Managerial warts become all too evident. New leaders emerge, often people unsung during the old regime, who thrive in the new empowered and teamwork environment. A high-energy core of employees who support the new order emerges.

Toward the end of phase 2, employees begin to emerge from their quagmire of muddled, depressed, and confused feelings. Desired new cultural attitudes and behaviors, such as a focus on customer service, begin to replace the old. Employees, witnessing their own and the organization's tangible strategic progress, buy into or at least accept the vision and plan and gain confidence in their newfound abilities.

Leadership

The CEO and top team increase their capacity to manage the strategic change and the ongoing business simultaneously. Many companies spend a good deal of time on the managerial process—teaching managers how to function as a team and supervise change. Team building is often needed to improve top-team functioning and to set an example for the rest of the organization.

Management also works to hone the organization by continuing to remove resisters and managers who block progress and by promoting and hiring key players—acts viewed positively by those supporting the change program. Team training and team building are provided for project teams. Where justified, the organization brings in external experts—for example, consultants in compensation, teams, or market research.

The CEO and top team remain in the driver role in areas where there is underperformance or new programs to be executed. They begin to make a transition to the role of coach, facilitator, questioner, prober, mentor, and intervener to individuals and teams that are able to manage their own projects and new jobs.

Implementation Keys

Significantly, the importance of the 18 implementation keys becomes clear during phase 2, and the company makes plans to install any that were previously neglected. Phase 2 usually sees effective accountability, review, and reward systems designed and begin to take hold. New or repositioned people replace those blocking progress and start to contribute. Teams become effective at senior levels. Departmental planning is installed for the first time. Thanks to a revitalized communication program, people at lower levels in the organization begin to understand how the plan is relevant to their work.

Tangible Results

Progress is made on fix-the-ship issues such as profitability and service. The beginnings of strategic progress are seen. For example, new systems are on-line or about to be, new products are just emerging, and entry is made into important new markets. Profitability improves. Downslides halt, and growth may start.

The accompanying exhibit shows management's top four priorities during phase 2.

Management's Top Four Priorities: Phase 2

1　Ensure that departmental planning is embedded and working.
2　Install remaining implementation keys.
3　Remove remaining resisters; complete people changes.
4　Ensure that selection, training, and development programs are working to meet near and future needs.

Phase 3: Structural Change

Hallmark

The hallmark of phase 3 is tangible progress in meeting strategic objectives and establishing the final configuration of the organization and its processes that will enable it to handle continuous strategic change.

Strategic Planning

The corporate planning process becomes one of detecting changes in the environment and updating and adjusting strategic priority issues as needed. The integrated process to develop strategic and operating plans and budgets from top to bottom functions relatively smoothly. The process emphasizes producing and executing good departmental operating and strategic plans that reflect the company's overall direction.

What People Are Asked to Do

The job is the same as in phase 2—accomplishing corporate strategic priorities and team and departmental plans—with two big differences. First, the job gets tougher. Priorities involve large strategic changes such as use of entirely new technologies or entry into new businesses, mergers or joint ventures, or acquisitions. Second, more and more responsibility is transferred down into the organization as people gain the capacity to act independently. Until now, for example, top officers scrutinized acquisition candidates in detail. In this phase, they delegate the details and recommendations, retaining only oversight and final decision making.

Organization Psychology

Both tangible results and people's feelings about themselves and the organization significantly improve as they develop skills in teamwork, cross-functional coordination, communication, management, and leadership. They become confident that they can continue to improve and that management will support their behavior and meet their needs. Fundamental changes in culture and skills that will ensure future success are becoming embedded in the organization.

Leadership

The CEO and top team continue to make progress in their transition from a directive role to that of coach, facilitator, questioner, mission communicator, and intervener. This transition is possible because people at lower levels in the organization can now sustain the basic business, with minimal appropriate attention from the top, and can help set and execute strategic direction.

Implementation Keys

The 18 implementation keys are in place and being effectively used, laying the structural groundwork for phase 4, continuous strategic change.

Tangible Results

The company now sees tangible strategic results, including the introduction of significant new products, entry into new markets, and incorporation of innovative service and production technologies. The organization is able to perform relatively independently at high levels of efficiency and in key areas where strategic results are demanded. Most structural barriers to progress (personnel, organization, systems) have been removed.

The accompanying exhibit shows management's top four priorities during phase 3.

Phase 4: Continuous Improvement

The CEO and top management staff can now begin to turn their attention, once again, to long-term strategy.

Hallmarks

The organization is configured for and achieving continuous strategic change. Managing change is a given duty. Continuous process improvement is considered everybody's job, and everyone is trained in process improvement techniques. Innovation is valued and considered imperative. Teams and teamwork are a way of life. Developing future

---

Management's Top Four Priorities: Phase 3

1 Don't allow the organization to backslide into old ways, slower tempo, or reduced effectiveness.
2 Applaud the positive results of planning to date.
3 Ensure that everyone from the CEO down has delegated as much as possible and empowered highly competent people to accept the delegation.
4 Begin to plot the next major strategic moves.

leaders and professionals is considered a primary duty of management. Senior management concentrates on broader issues affecting the company's future.

Strategic Planning

The planning process remains essentially the same as in phase 3—anticipating changes in the outside world and updating the company's responses to those changes through the development of strategic priority issues.

Management has enhanced its ability to scrutinize the outside world and think in terms of broader and more creative alternatives for the organization than in the past. At some point, the company will complete another thorough external and internal analysis from scratch. This analysis will look at all the company's strategic options, ranging from more of the same through sale and/or dismemberment. The world has changed since the change effort started. Nothing must be missed. Typically, such ground-up scrutiny is needed every three to five years unless the industry is rocked by a hot new invention or a turbocharged new competitor or company strategies just aren't working. Any of these requires an immediate, in-depth look. Companies in fluid, high-tech markets must constantly update their external analysis and their response to these findings.

What People Are Asked to Do

People must meet higher and higher performance standards while responsibility and accountability are pushed lower in the organization.

Organization Psychology

The organization is visibly confident. It knows its direction, its values, its capabilities, what kind of people fit, how they are to behave, and the results expected. People are confident that the culture will move them forward. They are open to change and new ideas.

Leadership

Top team members, by this time, have moved to a predominantly nondirective role. They are coaches, facilitators, questioners, supporters, and interveners. They focus on the health of the organization processes for producing strategic renewal—externally driven strategic planning, leadership, people, organization structure, and excellence in decision making and results.

The CEO can now pull away from day-to-day management and attend full-time to strategy and shareholder and financial community relations, ensuring that the organization has future needed competencies, the mission and vision are communicated, and the organization is motivated.

Management is confident that the company, by and large, can sustain needed growth and high performance levels to maintain or improve its market position.

Top-team members continue to participate fully in the development and implementation of long-term strategy. They lead their departments in the execution of departmental strategies and operating plans. They focus on continuous improvement of the business processes within their functional areas to meet or beat best-of-class standards.

Implementation Keys

The keys to implementation are fully operative and viewed as standard management tools and processes. Emphasis is on renewal tools such as process redesign and the selection, training, and development of people. Compensation systems are changed as needed to address structural changes in the business.

Tangible Results

The company is meeting its strategic objectives on a sustained basis and constantly raising performance standards at all levels in the organization.

Management's top four priorities in phase 4 are shown in the accompanying exhibit.

Speeding Up the Process

The speed of the strategic change process is governed by two factors. First, there is the difficulty of the business tasks to be accomplished. Reengineering several processes, for example, is far faster and easier

Management's Top Four Priorities: Phase 4

1 Enjoy the conquest and ensure that the organization does, too.
2 Continue to emphasize continuous change tools such as strategic planning and process redesign.
3 Continue organization building.
4 Plot and execute the next major strategic move.

than significantly restaffing the organization or restructuring markets and product lines.

Second, the speed of the process is also governed by the organization's ability to implement change. This capacity improves substantially when the organization moves quickly to (1) get strong leadership in leverage positions, (2) eliminate people who resist change, and (3) establish an accountability program for departments, teams, and individuals.

Do

- Understand the change pressures, change process, and the role that leadership must play at each stage.
- Educate your organization in the change process so that everyone understands the pressures, frustrations, and ultimate pleasures they will experience.
- Tell the organization what specific changes in the business and high performance standards you will be expecting so that they see the big picture and their place in it.

Don't

- Push the organization way beyond its capabilities. There has to be 25 to 35 percent stretch and psychological pressure and pain to change. But be careful about going over the brink.

What CEOs Say

When I started this book, my plan was to base it on the keys to implementation of strategic change we have developed in more than seventeen years of guiding organizations to successful strategic planning and implementation. But my curiosity overcame my intention to stick to my own experience, and I decided to talk to a number of chief executive officers to make sure that we were right or discover whether we had missed a trick or two.

The Sample

Ultimately, we interviewed twenty-two CEOs and sixteen other officers, principally vice presidents of human resources and senior and executive vice presidents. Though the sample was small, it was varied. It included large (multibillion-dollar) and small ($8 million) organizations, for-profit and not-for-profit, secular and nonsecular, privately and publicly owned, and even a midsize city. Most of them had one thing in common: They were successful in implementing change. For comparison, there were a couple of organizations that failed in their change effort.

Some of the organizations were "dead in the water" when they undertook their change programs. Although they weren't flirting with the financial coroner, many were significantly and painfully underperforming on important financial, competitive, or other performance dimensions according to their boards or chief executive officers or chief operating officers. Others were growing rapidly and were grappling with problems of how to organize and control their future growth. Still others, although successful, were looking for ways to increase future growth and profitability.

I limited my interviews to one hour, beginning by giving the CEOs the following questions:

- What pressures drove you to change?
- What outcome did you expect from the change program?

- What major issues were you compelled to address in order to effect needed change?
- How did you address these issues?
- Did you or did you not meet your initial expectations?
- How long did the process take? How did this time frame compare to your original expectations?

Then I sat back and listened

Where time permitted, we then closed by administering a ten-minute questionnaire to gauge the impact of the 18 implementation keys.

We could have gone on for hours, but CEOs have schedules that take precedence over interesting conversations with authors. Nevertheless, because most of the organizations were or had been clients, we had plenty of additional information on which to draw. In fact, because we had worked for many of these organizations, often for years, we had seen how their changes were made. Our knowledge of the organizations also made it hard for respondents to pull the wool over our eyes when describing what actually happened!

The Bottom Line

The results of our survey showed that we hadn't missed a thing. The 18 keys to implementation were the ones that the respondents used whether they were our clients or not.

The Techniques and Insights of First-Class Change Agents

What was intriguing were the war stories—the twists, techniques, and improvisations the CEOs used to get their organizations moving; the things in which they took joy; and the things that made them mad. So although all of the topics covered here are addressed in detail in subsequent chapters, I thought you might like to read some of the CEOs' experiences that really brought these topics to life for me.

What follows are some of the techniques and insights of first-class change agents.

Their Plans

Each successful CEO had an easily articulated vision and measurable objectives for the change plan. Even when I had no idea what the detailed plans looked like or who was involved in developing them, I had no trouble grasping their direction, which the CEOs expressed crisply, simply, and in a form that I—and their organizations—could understand.

A highly successful bank chairman in the process of resurrecting a very sick bank said, "Our objective is to become one of the sweet sixteen." (The sweet sixteen are the sixteen best-performing banks in the nation.) Everyone in his organization mentions that goal and knows how and when the CEO intends to get there. He must be doing something right. When he took over, the bank stock was selling at $3^1/_2$; it's now at 46.

A CEO of a company providing leased personnel and interim services and growing at 20 to 30 percent per year articulates his objective to be number one in his industry and specifies the financial metrics that will require. He also states six principles that he and his key people concluded stand for the great company it is to become:

1. *Great employees everywhere:* No tolerance for average players
2. *Highest expectations:* In performance and everything that we do
3. *Attention to detail:* The same process and the same outcome every time
4. *Empowerment:* Empowering employees within defined limits
5. *Great training:* Beyond product knowledge to employee wisdom
6. *Innovation:* Moving from the basic to the advanced to the truly innovative

The CEO of a very profitable bank, absorbing the acquisition of six banks that were underperforming by almost every possible measure, simply showed them the benchmark performance of the parent bank and gave them six months to increase their return on assets by 30 percent—a goal way below par but a trajectory the CEO felt was right. He presented them with a very tough goal but one that was achievable with extraordinary effort.

Broad Perspective

Teams don't develop the "grand-change-in-paradigm" strategies. CEOs do. This was a surprise to me. Virtually every radical shift in direction was the vision and insight of one person. The reason for this was quite clear. The CEOs viewed their jobs as understanding what was happening in their marketplace. They avoided getting so close to internal thinking that they were sucked into "common wisdom" or "operations-based" strategies. How did they keep their distance? Where did they get their information?

Most of the CEOs kept private counsel. The CEO of a Fortune 500 company has used a nationally known consultant as a confidant for years. Many of the CEOs used friends or members of advisory boards or other boards as sources of information and challenge. Several were voracious readers, some of business literature and others of everything in sight. There is no single formula except that these men and women had restless minds, searched out challenge and information, and were not satisfied with formulas.

Members of the Young Presidents Organization have another way to keep perspective. They universally laud the usefulness of their forums in which they meet at least monthly with the same five to seven individuals as long as they are members (until they are fifty years old). They credit a good deal of their business success to (1) the advice they receive at the forums from people who have experienced their problems and (2) the soft but ever-present "group pressure" to take the forum's good advice and make their businesses successful.

In another instance, I asked a human resources director about her chief operating officer, who had worked for twenty years in a company desperately in need of change. How was he able to keep his perspective, I asked, so that when he became chief operating officer he knew to introduce drastic change? She replied, "That's easy. Years ago, he sold his family company to our company, and he runs us now as if every penny were his and as if every inefficiency were lousing up his family business."

Paradigm Shifts

The most successful companies see and understand the implications of powerful business paradigm shifts for their industry and their company long before others do. Or at the very least, they see far better ways of dealing with the current paradigm. One CEO said, "The biggest problem people have is that they think that the present is the future."

So what kind of piercing, unusual insights do successful change agents have?

An executive who had been extremely successful in starting entrepreneurial health-care ventures had an exquisite sense of when to get into businesses and when to sell them. He was well into the tenth year of a venture that delivered outpatient services in stand-alone buildings when he saw the handwriting on the wall. Reimbursements for his company's services were going to be significantly cut, and hospitals were going to try to regain control of the type of outpatient work his units were doing. The result? Way ahead of the rest of the industry, the company developed profitable programs to put its services inside hospitals and make them partners.

The CEO of another company in the health-care field gave this example:

"We were growing by 40 percent per year, faster than I ever thought possible, and then the world changed overnight. Reimbursement rules changed, which changed the way our customers—doctors—had to do business. We had to reformulate the business quickly from one that provided doctors with oncology test data to one that provided a holistic package useful to the doctor and hospital alike. The new model was a patient management system. We provide test data, patient-tracking information, and clinical studies of therapeutic efficiency and help doctors cope with all of the bureaucratic paperwork the government now forces on them. We also use the Internet to get the data to the people who need it fast."

A former highly successful and nationally visible officer of a private company accepted an appointment to clean up a massive public utility. The utility had a simple formula for success: Raise electricity prices to cover the cost of whatever we want to do. The new CEO, after visiting every operation in the chain, returned and announced to his senior staff that 7,500 people were to be laid off, rates would not be increased for three years, the budget would be frozen for three years, and all project and capital costs must be justified economically, just as they are in business. Shocker? Yes. Rates constant for three years? Yes, for the first time in the organization's history.

A prescient CEO who started a business in a nascent field of child care service faced four simultaneous issues: getting the company in the black, attaining a defensible number one market position before someone else did, bringing in more venture capital to fuel the growth, and becoming profitable enough so that the company could go public while attaining sufficient critical mass to ensure sustained profitability in what is still a "thin" growth market. She proposed and executed two moves: first, a very large acquisition that solved the critical mass and profitability problem and, second, a change in product from "one-for-mula-fits-all" centers to a program that tailored the care format to each situation and included consulting in related areas.

One man saw a mundane business and turned it into a massive corporation. He observed that parking lots were universally dirty, poorly run with unreliable help, and the bane of the office building or the municipal agency responsible for them. Years after that insight, his is a very successful international public company.

Teams

Occasionally, teams do see the paradigm shift, though their usual role is to figure out how to cope strategically with the shift. The company here

puts exceptional emphasis on the team planning process and the necessity of having hard market data on which to base strategic decisions.

An executive vice president of a growing 2,000-store general merchandise chain said:

> "It just popped out at us during our annual planning meeting
> that our entire business concept should hinge around consum-
> ables and not on soft goods. The impetus really came from our
> consumer surveys—what they want and can't get at our stores,
> what is moving and what isn't, the shift in our sales and prod-
> uct profitability over the years, and what items were and were
> not repeat purchases."

Getting People to Think; Shaking Them Up

Every CEO seems to have a method for getting people to think "out of
the box." The head of a massive and growing retail business is well
known for attending meetings only briefly—but long enough to "turn
the question around 180 degrees" and give people who are dealing with
an important issue a set period of time to get back to him with their
conclusions.

When a complacent organization needs radical and lengthy change,
CEOs have to get and sustain their organization's attention. A couple of
techniques our survey discovered were unique.

A newly promoted CEO of a multibillion-dollar company knew
only too well that the culture of his company was one of entitlement to
the job, maintaining good people relationships rather than making
waves or progress, and a poor work ethic. He got his top thirty-five managers together with these messages:

> "We are no longer a people company. We aren't growing. We
> haven't added to our stockholders' value. We are a high-cost
> producer. Our product innovation is at an all-time low. We
> don't have the cash to grow. We have too many unproductive
> people."

The managers were shocked, but the CEO continued:

> "Let me make it clear. On one hand, we are still going to be a
> people company. The difference is that every person in every
> job is going to be a top-notch performer. And every job we
> have is going to be needed and high value-added."

He delivered the numbers that they had to make and the job that had to
be done in each of the primary functions. A major verbal fracas ensued,

with the chief operating officer and chief executive officer accused of being unfair, acting insensitively toward people, just looking for an excuse to downsize, and being too oriented to the bottom line.

The CEO told the managers to go away and think about it for a week and explained that they would hold a separate meeting to lay out the programs that would meet his objectives. His major motive was to find out who was with him and who wasn't. At the next meeting, a handful of people still vociferously resisted him. He went to work with the rest of the managers and, shortly, gave the resisters a good severance package. The company was gaining market share in eighteen months, and the bottom line was markedly improving in twenty-four.

The head of one of the health-care businesses mentioned earlier called his staff in one day, told them what the new paradigm was, and gave them ten days to work out a plan to move quickly in that direction. As he put it:

> "I created a hornet's nest of disbelief, anger, annoyance, and confusion because no one saw the world that way. I left town for ten days and told my staff I was unreachable. I explained that I would return to review their plans and see if they saw any fatal flaws in them."

Part of his purpose, too, was to smoke out the nonsupporters so they could be removed and the supportive staff could get on with the job. Predictably, a number of people strongly resisted his efforts; the others either bought into the concept or at least were willing to support it.

Another CEO in manufacturing observed, "I push people to look at customers and at the extent of competition."

Resistance

There was no subject that got CEOs angrier than resisters—people who for any reason did not support the corporate plans. The CEOs simply won't tolerate people who are not working in the best interests of the organization and are actively trying to hold it back. Most CEOs estimated the proportion of resisters in the general ranks at about 30 percent and claimed that very few of them were salvageable. The percentage of resisters can be even higher in senior ranks: CEOs reported that they got rid of 30 to 100 percent of their direct reports early in the change process.

Universally, the CEOs' advice is to oust resisters as soon as possible. Be kind and generous with severance pay, outplacement, and early retirements, but get them out. The higher in the corporate ranks they are, the faster they have to go. Not only can they slow down your change efforts, but they can take you under with them.

Indeed, the CEO of a Fortune 500 company and the general manager of another were sabotaged and ousted. The resisters were able to slow progress and ultimately poison the culture to the point that the board felt compelled to force the CEO out. His advice? "I'd go through the organization with a chain saw on day two and get rid of the whole lot of them."

The mayor of a midsize city said he faced a boarded-up downtown, lethargic economic development, a police department in turmoil with a record of terrible customer service, and disillusionment with the entire government process. Of the top forty officials, he had to retire thirty-five who resisted change or could not handle the pace. But in two terms, the mayor's approval rating has gone from 54 to 80 percent, and the public sector is completing more than 75 percent of its programs on time, up from less than 56 percent a few years ago.

The chief operating officer of a very successful and rapidly growing high-tech company has a very simple rule: New hires are evaluated at six and twelve months. If, at either of those reviews, the person is not an outstanding performer or clearly won't be, doesn't fit the culture, or shows signs of being a resister, he or she is let go. He never wants to be in the position of needing to execute a change program because he has kept unproductive people around.

Setting Objectives

Virtually every CEO dictated the overall change objectives and made it mandatory that every function in the organization (and ultimately every person, in most cases) have objectives tied to the top-level goals.

Often, their goals were linked to external metrics for the first time. Letting inbred people see what the outside world is like is a shocker and an eye-opener. A bank president observed:

> "I showed them that the top-notch performers in our part of the banking industry show a 1.3 percent return on assets. I gave our acquired banks one year to get from .6 percent to .9 percent and said that we would then talk about how to get the rest of the way."

Stated the former head of a massive manufacturing company:

> "I like outrageous goals—at least, outrageous to those who are now low achievers."

The CEO of a national multilocation service business noted:

> "Rather than try to change every unit at the same time because incremental growth was what they wanted and all that they thought they were capable of, I took a brand-new unit and raised the bar fifteen feet. I staffed it the way I wanted, with the people I wanted, and they showed the people who thought that fifteen inches was a big deal that fifteen feet was readily achievable. I put the company's mind in an entirely different place. Then I went to work on the rest of the company."

Rapid Growth

A lot of companies were unprepared for growth, usually because of inadequate "infrastructure"—the key middle to upper managers who must manage growth and information systems.

The chairman of a private multibillion-dollar retail chain explained his company's growth program:

> "We added 50 percent to our size overnight with the acquisition of a competitor's retail chain in our headquarters city. The acquisition and complete integration of management and facilities went extremely smoothly, and we're beating our profit expectations. I attribute this to the fact that we've been team planning for years and were able to put a team together quickly to plan the purchase and acquisition. We have excellent lower-level bench strength that we've been building over the years, in part in anticipation of such moves. This meant that we could staff the key leverage points of the acquired firm. In addition, our experience, some of it pretty costly and painful, with minor expansions gave us knowledge on how to move. Our cause, annoyingly, was made easier by the excessive time that it took the FTC [Federal Trade Commission] to approve the acquisition, so our planning was that much better."

Challenging Assumptions

Some people consider a key leadership trait the willingness to have your assumptions challenged and debated.

The CEO of a high-growth, high-tech health-care company explained that he welcomed challenges to his plan and change strategy:

> "The ability to question ourselves every year—to challenge our assumptions and ideas about the outside world—the abil-

ity to think outside of the company and put what we do for the patient, hospital, doctor, and community first is absolutely critical in health care's rapidly changing competitive markets."

As noted in the discussion of paradigm shifts, there are lots of ways to have your assumptions challenged with the objective of a better, more implementable plan.

Urgency

Passion for the job and a strong sense of urgency are unquestionably necessary leadership characteristics. As one CEO put it:

> "I have a fire in my belly, and I want one in everybody else's as well."

Commenting on the sense of urgency in getting a change program under way quickly, a CEO said, "You can't wait for all of this highly participative stuff. You have to set your objectives, clean out the resistance fast, consolidate support, and get on with the job. Otherwise, there are two dangers: The board throws you out, or it takes too long to get the job done."

A senior vice president of a large not-for-profit organization remarked:

> "We instilled urgency. The board gave us a well-publicized mandate to burn the house down if necessary to get the organization moving. People got the message after we developed a vision. I replaced four VPs who couldn't perform with people who held the new values that we wanted. I took a complete layer of managers out of the organization, rode one vociferous dissenter out by holding him accountable for results, installed objective setting and annual reviews for all, and just kept beating on the urgent need for change."

The CEO of a packaged-goods manufacturer explained:

> "International was a mess. I took the head of one of our [foreign country] subsidiaries and gave him twenty-four hours to come up with a plan to generate cash for growth, including the number of people and the businesses he would stay in and get out of. I wanted to see if I should keep him in the job or not.

He came up with a good plan. The other subsidiary didn't, and I ended up running [the subsidiary] myself for a while."

The CEO of the same company told how he got his company's attention:

"Removing fifty-five people from the R&D organization got people's attention. They really got the message that it was not business as usual when I met frequently with our sick R&D operations from four o'clock to eight o'clock in the evening to review where they were going, make quick decisions to throw out low-value projects, and punch away at getting the better, cheaper innovative products that were our high priority faster."

The CEO of a leased-help corporation said:
"I told one complaining group, 'If you don't like the new pace, leave, because the pace isn't going down. It's going up.' The incentive program washed a lot of people out who didn't want to work that hard or who were afraid they couldn't do the job."

Accountability

Universally, accountability was considered a primary force for aligning work with the plan, meeting objectives, and weeding out poor performers.

The CEO of a major utility noted his frustrations in dealing with an entrenched staff:

"People fought accountability in innumerable ways. Some are maliciously obedient—that is, they say yes and do something else, or they work strictly according to rules—all to help you fall on your face. Others give you half the facts so you have to work on a system to get information on what's really happening. Some slide completion dates on paper after you've signed off on a project. People not used to a professionally managed organization don't like to deal with facts and accountability. That's why I use the Baldrige (quality) program and reengineering initiatives that leave you naked with the facts to contend with."

To explain how he dealt with "significant problems in public safety, finance and accounting, public works, and five or six administrative processes," a mayor of a midsize city remarked:

"In a government environment used to little if any accountability, we established TQM [total quality management] teams,
a highly measurable process, to fix our problems. We put icing
on the cake: The team members could personally keep 10 percent of the savings they came up with. So far, the payout to
the teams has been $700,000."

Defining Events

Sometimes it took a defining event to get the organization moving. In
the case of two not-for-profit organizations and two for-profit companies, their defining moments were significant financial losses and loss
of market share.

One newly appointed CEO said, "The organization kept raising
prices even in light of declining unit volume. Then we lost $8 million.
That was the defining moment."

In another, the organization's market and financial performance deteriorated so badly that the board replaced the CEO and called in two
consulting firms to help get the organization and strategy straightened
out.

In a third, significant losses, the inability to come up with a plan to
correct them, and a marked deterioration of market position caused a
divided and contentious board to fire the CEO-founder and key vice
president and seek a new CEO from the outside.

None of the precipitating events would be welcome to any organization. Healthy organizations would never let performance get to the point
that such events would happen. In each case, an outsider was brought
in—belatedly—to run the organization.

Focus

All successful CEOs come across as focused. They articulate the business that they're in and their objectives very crisply. And they're quick
to peel off businesses or products that don't fit:

"We were always in focus," said the CEO of an outpatient-care business. "We had a small central staff, decisive officers, and immediate
access to capital." When changes in the marketplace became evident,
he explained:

"We were able to move quickly. When managed care came
along, we joined the enemy—the hospitals. They had access
to contracts with PPOs and HMOs that we didn't, and we
could run an outpatient surgical facility more efficiently than
they could and at a lower cost. So we did joint ventures. We

were quick to drop our HMO and PPO businesses when we found that they drained focus from our core thrust."

A high-growth broker of electronic parts and equipment started an adjunct proprietary business that used its formidable systems and Internet skills. The unit has not met expectations, and the broker is quickly studying the unit's future to see whether it stays and becomes a competitor for valuable resources or whether it goes.

Money

When asked to name the most potent force for getting results and enforcing accountability, CEOs universally answered, "Money." Money tied to objectives talks. Most CEOs were against traditional systems of merit pay, and virtually all used or were getting ready to use pay-for-performance systems.

The leader of a religious organization said:

> "I established a pool of 10 percent of salaries payable for meeting budget, with the conditions that the pool distribution would be based on results—agreed-on performance—and would not be equally distributed in each department. I got tremendous flack for not distributing the pool equally."

No one was more vocal on the subject of money as a motivator than the head of the parking system company. Everyone in the company is eligible for bonuses, and 34 percent of pretax profits are allocated to bonuses each year. Not only is the company's performance outstanding, but everyone in the company walks fast and talks fast—urgency.

Though this is a gut feeling and based on little specific evidence, it seems that companies with generous pay-for-performance systems and who spread incentive pay throughout the entire company (a) change the fastest with (b) greater focus and (c) make more at the bottom line.

Infrastructure

It was clear that lack of infrastructure can inhibit growth and that expanding without infrastructure in place is highly dangerous.

For the CEO of a child care service business, infrastructure was a serious problem. She remarked, "We didn't realize what we needed in systems and accounting as we grew to gain credibility with large clients and to run our growing business."

The CEO of a health-care business explained:

"Rather than barrel ahead opening five or six new units each year, which would have meant losing money, we sat tight building infrastructure—systems, staff, training programs for people managing remote field facilities. We hired two new executive vice presidents, one good at acquisitions and the other skilled in managing operations. Then we were able to move ahead relatively smoothly."

Mistakes

Growth will never be without mistakes. This subsection presents a few of those cited by the CEOs with whom I spoke.

Taking the advice of his senior staff proved to be a big mistake for the CEO of a major utility. He noted:

"I told the organization that we would cut overhead 40 percent and that it was up to them to figure out how. I accepted, wholesale, the organization that my key managers presented to accomplish the objective. I probably wouldn't do that again. I had to bite my tongue for a couple of years and then go back and change some of their recommendations."

For the CEO of a retail, wholesale, and manufacturing business, not acting quickly enough to get rid of resisters proved costly:

"I had three officers who fought change all the way. Two of them had been founders of an acquired business, and they simply couldn't work for or with someone else. I separated them in different parts of the business so they couldn't feed on each other, and they simply walled themselves off, badmouthed the corporate direction and me, and drove off some of our good people. I let this go on much too long. I should have fired them at the outset of their childish behavior and rid the company of its nonperformers and resisters long before I actually did. It cost us dearly."

Some CEOs found that success itself brought about costly mistakes. Rampant success severely damaged one company and came close to killing another. Both companies once had highly profitable products, dominant market position, complete flexibility to raise prices over the years, and weak competition. Success drove management's attention inward and created top-down, "we-know-all-we-need-to-know," inwardly focused cultures. An employee of the damaged company reported that the credo of his organization seemed to be:

- Don't move.
- Don't change.
- Don't challenge the formula.
- Don't challenge each other or the status quo.
- Don't, by any means—and particularly not close to bonus time—challenge management.
- Don't look outside the organization into the marketplace.
- Don't stick your neck out for anything.
- Don't make decisions. Wait for someone upstairs to tell you what to do.

One of these companies lost 10 percent of its market share before its management woke up. A formidable competitor took the other company to the cleaners. The chairman and a powerful sidekick, along with lots of innocent employees, lost their jobs, and the company is in critical care with an uncertain future.

A senior officer of a software company explained that not responding quickly enough to changes in the marketplace was a mistake they made:

> "We didn't sell out when we should have. We were blind to the impact of [a competitor's well-signaled actions]. There seems to be a window in these high-tech businesses when it looks like you're headed for oblivion or stardom, and oblivion says sell out while you can get good bucks for the business."

Communication

Communicating the message throughout the ranks was a given: "Pounding home the point" was how the CEO of the packaged-goods firm described his communication efforts during the change process. He observed:

> "There was an entitlement culture in the company—safety, security-oriented, work hard but safely, and when you work here, it's forever. The layoffs and early retirements took care of the 'forever' perception. But we had to pound home the point that we're pursuing a growth and efficiency strategy, that there is no such thing as a guarantee of full employment, and the way to have security is to perform and increase shareholder value."

The head of the child care service company said that she beats on the mission and vision every chance she gets:

"Say it often and say it simply. I use E-mail and monthly conference calls connecting all field managers so I can give recognition and reinforce the direction. I ask them to pass the
mission and vision down in the organization, and they are always supposed to give the message followed by 'And what
this means for you is . . .' "

Observations and Surprises

Here are some observations that we made and some things that surprised us as a result of the survey.

The Same Tools Across the Board

Remarkably, we saw no difference in the tools used by the different
types of organizations implementing change. They all had a plan, they
all set "tougher-than-expected" standards, they instituted accountability, and they got rid of the resisters and the people whose performance
was not up to par. Even the not-for-profits and religious organizations
used enforced accountability systems and monetary incentives, some
for the first time.

The *way* the organizations implemented the tools did vary. As you
would expect, family companies and companies such as banks in mature markets with a lot of long-service employees and a "family" atmosphere tended to take longer and be more gentle in cutting people than
other institutions. They were also more prone to let "encouraged attri-
tion" take its toll. This technique, which takes about two years to work,
holds people to tough standards and gives them very fair retirement
or severance packages when they can't live up to the new corporate
performance standards or simply can't take or don't like the new pace.

High-growth companies, particularly in high-tech markets, or companies in trouble, on the other hand, used every fair and legal technique
in the book to rid themselves of nonperformers.

Impact of the Change Keys

The survey asked the CEOs to rate on a scale of one to ten (with ten
being "extremely high") the impact of each of the change implementation keys. The variance of scores between the highest and the lowest
was extremely small. The conclusion? You have to use all 18, and most
of the respondents did. Although there was not much difference in the
impact scores, the CEOs made it very clear that the implementation keys

that cause the most change and have to be implemented quickly, thoroughly, and right are:

- *Accountability:* Establishing objectives and reviews
- *Reward:* Paying for performance
- *Leadership:* Covering critical leverage positions
- *Organization:* Getting the right people with the right skills in the right places
- *Resisters:* Finding them and getting rid of them fast

Advice to CEOs

We closed the interviews by asking for one piece of advice for a CEO just starting a change program. Here's what our interviewees said:

"Get as many people as you can involved in the planning process and then use small teams to work on pieces of the puzzle."

"Do it quickly. You're going to have pain. Get it over with so the wounds can heal as quickly as possible and you can get on with the job ahead. You must have the leadership 100 percent supportive of what you want to do or get the hell rid of them."

"Be flexible and open-minded. I can force change my way, but I can't make it effective that way. My way may be the right way to do things, but I have to let my employees go and do it their way because it's the only way it will get done."

"Go with your gut. The only time I have sleepless nights is when I get talked into something that I know is wrong. My last wrong decision on an R&D program is costing me $5 million at the bottom line."

"Once you've set your objectives and the key issues to be addressed in meeting them, bring your best remaining people together in a room and hash out a sound strategy. Paint what the world is going to be like and what your business will be like if you don't. Then communicate your plan daily until they've had enough."

"Get people with different skills. Don't take your friends into your venture just because you're comfortable with them. Make sure that the people you put in key positions in a change situation will be dedicated to the seventy-plus hours of work a week that it takes. Watch out for too many drummers. If everyone wants to be the bass drummer, you're in trouble."

"Communicating change is the most important job. Tell your staff that there is going to be change, here is what we are going to do, and here is how we'll measure success. The person whom the workers believe in most is their own supervisor, a credible person to them. You have to get that person on board, a believer, and get him to translate the message down. Tell the rest of the world what you're doing—the customer, media, audience—on a timely basis. It brings them in as helpers or at least minimizes negatives from the outside."

"The ability of the staff to execute is the most important issue. It is critical to appoint the caliber of people who can do the task, who can implement, who can organize—not just a nice person."

"Find one or two people outside your organization who have successfully led change and who will give you their ear."

"Don't ever underestimate the magnitude of the undertaking. You can't handle it by the seat of your pants. Make sure that sufficient resources are devoted to planning and executing your plan of action."

"Everybody and his brother will crawl out of the walls and try to talk you out of your plan. Don't let them. Stick to your guns.

PART II

The 18 Keys to Implementing Your Strategic Plan

Key 1

Develop an Accountability System

Introducing an Accountability System

What Is Accountability?

A sampling of executives defines accountability as:

- A management style that holds people's feet to the fire to accomplish strategic objectives

- Living the adage "It's what you inspect, not what you expect, that gets done"
- An objective accepted by an individual, a team, or an organization unit that is subsequently judged on its performance in meeting that objective and rewarded accordingly
- The only way to make sure that your plan happens
- Looking employees in the eyes and saying, "Did you, or didn't you? If so, great. If not, why not, and what are you going to do differently next time?"

But a definition, however useful to highlight and encapsulate a concept, fails to tell the whole story. It doesn't tell about the immense amount of effort it takes to mount an accountability system. It doesn't answer key questions: How do you arrive at *what* needs inspecting? *Which* of the eager troops do you hold accountable for achieving key plan objectives? *How much* rope (empowerment and resources) do you give individuals and teams to work with? *How* will you hold them accountable and *how frequently?* What are the *rewards* for high achievement or the *penalties* for not making the grade?

How Does Accountability Motivate?

People work to achieve their objectives for lots of reasons. Some *like* the challenge. They like to win. They experience real joy in accomplishment. Some want rewards in the form of money, promotion, accolades, peer approval (or envy), enhanced reputation, or the kudos from superiors. Others fear failure, lack of approval, or not getting the rewards they think due. They fear the loss of meaningful work and their current lifestyle.

Regardless of their basic drives, people are unquestionably motivated to achieve their objectives when they know you will regularly review their progress toward achieving them. Conversely, when objectives are loose and accountability is lacking, employees work on what they like, at their own sometimes less-than-blazing pace. Especially at the beginning of a change effort, few of them are really comfortable with the difficult challenges and new behavior they are asked to embrace. Given their choice, they'll take the slow road.

What Makes a System Work—or Not?

Accountability can, of course, be a sharp double-edged sword. An organization that announces a big, highfalutin strategic plan and accountability system must be willing to put the necessary time, money, and effort into making the system work. Otherwise, management loses credibility, and performance drops.

An accountability system works when:

- Top management treats it as the primary means of keeping the plan on track.
- The system is well designed, and managers and employees are thoroughly trained in its importance and use.
- Management uses paperwork, systems, and meetings to engage the people involved in execution, get information, evaluate successes, learn from failures, stimulate the players, redirect resources when necessary, rid the organization of noncontributors, and develop the skills of those who are committed and able.
- Top management holds managers accountable for the accountability system itself by judging their personal performance partly on their ability to make the system work for their people.
- The system is honest—separating the stars from the average performers from nonperformers and rewarding accordingly.

The system won't work if:

- Doing the paperwork is management's prime focus, at the expense of measuring actual achievement and redirecting people's work.
- Management doesn't put in the considerable time and effort necessary to make the system work.
- Managers are afraid to be truly, sometimes brutally, honest about people's performance—a cultural issue that must be addressed in many organizations.
- The accountability system's intent is distorted to get raises, bonuses, or promotions for favorites or rewards are simply given "across the board" instead of to those who are impartially judged to be doing the best job.

Although critical to success, accountability systems are hard and often dull work. That's why so many companies introduce them with great fanfare but lack the staying power to implement them completely, falling short of their strategic objectives.

How Messy Will It Be?

Be prepared. Even when you do all the right things to make accountability work, it's not going to be neat and predictable. Accountability systems are inherently messy because they are:

- *Complex,* touching many layers and functions within the organization, not only setting and reviewing objectives but tying many disparate functions together to achieve a unified, cross-functional, cross-organizational objective
- *Involved with people,* many of whom resist change and have the natural tendency to resist being judged
- *Time-consuming,* particularly in the first and second years, when systems are being developed and installed and people are painfully learning what accountability is all about
- *Initially costly,* given the time and money that must go into designing and debugging an accountability system and training large numbers of people in its use
- *Confrontational,* forcing management to deal with problem performers, give people bad news, push them in directions they don't want to go, and fire people
- *Flexible,* because you must make modifications in objectives, tasks, and resource allocations to reflect changes in business conditions and progress in plan implementation

---

The Eleven-Step Accountability Process

A complete accountability process, illustrated in Exhibit 1-1, has twelve key components:

1. Isolating the critical elements of the strategic plan, called *actionable* elements (that is, *elements requiring action*), and deciding which will be acted on first to implement the plan's intent
2. Defining which organization units—teams, functional departments, or individuals—will address the actionable elements
3. Establishing a format and system for turning priority issues into measurable program action plans
4. Developing scorecards to set and measure progress on corporate, departmental, and individual actionable items and other ongoing business
5. Designing and establishing the formal and informal accountability systems used to review accomplishments versus objectives and ask for program team, departmental, and individual strategic tasks
6. Gaining acceptance of objectives by the organization units that will accomplish them
7. Empowering those who must execute by giving them the

Exhibit 1-1 Twelve-Step Accountability Process

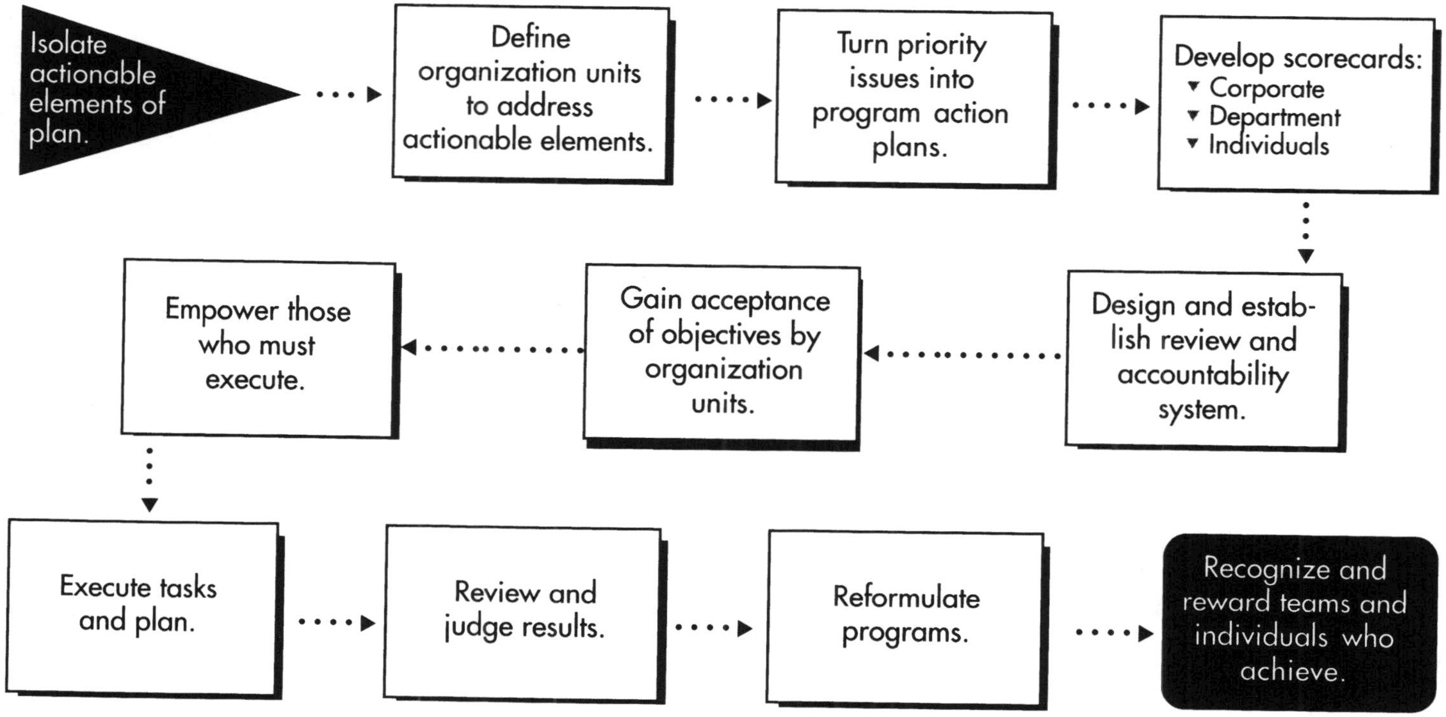

- Isolate actionable elements of plan.
- Define organization units to address actionable elements.
- Turn priority issues into program action plans.
- Develop scorecards:
  ▸ Corporate
  ▸ Department
  ▸ Individuals
- Design and establish review and accountability system.
- Gain acceptance of objectives by organization units.
- Empower those who must execute.
- Execute tasks and plan.
- Review and judge results.
- Reformulate programs.
- Recognize and reward teams and individuals who achieve.

> resources needed and a clear charter of what they can and
> can't do without senior-level approval
> 8. Executing tasks that will lead to achievement of the objectives
> 9. Judging whether or not the objectives have been achieved
> 10. Reformulating programs—making program, resource, and people changes when program reviews surface these needs
> 11. Recognizing individuals and teams according to how well they meet their objectives—rewarding and applauding those who succeed and withholding rewards from those who don't

This chapter covers items 1 through 4. The remaining components are addressed in subsequent chapters. Exhibit 1-2 shows how the whole system interlocks in a yearly cycle.

Isolating the Actionable Elements

Strategic plans generate a lot of data, thinking, and subsequent conclusions about actions you ought to take. But every organization has limits on its capacity to simultaneously run the everyday business and implement strategic change. So the smart company concentrates on only a handful of issues at a time. The question, then, is what will you account for now?

The elements that you select on which to take immediate action will come from the pool of twenty to thirty actionable elements contained in the following components of your plan:

- The strategic priority issues
- The direction statement
- The strategic measures and objectives

Exhibit 1-3 shows where actionable elements come from.

The actionable elements are highlighted in the strategic plan of a major national commercial real estate developer shown in Exhibit 1-4. Note that all priority issues, key result areas, and objectives are actionables as well as each statement of intent in the direction statement.

All the elements must be acted on, over time, but you have to decide which are the most important or urgent—the ones you will address *now.* You must consciously decide which to defer and why.

If this sounds like a formidable job, take heart. The strategic planning process is designed to funnel your thinking into those few elements

(Text continues on page 71.)

Exhibit 1-2 Corporate Accountability Cycle

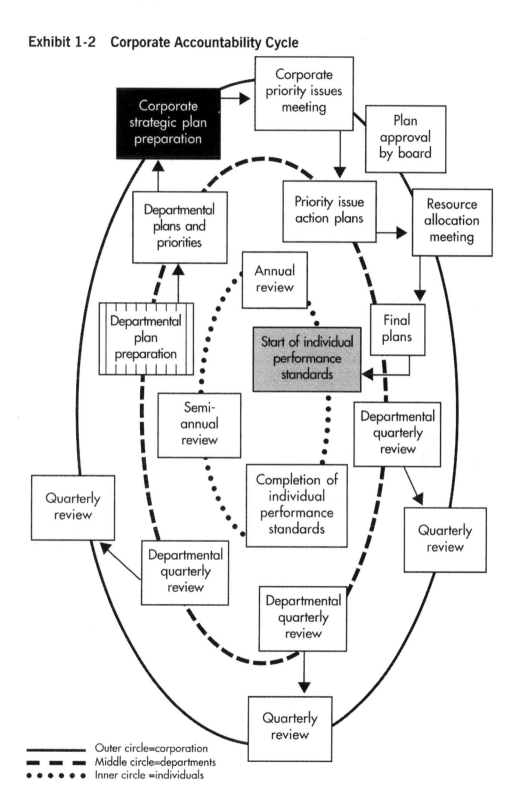

Outer circle=corporation
Middle circle=departments
Inner circle =individuals

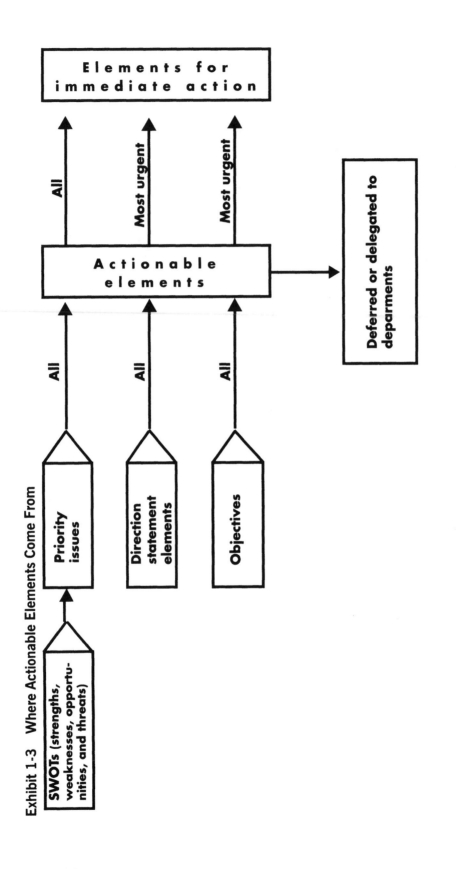

Exhibit 1-3   Where Actionable Elements Come From

Exhibit 1-4   Empire Commercial Realty's Priority Issues, Objectives, and Direction Statement

Priority Issues

> ### What priority issues must Empire Commercial address to achieve its objectives?

Empire Commercial's strategic priority issues are:

1. Site selection and acquisition

2. Construction management system

3. Tenant relationships

4. Cost and availability of capital

5. People and human resources

6. Information systems associated with development

7. Internal communications

▒▒▒▒ = Actionable

✔ = Addressed by priority issues for 1998
✗ = Addressed by delegated objectives for 1998

Exhibit 1-4   (*continued*)

Strategic Objectives

> **What are the key areas in which Empire Commercial must achieve superior results in order to be successful?**

Empire Commercial's overall objectives are:

- ˣ Size: $10 billion in assets

- ˣ Profitability: 16 percent return on investment

- ˣ Growth: Create approximately 3.5 million new square feet by year-end 1999

- ˣ Earnings: $7.20 per share by 2002

The other strategic areas in which Empire Commercial must set objectives and excel to achieve its overall objectives, together with the results expected, are:

- **Customer service**: Measured by (1) ˣproperties open on time, (2) key tenant management satisfaction with Empire measured by survey, and (3) repeat business

- **Product quality**: Measured by (1) continuing tenant satisfaction survey and (2) ˣoccupancy rate

- **Human resources**: Measured by (1) retention of key people, (2) productivity (employees, profit/employee), and (3) existence of succession plan

- **Employee satisfaction:** Measured by survey

- **Training:** Courses per year for key employees: (1) a minimum of one week's training per plan and (2) a development plan for key employees

Direction Statement

Mission and Vision

> ### What is Empire Commercial's purpose?
> ### What is Empire Commercial's future vision?

Mission

The mission of Empire Commercial Realty Company is to increase shareholder market value through the development and asset management of multistory, multitenant office buildings and office campuses.

Vision

The vision of Empire Commercial Realty Company is to:

- Be exceptionally profitable, with return on equity within the top 10 percent of commercial retail development companies in the United States.

- Provide a highly challenging and rewarding work environment for our people.

- Be recognized as a leader by the real estate, financial, and business communities by remaining financially sound. Provide quality and service while developing office facilities for a core group of leading corporate tenants.

- Be known by our key tenants for superior site selection and impeccable execution of the development process.

- Become a $10 billion assets company.

(continued)

Exhibit 1-4   (*continued*)
Business Definition

> **How do we define the dimensions of Empire Commercial's future business?**
>
> **What is Empire Commercial's market focus?**

Market Focus

Empire Commercial will continue to focus on new development with large or single key tenant and markets representing a predominance of Empire Commercial's asset investment over the next five years. Up to 20 percent of additional revenue could come from commercial campus structures and the acquisition of similar property types.

Competitive Advantage

Empire Commercial's competitive advantages are strong tenant relationships and on-time delivery of projects that meet or exceed the customers' needs and expectations.

Core Competencies

Our competitive advantages are delivered by three interrelated systems—core competencies that deliver the highest value in the industry to our customers and the highest return to our stockholders. The systems are:

- *Development*: Land acquisition, construction management, leasing of office space, and tenant relationships

- *Acquisitions*: Identification of acquisition opportunities, quick acquisition analysis and response to opportunities, tenant relations, and leasing of properties

- *Asset management*: Property Management, leasing, redevelopment, and disposition

The additional competencies that will fuel our success are our experienced and dedicated employees and access to capital.

Values

> **What are the values that will guide our behavior inside and outside Empire Commercial?**

We value:

- ✔ *Personal and professional development:* A workplace environment conducive to employees' professional development and subsequent attainment of career goals

- ✔ *Teamwork:* An environment that thrives on teamwork and cooperation among employees

- *Relationships:* Long-term relationships with suppliers, vendors, and professional service affiliates

- ✔ *Work:* A strong work ethic

- *Creativity:* A creative, flexible, risk-taking entrepreneurial spirit

- *Integrity:* The highest level of integrity, honesty, and ethical standards

- *Service:* Superior service to all of our internal and external customers

(continued)

Exhibit 1-4   *(continued)*

Action Plan Summary

> **What actions will we take to achieve Empire Commercial's objectives?**

- *Site selection and acquisition:*
  Plan 1: Acquire sufficient property for 14 office buildings to be built from 1999 to 2004.
  Plan 2: Acquire six urban office buildings meeting our specifications and demographics in 1999 including management contracts.

- *Construction management system:*
  Plan 1: Specify and install a construction management control system to manage cost, profit, time, and efficiency from material supply through completed building.

- *Tenant relationships:*
  Plan 1: Devise and test a tenant satisfaction survey. Complete one round of surveys to define where performance needs to improve and develop subsequent action plan for targeted improvement.

- *Cost and availability of capital:*
  Plan 1: New stock offering by July 1, 1999.
  Plan 2: Restructure short-term debt to reduce interest by 1/2 to 3/4 percent including improvement in bond rating.

- *People and human resources:*
  Plan 1: Hire a professional vice president of human resources to establish the function in the corporation with the initial emphasis on hiring, skill training, and compensation and accountability systems.

- *Information systems associated with development:*
  Plan 1: Complete finance, accounting, cost, and marketing system typing into priority issue above.

- *Internal communications:*
  Plan 1: Develop an annual communication calendar—what to whom from the top team, how, and how to get plan objections translated down into the organization.
  Plan 2: Have internet running by 1/6/99 with complete site for employee information including events, benefits, and company results and interaction group ware for use by teams.

that will have the highest potential impact on your organization. The process itself helps you choose the handful of actionable elements into which you must now breathe life. Of this select few, most will be addressed through your priority issues, with the remainder delegated to the organization for action. Exhibit 1-5 shows where actionable elements go.

Priority Issues

Priority issues are always the most important of the actionables. You've distilled all of your data and thinking into these three to five issues requiring action. If you do nothing else, concentrate your efforts here. Expand all your priority issues into action plans and delegate them throughout the organization to people who will be held accountable for addressing them successfully.

Priority issues are the locomotives of the plan. Although 75 percent of your strategic efforts will be devoted to your priority issues, they will affect strategic numbers in other areas. For example, you might establish a measurable priority issue objective "to increase customer satisfaction with improved product delivery and customer service." If properly executed, this will inevitably reduce cost even if you have not designated cost as a current actionable.

Priority issues are turned over to cross-functional program teams for planning and action. The ultimate responsibility for these critical teams and their programs, however, resides with the top team.

In working with more than 100 companies, my experience has been that virtually all the actions needed to address the most urgent and important direction statement elements and strategic objectives are contained in priority issue programs. Indeed, at the end of each client's resource allocation meeting every year, I run a "touch-back" exercise asking management these questions:

- Do the current priority issues address the elements of the direction statement that are the most important or in need of urgent attention?
- Will success in addressing these issues improve performance on the strategic objectives most in need of improvement?

Almost inevitably, the answer comes back yes. Still, it's worthwhile to reexamine the direction statement and strategic objectives looking for items that should be acted on, outside the current priority issues. Exhibit 1-4, presented in the preceding subsection, highlights actionable elements for a commercial real estate developer and also indicates those selected for the year 1998. Note that although most of these were already

Exhibit 1-5   Where Actionable Elements and Strategic Objectives Go

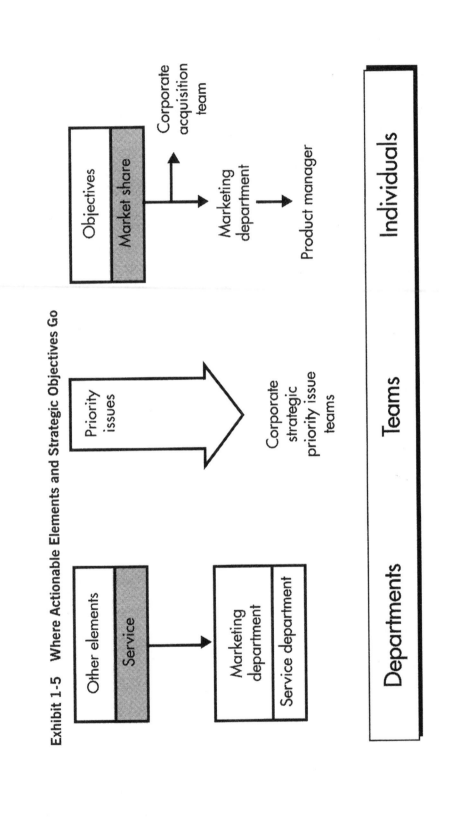

included in the company's priority issues, others were not. Two of these elements—acquisitions and asset management—were delegated to functions for execution as part of their ongoing job, and the rest were deferred.

Direction Statement

There will inevitably be one or two direction statement actionables that are important and require action but did not make the priority issue list. For example, the vision section of the direction statement might emphasize "market leadership," leading to the conclusion that the organization needs to upgrade its marketing knowledge, team leadership, and problem-solving and decision-making skills. This would be turned over to marketing and human resources for departmental plan implementation. Progress would be reviewed by the departmental vice presidents. Other actionable items of lesser urgency would be deferred.

Strategic Objectives

All of the direction statement's key actionables must, as soon as possible, be turned into strategic objectives, with performance measured *somewhere* in the organization. Even though the top team is ultimately responsible for all of the objectives, administratively, they fall into the four categories shown in Exhibit 1-6.

1. *Top team:* Objectives that are the direct responsibility of the top team, such as growth by acquisitions or the completion of a succession plan.

Exhibit 1-6   Where Strategic Objectives Go

▼ **Top team:** The top team is ultimately responsible for all of the plan's strategic objectives and the successful implementation of the priority issue programs supporting them. The top team may, however, "share" or delegate some or all of these objectives.

▼ **Shared:** The objectives are shared between two organizational units. For example, a team reporting to the top team may be required to gain five market share points via acquisition while sales and marketing are assigned the remaining 5 percent to gain through normal sales efforts.

▼ **Delegated:** Objectives for important actionable plan elements that weren't top-ranked but require action are delegated to an organizational unit such as a department. For example, the development of a human resources information system would be delegated to the human resources department.

▼ **Deferred actionables:** Performance is satisfactory, or the actionable item is not important enough for action at this time.

2. *Shared:* Objectives that are shared between the top team and a functional area. For example, an objective for market share growth may have two elements:

- Increases through product line extensions, distribution system restructuring, and penetration of new customer segments
- Acquisition of competitors and complementary product lines

The first shared responsibility is delegated to marketing, and the second remains with the top team. Both are necessary to achieve plan objectives.

3. *Delegated:* Strategic objectives that are and can be met by ongoing operations—for example, market share gains by marketing. Objectives such as these are delegated to the appropriate functional area, which is expected to develop and execute any strategic and operating plans needed to meet them. Imagine, for example, an organization that continuously meets its cost-per-unit objectives through cost containment and reduction methods at the manufacturing level. The top team sets cost objectives, but it doesn't review the programs or the details of progress. This falls to the vice president of manufacturing and his or her organization.

4. *Deferred:* Objectives on which no action will be taken at this time. Inevitably, strategic planning results in direction changes and new actionables. It can take considerable time to establish how such actionables will be implemented and measured. For example, it took almost a year for a manufacturing company, with a new thrust of quality and service, to establish the meaning of the concepts to the customer and begin to design measurement mechanisms.

Actionable Items That Don't Make the Cut

Many important potential actionables won't be acted on for a number of years. As a matter of course, each year our clients review every single concept in the priority issues, direction statement, and strategic measures and objectives and rate them as follows:

- \+ We are doing a good job.
- 0 We are doing OK.
- − We are doing a poor job or nothing.

This information becomes grist for the mill for strategic programs for the coming year. Over the years, every actionable should be addressed through a program action plan, a departmental program, an individual action, a policy or procedure, or someone's ongoing work.

Determining Who Is Responsible for the Actionable Elements

To summarize who is accountable for what:

- The *top team* picks the "actionables" for the corporation.
- The *top team* establishes, oversees, and is ultimately responsible for programs that address the strategic priority issues. These programs are delegated to a cross-functional team for development and execution.
- The *top team* is responsible for achieving the strategic objectives. Some or parts of those objectives may be delegated to or "shared" with functional departments.
- The *actionable items of lesser impact* or areas where the company is already performing adequately are delegated to *functional departments* or individuals for execution, management, and accountability.
- The *remainder of the potential actionable elements* are not acted on during the first year of planning but are reevaluated during the next planning cycle.

But as we'll see, it's not that simple.

Turning Priority Issues Into Program Action Plans Without Getting Overwhelmed: Organizational Clutter and the Objectives Maze

The typical company has three to five priority issues yielding ten to fifteen action plans, with the business to run as well. There will probably be five teams addressing the priority issues (program teams), with a total of twenty-five team members and five sponsors—top-team members who help and mentor program teams. (Teams are discussed later in Part II; see Key 9, "Use Teams [Appropriately].") They will involve to a greater or lesser extent managers of five to seven departments and about ten members of those departments helping them meet their goals. In short, you are unleashing an army of fifty or more people to work on your strategic issues.

Exhibit 1-7 shows the organization maze created as one typical priority issue program—acquisition of new businesses and products—wends its way through an organization. This program involves a team drawn from six functions, a team leader who reports to the top team, and a corporate sponsor. Only some of the innumerable formal and informal lines of communications are shown here. In addition, throughout

Exhibit 1-7 Departmental Participation and Communication for a Priority Issue Program Team—Acquisition of New Businesses and Products

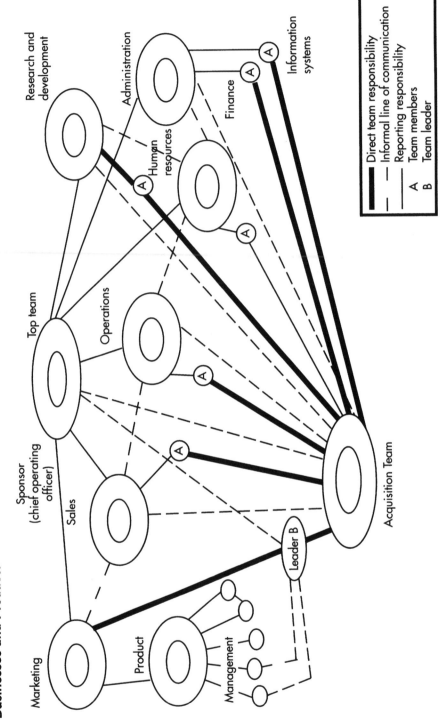

the program, the team will call on specialists such as financial analysts, investment banking firms, and market analysts, not shown on the chart.

You can imagine the havoc, confusion, and frustration, not to mention the lack of action and results, that would occur if you allowed uncontrolled, "just do it" delegation of strategic plan elements, fuzzy definition of the job to be done, unclear definition of authority, vague objectives, inadequate attention to the resources needed, and no management mechanism to surface problems as they arise.

For such a complicated system to work, the acquisition team must have a clear written charter from the top team—empowering it and delineating its mission, objectives, responsibilities, and authority—and a scorecard by which its results will be judged. Although team members need plenty of latitude to work in the manner most efficient for them, they must be trained to act as a team and understand how to operate within the organization. And because no team operates in a vacuum, its work must be explicitly "interlocked" with the major functions that must provide support work throughout the program.

Developing Interlocking Scorecards

One tool that allows you to delegate and disperse actionable elements, ensure cooperation among the work units and individuals who must support each other to get the results you want, and maintain control over the entire process is interlocking scorecards.

To develop interlocking scorecards, you must take the following steps:

1. *Establish strategic and operating objectives for each organization unit that must execute the plan,* ensuring that those objectives are aligned with the corporate plan. These units are:

- The top team, which is ultimately responsible for the corporate objective and priority issue programs
- Functional departments
- Program teams
- Individuals

2. *Identify interlocks*—those objectives that must be accomplished in concert with other units.

3. *Lock those interdepartmental objectives into unit objectives and plans.*

4. *Allocate resources* to each unit carrying out a strategic or operating effort, ensuring that the unit understands the extent to which it is empowered to accomplish the effort.

How the Scorecards Interlock

The scorecards have to interlock in different departments and on different levels to pull together the resources needed to accomplish critical tasks. Exhibit 1-8 illustrates how the scorecards interlock for an acquisitions program. Responsibilities at each level are:

- *Top team:* Approve candidates, make key decisions, and approve final acquisitions.
- *Team sponsor:* Ensure that the team's process has the necessary resources and is running well.
- *Priority issue program team:* Identify, screen, and make the acquisitions.
- *Marketing department manager:* Serve as team leader.
- *Product manager:* Participate as a team member.
- *Market analyst:* Although not a team member, be on call for market, competitive, and product analysis.

Of course, there will be representatives from finance, operations, human resources, engineering, research and development, and legal as well.

Let's look first at a basic system for setting objectives, accountabilities, and interlocks and then briefly discuss how to apply the system to each of the four organization units noted earlier in this section, including how and when interlocks take place. Subsequent chapters examine the detailed process of setting objectives and establishing accountabilities for three of the units—departments, teams, and individuals.

Setting Objectives: The Buck Starts Here

There is no better, more logical system for setting objectives that I'm aware of than that taught by the American Management Association for the past twenty-five years. The system works like this:

- *Key result areas:* Identify the key areas in which you must get results. For the most part, these key result areas (KRAs) will be actionables from your strategic plan. For example, three actionable elements from Empire Commercial's plan are product quality, customer service, and employee satisfaction.
- *Measures:* Decide on the measure(s) you will use to determine success for each KRA. In the area of service, for example, Empire has

Exhibit 1-8   Interlocking Scorecard—Acquisitions

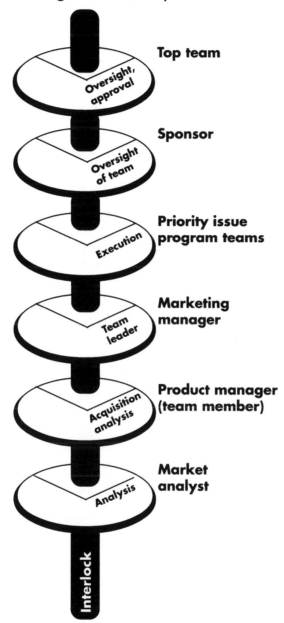

three measures—customer satisfaction as measured by an independent market survey, percentage of properties open on time, and repeat business.

■ *Objectives:* Write measurable objectives for each of the measures—for example, an increase in the customer satisfaction index from 91 in year one to 96 in year three.

This system works for corporate, departmental, individual, and team objectives. Exhibit 1-9 shows a traditional set of KRA measures and objectives for a manufacturing business. We call such a set of objec-

Exhibit 1-9   Key Result Areas and Objectives for a Consumer Packaged-Goods Manufacturing Division

Key Result Area	Measure	Year 1 Objectives	Year 3 Objectives
Cost	Cost per case	$79.50	$71.00
	Cases per employee per year	15,000	24,000
Safety	Work time loss per year (hours)	25	10
	Plant safety index	94	96
Quality	Complaints per million units	0.9	0.6
	Index of distributor and end-customer perception	TBD	TBD
Service	Error rate	0.8%	0.1%
	Index of distributor and end-customer perception	TBD	TBD
Morale/Attitude	Index based on internal employee survey	3.22	3.60
Planning	Performance on each manufacturing priority issue program	Program by program	
	Annual strategic plan accepted by management	9/1 each year	
Capacity	Capacity to allow steady-state production of strategic plan demand forecast with 15% excess for demand spikes	675 million cases	850 million cases

Note: TBD = to be determined after measurement methods are baseline are established © 1998, C. Davis Fogg Management Consulting, Inc.

tives a "scorecard." Note that it is not uncommon for companies new to planning to have several measures whose initial data must be collected to establish a baseline measurement and initial objectives. They then have to provide a system for collecting continuing performance data.

But although the system works fine, it is often applied in a vacuum, with each organization unit considering only its own objectives and needs. Traditional scorecards rarely incorporate the needs of other units or recognize the needs of a particular unit for work and cooperation from others.

That's why we need interlocking scorecards in which mutually dependent tasks are accounted for. We'll therefore look at scorecards for the top team, functional departments, priority issue teams, and individuals and show how we interlock the mutually dependent tasks.

We also need to rearrange traditional scorecard dimensions to ensure that (1) short-term-payoff tasks are separated from long-term strategic and infrastructure-building initiatives and (2) interlocking efforts between organization units needed to accomplish the plan are explicit These dimensions vary, as we'll see below, depending on whether goals are being established for the top team, departments, teams, or individuals.

Top-Team Scorecard

Exhibit 1-10 shows graphically the following dimensions of the top team's scorecard:

- *Financial performance:* The traditional measures of current performance, such as return on investment.
- *Strategic numbers:* Performance on strategic measure such as market penetration, customer satisfaction, the percentage of sales that are new products, employee morale, service, and quality.
- *Strategic priority issues:* The performance of strategic priority issue program teams on meeting their objectives.
- *Creation:* The performance in creating new value for the organization, such as geographic diversification, and entry into new categories or businesses not included in priority issues.
- *Internal drivers:* Internal indicators and plans that lead to current high performance (cost efficiency) and long-term strategic success—such as a succession plan, training and development, and world-class core processes—and are not included in priority issues.
- *Functional performance:* The performance that is the province of the functional vice presidents and spelled out in departmental plans. But the top team reviews performance on departmental

Exhibit 1-10   Top-Team Scorecard

Financial Performance
Strategic Numbers
Strategic Priority Issues
Creation
Internal Drivers
Functional Performance
Team Operations

plan objectives because they are the single most important element in short- and long-term success.

- *Team operations:* The functioning of the team process that is charged with making strategic progress.

Exhibit 1-11 shows KRAs for each level of the organization, including those that apply to the top team. Remember the earlier illustration (Exhibit 1-7) showing how one priority issue permeated an entire organization? Think of these KRAs as belonging to the top team of that organization. That's why the top team is allocating a slice of its work pie to acquisitions as shown in Exhibit 1-8. The top team's objectives

Exhibit 1-11 KRAs From Strategic Plans for Top Team and Departments

	KRAs	Measures	Weight
TOP TEAM			
Current performance	• Current financial performance	Stock value added EPS growth ROI	33% 33% 33% ——— 100%

Strategic performance	• Strategic numbers
	  Service
	  Quality
	  Innovation
	  People
	  Market position
		
		Index
		Index
		Percentage new products on
		  market
		Strategic succession plan
		Satisfaction and values index
			30%

		Market position or share	20%
	• Priority issue program teams	Extent met objectives	20%

	• Departmental plans	Extent met strategic objectives
		  Delegated
		  Departmental
		  Infrastructure
			20%

	• Team operations		10% ——— 100%
DEPARTMENTS	Numbers		
Departmental ongoing tasks (marketing and sales aepartment)		Sales Gross margin Average price Expense budget performance Service index	25% 5% 10%
	Operating priorities	Market penetration	20%
		New-product launch sales goals met	20%
		New products slated for next year ready	20% ——— 100%

(continued)

Exhibit 1-11 **(***continued***)**

	KRAs	Measures	Weight
Departmental strategic tasks	Numbers	Revenue Gross profit Average price Growth in share Market share Service index	10% 15%
	Delegated strategic objectives	5% market share increase, market A	15%
	Departmental strategic priorities	New products worth 40% current sales in 3 years	15%
		Distribution expansion to Europe with 10% share year 3	15%
		Add European Manager to manage expansion	
	Departmental infrastructure	Risk analysis techniques and training in place	5%
	Departmental team obligations	Market expansion team New-product development team	15%
	Department owes others	Time to information systems team on management and marketing information system (30 man-days)	5% — 100%

© 1998, C. Davis Fogg Management Consulting, Inc.

and activities for this acquisition must interlock with other acquisition events in the company.

Departmental Scorecard

The most critical organization unit is the functional department. Departments have the people and dollar resources both to make the existing business happen and to execute strategy. As a result, they have the most important and complicated scorecard, one that requires careful development during strategic and operating planning. In addition, the departments are the focal point for coordinating tasks between functions and thus very much control whether or not interdepartmental tasks are efficiently executed. Departmental scorecard categories, illustrated in Exhibit 1-12, include:

- *Delegated corporate priorities:* Strategic priority issues or objectives delegated from the corporation for execution by a lower-level unit.
- *Departmental strategic priorities:* Priorities and objectives for the unit's own strategic priorities. For example, a manufacturing department may have a three-year program to install an entirely new high-efficiency manufacturing process.
- *Departmental operating priorities:* Annual priorities and objectives for the unit's ongoing job, such as the launch of a new product line for a sales department.
- *Departmental infrastructure priorities:* Priorities and objectives that will build the core capability of the unit to fulfill its purpose in the future. For example, a human resources department might design and install a human resources information system (HRIS).
- *Interlocks:*
  —*Owed us:* Actions needed from another unit to fulfill the department's plan. For example, human resources may require 500 hours of systems work and 2,000 hours of programming work from information systems to establish the human resources information system.
  —*We owe:* Actions the department owes another unit to fulfill that unit's plan. For example, human resources may be required by the top team to structure and oversee thirty weeks of leadership training throughout the company to help fulfill the top team's leadership development program.
- *Team participation:* Time committed to cross-functional strategic priority issue program teams as well as objectives for what the department will contribute.
- *Numbers:* Numerical operating measures appropriate to the department, such as sales, gross margin, net profit, expenses, or cap-

Exhibit 1-12   Departmental Scorecard

Delegated Corporate Priorities
Departmental Strategic Priorities
Departmental Operating Priorities
Departmental Infrastructure Priorities
Interlocks

Owed Us	**We Owe**

Team Participation

Numbers

Operating		**Strategic**

ital; strategic measures as well, if appropriate, such as customer satisfaction index or percentage of revenue from new products.

"We owe" and "owed us" are the interlocks that tie different functions or project teams together in implementing a complicated strategic plan. The interlocks are negotiated function-to-function, individual-to-individual, or by functional members of a team. They become objectives by which an individual or organization unit will contribute to a strategic initiative "owned" by someone else.

Individual Scorecard

Exhibit 1-13 shows graphically the following dimensions of an individual's scorecard, using a product manager in a marketing department as an example. Note that some individual issues and objectives may be portions of or direct "lifts" from the departmental plan.

- *Delegated corporate strategic priorities:* Issues delegated to the individual or the individual's role in addressing corporate strategic priority issues
- *Departmental strategic priorities:* Participation and results expected in resolving departmental strategic issues
- *Departmental operating priorities:* Participation and results expected in resolving departmental operating issues
- *Departmental infrastructure priorities:* Measurable contribution to departmental infrastructure activities delegated to the individual
- *Individual's ongoing job:* Key measurable elements of the individual's ongoing job that are expected to contribute to current operating results
- *Team objectives:* Participation and results expected in strategic or other team efforts
- *Interlocks:*
  —*Owed me:* Actions needed from another unit to fulfill the individual's plan
  —*I owe:* Actions needed from the individual by another unit to fulfill that unit's plan
- *Behaviors and values:* Development objectives in fulfilling corporate behaviors and values
- *Personal development:* Objectives for development in a content area such as market research techniques or other skills such as leadership or team management
- *Numbers:* Numerical results, operating or strategic, for areas under the individual's control or influenced by the individual's actions

Team Scorecard

Finally, teams have scorecards, too, the dimensions of which are outlined in the following list and graphically illustrated in Exhibit 1-14.

Exhibit 1-13   Individual Scorecard

Delegated Corporate Strategic Priorities
Departmental Strategic Priorities
Departmental Operating Priorities
Departmental Infrastructure Priorities
Individual's Ongoing Job
Team Objectives
Interlocks

Owed Me	I Owe

Values and Behaviors
Personal Development

Numbers	
Operating	Strategic

Exhibit 1-14   Team Scorecard

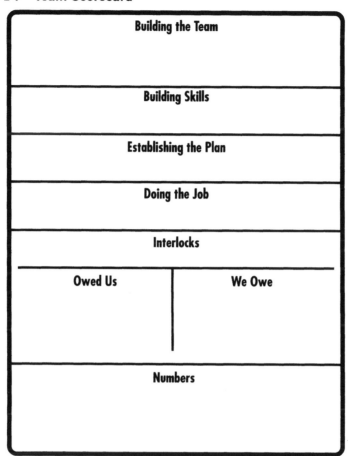

In the example shown in the exhibit, the team is charged with external growth.

- *Building the team:* Ensuring that the team has the proper leadership, membership, teamwork skills, and understandable rules of operation
- *Building skills:* Training that the team needs to ensure that it has the process and analytical skills required to do the job
- *Establishing the plan:* Defining the team's mission/vision objectives, strategies, and detailed action plans
- *Doing the job:* Specific objectives and the specific steps that will lead to their accomplishment
- *Interlocks* (teams are the key consumers of interlocks):
  —*Owed us:* Actions needed from others to fulfill the team's plan
  —*We owe:* Actions the team owes others to fulfill their plan

- *Numbers:* What is expected of the team—for example, revenue from new external ventures in the next three years

Building Interlocking Scorecards Into the System

Interlocking the efforts of all these organizational units requires careful attention at each stage of the planning process. Exhibit 1-15 shows when in the planning process interlocks take place. In brief, this process includes:

- *Departmental plans:* In the first step, each department develops (1) the strategic priority issues that it feels should be addressed by the corporation and (2) a first pass at its own plan and scorecard, including strategic, ongoing business, infrastructure, and team priorities as well as one- and three-year performance numbers. Even at this early stage, the plan should include support expected from others and support that the department expects to give others, as negotiated by the department manager and members at this point. Because department staff participate in the development of these plans, they have a good idea of what their individual responsibilities will be.

At this stage, not all issues will be measurable. For example, a departmental issue may be manufacturing cost reduction. The "from" and "to" numbers for which the department will be accountable will come later in the process.

- *Corporate priority issues meeting:* The top team reviews all corporate strategic priority issues submitted and agrees on four to six corporate issues to be addressed now. It selects teams to develop action plans for these issues and identifies team leaders. The top team also approves, modifies, or disapproves parts of the department plans, sending them back to the departments for completion and inclusion of firm measures. During this meeting, the interlocking work issues are squarely addressed, and every department should go away knowing its obligations to others.

- *Final plans:* The strategic program teams flesh out their action plans and resource requirements. The departments hone their plans.

- *Corporate resource allocation meeting:* The top team, knowing long-term profit requirements and the amount of money available for investment in strategic programs, meets to allocate resources. During this meeting, the top team views all strategic program action plans along with the final departmental plans, allocates money and people to programs and departmental plans of merit, and addresses the interlocking of scorecards once more.

- *Individual performance standards:* Many individual standards—like those for the individual participating in the acquisition program—

Exhibit 1-15   When the Interlocks Take Place

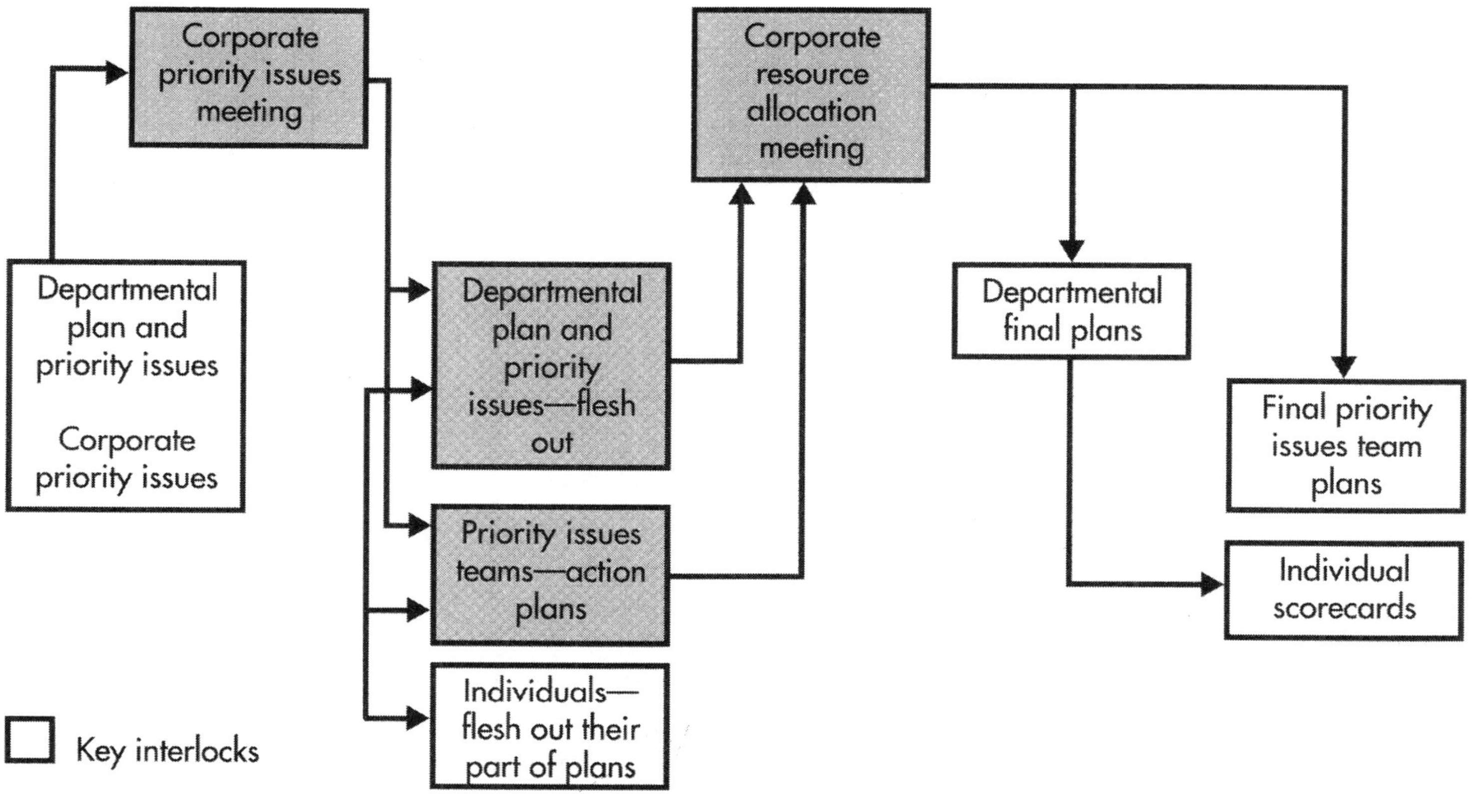

Corporate priority issues meeting

Departmental plan and priority issues

Corporate priority issues

Corporate resource allocation meeting

Departmental plan and priority issues—flesh out

Priority issues teams—action plans

Individuals—flesh out their part of plans

Departmental final plans

Final priority issues team plans

Individual scorecards

Key interlocks

are lifted directly from the departmental plan. These are already interlocked with the appropriate other resources. Planning for their on-going duties, individuals are expected to make their own interlocks with resources needed to help them achieve their goals. With these connections made at the individual level, the interlocking system is complete.

In the succeeding chapters, we examine these planning efforts in detail.

Do

- Design a comprehensive accountability system using inter-locking scorecards before you implement your first plan.
- Implement the system initially and quickly in those parts of the organization critical to strategic success and then phase in the system throughout the entire organization as soon as practical.
- Pay close attention to interlocks during your planning cycle so that the shared resources needed for so many strategic programs are available.

Don't

- Announce accountability systems with fanfare and let them fizzle by delegating execution to human resources and "the rest of the organization." It's the top team's job to see that the accountability initiative works.

Key 2

Turn Strategic Priority Issues Into Assigned, Measurable Action Plans

Principle: Strategic priority issues are best addressed through cross-functional teams, which plan and manage programs and are accountable for results.

Why it's important: Priority issues and programs to address them are the primary vehicles for strategic change.

How it's applied: The top team develops the priority issues during the strategic planning meeting, then delegates them to project teams, which prepare detailed action plans. At the second strategic planning meeting, devoted to resource allocation, the top team reviews the plans and assigns resources to those it approves.

Expected results: The entire organization will be focused on accomplishing the objectives of these issues, resulting in lasting strategic change.

I stated in Part I (see "The Strategic Plan Process") that strategic priority issues are the single most important output of the planning process. They must be addressed if the organization is to succeed in the future. So how do you make sure that these issues are turned into appropriate actions? That resources are allocated to them? That you get the results you want for each one?

To start, you need priority issue program action plans. The top team usually delegates the task of developing these to multifunctional teams called program teams. The same teams will run the priority issue programs when they are approved.

One priority issue may spawn two or three action plans. For example, if cost is a priority issue, it may yield three plans: overhead cost, operating cost, and selling and marketing cost.

What's in an Action Plan

Each action plan will show:

- One- and three-year objectives for the overall priority issue.
- One- and three-year objectives for the program action plan addressing part of the overall issue.
- Definition of the program; why it's important.
- Scope of the program.
- Key first-year steps to move the program forward—who must do what, when.
- Interlock requirements—required actions and resources that are outside of the team leader's power to command. Obtaining these resources requires a sign-off from the person "owning" them.
- Calculations of the anticipated incremental cost and gain.
- People and skills required to carry out the program, particularly scarce leverage people.

The plans are brief—just two pages—but they contain the key information the top team needs to assess them, approve the worthy ones, allocate resources, and ultimately review progress against each plan as it's being executed. Exhibit 2-1 gives an action-planning format and Exhibit 2-2 a completed plan.

The Action-Planning Process

Top Team: Objectives and Delegation

The top team generates priority issues during the first strategic planning meeting—named, appropriately, the priority-setting meeting. The top team develops broad one- and three-year objectives for each priority issue and generates ideas for addressing them. To flesh each idea into an action plan and execute the program once it is approved, the top team names a project team leader and cross-functional team members. Usually, one priority issue is assigned per team.

For a few priority issues, the impact of the issue is isolated to one department, which holds most of the resources needed. When that happens, the issue is assigned to that department and incorporated into the departmental plan. If, for example, a company identified manufacturing cost as a priority issue, it might assign that issue to the manufacturing department for action.

(Text continues on page 99.)

Exhibit 2-1   Program Action Plans Format

PROGRAM ACTION PLAN

Program no. _____   Program manager: _____
Program name: _____
Priority issue: _____
Objective: Year 1 _____
_____

Year 3 _____
_____

Description and scope of program: _____
_____
_____

Step	What	Who	When

IMPACT ESTIMATE

Record incremental impact only—resources beyond those currently available to the program.

	Year		
	1	2	3
Revenue			
Sales:			
Gain			
Profit:			
Cost savings:			
Total:			
Cost			
Expense:			
Capital addition:			
Working capital changes:			
Net results			
Cash flow:			
Present value:			
Profitability index:			
People			
Number:			
Time required:			
Special skills:			

INTERLOCK REQUIREMENTS

Group/Division/Person	What's Required	When		

Exhibit 2-2   Completed Action Plan, Including Impact Estimate and Coordination Requirements

PROGRAM ACTION PLAN

Program no.:   3   Program manager: Schwartz

Program name: Tuncon Plant

Priority issue: Long-range capacity plan

Objective: Develop long-range manufacturing facilities that will:

* Meet forecast demand 1998–2007

* Accommodate testing and manufacture of new products

* Achieve dramatic improvement in quality, cost, and customer service

* Be configured for continuous improvement of quality, cost, and service, and expansion or reconfiguration for new-product lines

Year 1: Design plant and begin construction.
Year 2: Complete construction and start up.
Year 3: Achieve running rate of 177 million units per year at a cost of $.325 per unit.
Design capacity: 600 million units, one shift, cost of $.22 per unit.

Step	What	Who	When
	Establish design specs based on marketing forecast, product mix, research requirements	Team. Engineering lead.	Feb. 1997
	Approval specs	Top team.	March 1997
	Flowchart and system design. Costing.	Team. Engineering and finance lead.	July 1997
	Detailed drawings for bid purposes. Costing.	Team. Engineering and finance lead.	Sept. 1997
	Approval	Top team.	Sept. 1997
	Bids	Purchasing and construction.	Nov. 1997
	Construction start	Construction team from manufacturing and facilities takes over.	Jan. 1998
INTERLOCKS			
	Central safety, quality, environmental, and engineering	Review plans and drawings for compliance.	Prior to each major corporate review
	Information systems	Project management systems; internal plant systems and communications.	Shown on separate schedule
	Human resources	Temporary help during construction, hiring, and training.	Shown on separate schedule

IMPACT ESTIMATE

Record incremental impact only—resources beyond those currently available to the program.

		Operating Year		
		1	**2**	**3**
Revenue		**2000**	**2001**	**2002**
	Price/unit	$.425	$.420	$.400
	Cost/unit	$.325	$.295	$.270
	Units	177	350	525
	Revenue	75	147	210
Gain				
	Manufacturing cost (x $1 million)	57.5	94.5	45.0
	Gross margin (x $1 million)	17.7	52.5	95.0
	Gross margin (%)	27.6%	35.7%	45.0%
	Cost (million)	40	48	52

Cost

1. Expense capital $125 million
2. Capital $125 million
3. Equipment $250 million
    Total investment $500 million

Net results

10-year ROI = 19% per annum
5-year ROI = 17% per annum

People

Key skills: One key construction manager
                     One plant manager from groundbreaking on

(continued)

Exhibit 2-2   (*continued*)

INTERLOCK REQUIREMENTS		
Group / Division/ Person	*What's Required*	*When*
1. Construction Division	Manage entire construction process	Start 1/1
2. Safety and hygiene	Plan security and buyoff, write safety procedures, cost by plant	Start 3/1
3. Legal	Handle all licenses, liability assessment, and insurance	Start 4/1
4. Vendors	Call on appropriate vendors—company committee to design receipt and shipping systems	Start 5/1
5. Customers	Form customer committee to design order-entry shipment systems	Start 5/1

Project Team Responsibilities: Strategies and Implementation Methods

The teams follow the process shown in Exhibit 2-3. At a kickoff meeting, a top-team member provides direction on the scope of the work. Each project team begins by brainstorming ideas on how best to address its assigned priority issue. The team then condenses this list to a handful of ideas that members feel have the best chance of meeting their assigned objectives.

Project teams require your best people. After all, a good deal of the future of the company is in their hands. You can expect a project team with the right mix of disciplines and creative, motivated people to generate good ideas and good plans. If you settle for anything less, you risk mediocrity.

To illustrate the process, here's what might happen when a hypothetical project team takes on the priority issue of new-product expansion. The team identifies a host of possible implementation strategies, ranging from invention and internal development through licensing, joint venture, and acquisition. After selecting a few strategies that best address the issue and fit the company's direction and competencies, the team prepares a separate action plan for *each* recommended strategy, stating who must do what, by when, to move the program forward in the coming year.

Let's say one recommended strategy is internal new-product development. The team's action plan includes several crucial steps: market segmentation and positioning of the current and potential product lines, identification of new products and their rough specifications, concept testing with customers, and recommendations to the top team on which products should actually be developed. (After this plan is approved and implemented, the program team would then generate another action plan for developing and launching the approved products.)

After drafting the action plan, the team undertakes two tasks in parallel. One is to calculate the cost and potential gain from the program. For some programs, a project team would involve the finance department in preparing investment and return calculations. For our new-product development program, only the initial incremental expenses such as market research, travel, and perhaps some early research and development costs can be detailed at an early stage. The anticipated revenue and return on investment can't be calculated until the initial stage of the project is completed, although the overall revenue objectives and return would be part of the project objectives.

At the same time, team members detail their interlock requirements—time and resources needed by the program that are outside team

Exhibit 2-3   Developing Action Plans From Priority Issues

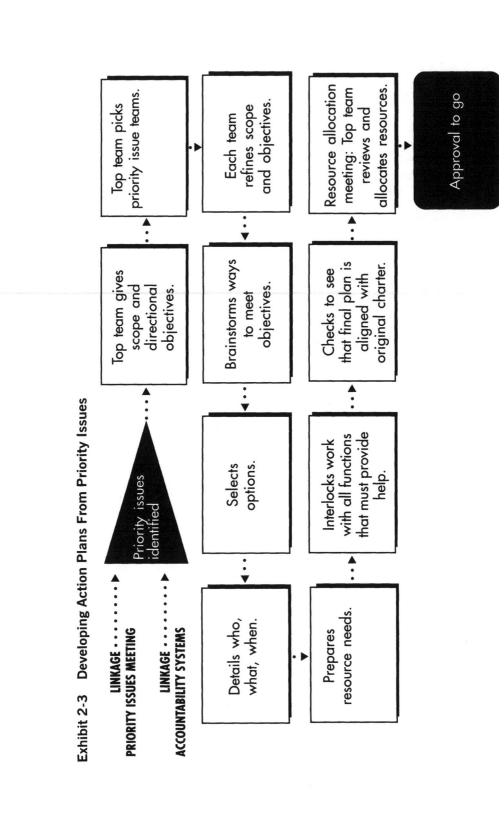

members' control. For example, a team member from marketing may be able to commit market research resources, but the team will have to get a commitment from information systems to process the research data. If, in a worst-case scenario, this "sign-off" is denied, the project team can appeal that decision to the top team during the forthcoming resource allocation meeting.

The team must also identify new hires needed and incremental time required from people already in the organization to carry out the project. The latter is particularly important and, again, needs to be coordinated with the functional areas that will provide the services.

Top-Team Approval

The project team is now ready to present its action plan to the top team for its review, which takes place at the second major corporate strategy meeting, the resource allocation meeting. Before that meeting, project teams should circulate summaries of their plans to top-team members. At the meeting, the top team decides whether to go with each plan, scrap it, or modify it. Here, the most desirable programs are funded, resource conflicts adjudicated, or programs and priorities altered.

When its plan is approved, the project team receives a charter from the top team and the program sponsor. The teams get training in team management, facilitation, and development and are off and running.

Resource allocation and the team process are covered in depth later in Part II (see Key 11, "Allocate Resources Effectively, Putting Your Money and People Where Your Future Is," and Key 9, "Use Teams [Appropriately]").

Action Plan Detail

How much detail goes into the final action plan? Very little. Just enough so that management can review team progress and know where to dig more deeply if it chooses. Stick to a two-page format. Otherwise, the top team will be buried in paperwork, making it difficult to ferret out needed information quickly, compare programs addressing different issues, and make good resource allocation decisions. After all, you are likely to have fifteen to twenty action plans to monitor.

What belong in the plan are the program's objectives and four or five key action steps the team commits to accomplish during the next year. The steps to include are those that need top management input or significant resources. The team, of course, may back up this bare-bones plan with exceedingly detailed action and work plans that it will use to direct the work of the program.

Potential Problems

Watch out for these three flaws that action plans commonly exhibit:

1. *Objectives and action steps that are not measurable:* Broad generalities—such as "significantly improve service," "reduce manufacturing costs," or "improve organization morale"—aren't good enough. How would you know when you'd accomplished them? Demand specific measures as soon as reasonable guesses can be made. If the project team doesn't provide measurements, then the top team will have to do it for them or, better yet, work with the project team to do it jointly. Remember, all objectives and action steps must have a time measure: "completed by [date]." Use numbers to measure revenue, cost, units, profit, service, or quality level.

Is it ever acceptable to go with a directional objective like "significantly improve customer service"? The answer is a reluctant and qualified yes. Early in the process, you may not have an adequate definition of what service is and how to measure it. But in such instances, you must establish a date by which more precise measures will be available.

2. *Too much detail:* Discipline your troops early to give you the three to five most important steps and keep the detail to themselves. If they can't pick out the key steps, help them.

3. *Narrow thinking:* There is a tendency to think in terms of incremental extensions of today's business instead of broad, even iconoclastic, methods to address priority issues.

Review

The top team will review progress on strategic priority issue programs at least quarterly. The review process is covered later in Part II (see "Key 17: Review Performance").

From objectives to review, action planning is a low-tech, paper-driven process, but it's the best way to put the most important part of your strategic plan into motion. It works because it forces the players to focus on the key elements. And because most people have used action plans and understand their format and method, they can get right to work on the issue without having to learn a new process or system first.

Do

- Limit your plan to three to five priority issues. Each will generate one or more action plans requiring time and resources from your organization. Too many plans will splinter your efforts and hamper progress.
- Use multifunctional program teams to generate and select ideas on how to address your priority issues. Many minds and disciplines develop superior solutions.
- Insist that objectives and action steps be measurable.

Don't

- Allow infinite detail on submitted plans. You have to manage ten to fifteen action plans and need to focus only on the "bottom-line" objectives and action steps for tracking.
- Allow people to use their own format for action plans. Instead, develop one format for your organization and insist that it be used consistently so that you can find the information you need and track it easily.

Key 3

Embed Departmental Planning

> **Principle:** Second only to people, functional departments are the single most important element in effectively executing your plan.
>
> **Why it's important:** Departments have the money, the people, the skills, and hopefully, the leadership needed for effective execution. They also have the power to sabotage the plan. The organization goes as the departments go.
>
> **How it's applied:** Develop well-thought-out, resourced, and measurable departmental plans.
>
> **Expected results:** With good departmental plans, you will achieve superior integration of corporate objectives and strategic priority issues into ongoing departmental tasks as well as superior coordination of efforts between or among departments that must work together to execute the plan.

Functional departments are the implementation centers of organizations. They have the people; they have the dollars. They house the bulk of the leadership, and they are the repository of the company's skills and collective learning. They have the ability to carry out corporate plans to a T or to go their own merry way, hiding efficiency-sapping unaligned activities deep in the department, where they're nearly impossible to discover.

So what is the role of the departments in implementing corporate strategies? How do you ensure that departmental actions are in line with the corporate plan? What process do you use to ensure efficient planning at the departmental level?

To answer those questions, this chapter examines departmental planning, fitting it into the context of the corporate strategic planning process.

The Departmental Planning Process

Objectives

The objectives of departmental planning are to:

- *Define, monitor, and measure the department's performance* on the following overall scorecard introduced in the Key 1 chapter:
  —Corporate priorities delegated to the department
  —Departmental strategic priorities
  —Departmental operating priorities
  —Departmental infrastructure development
  —Interlocks owed to others
  —Interlocks owed to us
  —Strategic program team involvement
  —Numbers that quantitatively measure the department's performance
- *Establish accountability* for the plan at the departmental level and for individuals within the department.
- *Ensure alignment* of the department's actions with the corporate plan.
- *Coordinate the department's plan* with others in the organization who must provide help or to whom the department must provide resources, including strategic program teams to agree on interlocks.

Advantages

Organizations using departmental planning get results superior to those that don't. The plans resulting from the departmental planning process are usually realistic and measurable, allowing you to hold people accountable for results. Plans based on this process therefore propel a higher rate of execution of assigned tasks than do loosely drawn plans or those based strictly on budget numbers, historical results, and the traditional unchallenged role of a department.

Ironically, adding formal departmental planning to existing strategic, operating, and budgetary planning processes actually cuts down on the time, detailed numbers work, and hassle needed to put all three together because:

- Strategic tasks and operating tasks are developed in parallel.
- Strategic numbers and operating numbers are task-based.
- Top-down budget numbers fall easily out of the resource allocation process that follows departmental planning.

In addition, the system forces coordination between departments and teams that must help each other. Mutual work and goals become inter-locked—a critical step in effective plan execution.

More than any other tool that we've observed, departmental plan-ning builds enthusiasm and commitment to both the departmental and the corporate plan. People feel included when they have an opportunity to influence policy and action at both the corporate and departmental levels. They like seeing the big picture, and they like the stimulating interaction that the process requires.

Disadvantages

The departmental planning process has only one disadvantage. As with any new process, it takes time to design the process, train people in its use, and get people through the learning curve during the first and sec-ond planning cycles.

Departmental Roles

Before going into the planning process itself, we need to expand on the functional roles introduced in the Key 1 chapter so that you will have a detailed understanding of the roles included in the departmental score-card.

Most functional departments have the following three overall func-tions, divided into eight roles, which are presented with examples in Exhibit 3-1:

1. Corporate work
2. Departmental work
3. Work with others

Corporate Work

Delegated Corporate Strategic Priorities/Priority Issues. A department's first responsibility is to implement delegated corporate plan priorities, objectives, and tasks. Marketing might be asked to lead a formal project team reporting to the top team whose objective is to acquire competitors that will add at least five share points in niches in which the company is now weak.

Delegated Corporate Objectives. To fulfill a corporate strategic objec-tive to dominate certain market niches, marketing, for example, might be asked to gain five market share points over three years by extending its ongoing marketing, sales, and product line introductions. Marketing,

Exhibit 3-1   Departmental Roles

Role	Definition	Example
1. CORPORATE WORK		
Delegated corporate strategic priorities/ priority issues	Department is given a corporate priority to execute using its own resources.	Manufacturing is given a cost-per-unit objective to achieve as part of a corporate "cost reduction" priority issue.
Delegated corporate objectives	Department is given a corporate strategic objective to meet.	Customer service is assigned a customer survey satisfaction rating to achieve, with the detailed means of doing it left to the department.
2. DEPARTMENTAL WORK		
Departmental strategic priorities	Long-term structural strategic priorities specific to the department's charter	Marketing priority of developing alternative distribution channels for current products
Operating priorities	Critical priorities and tasks to be addressed to make the next year happen	Products and services scheduled to be released in the next year
Infrastructure priorities	Priorities that address building the department's future capacity to deliver	Installation of a human resources information system for human resources to allow planning for succession and future developmental needs
3. WORK WITH OTHERS		
Interlock—owed to others	Priorities and tasks to be addressed for other departments to help them with their plan	Human resources designs specific training courses at another department's request.
Interlock—owed to us	Tasks that the department needs to perform requiring the help of others	Marketing needs information systems to help build a customer-market-product profitability model.
Team obligations	The department's involvement in corporate teams	Two members of the finance staff each work half-time as members of new-product teams.
4. NUMBERS	Strategic and operating numerical measures appropriate to the department's function	Sales revenue, spending, profitability, percentage of revenue from new products, market share

in turn, figures out how to meet these objectives without a formal project team. Formal reporting to the top team is limited to periodic reporting of market penetration numbers.

Departmental Work

Departmental Strategic Priorities. Departments have long-term strategies, too. At least, they should. They are the priorities and tasks that will strategically and structurally move the department toward fulfilling its own mission and vision. A department might plan to grow a nascent market, for example, by adding direct-to-the-customer Internet distribution to supplement already successful retail stores. A retail chain might plan to systematically build distribution capacity and "bank" trained store managers well in advance for planned expansions. Exhibit 3-2 shows departmental priority issues from a variety of companies and functions. The department's strategic priorities usually result in project work that causes major structural change in the way the department will conduct its future business.

Operating Priorities. Operating priorities are usually addressed in the departmental operating plan or annual plan, which covers the department's most important ongoing responsibilities, prescribing tasks with short-term spending and payoff. Included would be the sales department's sales, new-customer, and market-penetration goals; finance's goal for debt and equity financing in the next year; operation's cost and efficiency goals and the initiatives to support them; and new products to be released in the coming year.

Note that you're only looking at the tip of the iceberg here—the four or five operating or ongoing tasks with the biggest impact. Obviously, every department member has dozens of job description tasks that have to be performed to keep the company running. Said another way, a major product launch belongs in the departmental plan. The items needed to support it—pricing, market research, advertising, and promotion—don't. These belong in individual job descriptions.

Infrastructure Priorities. Infrastructure is the heart and vasculature of the department—the assets, systems, and knowledge that keep it alive and allow it to do its job.

In those departments that drive the company's core competencies and competitive advantage, the infrastructure has to be first-rate. It would be hard to imagine American Express letting its marketing department and information systems deteriorate or Rubbermaid allowing its product development methods to calcify.

Too often, companies do leave infrastructure building to chance.

Exhibit 3-2 Departmental Priority Issues From a Variety of Companies and Functions

Human Resources

▼ Training
▼ Compensation systems
▼ Accountability systems
▼ Staffing levels
▼ Labor relations

Finance

▼ Cash flow
▼ Asset return/utilization
▼ Overhead cost
▼ Reporting/control/timeliness
▼ Financial structure/capital
▼ Receivables management

Sales

▼ Penetration
▼ New customers
▼ Order entry/service
▼ Training/skills
▼ Sales force efficiency
▼ Selling configuration

Research and Development

▼ New products
▼ Technical core competencies
▼ Technical career ladder
▼ New-product process
▼ Future technologies
▼ Innovation

Operations

▼ Cost
▼ Quality
▼ Waste
▼ Maintenance
▼ Cost systems
▼ Standards, standard operating procedures
▼ Capacity
▼ Raw materials supply

Management Information Systems

▼ Processing capacity
▼ New computer systems
▼ Response to internal customers
▼ Financial reporting
▼ Market reporting

Marketing

▼ New products
▼ Distribution systems
▼ Emerging segments
▼ Market penetration
▼ Pricing
▼ Customer satisfaction
▼ Marketing profit

Nevertheless, examples abound of infrastructure improvements that support department work day in and day out, cumulatively adding to the department's performance. We've seen programs that include reengineering a customer service system from start to finish; revamping the new-product development system to reduce cycle times and improve market "hit" ratios; training all manufacturing personnel in continuous improvement methods prior to installing such a program; training engineering, product development, and marketing people in teamwork and team management as part of a system to improve the product development cycle time and product innovation and quality.

Work With Others

Interlock—Owed to Others. These priorities are agreed-upon work owed to other departments to aid them in accomplishing their operating or strategic plans. The role of many departments is to be a resource, in part or in whole, for others. Unfortunately, departments frequently don't consciously define that role, talk to their potential customers about their needs, or identify the resources needed to fulfill them. Once the year is under way, the battles begin over resources, time, and scheduling.

Look at how often information systems (IS) is the whipping boy for operating departments—sometimes for good reason but often not. Frequently, users have not defined their expectations for IS early in the planning cycle, particularly for the unexciting, time-consuming little things like system modifications. This example underscores the need to solicit the requirements of customers and peers early in the planning cycle so that there are fewer surprises during implementation and so that resource allocation and acquisition can be intelligently planned.

Every organization has plenty of examples of "work owed to others" roles: Human resources sources or designs training for other departments; information systems completes a dedicated human resources information system for human resources; product development produces prototypes for marketing for a market test; operations runs prototypes for product development for the market test; communication provides advertising, packaging, and collateral support for a new-product launch.

Interlock—Owed to Us. The flip side of the department's work that is owed to others is the work needed *from* others to achieve department goals.

A hospital administrator, for example, might be committed to reducing cost and improving efficiency. To accomplish that task, she requires help from information systems at the parent company to install a "procedure profitability" model. The agreement on what is to be done and its timing and cost is worked out in advance and made part of the plan.

Team Obligations. This defines the department's obligation to support strategic program teams. An acquisition team, for example, may require 25 percent of a marketing vice president's time. New-product teams may require significant effort from three product managers. A cost reduction team may require the full-time attention of three analysts from finance for six months.

Because planning and interlocking for interdepartmental needs are often neglected, they frequently become a cause of conflict when plan execution is under way. It's better to estimate the time needed up front as part of the overall resource allocation scheme than to tack it on later in the year.

Numbers in the Departmental Plan

The departmental plan must include numbers and other metrics that measure the department's overall strategic and operating performance. The department manager and controller should provide a three-year history of department spending and—for operating units—revenue, margin, and profit, as well as a tentative three-year projection. The projection numbers are best guesses, with the first year intended to be a relatively "tight" guess on which budgets can be based.

Scorecard Format

Exhibit 3-3 shows a marketing department scorecard. Using this format, a departmental plan can be presented on two concise pages. Usually, this plan becomes the department manager's individual objectives; it is used to hold the manager accountable for his or her performance. The scorecard is also used to delegate priorities and objectives to people in the department. Those objectives are incorporated into their individual objectives. The individual objective-setting process, the final piece in the loop of accountability, is covered in the Key 4 chapter.

Putting Together the Annual Departmental Plan

How do you produce the perfect departmental plan? Unfortunately, there is no magic process. But there are a series of steps that, if implemented competently, will go a long way toward aligning department activities with the corporate plan and dramatically increasing plan buy-in.

Exhibit 3-3   Marketing Departmental Scorecard

DELEGATED CORPORATE STRATEGIC PRIORITIES

Through external means (acquisition or joint venture), add 10% market share by 1/1/2000.

DEPARTMENTAL STRATEGIC PRIORITIES

E-commerce: Add electronic commerce as a distribution method. Achieve number one channel position with a minimum of 10% of business electronically processed by 1/1/2001, 20% by 1/1/2002.

Alpha launch: Launch the alpha line of digital circuits by 6/1/2002, with first-year volume of $100 million and 18% market share.

New prototypes: Concept and customer testing on two new prototype circuits and one new subsystem and go/no go for full development by 6/1/2000.

Breakthrough products: Completely reposition our capabilities. Develop new-product concepts and marketing plans that can result in revenue and profits equal to next year's budget three years after launch for top management approval by 1/1/2000.

Service reengineering: Reengineer the sales service department. Objectives: Reduce customer wait time to 30 seconds maximum; lower transaction cost 40%; allow orders placed by midnight to be received the next day. Customer service index improvement from 92 to 97.

DEPARTMENTAL OPERATING PRIORITIES

New products: Beta line extension launch 4/1/2000. First-year revenue/gross margin = $55 million/ 32%.

Sales and profits: Achieve unit sales increase of 22% at average selling price of $32 and gross margin of 38%.

Productivity: Zero-base-plan our selling and distribution system to remove inefficiencies and unproductive distributors and reps. Achieve productivity increases of at least 33% and increases in customer satisfaction ratings.

DEPARTMENTAL INFRASTRUCTURE PRIORITIES

E-commerce: Add electronic commerce department by 1/1/2000 with experienced internal management and a sourcing plan for graphics, promotion, customer development, and systems.

Education: All marketing personnel to be trained in scenario and probabilistic decision-making tools by the current year's end.

Satisfaction surveys: Design new, less intrusive, and more effective customer satisfaction survey methods for distributors, reps, end customers, and suppliers. Model for evaluation and approval 6/1/2000. Roll out 7/1.

Profitability evaluation system: Complete mechanization of system to evaluate product, customer, and distribution system effectiveness and profitability by 1/1/2000.

INTERLOCKS

Owe

Internal research: Internal customer research programs for (1) information systems, (2) human resources, and (3) purchasing. Due 2/15, 5/30, and 7/1, respectively.

Planning analysis: New-customer and competitive research data, analysis, presentation, and interpretation for top management planning retreat 6/1.

Owed to Us

Information systems: Information systems effort of 200 work-hours to complete product profitability system by 1/1/2000.

TEAM PARTICIPATION

Acquisitions: Department manager and one analyst on acquisition team. Commitment for one year at approximately 25% of time each.

Information systems: Department manager member of corporate information systems team. Commitment for one year at 10% of time.

NUMBERS*

	Year		
	1	2	3
Sales (x $1 million)	1,000	1,200	1,600
Profit	38%	40%	40%
Penetration overall	32%	34%	36%

*Include only products currently on the market and their extensions, distributed through existing channels.

Exhibit 3-4 illustrates the annual departmental planning process, locking departmental actions into the corporate plan and individual standards of performance. (Exhibit 1-2 in the Key 1 chapter shows how departmental planning fits into the entire corporate accountability cycle.)

The key steps in annual departmental planning that we will review in detail now are:

1. *Departmental prework, part 1:* The department head and direct reports individually prepare their lists of corporate and departmental priority issues, involving direct reports in the process.
2. *Departmental priority-setting meeting:* The departmental staff agrees on corporate priority issues; departmental strategic, operating, and infrastructure priorities; anticipated participation on teams; work owed to others; and work required of other departments.
3. *Corporate priority-setting meeting:* The top team agrees on corporate strategic issues, teams to address them, and approval or modification of the departmental plans and priorities.

Exhibit 3-4   Annual Departmental Planning Process

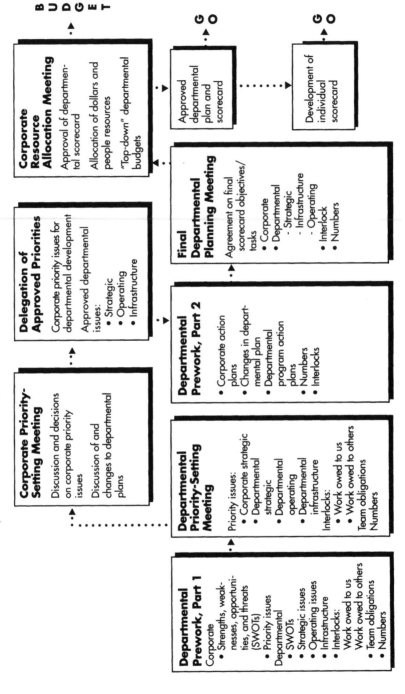

Departmental Prework, Part 1

Corporate
- Strengths, weaknesses, opportunities, and threats (SWOTs)
- Priority issues

Departmental
- SWOTs
- Strategic issues
- Operating issues
- Infrastructure
- Interlocks:
  Work owed to us
  Work owed to others
- Team obligations
- Numbers

Departmental Priority-Setting Meeting

Priority issues:
- Corporate strategic
- Departmental strategic
- Departmental operating
- Departmental infrastructure

Interlocks:
- Work owed to us
- Work owed to others

Team obligations

Numbers

Corporate Priority-Setting Meeting

Discussion and decisions on corporate priority issues

Discussion of and changes to departmental plans

Delegation of Approved Priorities

Corporate priority issues for departmental development

Approved departmental issues:
- Strategic
- Operating
- Infrastructure

Departmental Prework, Part 2

- Corporate action plans
- Changes in departmental plan
- Departmental program action plans
- Numbers
- Interlocks

Final Departmental Planning Meeting

Agreement on final scorecard objectives/tasks
- Corporate
- Departmental
  - Strategic
  - Infrastructure
  - Operating
- Interlock
- Numbers

Corporate Resource Allocation Meeting

Approval of departmental scorecard

Allocation of dollars and people resources

"Top-down" departmental budgets

→ BUDGET

Approved departmental plan and scorecard

→ GO

Development of individual scorecard

→ GO

4. *Delegation of approved priorities:* Corporate priority issues and approved departmental issues are delegated to departments and cross-functional teams to enable fleshing out of details.
5. *Departmental prework, part 2:* Departmental plans are completed, incorporating corporate inputs.
6. *Final departmental planning meeting:* The departmental staff agrees on the plan that will be presented to the top team.
7. *Corporate resource allocation meeting:* Strategic priority issue action plans and departmental plans are given final approval. Dollar and people resources are allocated to the ongoing business and strategic programs.
8. Individual objectives are set at the departmental level based on approved plans.

Departmental Prework, Part 1: "Dip-Down" to Develop Priority Issues

The first step is traditionally called a "dip-down" because, from the top team's point of view, it's an opportunity to delve into lower levels of the organization to get their thinking about corporate strategic priorities.

This step establishes priority issues for each of the department's role areas as well as the department's view of what the corporate strategic priorities should be. Remember that a priority issue is a broad area to be addressed that will later be turned into objectives and detailed action plans. The purpose here is to identify the critical issues and avoid getting "micro," which is the immediate tendency of most departments. A priority issue for a health-care facility, for example, would be delivery cost per patient. Later, the department would set objectives and formulate detailed action plans for reaching them.

Homework

Each department staff member individually completes the following homework before the department's priority-setting meeting. Staff members who have people reporting to them involve their staff in the preparation of the prework. Each staff member lists:

- The top three or four corporate strengths, weaknesses, opportunities, and threats (SWOTs) and three or four corporate priority issues. These may be new issues, continuations of old ones, departmental issues that the staff member feels should be handled at the corporate level, or issues far beyond the department's boundaries.
- Three or four departmental SWOTs

- The top three or four departmental priority issues, derived from the SWOTs, for each of the following categories:
  —Strategic
  —Operating
  —Infrastructure
- Commitments that affect the department:
  —Interlocks, including work needed from others and work owed to others
  —Team commitments

The department may agree in advance of prework that certain criteria will be used to guide the selection of issues. Typical criteria include long-term impact on profits, fit with the corporate and departmental direction statements (if they exist), and extent to which addressing the issue will bolster a competitive edge or enhance a core competency.

The SWOT exercise will usually yield most of the data needed to establish issues to be addressed in all of the categories listed. If it doesn't, department members will need to think out of the box and ensure that they have covered key issues in each category.

Most departments need to go through a complete SWOT exercise for both the department and the corporation every three years. In the intervening years, it is usually sufficient to update the priority issues by asking, "In light of last year's progress and changes in the environment and internal operations, (1) are the existing issues still valid, and (2) are there others that should be considered?" The new priorities can then be picked from this list.

Departmental Priority-Setting Meeting

The agenda for a departmental priority-setting meeting is shown in Exhibit 3-5. The meeting, well-facilitated, takes about three-quarters of a day.

For the departmental-level items, the planning team should agree on the two to three issues to be addressed in each category and, where possible, set provisional objectives for those issues. For example, if a critical operating issue is sales revenue, the revenue growth and sales levels should be tentatively set.

Here are some examples of acceptable ways of incorporating measurements into each issue:

- *Measurable objective:* "Achieve fully burdened unit cost of $0.44 for 1999."
- *Time-based task:* "Complete a survey of the future digital camera market and recommend our entry strategy by February 1, 1999."

Exhibit 3-5   Agenda for a Departmental Priority-Setting Meeting

▼ Corporate SWOTs
▼ Corporate strategic priority issues
▼ Departmental SWOTs
▼ Departmental strategic priority issues
▼ Departmental operating issues and tasks
▼ Departmental infrastructure issues and needs
▼ Departmental numbers
▼ Interlocks
    Work owed to others
    Work owed to us
▼ Team tasks

- *Priority issue:* "Complete an action plan to address the priority issue of advanced programming capability by February 3, 1999."
- *Directional tasks:* "Improve service significantly beyond competitors' levels and customer expectations by 2002. Measures and action plans to follow when service database is complete in April 1999."
- *Resources provided:* "Provide four worker-years of programming assistance to the chief financial officer between January 1, 1999 and July 10, 1999 to complete installation of new general ledger system."
- *Team tasks:* "Provide 25 percent of one product manager's time to participate on the service system's team. The expected end result of this team is to reach better-than-competitive service rates in 1999 as measured by a to-be-conducted satisfaction survey."

It's not OK to use:

- *Vague directional tasks:* "Grow sales significantly" or "Significantly improve our image among electronic component brokers." There are no numbers or suggestions of how you're going to get them.
- *Priority issues without detailing objectives and action plans:* "Our top priority is manufacturing efficiency." Again, there are no numbers or suggestions of how you're going to get them.
- *Ongoing tasks:* "Continue to build our customer base." This is basically a job description, not a measurable objective.

The toughest issues to make measurable are those we often call "soft."

"Establish a team-based, empowered culture in the organization," for example, is only a vague, unmeasurable statement of intent. Acceptable ways of measuring this issue might be:

- "Ensure that five strategic program teams receive training in team management and facilitation and have an outside facilitator on call whenever required to help them by May 1, 1999."
- "Have an off-the-shelf team-training program approved by top management and ready for use by any new team by May 1, 1999. Require that all new teams take such training."
- "All employees will attend training courses on empowerment, job descriptions, writing performance standards, and performance reviews by January 1, 2000. Seventy-five percent of all positions will have job descriptions and subsequent individual performance standards in place by June 1, 2000. Audit will determine the extent to which job standards have been set according to human resources empowerment standards of giving employees adequate latitude, resources, and skills to do their job."

The output of the departmental priority-setting meeting should be a consensus on the three to five corporate priority issues and the key department-level issues, with associated measurable objectives. Placed in the departmental scorecard format shown in Exhibit 3-3, these form the departmental plan that the department manager takes to the upcoming corporate priority-setting meeting.

Corporate Priority-Setting Meeting

At the corporate priority-setting meeting, the top management team makes several corporate-level decisions that affect departmental plans:

- What will the corporate priority issues and their objectives be?
- Who will handle them? Usually, they will be addressed by a cross-functional team headed by an individual from a functional department.
- Which corporate issues and objectives, if any, will be delegated to a department exclusively for execution?

The top team also addresses each department's plan, approving or rejecting individual priorities and accepting or adjusting objectives. The team pays particular attention to (1) the alignment of departmental tasks to the corporate direction statement and priorities; (2) additional resources probably required for the new priorities; and (3) coordination, or lack thereof, among departments needed to address specific priority issues.

Finally, the top team determines a tentative budget for each department. For each department, the outcome of the meeting will be a complete departmental scorecard, similar to that shown in Exhibit 3-3, with the corporate objectives added.

Delegation of Approved Priorities

Departmental Prework, Part 2: Putting Flesh on the Plan

The revised priority issues go back to departments to:

- Prepare program action plans for corporate priority issues dele-gated to the department for execution. An action plan should include one- and three-year objectives; a description of the scope of the program; a schedule; and the human, dollar, and other resources required, includ-ing the help needed from other departments. An example of a completed program action plan is shown in the Key 2 chapter (see Exhibit 2-2).

- Assist in the preparation of strategic priority issue action plans that are the responsibility of another department but need this depart-ment's input or assist a department member in preparing the action plan for a strategic program team on which he or she is serving.

- Incorporate corporate strategic objectives into the department's ongoing business. This could, for example, lead to one- and three-year market-penetration goals for existing products and their extensions or to one- and three-year manufacturing efficiency goals.

- Prepare, at the department manager's option, action plans for de-partmental-level priority issues. These will not be reviewed at the cor-porate level but provide a department management tool.

- Prepare final one- and three-year budget numbers and summarize incremental resources required for the plan.

Final Departmental Planning Meeting

Exhibit 3-6 shows an agenda for a final departmental planning meeting, attended by the department vice president and his staff. The output of that meeting is a final plan in the departmental scorecard format, accom-panied by a summary of resources required and one or more action

Exhibit 3-6   Agenda for a Final Departmental Planning Meeting

▼ Review assigned corporate priority issue programs.
▼ Revise the departmental plan and make it measurable.
▼ Review departmental priority issue action plans.
▼ Complete tentative budget.
▼ Complete final scorecard.

plans backing up each corporate strategic priority issue delegated to the department.

Corporate Resource Allocation Meeting

A single corporate resource allocation meeting is used to allocate funds and human resources to corporate and departmental strategic and operating funding requests. More than any other tool, this meeting helps align corporate strategy with departmental action. In the resource allocation process, detailed in the Key 11 chapter, management:

- Scrutinizes corporate and departmental plans.
- Selects and funds corporate priority issue programs.
- Approves or disapproves departmental plan priorities and scorecards.
- Allocates the time of valuable leverage people.
- Allocates funds while establishing a one- and three-year budget. Approved projects are a go, funded from this day so work can start or continue.
- Ensures that all corporate strategic plan issues and objectives are incorporated into a departmental plan or are assigned to a department manager/team leader or team.
- Sees that all departmental plan elements are aligned with corporate priorities.
- Lists and coordinates interdepartment interlock requirements, arbitrating any conflicts over availability or timing of resources required.

Setting Individual Standards of Performance

The final step in the departmental planning process is to turn departmental priorities and objectives into individual performance standards. This is covered in depth in the Key 4 chapter.

Motivational Value of Departmental Planning

Departmental planning has extremely high motivational leverage. Departments involved invariably are enthusiastic about participating in setting corporate priorities. It helps them see the big picture. It makes them rightly feel important. Its direct tie to the corporate plan makes their jobs more understandable and important. Furthermore, departments that have had budgets but not true plans relish the opportunity to thrash out departmental business and then have a scorecard that they can use to judge their progress.

Developing a Complete Departmental Strategic Plan

During the first and sometimes second year of a strategic change program, most departments concentrate on defining departmental and corporate issues in an "annual departmental plan," described in the preceding section. In the second or third year, they should develop a departmental strategic plan. Exhibit 3-7 is a chart showing the departmental strategic planning process. The process is the same as the corporate process but applied at the department level. It assumes that the department manager and his or her staff are the planning team. The highlights of the process are as follows:

Departmental Prework, Part 1

- *Target markets and strategy:* Assign a subteam to:
  —Identify and segment the department's current and future markets. Some departments, such as sales, have predominately external markets. Their market segments, their customers, and their customers' needs are usually primary to corporate strategy and are covered during the corporate planning process as a matter of course. Other departments, such as finance, human resources, and information systems have predominately internal markets whose customer needs must be examined. Information systems, for example, has the functions of (1) worldwide corporate communications, (2) responsive requests from divisions for unique systems, (3) repair and help desks, (4) operations, and (5) R&D, each with a different set of customers with different needs and potential competitors.

  —Identify the needs and satisfaction of these markets with the department versus the competition. (Internal departments can compare their services with those of outside vendors—corporate communications with public relations firms, product design with independent design companies, and so forth—or survey their in-house customers.)
  —Evaluate the performance of the department's product/service and future market needs.
  —Select target markets and strategy for satisfying these needs.
  —Explore any new opportunities or optimal ways of configuring your business to be more effective in the future.
- *Financial information:* Assign the jobs of:
  —Evaluating spending history by type of program or service
  —Determining the return by service
  —Performing a portfolio analysis of desirability of services

Exhibit 3-7   Departmental Strategic Planning Process Flowchart

Departmental Prework, Part 1

Assigned prework:	**Assigned and circulated— financial information:**	**Individual work— departmen- tal:**
• Market identification • Market segmentation • Customer needs; satisfaction versus competition • Service/product performance evaluation • Target markets and customer satisfaction strategy • New opportunities; strategic options	• Spending history • Spending by program versus return • Portfolio analysis, desirability of services • Baseline forecast	• Strengths • Weaknesses • Opportunities • Threats • Priority issues

Priority-Setting Meeting

Discussion:
- Product/customer analysis
- Financial/history/forecast
- Customer/market strategy

Consensus:
- Strengths, weaknesses, opportunities, threats
- Mission, vision, business definition, and values identified
- Priority issues
- Key result areas and scorecard format
- Strategic programs for priority issues
- Interlocks
- Action steps for resource allocation meeting

 Corporate approval of strategic priority issues scorecard

Departmental Prework, Part 2

Individuals/teams:
- Programs to address priority issues

Assigned/circulated:
- Draft mission statement
- Draft scorecard
- Draft overall strategy statement

Resource Allocation Meeting

Consensus on:
- Direction statement
- Strategy statement
- Action plans
- Scorecard
- Resource allocation system
- Review
- Changes in organization structure
- Communication of plan

 Corporate approval of scorecard, action plans, and resources

Postmeeting Work

- Completion of action plans
- Coordination of interlocks
- Delegation of objectives/steps

—Preparing a baseline forecast of revenue, demand for the department's services, people required, and spending
- *Individual preparation:* Each team member, after meeting with her people for a dip-down, prepares her view of the department's SWOTs and strategic priority issues.

Departmental Priority-Setting Meeting

- *Discussion:* Discuss the market analysis made by the marketing subteam and agree on:
  —What market segments you will serve and why
  —What customer needs you will meet
  —What your competitive advantages will be
  —New products, services, or organization configurations you will use to facilitate meeting customer needs
- *SWOTs:* Discuss and agree on the department's SWOTs and strategic priority issues.
- *Direction statement:* Agree on the key concepts within each category of the direction statement—mission, vision, business definition, values, core competencies, and competitive strategy. The department manager will "wordcraft" the statement for the next meeting.
- *Priority issues:* Develop strategic priority issues.
- *KRAs/scorecard:* Agree on key result areas and measures and the departmental scorecard format. Assign one team member the job of tentatively setting objectives for each measure and completing the scorecard by the next meeting.
- *Action steps:* Assign priority issues to individuals or teams to prepare action plans for the resource allocation meeting. Assign other actions.

Departmental Prework, Part 2

Steps after corporate approval of departmental strategy, priority issues, and scorecard are:

- *Individuals/teams:* Assigned individuals or teams complete priority issue action plans for presentation at the resource allocation meeting.
- *Assigned/circulated:* The department manager drafts the direction statement and a summary of market strategy and competitive advantage. The assigned individual completes the statement of strategic objectives and the individual scorecard.

Resource Allocation Meeting

- The department reaches consensus on:
  —The direction and strategy statements
  —Priority issue action plans and the resources to be allocated to them
  —How the plans will be reviewed
  —Any changes in the organization as a result of the plans
  —The schedule that will be used to communicate the plans and their results throughout the next year

The departmental final scorecard approves priority issue programs. Allocation of strategic resources and tentative requests are agreed upon during a corporate resource allocation meeting.

Postmeeting Work

- Complete action plans, interlocking of programs with others, and delegation of objectives.

The outline of a departmental strategic plan is shown in Exhibit 3-8.

How often does a department develop a complete plan? Usually, once every four or five years, about the same frequency with which a corporation will do a ground-up plan. If the environment changes dras-

Exhibit 3-8   Departmental Strategic Plan Outline

Plan
▼ Direction statement: mission, vision, business definition, values, competitive strategy, core competencies ▼ Strategic priority issues (department) ▼ Summary of action plans to address each (three sentences per action plan) ▼ Department scorecard ▼ Strategy summary

Appendix
Very brief summaries of analytical work done prior to plan completion: ▼ Market segments, needs, and strategy ▼ Strategic options and choices ▼ Portfolio analysis of business segments and choices

Note: The plan format is suitable for departments such as information systems, with a predominantly "inside" market, as well as for marketing, with a predominantly "outside" market. Slightly different emphasis and analyses would be used by each.

tically or the corporation changes direction or begins ground-up planning again, the departments will be obliged to follow.

Relationship of the Departmental Strategic Plan to Annual Departmental Planning

Most companies find it expedient to develop only the corporate and departmental priority issues during the first year of planning. They do departmental strategic plans, as noted above, in year two or three. Although this appears to put the cart before the horse, it is often the only way to keep the departmental workload down to a manageable level, thereby helping rather than hindering the acceptance of planning at the departmental level.

Once departments have developed a departmental strategic plan, in subsequent years they need only cover the following checklist prior to developing new priority issues for the annual planning cycle:

- *Environmental changes since the last plan was developed:* What changes in the outside world and within the corporation are helping (opportunity) or hurting (threat) the department? One designated department member usually prepares this data, sometimes relying on a survey of internal customers' opinions.
- Scorecard *numbers:* It is usually the department manager's job to measure cost, efficiency, revenue, or financial return over the past three years and forecast performance, assuming "business as usual," for the next few years.
- *Scorecard performance review:* How well did the department do on its scorecard— particularly with regard to corporate and departmental strategic programs?
- *Direction statement review:* Each individual on the departmental team is asked to evaluate the department's progress in fulfilling each statement of intent in the direction statement, indicating good progress (+), satisfactory condition (0), or needs work (−). The department will list the results and use the input when it develops its priority issues for the next year.

Do

- Make annual departmental planning an expected part of your planning process right from the beginning and implement it as soon as practical.
- Enforce a uniform format and process for departmental planning that embraces both strategies and operating plans, and

uses the interlocking scorecard as its hub. The system described here works.

- Require departments to develop a strategic plan in year two or three of the change process.
- Listen to the "dip-down." You'll hear a lot of important things, including some that you don't want to hear but need to. Your attention to department inputs motivates the people who must execute all of your plans.

Don't

- Make this a paperwork exercise. Most department plans can be summarized in bulleted-list form on two pages. You can talk the detail.
- Bloat the plan with more than two to three issues in each category.
- Approve priority issues or objectives without good measures. Measures are your ultimate (and only) control of plan progress.

Key 4

Negotiate Individual Accountabilities

Principle: Individuals who accept clear accountabilities and are judged on the results perform better than those who don't.

Why it's important: Ultimately, it is individuals who perform the work of strategy, and they must be assessed and held accountable.

How it's applied: Through a performance management system, the objectives and work of the organization are dispersed to individuals, their accomplishments are measured and judged, and their compensation and future with the company are determined.

Expected results: Far superior quality and speed of implementation can be expected than would be the case without individual accountabilities.

Individual Accountabilities

What Is an Individual Accountability?

An individual accountability is an objective or a task for which an individual is held responsible. It does not mean that the individual performs all of the work. A sales manager who is accountable for $100 million in sales may parcel the work out to five sales associates. Although he holds his people accountable for each delegated piece, he remains accountable to upper management for the entire amount. A solo market researcher, on the other hand, may indeed do all of the work himself. For a member of a strategic priority issue team, accountability is twofold: She will be judged on the overall team results as well as on her functional contribution to that team.

Where Do Individual Accountabilities Come From?

Individual accountabilities come from the sources shown below and in Exhibit 4-1. We've illustrated them in Exhibit 4-2 with the specific accountabilities of a marketing manager who reports to a vice president of sales, marketing, and business development.

Department managers, of course, are entirely responsible for all of their department's tasks and objectives and therefore the departmental scorecard. He or she will have additional operating, personal, and behavioral objectives supplementing the departmental scorcard and yielding their individual scorecard.

Individuals within the department will have separate departmental goals delegated to them and will be responsible for their own strategic, operating, personal, and behavioral objectives:

- *Corporate strategic priorities:* These are delegated to an individual or her department for execution of which there are none in this example.

- *Departmental strategic priorities.* The most important of those developed by her own department and approved by upper management, as well as those delegated from the sales, marketing, and business development function.

- *Departmental operating priorities.* The most important short-term objectives to be met, here, the launch of a new product and the volume and gross profit of the overall business, have extensive new product development, testing, and launch.

- *Departmental infrastructure priorities.* Those issues that must be addressed to give the department both the capacity, systems, and skills needed to carry out its function in the long term—here, the mechanization of a product distribution system customer profitability analysis.

- *The individual's ongoing job:* The ongoing job, defined in the job description, is the individual's principal mission in the corporation. For the marketing manager, key ongoing accountabilities are market penetration; market strategy; sales, advertising, and promotion campaigns; new-product development; and development of the marketing organization. Here, the marketing manager is charged with a profitability analysis of customers and product channels with the purpose of "cleaning up the marketing value chain" and improving profitability.

- *The departmental plan:* The plan of the individual's department includes corporate strategic tasks assigned to the department. The marketing manager is assigned two tasks from the departmental plan: (1) development and launch of a new product line and (2) a profitability

Exhibit 4-1   Sources of Data for Individual Accountability

CATEGORY	DATA SOURCE
Corporate strategic priorities and corporate objectives for departmental execution	Delegated from corporate to departmental plan to individual
Departmental strategic priorities	Delegated from departmental plan to individual
Departmental operating priorities	Delegated from departmental plan to individual
Departmental infrastructure priorities	Delegated from departmental plan to individual
Individual's ongoing job	Derived from individual's job description
Team obligations	Delegated from departmental plan or corporate team or derived from individual's job description and functional commitments
Interlocks: **Owe to others**	Delegated from departmental plan or individual's commitments to others
Owed to us	Delegated from departmental plan or commitments to individual from others
Behavioral values	From the corporate value statement and the individual's expected competencies and behaviors
Personal development	Agreed upon with management
Numbers	Key result areas with measures and numbers by which the person is ultimately judged

*Note: The individual may manage a department and keep delegated goals as his or her own or pass them on to other individuals.

Exhibit 4-2   Marketing Manager's Individual Scorecard

CORPORATE STRATEGIC PRIORITIES

None

DEPARTMENTAL STRATEGIC PRIORITIES

- Complete concept testing on three new products by 6/1/99 with recommendation on which to develop for market.
- Establish six new products in development that could come to market in late 1999 or in 2000.
- Complete entry plan for West Coast market by 3/1/99. If positive financially, be open for business by 9/1/99.

DEPARTMENTAL OPERATING PRIORITIES

- Achieve an average selling price of $32 per unit on a unit volume of 7.7 million for entire year 1999 yielding gross margin of 38%.
- Launch product A in second quarter with unit sales of 1.4 million through year-end and gross margin of 32%.

DEPARTMENTAL INFRASTRUCTURE PRIORITIES

- Mechanize product, customer, distribution system profit and cost analysis.

INDIVIDUAL'S ONGOING JOB

- Complete profitability analysis of products, markets, and customers by 6/1/99; recommend cuts and value chain emphasis.
- Recruit two new market analysts from B school with leadership potential.

TEAM OBJECTIVES

Member of corporate information systems team. Project recommendations on system due 5/1/90.

INTERLOCKS

Owed to Me	I Owe to Others
Information systems: 100 work-hours for product profitability system	25% time to corporate systems team

VALUES AND BEHAVIORS

See separate sheet.*

PERSONAL DEVELOPMENT

See separate sheet.*

* Not appended

NUMBERS

KRA	MEASURE	BUDGET		
		1999	2000	2001
Market penetration (existing products only)	Units % Market	41	43	47
Sales	$ million	246	277	360
Gross margin	%	36%	37%	37%
New products	Unit percentage of total production	25	30	35
Service	Survey index	94	95	96
	Complaints per million units	1.0	0.8	.06
Employee morale	Survey index	91	93	93
Succession	Number promotable two grades	1	2	2

analysis of products, channels, and customers with the purpose of "cleaning up the marketing value chain" and improving profitability.

- *Team assignments—corporate or departmental:* The marketing manager's assignment is to a corporate information systems team revamping the corporation's order-entry, production-scheduling, and fulfillment system.

- *Interlocks.* These are tasks the marketing department owes others. Interlocks here are marketing department times for corporate priority issue program teams projects and tasks that others owe marketing, such as information systems programming time for a new product and a market profitability tracking system.

- *The value, behaviors, and competencies that the organization expects of individuals:* Recall that values such as innovation and teamwork come straight from the direction statement and apply to everyone. Competencies are directly related to the job and for a marketing manager might include the ability to influence and persuade as well as self-confidence. They are derived from the competencies needed to perform a specific job at a high performance level and are explained below.

- *The individual's personal development goals:* The marketing manager has high potential and is expected to participate in internal and external leadership development courses and coaching. He also needs a course in quantitative methods for decision making to bolster a weakness in that area.

Values and Competencies

We spent a lot of time in the strategic planning process describing corporate values but none on this new concept—job competencies—which has crept into the corporate lexicon in the past few years. The behaviors and tangible results that people get from their job competencies influence management development needs and ultimately career paths and promotions. Let's look at competencies and corporate values this way.

Values vs. Competencies

The overriding corporate values and resulting desired behaviors are expressed in the direction statement. They are the handful needed to get a competitive advantage in the future and establish the internal atmosphere in which future employees will be motivated to be top-notch producers and achieve your vision.

External
World
Critical → Values → Competitive Advantage → Market Performance → Fulfilled Vision
Success
Factors

Everyone in the organization is expected to hold these values and practice them, as appropriate, in their own job.

Competencies (sometimes called behaviors or capabilities) have been defined in many ways. I prefer the simple definitions of David D. Dubois, which I've paraphrased here:

> *Job competence:* An employee's capacity to meet (or exceed) a job's requirements by producing the job outputs at an expected level of quality within the constraints of the organization's internal and external environments. In other words, job competence is fulfilling the conditions of the job description.
>
> *Job competency:* An underlying characteristic of an employee—motive, trait, skill, value, aspect of self-image, social role, or body of knowledge—that results in effective and/or superior performance in a job.[1]

Exhibit 4-3 shows selected job competencies for a director at American Express. Note the behaviors expected as a result of the competencies and that these competencies are tied to the job, not to the overall organization. In short, they are a behavioral job description.

[1] David D. Dubois, Ph.D., *Competency-Based Performance Improvement: A Strategy for Organizational Change* (Amherst, Mass.: HRD Press, 1993).

Exhibit 4-3 Mallinkrodt Executive Competency Model

Core Competencies

- ▼ Act with integrity
- ▼ Effective decision making
- ▼ Drive and commitment
- ▼ Building relationships and teams
- ▼ Adaptability
- ▼ Focus on customers

Role Competencies

Executives

- ▼ Visionary thinking
- ▼ Shaping strategy
- ▼ Entrepreneurial risk taking
- ▼ Global perspective
- ▼ Driving execution

Middle Management

- ▼ Provide direction
- ▼ Manage execution
- ▼ Champion change
- ▼ Establish plans

First Line Management;
Team Leaders

- ▼ Lead others
- ▼ Work efficiently
- ▼ Commit to quality
- ▼ Delegate and monitor

Individual Contributors

- ▼ Work efficiently
- ▼ Commit to quality
- ▼ Manage execution
- ▼ Establish plans

Source: Courtesy Human Resources Department, Mallinkrodt Inc.

Competency Model

A competency model includes those competencies that are required for satisfactory or exemplary job performance within the context of a person's job roles, responsibilities, and relationships in an organization and its internal and external environments. Exhibit 4-4 shows a generic menu of competencies for a sales manager. This, in essence, becomes a behavioral job description. Competencies will vary and therefore must be defined function by function and sometimes job by job because the success criteria will differ from job to job. A critical competency for a salesperson—for example, customer orientation, ability to influence— has far less relevance to the laboratory scientist, to whom creativity, conceptual ability, and perseverance are high on the competence scale.

In addition, competencies are defined for key classes of jobs, such as leaders, managers, and supervisors. These definitions are used to select people for leadership development programs and leadership positions and to give aspiring leaders a behavioral model to "shoot for."

Exhibit 4-4   Generic Competency Model for Salespeople

WEIGHT	COMPETENCY	WEIGHT	COMPETENCY
XXXXXXXXX	**Impact and Influence** Establishes credibility Addresses customer's issues, concerns Indirect influence Predicts effects of own words and actions	XXX	**Self-Confidence** Confident in own abilities Takes on challenges Optimistic style
XXXXX	**Achievement Orientation** Sets challenging achievable goals Uses time efficiently (Improves customer's operations) (Focuses on potential profit opportunities)	XX	**Relationship Building** Maintains work-related friendships Has and uses networks of contacts
XXXXX	**Initiative** Persists, does not give up easily Seizes opportunities (Responds to competitive threats)	XX	**Analytical Thinking** Anticipates and prepares for obstacles Thinks of several explanations or plans
		XX	**Conceptual Thinking** Uses rules of thumb Notices similarities between present and past
XXX	**Interpersonal Understanding** Understands nonverbal behavior Understands others' attitudes, meanings Predicts others' reactions	XX	**Information Seeking** Gets information from many sources
		XX	**(Organizational Awareness)** Understands functioning of client organization
XXX	**Customer Service Orientation** Makes extra efforts to meet customer needs Discovers and meets customer's underlying needs Follows up customer contacts and complaints (Becomes a trusted advisor to customers)	Threshold	**Technical Expertise** Has relevant technical or product knowledge Takes on challenges Optimistic style

Source: Lyle M. Spencer Jr., Ph.D., and Signe M. Spencer, *Competence at Work* (New York: Wiley, 1993), p. 173.

"Weight" refers to the relative frequency with which each competency distinguishes superior from average performers.

Note: Items in parentheses are relevant only to some sales positions.

Exhibit 4-5 shows the leadership competencies at General Electric Power Systems.

Defining Job Competencies

There are several methods of defining job competencies:

- *Interviewing individuals:* People within a function are interviewed to establish what the competencies have been and what they need to be in the future to meet the organization's strategic objectives.

- *Behavioral interviews:* Both average and outstanding performers are asked to cite incidents in which their performance was particularly good or they overcame significant obstacles to achieve their goals. Out of the "stories," the interviewer distills the actions and underlying competencies separating the average from the outstanding performers.

- *External assessment.* This refers to assessing the competencies (in the broadest sense, including values, job competence, and knowledge) that will be required in the long term. Although overall competencies and values are important, particular attention must be paid to high strategic leverage positions and those where potential incumbent development time is long. The leverage competency areas include leadership, hubs of innovation such as scientific or marketing personnel, and keepers of systems and processes such as information and human resources systems.

- *Management consensus:* Ultimately, management must come to a consensus that the resulting behaviors are "correct" for the jobs in question and are in alignment with the corporate direction.

Competencies and Corporate Values

Corporate values are simply corporatewide competencies. Every position's competency menu is expected to include the corporate values. The relative weight of those values and the behaviors expected as a result will vary from job to job. The value of enhancing shareholder value is at the top of the CEO's list, and the tabulation of things that he needs to do to accomplish it is long. It starts with crucial items such as executing a strategy that will result in high value added but includes indirect value-added items such as relationship with the financial community. Enhancing shareholder value is relatively high on a manufacturing manager's list, with her associated behaviors being cost management, quality, and customer service.

In practice, competencies are added to the performance manage-

(Text continues on page 138.)

Exhibit 4-5 Leadership Competencies at GE Power Systems: GEPS 360-Degree Leadership Assessment Ratings

Leader's Name _____

Coach Name/Address _____

Characteristic	Performance Criteria	Mgr.	Peers	Staff
Vision	• Has developed and communicated a clear, simple, customer-focused vision/direction for the organization. • Forward thinking, stretches horizons, challenges imaginations. • Inspires and energizes others to commit to vision. Captures minds. Leads by example. • As appropriate, updates vision to reflect constant and accelerating change impacting the business.	4.3	3.8	4.0
Customer/ Quality/Cost	• Listens to customers and assigns the highest priority to customer satisfaction, including internal customers. • Inspires a passion for excellence in every aspect of work. • Committed to achieving highest product/service quality at competitive market price by streamlining structure/processes. • Demonstrates a service mindset and unyielding cost consciousness throughout the organization. • Integrates internal and external customer feedback into business management. • Challenges existing process capability and encourages alternative solutions. • Understands the underlying theories, principles, and practices of Six Sigma from a management and technical perspective.	4.4	4.3	4.1
Integrity	• Maintains unequivocal commitment to honesty/truth in every facet of behavior. • Follows through on commitments; assumes responsibility for own mistakes. • Practices absolute conformance with company policies embodying GEPS commitment to ethical conduct. • Actions and behaviors are consistent with words. Absolutely trusted by others.	4.4	4.5	4.1
Accountability/ Commitment	• Sets and meets aggressive commitments to achieve business objectives. • Demonstrates courage/self-confidence to stand up for beliefs, ideas, coworkers. • Fair and compassionate yet willing to make difficult decisions. • Demonstrates uncompromising responsibility for preventing harm to the environment.	4.4	4.2	4.0
Communication/ Influence	• Communicates in open, candid, clear, complete, and consistent manner—invites response/dissent. • Listens effectively and probes for new ideas. Uses facts and rational arguments to influence and persuade. • Breaks down barriers and develops influential relationships across teams, functions, and layers.	3.5	3.2	3.1

Source: Corporate Leadership Council, The Next Generation: Accelerating the Development of Rising Leaders (Washington, D.C.: Corporate Leadership Council, 1997), 142–143.

(continued)

Characteristic	Performance Criteria	Mgr.	Peers	Staff
Shared Ownership/ Boundaryless	• Self-confidence to share information across traditional boundaries and be open to new ideas. • Encourages/promotes shared ownership for team vision and goals. • Trusts others; encourages risk taking and boundaryless behavior. • Champions Work-Out as a vehicle for everyone to be heard. Open to ideas from anywhere.	3.9	3.1	3.5
Team Builder/ Empowerment	• Selects talented people; provides coaching and feedback to develop team members to their fullest potential. • Delegates whole tasks; empowers teams to maximize effectiveness. Is personally a team player. • Recognizes and rewards progress toward achievement of Six Sigma threshold/objectives. • Resources Six Sigma projects and drives Six Sigma culture change. Creates positive work environment.	3.7	3.0	3.0
Diversity	• Demonstrates personal commitment to diversity in staffing, training, development, retention, and related processes. • Uses contemporary change processes to ensure diverse employee participation in continuously improving the business. • Actively seeks and considers diverse ideas/approaches in developing alternatives to solve problems/leverage opportunities. • Supports employees in balancing work/family demands consistent with personal values and the needs of business.	4.4	4.2	4.5
Knowledge/ Expertise/ Intellect	• Possesses and readily shares functional/technical knowledge and expertise. Constant interest in learning. • Demonstrates broad business knowledge/perspective with cross-functional/multicultural awareness. • Quickly sorts relevant from irrelevant information, grasps essentials of complex issues and initiates action. • Demonstrates competence and understanding with details of data. • Utilizes data to strategically manage the business. Makes good decisions with limited data. Applies intellect to the fullest.	4.5	4.2	4.6
Initiative/Speed	• Anticipates problems and initiates new and better ways of doing things. Creates real and positive change. • Hates/avoids/eliminates "bureaucracy" and strives for brevity, simplicity, clarity. • Understands and uses speed as a competitive advantage.	4.0	3.9	4.2
Global Mindset	• Demonstrates global awareness/sensitivity and is comfortable building diverse and global teams. • Considers the global consequences of every decision. Proactively seeks global knowledge. • Treats everyone with dignity, trust, and respect.	4.3	4.2	3.7

Rating Scale

Significant
Development Need 1 —— 2 —— 3 —— 4 —— 5 Outstanding
Strength

ment system, along with corporate values and performance judgments made during an individual's annual review.

A New Take on Job Descriptions

I covered most of the important sources of accountabilities in earlier chapters, but here, for the first time, I've inserted job descriptions into the mix. Fully anticipating scowls and groans, here's where I stand on the subject:

First, job descriptions are absolutely critical. Without job descriptions, individuals have no clear picture of the activities they are to carry out and how their success will be measured. So don't be surprised if they sometimes fail to get the basic job done, cause conflict and organizational chaos by wandering over the boundaries of others' jobs, or indulge in tasks that are interesting but unnecessary for corporate success.

Second, don't even bother to dig your job description out from the back of the bottom drawer and dust it off, because it's probably useless. The trouble with typical job descriptions is that they are archival lists of outdated tasks and activities. That's not the kind of job description I'm talking about.

A potent job description lists the measurable outputs of the job and explains their relationship to corporate strategy. This kind of job description would look like the one in Exhibit 4-6, drawn up for our marketing manager.

Individual Performance Management Systems

The organization's performance management system provides the framework for establishing and tracking individual accountabilities. In broad terms, a performance management system for individual employees consists of three steps:

1. *Delegate corporate and departmental objectives.* Parcel out top-level and departmental objectives to the individual who must take action.
2. *Establish individual objectives.* Establish measurable objectives for each employee and hold the person accountable for those objectives.
3. *Monitor progress against objectives.* Get desired results by tracking progress and taking corrective action when needed to get goal trajectories back on track.

Exhibit 4-6   Marketing Manager's Job Description

OVERALL

Purpose of the job: Meet current and future market penetration objectives of the corporation.

Job scope: North America; electronic components; all distribution channels.

QUANTITATIVE MEASUREMENTS

KRAs, measures, and alignment with corporate priorities and strategy.

KRA	WEIGHT	MEASURE
Sales	20%	$
Profit	Gross margin	
Penetration By product group By channel	10%	Unit market share % by market
New products	10%	Launched according to schedule, meeting revenue and profit projections.
Innovation	10%	Percentage of product sales that are new products on market less than three years.
Marketing strategy		One-year and long-term competitive strategy, product, and marketing plan accepted by top team.
Customer satisfaction	10%	Overall satisfaction with product, service, marketing efforts, and quality as measured by periodic survey.
Employees	15%	Morale, attitude, and adherence to values as measured by annual survey. All employees are B-level performers or higher. Any C-level performers are on six months or less performance notice.
Competitive advantage	10%	Meeting top customer needs significantly better than competition as measured by objective survey and market share.
Competencies	15%	Performance on the corporate value scale. Mutual agreement between supervisor and employee.

Direct job responsibilities: Day-to-day administration of product management and personnel to support the marketing plan; pricing, advertising and promotion, packaging, and market research.

Shared responsibility: Jointly responsible with the sales manager for meeting sales, targets. Responsible with engineering and public relations for developing technical product performance information and sales collateral needed by the sales force and customers.

Team and interlocking requirements: Lead the new-product development team, consisting of marketing, finance, manufacturing, and R&D representatives. Coordinate marketing efforts with sales. Performance will be judged by the achievement versus objectives of that team.

Exhibit 4-6 *(continued)*

EMPOWERMENT

Unqualified (what you may do without consulting anyone): Spending within budget. Approval of all artwork, advertising, and collateral campaigns. Price quotes that yield at least 34% gross margin. Product line extensions returning 34% gross margins or above, fully burdened ROI of 38% or above, and less than $20,000 in capital each.

Inform later: May quote prices yielding 30–34%; may approve product extensions with 34–38% ROI but must inform VP of marketing later.

Qualified: Hire and fire nonmanagerial or supervisory personnel after clearance by human resources.

Requires approval of VP of marketing: Significant additions to or deletions from distribution system. Price quotes yielding less than 34% gross margin and product extensions yielding less than 38% ROI. Hiring and firing of managerial and supervisory-level personnel. Budget variances. Any capital spending in excess of $20,000.

Requires "upstairs" approval by top team: New product line definition, funding, scheduling, and ultimate launch decision.

Any other decisions not specifically excluded are yours to make.

Increased empowerment: One additional year's experience combined with new knowledge of probabilistic decision-making methods will significantly expand decision-making latitude in areas of pricing and launch of new products without approval.

A well-designed and consistently implemented performance management system is a vehicle to:

- *Improve performance:* Upgrade the performance of individuals not meeting their objectives.
- *Determine rewards:* Establish base and incentive pay levels for individuals.
- *Identify employees who are eligible for promotion:* Pinpoint those whose performance signals promotability.
- *Eliminate poor performers:* Weed poor performers out of the corporation quickly.
- *Develop employees:* Establish development programs for all employees who have growth potential; determine remedial action for those who are valuable but underskilled.
- *Implement your organization's succession plan:* Use performance reviews to identify pools of individuals ready to step into important management slots.

Scorecards for Individuals

At the center of performance management for each employee is the individual scorecard, a set of measurable objectives for which the person is accountable. The marketing manager's scorecard in Exhibit 4-2 is a typical individual scorecard. To create it, we simply "lifted" the departmental scorecard categories and modified them for the individual.

Consistent scorecard formats from top to bottom in the organization make it easier to align work and examine performance data at all levels. Not everyone has a task in each category of the scorecard. For most, the individual's objectives will cluster in the ongoing and departmental task sections. Keeping all of the categories on every scorecard, however, helps people understand the nature of the overall job of the department and the corporation.

Installing a Performance Management System

Exhibit 4-7 shows the process of designing and installing a performance management system. The fourteen-step process is as follows:

1. *Select a team.* Its members will be responsible for the design of the system. The five- to seven-member team usually consists of people from different functional areas and levels within the organization. They are supplemented by someone from human resources and an outside consultant expert in performance management systems and developing competency profiles.

2. *Survey values and competencies.* The team, supplemented by subteams if necessary, ensures that the corporate values are understood and that the future needed competencies are determined for at least high-strategic-leverage jobs within the company during the first round of the program.

3. *Interview the organization.* This will enable the team to understand current job performance standards for key jobs and how they are set and reviewed. The team also gathers information regarding what various constituencies see as (1) the objectives for the system, (2) key barriers to its success, and (3) what they personally will get out of it.

4. *Survey the best of class.* Visit companies that perform at the top of their industry and are known for good performance management systems in order to collect and evaluate information on their systems.

5. *Write system specifications.* Define the system. Include a flowchart of timing and events, a statement of objectives and probable outcomes, the system that will be used to process the resulting data, and

(Text continues on page 144.)

Exhibit 4-7   Designing and Installing a Performance Management System

SELECT TEAM
Select team to design performance appraisal system. Select consultant for behavior survey and performance management system if needed.

SURVEY VALUES
Survey and select future values and behaviors.

LINKAGE: OVERALL ACCOUNTABILITY PROCESS

LINKAGE: CULTURE

TRAIN AND LAUNCH
Provide training for senior management and leverage managers and critical strategic personnel using system in year one.

DEBUG THREE-SIX SYSTEM
Conduct three-month trial of system. Design training course. Tie to compensation system.

LINKAGES: DEPARTMENTAL AND STRATEGIC PLAN OBJECTIVES

SET SCORECARDS
Supervisor and subordinate complete subordinate's scorecard based on corporate and departmental scorecards. Empowerment limits set.

ASSIST
Provide postlaunch help to those requesting it. Conduct sample quality control survey to judge quality of system implementation.

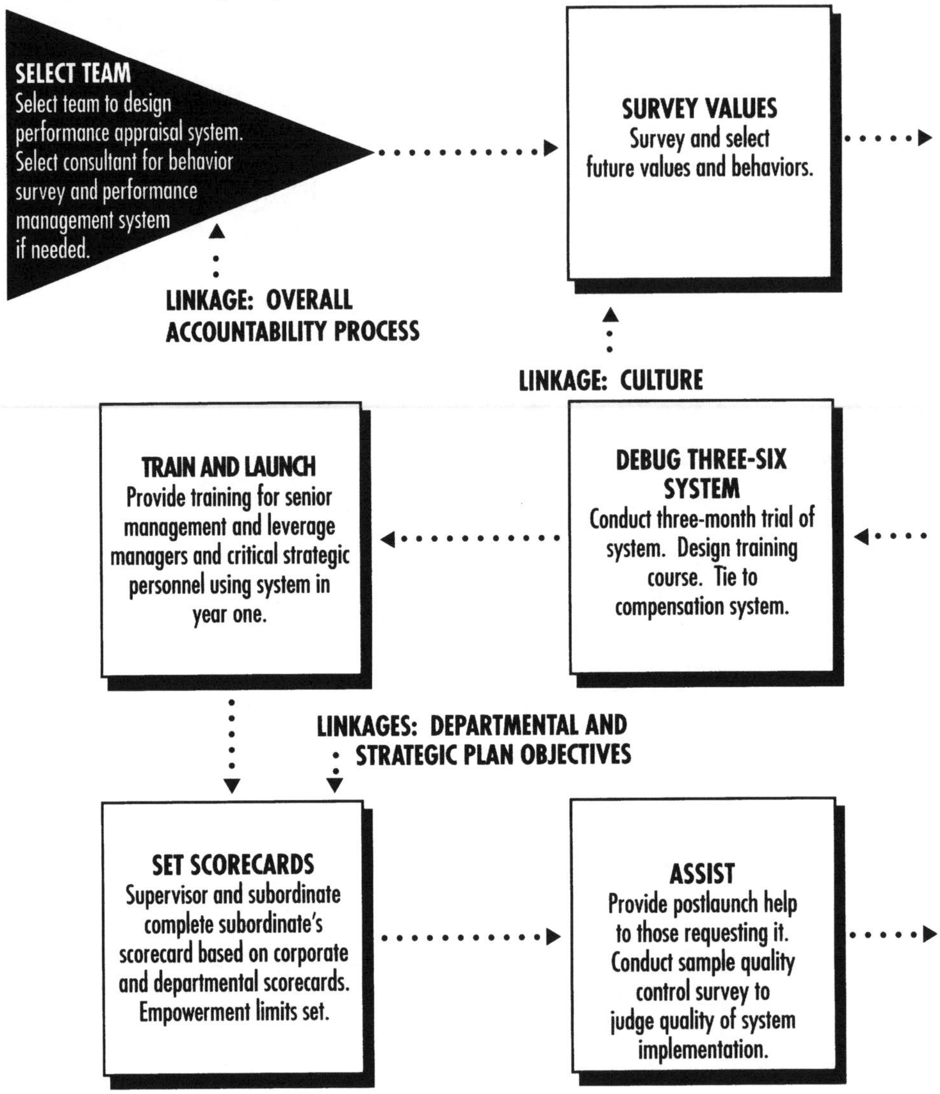

INTERVIEW ORGANIZATION
Interview top management and sample of employees to understand job, current performance standards and methods of review, their objectives for the system.

SURVEY BEST OF CLASS
Collect and evaluate information on systems from "best" companies.

LINKAGES: COMPENSATION AND TRAINING

DESIGN SYSTEM
Design system and get feedback from those originally interviewed.

WRITE SYSTEM SPECS
Define system specifications and get top team's approval to proceed.

AUDIT EFFECTIVENESS
Conduct fourth-month audit on effectiveness of job descriptions, objective setting, and empowerment.

ASSIST DURING REVIEWS
Help as requested during semiannual and annual reviews.

LINKAGE: OVERALL ACCOUNTABILITY PROCESS

LAUNCH YEAR TWO
Provide training for second group of participants. Launch second group on system.

AUDIT EFFECTIVENESS
Conduct audit of effectiveness of system after 9–12 months and first group of reviews. Make system changes if needed.

mock-up formats of job descriptions and scorecards for key representative jobs. Determine who will administer the system, quality-control its use and design, and execute training. Get management's approval to proceed.

6. *Design the system.* Turn the approved specifications into a firm system. Design a training course for the performance management system and its exact tie to the compensation system.

7. *Debug the system.* Run a three- to four-month trial of the system with a select team whose job is to debug it. The team should be representative of the levels and functions in which the system will be used.

8. *Train and launch.* Apply the system to the top team, program teams, all leverage managers, and centers of strategic change who are responsible for strategic tasks, regardless of their position in the company. These are the change agents whom you must stimulate and monitor during the early periods of strategic plan execution.

9. *Set objectives.* Supervisor and subordinate agree on the subordinate's job description and empowerment limits. They then complete the subordinate's scorecard based on corporate and departmental strategic objectives and the individual's ongoing responsibilities and measures.

10. *Assist users.* The team or human resources provides postlaunch help interpreting the system for those requesting it.

11. *Audit effectiveness.* After four months, the team runs an audit on the system to identify flaws and barriers to effectiveness. Team members interview pairs of supervisors and subordinates to determine the process they used to mutually set goals, their satisfaction with the method, the realism of the goals, and their support of the system.

12. *Assist during reviews.* The team provides consulting and counseling during semiannual and annual reviews. Courses are held in how to conduct reviews.

13. *Audit effectiveness.* A second effectiveness audit is held after nine to twelve months so that the system and process can be revised, if necessary, before the second group of employees is introduced to it.

14. *Launch year two.* At six- to twelve-month intervals, install the system in successive layers, moving down from the top team. Use the six months preceding launch to put the initiates through training, job description writing, objective setting, and performance review. This will make them familiar enough with the system to take it down to the next layer.

System for Accountabilities: Who Does What, When

Exhibit 1-2 in the Key 1 chapter shows when individual accountabilities are set in conjunction with the corporate planning cycle, and Exhibit 4-8 shows how individual accountabilities are established.

Exhibit 4-8 Establishing Individual Accountabilities

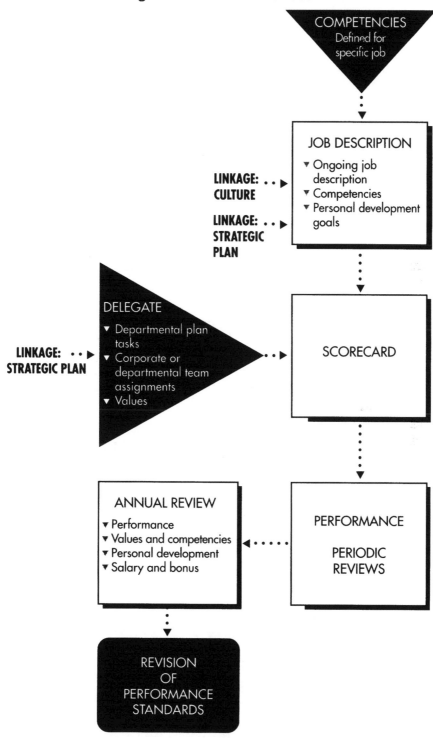

Job Descriptions

The employee and the supervisor jointly work out the job description and measures. This is usually done when an individual moves into a position. The specific objectives may change annually, but for most jobs, the rest of the job description changes little over time. As the individual's capabilities expand, however, empowerment can increase. And when an individual receives assignments outside of the original description, the expanded job scope should be noted for the record and relevant performance standards established.

Annual Scorecard

Individual scorecards for the coming year are formally prepared immediately after the second planning meeting—the resource allocation meeting. By now, the corporate directives have been decided and delegated, departmental priorities and numbers finalized, and individual assignments made.

In reality, individuals will already have done much of their thinking about their jobs. At the very beginning of the process, during the "dip-down," they contributed what they thought corporate, departmental, and their own priorities must be. They also have a pretty good idea of what the key numbers will be since these were suggested at the beginning of the process. Therefore, after the priority-setting meeting, most people are in a position to start preparing their individual accountabilities. Following the resource allocation meeting, they'll probably just need to make a few adjustments and polish up what they've been working on.

Although individual accountabilities are worked out between an individual and her boss, they should be circulated to her subordinates and peers to make sure that tasks are coordinated, that people understand each others' commitments, and of course, to increase accountability by giving the goals widespread visibility.

How Individual Accountabilities Affect Performance

Individual accountabilities are a three-in-one weapon in the war for high performance:

1. They stimulate and get superior performance from excellent people.
2. They are a development tool to make those people even better in the future.
3. They are a tool to get weak people out of the organization.

You couldn't devise a better managerial Swiss Army knife if you tried!

Do

- Install an individual performance management system from day one of your plan for your leverage people and centers of strategic change.
- Use a uniform interlocking scorecard system from top to bottom for recording objectives and measuring results.
- Make sure that the tie between scorecard results and salary, incentive pay, promotions, and the removal of poor performers is crystal-clear.

Don't

- Let the system degenerate into a paperwork mill.
- Let grumbling about the system and the resisters stop you from using it immediately.
- Use any old system. Tailor an interlocking scorecard system to your needs and specifications.

Key 5

Change the Organization Structure – Fast

Principle: Organization structure and its related competencies must be perfectly aligned with strategy if that strategy is to be well executed and result in a formidable competitive advantage.

Why it's important: Misalignment yields an organization that is inefficient, costly, and does not react quickly to changes in the marketplace. This can put the company at a significant competitive disadvantage.

How it's applied: Evaluate the future work and the competencies required to implement your strategy. Build the structure around future competencies, not simple extensions of what you now have.

Expected results: Significantly better execution of strategy than the competition can be expected as well as the ability to attract better people, which keeps competencies up to date and stimulates continuous positive change.

What is organization structure? In the past, when we talked about structure, we put the emphasis on the boxes in the organization—which boxes report to which, who heads the boxes, what people and jobs are in each box. We call the pictorial representation of these interrelationships the "wiring diagram." Despite new trends, most wiring diagrams look like pyramids—the traditional hierarchical system.

But what makes the organization productive and effective is less the placement of the boxes than the presence of strong leaders, skilled workers, and "lubricant": organizational support systems—both formal and informal, tangible and intangible—that facilitate purposeful interactions and efficient processes. Lubricants include cross-functional teams, which promote cooperation and coordination among the boxes; management practices that speed up decision making and the transfer of information among the boxes; top-level actions that model and encourage informal interpersonal interaction; and the interlocks among functions that help ensure the coordination of tasks. Corporate policies and procedures governing hiring, firing, promotions, and funding lubricate the structure, as do information systems that provide decision-making and performance evaluation data at the corporate, departmental, and individual levels. These structural lubricants are highlighted in Exhibit 5-1.

Designing Your Organization Structure

You can't implement new plans and accomplish new goals if you have to slog through an outmoded organization structure that obstructs decision making and impedes new processes. When structure gets in the way of strategy, you need to change that structure—fast.

The best way to plan a new structure in a dedicated meeting of the top management team, before an implementation plan meeting. Expect to spend two intensive days, using the following step-by-step process, which is shown in Exhibit 5-2.

Step 1: Post the Elements of Your Strategic Plan

Structure follows strategy. It's an old rule and still a good one. Your strategic plan should contain the competitive strategies that you will use to win and the quantified results you want to achieve in the future. These will guide what and how much change is required in your organization. As you design your structure, you have to ask, "What will significantly improve performance in each of the plan's internal and external objectives and other critical performance factors?" And you'll want to confirm that any resulting organization structure and operating rules are consistent with the mission, vision, business definition, competitive strategy, and values in your direction statement.

Exhibit 5-1 Structural Lubricants

- ▼ Cross-functional teams
- ▼ Decision-making rules, practices, and speed
- ▼ Interfunctional communication practices
- ▼ Interlocking requirements
- ▼ Hiring, firing, and promotion policies and procedures
- ▼ Informal communication
- ▼ Ease of getting justified funding
- ▼ Information systems

Exhibit 5-2 Steps to a New Structure

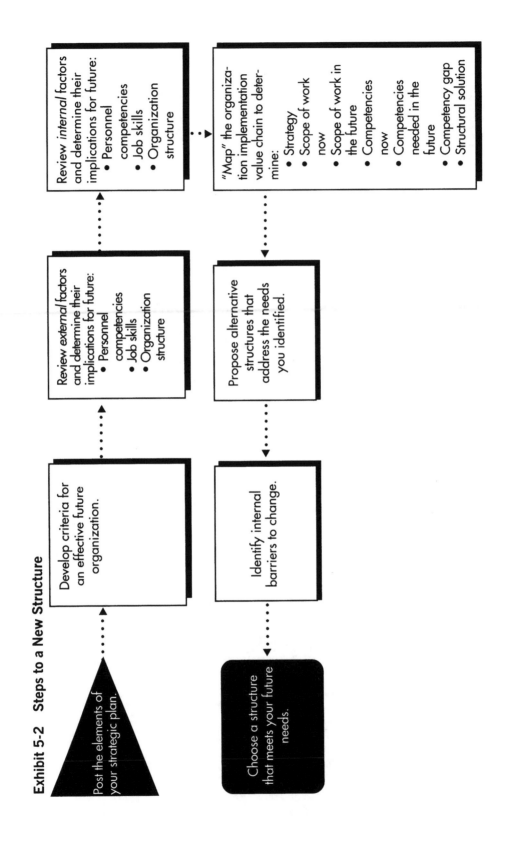

Post the elements of your strategic plan.

Develop criteria for an effective future organization.

Review *external* factors and determine their implications for future:
- Personnel competencies
- Job skills
- Organization structure

Review *internal* factors and determine their implications for future:
- Personnel competencies
- Job skills
- Organization structure

"Map" the organization implementation value chain to determine:
- Strategy
- Scope of work now
- Scope of work in the future
- Competencies now
- Competencies needed in the future
- Competency gap
- Structural solution

Identify internal barriers to change.

Propose alternative structures that address the needs you identified.

Choose a structure that meets your future needs.

Step 2: Develop Criteria for an Effective Future Organization

Criteria will help you design a structure that is right for you. Later, when you have reached some decisions about structural changes or are considering alternatives, your criteria will provide standards against which you can measure your choices. Criteria may vary depending on your strategic objectives and plans, but some typical ones are shown in Exhibit 5-3.

Step 3: Review External Factors and Assess Their Impact

Review *external* factors and determine their implications for changes in the work to be done, people competencies, and structure.

Answer the questions in Exhibit 5-4, referring to the following components of your strategic plan:

- *Marketplace trends:* Developments in areas such as customers, customer needs, competitive action, and technology.
- *Critical success factors in the marketplace:* Those few things that you have to do well in the marketplace to win.
- *Competitive strategy:* Those customer needs that you'll consistently meet better than the competition—for example, product performance and innovation, service, and quality.
- *External key result areas and measures:* Factors that will lead to success, such as market share, service levels, and overall customer satisfaction.
- *Environmental trends:* Forces in the outside world that drive structure. While you are thinking externally, you'll also want to take into account at least some of these trends:
  - *Accelerated response time:* Markets and the competition are changing rapidly. Rigid organizations can't compete effectively in such markets.
  - *Global markets:* Many markets are global and require different skills and structures to operate in them.
  - *Partnerships:* The need to cooperate or be partners with outside firms, vendors, and business associates is growing. Companies are leveraging their assets with partnerships in product development, technology, marketing, and geography.
  - *Workforce ethic:* Young employees expect more autonomy and more say in defining their jobs than ever before—coupled with virtually no loyalty to the organization.
  - *Legislative action:* Legislative control and government intervention are increasing in many industries.
  - *Segmented markets:* Markets continue to be segmented, with

Exhibit 5-3   Criteria for an Effective Organization

STRATEGY
- The organization is aligned with external and internal strategies.
- Its core processes are best of class, far superior to the competition.
- It is positioned to win in the long term.

COMPETENCIES
- The organization allows opportunities for development of leaders and other key employees to meet long-term strategic needs.
- It provides the best structure to utilize and build core competencies.
- Constant learning and skill improvement are required.

REACTION TIME
- The organization can react faster to changes in the marketplace than the competition.
- It is flexible enough to change parts rapidly if strategy and the marketplace dictate.

WORK
- The work and work flow are organized efficiently.
- Productivity per employee is far higher than the competition.

SYSTEMS
- Sophisticated, user-friendly systems for information, decision-making, and control are utilized.
- There is control without bureaucracy.

COORDINATION
- A high level of vertical and horizontal coordination and teamwork is encouraged.
- The structure is well suited for teams.

PEOPLE
- The structure empowers people.
- It encourages informal interaction.
- The organization has the best possible people, outstanding leverage leaders.

EFFICIENCY
- The organization has the most efficient structure in the industry.
- The organization has the best structure to utilize and build core competencies.

FOCUS
- People are forced to look outside so that they never lose sight of customer or the marketplace.
- The organization is consistent with its business definition.

PERFORMANCE
- The organization will give current and future competitive advantages in internal and external key result areas and core processes.
- It is likely to be the most profitable.

Exhibit 5-4   Analyzing External and Internal Factors

▼ What are the key trends in the marketplace that could affect structure?
▼ Where is the organization performing adequately to meet strategic objectives?
▼ Where is it not?
▼ What is the root cause of the problem?
▼ Bottom line, what and where does this mean that we need to improve in the organization: people? competencies? structure?
▼ What are the probable means of improvement?
▼ What structural or procedural changes are indicated?

---

special offerings made to smaller and more specialized segments.

—*Electronic commerce:* More and more can be bought and sold electronically. The entire value chain, from raw materials through operations to the customer's cash register, can be interconnected.

Step 4: Review Internal Factors and Assess Their Impact

Applying the same questions you used in step 3, consider the following *internal* factors and determine their implications for structure:

- *Core competencies:* Assets and intellectual skills needed to yield superior performance on critical success factors and competitive strategy.
- *Core processes:* Processes needed to deliver your competitive advantage. Though often thought of as a core competency, these are important enough to warrant separate scrutiny.
- *Internal key result areas:* Indicators that the organization is capable of producing what you want in the marketplace. Such indicators include innovation, employee satisfaction, morale and productivity, and cost structure.
- *Financial measures:* Measures such as profitability, return on assets, and shareholder value.

And just as there are environmental trends that will drive your structure, so, too, are there trends in management and systems that you should weigh as you look internally. These include:

- *Direction/accountability:* Strong planning gives direction to the organization in the form of overall priorities and objectives. These are turned into objectives at lower levels with a tough accountability chain up to the top. The philosophy is "I'll empower, I'll leave you alone, but I'll hold you strictly accountable for what we agree you must do."

- *Core-process orientation:* This approach ensures that the core processes that create the company's competitive advantage and customer and stockholder value are the focal point of the business.
- *Use of teams:* Project teams, quality teams, continuous improvement teams, self-directed work teams, and business teams are all used with the objective of better coordination of work, superior output, and lower cost.
- *Empowerment:* Decision making and responsibility for performance and variances are pushed down to the lowest level possible.
- *Cross-training:* Each employee is trained to do multiple jobs.
- *Information systems:* Systems are geared toward spotting variances to standards and quickly making decisions at all levels. Systems are developed that allow people to collaborate on work via intranets.
- *Reward systems:* Financial reward is structured to pay for performance and to fit new team and process-oriented work structures.
- *Top team:* Top management works to truly become a team and focus more and more of its attention on strategy and process rather than day-to-day decisions.
- *Philosophical management:* People learn and are imbued with a set of values and operating principles that enable them to become self-directed in their work rather than relying on the hierarchy to make decisions or give constant direction.
- *Flexibility:* There is a willingness to change organization structure or people quickly to respond to change.

Step 5: Map the New Work and Competencies Needed

Go through every value chain in the organization, as illustrated in Exhibit 5-5, and determine:

- Strategy
- Scope of work now
- Scope of work in the future
- Competencies now
- Competencies needed in the future
- Competency gap
- Structural solution

The most important externally driven value chains are usually geographic focus, development of new products/services, sales, distribution, customer fulfillment, customer service, and purchasing. The most

Exhibit 5-5   Value Chain: New Work and Competencies Driven by New Sales Strategy

Strategy	Work	Competencies	Structure	Action
NOW Domestic scope	Direct sales distribution	OK	VP sales	Grow from within

FUTURE International scope	**NEW**
	• Electronic commerce
	• Foreign
	  - Direct
	  - Distributors
	  - Reps
	  - Agents
	• Joint ventures
		GAPS
		• Languages
		• International experience
		• Electronic commerce
		• International negotiating and deal making
		• Multiple distribution methods
			NEW
			• VP domestic
			• VP international
			• Director of electronic commerce
			• Director of ventures
				• Outside hires
				• Grow from within
				• New divisional structure

important internal value chains are information systems, human resources and development, and marketing.

Step 6: Propose Alternative Structures

Examine alternative organization structures and identify those that best address the needs you have identified. The "Structural Options" section later in this chapter examines some common approaches to organization structure and discusses what company presidents actually do about structure and reporting relationships.

Step 7: Identify Internal Barriers to Change

Based on survey work, which internal barriers to change must be removed to make both the current and any new structure work? What should you do to remove them? Often, the "lubricants" in an organization get a bit dry or sand-filled and cause significant inefficiencies. Barriers can be bureaucratic policies and procedures that concentrate decision making at the top or make it time-consuming or difficult to hire and fire people or constrain spending of modest amounts of money without lengthy multiple permissions. Barriers may be insufficient functional resources such as information systems. They may be incompetent resources such as public relations, advertising, and communications.

While you're designing a new organization and its policies and procedures, it is important to make sure that you remove all the barriers to rapid change that you can identify. A simple "barrier" survey will be helpful. One of the best techniques for finding out what's in people's way is to ask them. They'll give you the barriers and most likely a solution. During representative individual interviews and a number of focus groups conducted by a consultant or human resources specialist, people are asked the simple questions shown in Exhibit 5-6. Once the barriers are identified, the top team can go about fixing some immediately and making sure that all those that should be removed are cleared away by the time the new structure goes into effect.

Step 8: Choose a Structure That Meets Your Future Needs

By the time you finish the analysis of success criteria, external and internal factors, internal barriers, competencies required in the future, and

Exhibit 5-6   Questions to Ask When Identifying Barriers

▼ What are three words that describe the culture at our organization?
▼ What are three words that describe parts of our culture or operations that impede change?
▼ What are three things that we could do to improve plan implementation and speed up change?
▼ What are the three major barriers to plan progress that we should change or remove—such as policies, procedures, functions, or people resisting the plan?
▼ When was the last time that an action of yours meant to drive the plan forward was slowed down or thwarted? How and why? What should be changed to prevent this from happening again?
▼ Explain how your job helps fulfill the company's direction and strategic objectives. Be specific about the parts of the direction statement and objectives that you influence. (Have statement available.)
▼ What skills or resources are needed to speed up or do a better job on your strategic tasks?
▼ What has the top team done that is helpful to plan implementation? Where is the team throwing up barriers? Where could the team do a better job?
▼ If you're on a project team, how helpful has your sponsor been? What does she do that is helpful? What could she do to improve?
▼ How do you feel about the change program? What are the chances that it will yield good and lasting results?
▼ Summarize by telling me three things that you'd like me to ask the CEO to do to speed up the change process and make it more effective.

This questionnaire was designed to be administered six months after the change process is under way. The same questions can be rephrased and the questionnaire used during the planning process to discover anticipated barriers to change.

competency gaps, you will probably have determined many of the components of your ideal structure. Now's the time to combine them into a total organization structure—or better yet, one or two alternative structures—to evaluate against the criteria you established in step 2. The next section examines the array of options from which you can choose.

Structural Options

Let's start by looking at your options as if you were building a structure from scratch. Then we'll examine the more likely scenario that what you'll really do is modify the structure you've got to meet your updated needs.

Basic Structures

Virtually all structures are some variation of these three traditional forms:

1. *Functional structure:* The individual functions—such as marketing, operations, and research and development—report to the president, with general staff support such as human resources and finance reporting to the chief executive officer. Functional organizations, usually a business's first stop after the entrepreneurial stage, have the advantage of developing strong functional expertise. Their disadvantage is that the functions, given a chance, become silo organizations that communicate poorly among themselves and pass information to the top for integration and decisions rather than working out issues at lower levels. A functional structure can also be a *flat organization* when organization layers are removed to improve communications and lower costs.

2. *Corporate structure:* A number of self-contained divisions, each focusing on one or more businesses, are responsible for the profit and

Exhibit 5-7   Questions to Ask When You Choose a Structure

▼ What organization structure or structures make sense?
▼ What are the pros and cons of each versus our criteria for an effective organization?
▼ Do the alternatives include all of the future competencies needed to be effective?
▼ How big will the impact of each be on our future strategic results?
▼ What is the cost and financial gain of each?
▼ For the highest impact, when and how would be implement the changes?
▼ What short-term negative impact will the changes have on performance and morale?

loss and the future of their businesses. The divisions report to the chief operating officer of the company, while staff functions such as finance, treasury, and administration probably report to the chief executive officer. Divisions have the strong advantage of complete resources to address a very focused product and market. This should increase penetration, innovation, and profitability. The downside of the divisional structure is that divisions become fiercely independent of both corporate headquarters and each other, making synergy among them difficult and strategic decisions at the corporate level sometimes conflictual and painful.

3. *Entrepreneurial structure:* Although people have titles and functional responsibilities, this is really a fluid, loose organization in which people play multiple roles and make decisions as needed. There may be individual functions, but people often fill more than one permanent or temporary role. The advantage of this structure is that it allows extremely rapid response to the market and produces a highly motivated workforce because workers are so close to the action. The disadvantage is that communication and control become difficult as the company grows beyond the 200-person level, forcing it to institute more formal organization structure, information systems, and controls.

Overlays to Basic Structures

You can overlay the basic structures with various embellishments:

■ *Business units:* These units, sometimes called *strategic business units,* focus on individual businesses in a functional organization that has more than one business. They are usually cross-functional teams having profit-and-loss responsibility, often headed by a marketing manager with marketing and product development reporting directly to him. The rest of the business functions, such as sales, manufacturing, finance, and human resources, are shared with other businesses who are represented on the team. The primary advantage of business units is that they provide strong cross-functional coordination of a specific business. Their disadvantages are that they take team members' time away from the functional areas represented on the team and most share resources with the other teams.

■ *Coordinating teams:* These teams, which can be either permanent or temporary, oversee multifunctional processes or projects. A permanent team, for example, might coordinate the operation of an order-entry and -fulfillment core process that crosses many organization boundaries. The more common temporary teams are chartered to accomplish one purpose, such as bring a new product to market. Continuous improvement teams are permanent teams charged with continuously improving a work process.

Coordinating teams break down the barriers to cross-functional efficiency posed by functional silos. Although they require no additional personnel, they do require the organization to put time and resources into teaching team skills to members. Once learned, however, these skills are invaluable to the individual and the organization.

■ *Subsidiaries, joint ventures, spin-offs and "satellites":* Cooperative ventures that are separate from the parent organization each have their own specialized reason for being. A spin-off, for example, can isolate an incubator unit or a business of different character from the parent. Joint ventures take different forms, depending on how close an a organization wants to get to its joint venture partner and on legal considerations.

What Company Presidents Really Do About Structure

During strategy seminars with hundreds of company presidents, we've asked three basic questions:

1. Have any of you reorganized lately, or are you considering it?
2. If so, why? How does the new organization structure align with your competitive and corporate strategy?
3. How well does it work (or not work)?

We discovered that few companies reorganize dramatically to implement their plans. More often, they simply fine-tune their existing structure to support the new strategies. The boxes don't change much, but there are a few policy and procedure changes. The most significant change is that they report extensive use of teams.

Levels of Structural Change

Here are the three levels of structural change that we see, together with their frequency:

1. *Drastic:* The organization moves from one existing structural extreme to another (one percent).
2. *Fine-tuning:* A function is moved, split, or added (19 percent).
3. *None:* The structure's fine. Making it work is the problem (80 percent). As we'll see in later chapters, the major changes are in people, use of teams, accountability systems, and reward structures.

If your organization is among the 20 percent needing change, the categories described in this subsection may offer lessons for you.

Drastic. Drastic changes usually have radical purposes. The first is to shake up an established cultural order that is way out of whack with the new world that you're entering. The second is to put the organization back together in a form that will excel in the new environment.

A classic example is Saturn Corporation. Established virtually independently of General Motors, Saturn's charter was to break the culture that had so sapped GM—entitlement, management-worker-union conflict, slow decision making, lack of customer focus, poor teamwork. Saturn used, for the first time within the GM organization, extensive cross-functional design and production teams that included United Auto Workers members from the factory floor. The results were very good union-management relations and considerable innovation in design, manufacture, and marketing (through a new independent dealer organization).

This example unfortunately provides a cautionary lesson. GM went through all the work and agony of setting up Saturn only to back away from its original strategy as time went on. The parent turned down Saturn's repeated requests for funding for model changes desperately needed to reach breakeven. Although it worked well at first, Saturn's revolutionary organization is now slowly degenerating into something not yet predictable except in one respect: It will underperform the original concept.

Before you consider anything drastic, think twice. Think about all you must do to implement it now and support it in the future. Anticipate all the forces that can potentially pull it apart and sink it. Is it truly the best thing to do? Will you have the resolve to support it long-term? Drastic organizational changes that fail or whither from neglect are hard to recover from.

Fine-Tuning. Most structural changes have no grander design than to make what you have more effective and to focus your strategy better. Fine-tuning includes changes such as the following:

- *Adding new functions that didn't exist before the plan:* The publishing arm of a large religious not-for-profit organization had been losing market share to for-profit publishers. The complacent culture of the religious publisher had difficulty incorporating the need for market focus, cost reduction, increased innovation, higher quality, improved service, and better market access. The CEO, himself a minister, didn't think he had the ability, experience, and particularly the interest to run the business effectively. So the organization added a chief operating officer, recruited from industry, to run the entire organization. Formerly the chief operating officer of a major division of a Fortune 500 company, the new hire is beginning to make key changes in pivotal places, which will cascade other needed changes in the organization.

Other functions often added to organizations are marketing, product management, and human resources.

- *Changing one or more people blocking progress:* The key to making an existing structure work is often simply to change one or two top-level people who cannot operate under the new marching orders. This is covered in depth in the Key 6 chapter.

- *Splitting departments to get more focus on specific activities:* A printing company took both order entry and sales service out of their traditional resting place in manufacturing. Wanting to be more customer focused, the company was responding to customer dissatisfaction that resulted from manufacturing's inclination to make life easy for itself with long production runs.

One not-for-profit split its new-product department into new-product development and marketing, both reporting to the chief operating officer. The reason was twofold. First, marketing was a new thrust and getting inadequate emphasis—in part, because the department head neither liked nor was skilled in the function. In addition, the organization wanted to attract a high-caliber marketing vice president. To do that, the job had to report to the top.

- *Using teams:* A Fortune 500 company's new-product releases were driven by the schedule that worked for product development, research and development, and manufacturing. Each function tossed the product over the wall to the next when it had completed what it viewed as its charter. Product development cycles took up to two years—much too long. The chairman of the company set a nine-month deadline to get the next product out. After screams of protest and "It can't be done," the company formed a product team that included all of the relevant functions—manufacturing, R&D, sales, marketing, and product development. Early on, members got training in team management and facilitation. They got the product to market in nine months and two weeks.

- *Changing the hierarchy, such as by moving a department up or down in the reporting order:* The manager of the strategic planning and new-business development department of a high-growth division of a Fortune 500 company was taken out from under the vice president of marketing and made a peer, reporting to the divisional vice president, and a member of the divisional top management team. The new-business development job was so important to the division's future that the necessary communication was already predominantly with the top divisional team and corporate senior management. The change also responded to external forces because prospective acquisitions and investment banks didn't want to deal with anyone below the top team.

- *Removing layers:* One of the first moves of the new CEO of a Fortune 500 company was to remove a layer of group vice presidents to whom the operating divisions reported. They simply served as information filters up and down, adding very little value to the process of management. Without stretching the span of control of the chief executive officer and chief operating officer, the change brought the operating vice presidents closer to the top planning and decision-making loop.

- *Spinning off units with low strategic importance; cleaning up the rest:* A Fortune 500 chemical company, plagued by low margins and under pressure from the board and the financial press, took eight major groups and divided them into three strategic postures: (1) our future growth, which would consume cash; (2) our cash generators, which would provide the cash for the former; and (3) the drains, which were doing poorly or had no prospects for significant improvement. The drains, or parts of them, were spun off to employees, sold, or shut down.

Successful senior executives from other operations moved in to clean up the cash generators. They developed a plan and set clear priorities. They cleaned house of poor products, businesses, and people and repopulated key slots with good people. They removed organization layers, tempered expansion, and reduced research and development to the minimum needed to be good cash generators. The approach worked. They achieved a two-year turnaround and significant profitability in the third year in previously marginal cash-generator groups.

- *Eliminating low-value-added units:* A company specializing in high-performance printers for networks and offices decided that a business unit experimenting with imaging techniques was potentially of low value to the company's future and a high cash drain. It gave the business to a group of employees still interested in pursuing the field with no promises of long-term future support.

- *Creating focused business units:* Established in the early 1960s, Corning's Electronic Products Division managed three businesses—resistors, capacitors, and tantalum capacitors. In a climate similar to today's electronics markets, the division was faced with stiff competition, very high growth, extreme swings in demand, and the need for rapid product innovation. Its functional operation could not respond rapidly enough to make critical decisions, particularly on products to be developed and launched.

An early pioneer in the use of teams, the division formed business units in the mid-1960s—each a team headed by a person from marketing, with representatives from manufacturing, sales, product development, and finance and assistance from a corporate facilitator-psychologist. The teams had profit-and-loss responsibility and were responsible to the top management team for developing and executing their strategic and operating plans.

They achieved a degree of coordination, innovation, and rapid action that would never have occurred under the functional umbrella. The division grew from $18 million to more than $150 million—due, in part, to the business-unit structure.

- *Establishing formal or informal ventures with other companies:* One of the nation's largest market research companies used joint ventures in Europe to leverage its leadership technologies and domestic market position in customer satisfaction measurement and management. The company did not have the time, language ability, market contacts, or capital to go into Europe on its own. Joint ventures provided a way to penetrate the market during the narrow window in time when the market was just beginning to develop and competition was slight.

Real-Life Results of Structural Change Efforts

A Design Success

An extremely conservative Fortune 500 company found that it had the scientific capability to exploit part of a niche in the biotechnology market. The problem was that the company was bureaucratic and took weeks to make the most fundamental decisions. The organization culture was risk-averse, basically taking the attitude that "if there's much risk, don't do it." Worse yet, the top people were micromanagers who often got involved in downstream operations in an invasive and nonproductive way. This was obviously not the atmosphere in which a high-tech venture could flourish.

What was the solution? The company chose to separate the new venture from corporate headquarters, hired an exceptionally well connected biotech scientist/manager, and put his headquarters 1,200 miles from corporate headquarters. His corporate mentor was the senior vice president of research and development, a biotechnologist himself who understood what it took to build an entrepreneurial business. To protect its interests, the company assigned a very astute, positive, and pro-growth chief financial officer to be part of the biotech team.

Although reluctant at first, management became convinced up front of the speed with which the venture would have to move to obtain patent rights, make alliances, and acquire other companies. After three years, the venture is on track, with patents tied down and two basic acquisitions needed to secure the venture accomplished. Although there was lots of hand-wringing at headquarters, the organization structure worked, and timely decisions are being made.

A Design Disaster

An information systems company installed a "matrix" organization in a moderate-size company to implement a new strategy of geographic expansion on the one hand and market/product focus on the other. In a matrix such as this, one person is responsible for the market and its development, and another is responsible for product. They both report to the same level in the organization—in this instance, the president. Other functions that they need in order to perform their jobs are drawn from operations, finance, and sales as necessary.

A little over a year later, the president dismantled the new organization, terming it a mess, unworkable, and devastating to progress. Designed by an academic, this theoretically profound structure paralyzed the company and so diffused managerial authority and responsibility that it plunged from reasonable profitability well into the red. It lost leadership market share for its number one product, and poor morale was worsened by the necessity of making deep personnel cuts to keep the company viable.

A quick return to a conventional product management organization, combined with two changes at the top, at least reversed the decline, but the company never completely regained market share losses. Once lost, they are rarely regained.

The Cost of Structural Mistakes

Remember, even the smallest organizational change takes time to be effective—or prove ineffective. To become effective, a new organizational unit battles two wars. First, both new and old players have to figure out what their jobs are and get to know one another. Second, they have to establish or modify their relationships with other organization units. This takes about a year—sometimes longer.

A mistake takes even longer to correct. Dismantling an organization and returning to the former structure—or imposing another one—stalls progress, causes chaos, costs money, unsettles everyone, drives out good people, and has the organization questioning whether management really knows what it's doing.

Organization design doesn't have to be complicated. As you work through the questions about the effectiveness of your organization versus strategy, structure "falls out." When you look at your list of barriers to success, there will be a handful that, if fixed, will do what is needed to make the structure effective. Then you have to deal with the leadership, people, accountability, and compensation issues so that all the pieces of the puzzle fit together.

The Gains of Cleaning House

Finally, getting rid of and not replacing your resisters and incompetents has significant cash flow benefits. One company with $1 million in revenue and a payroll with associated taxes and benefits of $260 million figured it stood to gain $80 million (30 percent of payroll costs before one-time severance costs) in sustained additional cash flow and an additional pickup in personnel efficiency of 10 percent or a total of $100 million per year. This cash flow is available for funding a better future including product innovation, market penetration, geographic expansion, incentive payments, better facilities and surroundings for employees, debt reduction, and acquisitions. The very act of creating these savings will increase shareholder value, not even counting the future benefits of a lean, strategically focused organization.

Given these numbers, why would anyone *not* clean house and keep it clean?

Do

- Be cautious in reorganizing the boxes in your organization. Most needed changes are small.
- Go through the entire analytical process when you're thinking of changing your organization. Be sure to focus on the value chains that give you your competitive advantages and the subsequent competencies required in the future to accomplish that work.
- Make sure any structural changes enhance your ability to achieve your strategic objectives and fit your criteria for an effective organization.

Don't

- Rush into structural change. Once a company's structure is changed, it is expensive and disruptive to redo.
- Attempt radical change in the structure unless it's truly indicated.
- Make structural changes until all of the other elements of the organization—leadership, people, accountability, compensation, and reward—are thought out.

Key 6

Change the People – Fast

> **Principle:** The change rate of your business is directly tied to the percentage of "leverage jobs"—those critical to achieving the plan—held by superb change agents.
>
> **Why it's important:** Your change agents will get their own jobs done and inspire others to do theirs better.
>
> **How it's applied:** Before plan execution starts, identify the leverage positions and fill them with A-rated players. Then empower them to succeed.
>
> **Expected result:** Your organization will have a faster, smoother trip through the white water of change.

Everyone agrees that people are the key to change. *People* doesn't mean warm bodies at the work bench. It means accomplishment or lack of accomplishment; a positive, achieving culture or a self-defeating culture. It means good earnings and stock market valuation or poor.

Whenever you start a major change effort, you're given a "deck" of people to use. Although you may be tempted to try, you can't immediately throw out all those who don't perform to new standards and import perfect replacements. That's a dream solution, but reality doesn't work that way.

Instead, there is a continuum of actions you must take to hone your organization to fit the new direction. It starts with putting your stars in key leverage positions and removing those who are dedicated to destroying your efforts. It continues with culling poor performers, adding select outsiders, and gradually training, developing, and upgrading the human machine base with which you started.

People Issues During the Change Cycle

What people issues predominate during each phase of the strategic change cycle? The following list shows a typical pattern. Later in the chapter, I'll cover how to expedite changes in people to speed up your progress through the cycle.

- *Phase 1: Recognition—hemming and hawing:* Most companies are too slow to make needed organization changes. They want to support the loyal old guard and give problem people a chance, even if they were not contributors under the old business order and are much less likely to be under the new. Although the company may plug a few glaring gaps between existing and needed competencies, for the most part, management hopes to accomplish the impossible and implement revolutionary change through incumbent personnel, whether appropriate or not. It never works.
- *Phase 2: Unfreezing—good guys in, deadwood out, poor structure disassembled:* The penny drops. Frustrated by the laggards, management gets the deadwood, poor performers, and resisters out of the firing line and mostly out of the organization. All top departmental managers, leverage managers, and staff throughout are of the new order.
- *Phase 3: Structural change—mostly there:* The organization is self-selective. The good people in key positions pick others like themselves for new jobs, projects, and departmental personnel. The organization indoctrinates them well.
- *Phase 4: Continuous change:* The organization is well aware of the need to train and develop its people internally so that the balky, expensive, strategy-slowing process just completed will never happen again. Formal training and development programs, covered in the Key 14 chapter, are established.

People as the Key to Implementation

I can't remember the number of times that I've heard observations like the following:

- "If I'd only got rid of him two years ago" (or variations on that refrain).
- "Life has been so much easier and progress so vastly improved since we shook up that arrogant, inbred, and underled bunch of development engineers who thought their talents so indispensable."
- "I can't tell you how fast the project has moved since we brought in Sam to run it."
- "Fewer people, far more progress."

One corporate executive vice president dubbed himself a late learner. He inherited and put up with a verbal and virulent salesman who accounted for 60 percent of the company's sales. Although he brought home the sales, he let customers know how screwed up the company (not he) was. He lorded it over and disrupted internal operations to his sole advantage and to the disadvantage of others needing shipments. He held the company hostage. He had a can't-do attitude with respect to strategic change unless the ideas were his.

The new executive vice president finally had enough. He and the president got to know the customers well over the course of a year and retired the nemesis. They didn't lose a penny in sales and cleared the way for a new professional sales force.

People are key because they are the only organization asset capable of thinking conceptually and translating your direction into action. Most important are "leverage" people—the drivers of your plan.

Does anyone doubt it?

The People Planning Process

To get the people equation right and expedite your way through the change cycle, use the steps detailed in the following list and illustrated in Exhibit 6-1:

1. *Pinpoint leverage leadership positions.* On your organization chart, map key leverage leadership or managerial positions, along with the positions reporting to them. A leverage position is one that is directly responsible for carrying out a key strategic objective or program. Exhibit 6-2 lists the typical characteristics of leverage people.
2. *Determine job qualifications and competencies.* Identify what is required for each leverage position under the new structure and strategy. Do this without reference to the qualifications of the incumbents.
3. ABCD *your managerial and supervisory people.* Rate them from A (superb) to D (must go). See Exhibit 6-3.
4. *Establish leverage competency gaps.* Pinpoint the gaps between the incumbents and the "new" leverage job descriptions.
5. *Fill leverage positions.* Decide who will fill the high-leverage slots, preferably all A's.
6. *Remove the D's.* Get rid of any D-level performers who can be identified at this time.
7. *Identify any non-value-added operations.* Quickly spot the

Exhibit 6-1 The People Planning Process

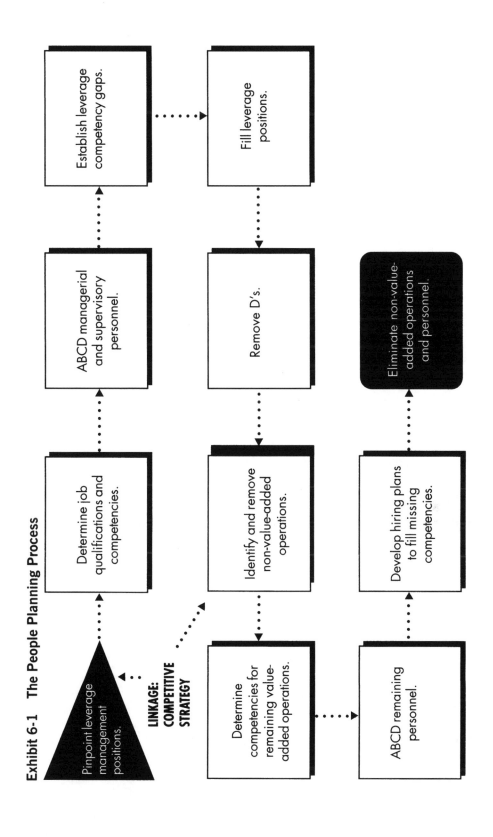

Exhibit 6-2   Typical Characteristics of "Leverage" People

▼ Are overachievers.
▼ Are always asked to do difficult projects.
▼ Are respected and accepted by peers.
▼ Have demonstrated leadership abilities.
▼ Have strong content skills in one or more areas.
▼ Have natural or acquired team skills.
▼ Have management's confidence.

deadwood by examining departments, processes, functions, and people.

8. *Determine the competencies required for the remaining high-value-added operations.*
9. ABCD *the remaining personnel.*
10. *Develop hiring plans to fill any missing competencies.*
11. *Eliminate non-value-added positions and personnel.* Get rid of unnecessary positions and release surplus personnel, including D's, low C's, and identified resisters.

In the following subsections, we'll take a closer look at each of these steps.

Pinpoint Leverage Positions

Leverage positions are the critical spots where you expect change to take place. There aren't very many of them. We usually see ten to twenty, with the larger number at larger companies.

Here are a few typical leverage positions:

■ *The top team:* To a person, all had better be first-rate. They have to be leaders, not just managers. They supervise the departments where the work gets done. They participate in policy making. They are the final court of review for strategic initiatives and their own summary strategic work.

■ *Project team leaders:* You will likely use teams for plan implementation. Team leaders need to be technically competent in their functional area, respected by the organization for their abilities, and models of the key aspects of the new culture. If they haven't already demonstrated good leadership skills, they must have clear potential. It will be up to them to bring their team members around or cull them.

■ *Key department heads:* One or two functional areas will be the vanguard of your change efforts. Whatever the lead departments are in your change plan, the heads must be top-notch, backed up by highly

Exhibit 6-3 Personnel Ratings: Sales-Service Organization

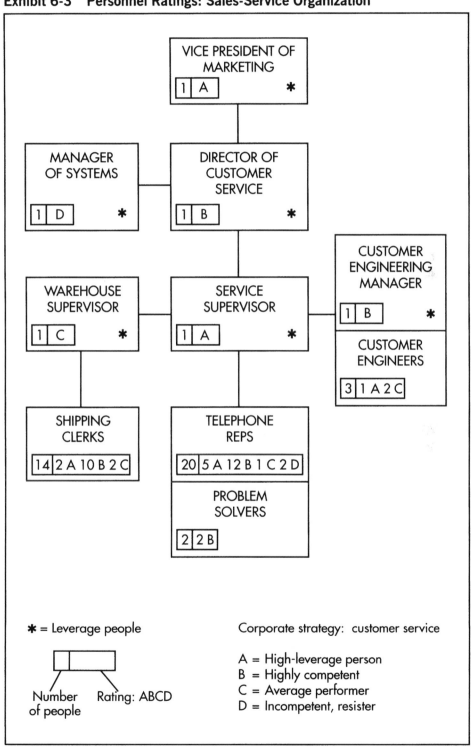

competent successors in supervisory and key employee ranks. If your change is manufacturing reform, key managers must be modern-age in manufacturing, team skills, and problem-solving techniques. If it's a market-driven plan, your vice president of marketing, key product and marketing managers, and sales supervisors need a comparable set of characteristics.

- *Key staff:* There are also individual contributors who will spark the change effort in functions that lead your efforts. In one company, where product development was a major thrust, a few development scientists, engineers, and manufacturing and marketing staffers were key. In another, where information systems reigned, a handful of the finance and information systems staff were critical to success.

- *Support:* A handful of people in support functions such as human resources can be high-leverage people—for example, those charged with recruiting, personnel assessment, and creating training and development programs to support the change effort.

Determine Job Qualifications and Competencies

For each leverage job, define (1) the strategic objectives of the job; (2) the environment in which the person must operate, particularly team and collaborative situations, and interface with key management; (3) the technical and managerial skills needed to do the job at a superb level; and (4) the personal characteristics and competencies needed. If competencies have not been determined at this point and there is no time to do a behaviorally based survey, at least define the job skills and competencies required as seen by the incumbent, peers, subordinates, and supervisors.

At a planning meeting, present data on the competencies required in each of the key leverage positions in the organization. Discuss the qualifications of *each* manager and supervisor, not just those currently in leverage positions. You will need to categorize them by some rating system.

ABCD Your Managerial and Supervisory People

How do you determine each person's rating?

How about the same way that Thomas Jefferson and Meriwether Lewis trimmed the bloated federal army when Jefferson first took office?

Jefferson and Lewis established objectives for their military culling:

- Save money (always a nice thing).
- Get rid of as much incompetence in the officer corps as possible (move the plan forward).

- Get rid of as many politically unacceptable Federalist officers as possible, but not at the expense of competence (those who were out of line with the "corporate values" as well as potential internal enemies).

Their technique was to rank the officers, based on their fitness to carry out a commission, into nine categories. The top category "denotes such officers as are of the 1st class, so esteemed from a superiority of genius and military proficiency." The bottom category denotes those who are "[u]nworthy of the commission they bear."[1]

They discussed the merits of each of 1,400 officers and made their decisions in one day, if I recall my history. They carried out their plan, and they didn't lose any wars.

If you're entering into the unexplored territory of a strategic change program for the first time, you must do as Jefferson and Lewis did. Divide your people into well-thought-out categories based on their ability to contribute to your new direction. Then, having done your assessment, act on it.

Jefferson's nine categories might prove cumbersome, but the following four-category rating system should work for most organizations:

A. *High-leverage person:* Has or can quickly get the rounded skills necessary to carry out a high-leverage strategic leadership job.

B. *High-competence person:* Forms part of the company's backbone that gets the work done.

C. *Average performer:* Will work, but within sometimes marginal capability limits. Ultimately, must improve or leave.

D. *Destroyer:* Is among the malevolent force of passive-aggressive and openly aggressive people who vehemently resist change and those who lack the competence to do the job.

Establish Competency Gaps

Once you have determined job qualifications and assessed the capabilities of those filing your leverage jobs now, note where there are competency gaps between each key job and the incumbent.

Fill the Leverage Positions

Select the people to fill the leverage positions. Here's where you'll put your A's, because these people will play a crucial role in implementing your strategic priority issue programs and staffing the accountability

[1] Stephen Ambrose, *Undaunted Courage* (New York: Simon and Schuster, 1996), 61

structure that keeps you on course. They need confidence, good functional knowledge, and successful prior performance. They should be aggressive achievers and appropriate risk takers. They need the respect of their colleagues and should be good at working with people. One of their prime jobs will be to ensure that you have nothing but A and B performers throughout the organization in short order.

At this point, some organizations have done a complete crossruff—assessing the competency of every job and person in the organization and shuffling people into jobs best matching their skills.

Where there are still competency gaps in your key leverage positions, decide what you will do about each weak person—from training to supplemental leadership and help to substituting another person to recruiting outside for a replacement.

Profile of a Leverage Manager

George was recently hired as chief financial officer in a large publishing company. He was given the responsibility for coordinating planning and was made part of the top team charged with implementing the company's slowly progressing plan. He inherited a mess in strategic information systems programs.

George was masterful at getting people to do things whether they worked for him or not. How? Astutely political, he didn't ruffle feathers (much) but knew virtually everything going on in the organization. He was willing to confront, appropriately. Colleagues and subordinates trusted him because he helped facilitate issues and did not breach confidences. He exuded energy and kept very long hours. George allowed no major issue in his or anyone else's program to go unresolved. He often used his position on the top team to push the team to confront, to move faster. He had little fear.

He assembled and motivated an excellent staff and promoted their presence in the company. Unlike the rest of the organization, he did not hesitate to fire poor performers or move them out of the way—even when they were his own picks.

Remove the D's

Destroyers fall into two categories. The first are unbelievers. They don't buy you, your program, the culture, or the organization. They are self-believers—in their agenda, which usually revolves around their ego and building their own empires. They are defensive. They do not communicate or collaborate well with the organization. They may be very bright and able, harboring personal agendas that dangerously influence their job interface. They become poisonous resisters (see the Key 8 chapter).

The second group of destroyers are those without the competence or the capability to do the new job. The were probably marginal to sub-marginal employees before the new plan and will not be able to contribute adequately to the new direction.

Profile of a Destroyer

Jim was vice president of marketing for a fast-paced electronic equipment firm undergoing a painful turnaround. He was very smart, exceedingly knowledgeable, with a powerful personal presence—traits that he would soon render useless for his new employers. After bringing Jim in from the outside to fix their sales and distribution problems and help with plotting future strategy, his employers discovered a Judas, if not the devil himself.

Jim's method of fixing field performance was to set probably unreachable quotas and then berate the salespeople for not meeting them. He managed by intimidation: "If you don't like it, leave. I can replace you tomorrow." In strategy meetings, he issued absolute statements of "truth" with no willingness to participate in dialogue. In fact, he never entered into two-way conversations, and soon all of the functions that needed to work with him—product development, research and development, and manufacturing—refused to do so.

Nine months after Jim arrived, and as sales seriously deteriorated, he was fired. He cost the company more than a year of strategic rebuilding.

Sound familiar?

The destroyers always get it in the end. So why wait to see the damage?

Your options for dealing with D's range from removing them from the priority programs to ridding the organization of them, with the latter approach ultimately being the most productive. Either way, you have just improved your plan prospects, signaled the organization that their type of destructive ways or incompetence won't be tolerated, and begun to build the new culture by example.

Identify Any Non-Value-Added Operations

The deadwood can consist of departments, processes, functions, or people. Ferreting it out doesn't require extensive reengineering, which you may be doing later in the change process. Use your leverage managers to determine—either in their own departments or, as part of a team, in other areas of the company—where there is redundant, unimportant, or extremely inefficient work. The simple questions asked are: "What is the output of this department? Who is the internal or external customer?

What is its benefit? How important is the benefit to sustaining our competitive advantage? To get that benefit, what are we spending/putting in? What would happen in the long term if the activity went away?" Many companies interviewed eventually released one-third of their employees, and the amount produced and productivity of the remaining assets and people went up, sometimes 10 to 15 percent. The quantity of deadwood you identify reflects unproductive activities and people that can accumulate over the years if not carefully watched.

Determine the Competencies Required for the Remaining Jobs and ABCD the Remaining Personnel

Decide which operations to cut and the number of people associated with them. Leverage managers should then ABCD the supervisory and nonsupervisory people now under their command. The objective is to rate every single person in the company. Leverage managers should look at the competencies required for each job (first identifying those competencies if this hasn't already been done) and then rate the individual's performance and his or her potential. Where the people have or will have personnel deficiencies, leverage managers must determine with whom they will be replaced. This "second-round" rating of people should to be carefully timed and coordinated so you can make your large, initial personnel cuts simultaneously.

Such cuts usually take place within four to eight months of the time that leverage management is in place. You will then end up with your largest cut list of operations and personnel and a pool of relatively productive employees to be used from this point forward. The remainder of your unproductive employees will be smoked out later when they consistently fail to meet new, higher performance hurdle rates.

Develop Hiring Plans to Fill Any Missing Competencies

If you're taking a new direction or altering course significantly, chances are there are skills missing. One manufacturing company found that the key skills missing were—guess what?—in manufacturing. Its supervision was hopelessly out of date and lazy to boot. The company ended up hiring two topflight managers to shape up the organization, and shape and shake it up they did, replacing the C and D supervisors they inherited.

Make Your Cuts

When the planning is over, make your initial cuts in operations and people quickly.

The Rest of the Cast

How about the rest of the players? They fall largely into two camps: competent believers and competent skeptics. Both can be positive contributors.

1. *Competent believers—your B's:* They are your highly competent to potentially outstanding performers. They probably know their stuff, and what they don't know, they'll learn. They will take initiative within the limits of their competence and comfort level and will adapt within the new culture even if they are not completely comfortable with it. Many aren't risk takers, but they won't screw things up. They are the backbone of your organization, but they have to be led well.

(What about your C's? The average performers eventually have to move up to the B category or get out.)

2. *Skeptics:* As I point out in the Key 8 chapter, about 50 percent of your overall population will view your plan with healthy skepticism or disinterest. Their attitude is, I'll do a job, but you'll have to show me, persuade me, that what we're doing is right. Naturally, a similar percentage of your B's and C's will be skeptics. Assuming you weed out the resisters, then this population is a prime target for communication and persuasion to bring their attitudes onboard 100 percent. If they stay skeptical or slip into the resister category, they will have to go.

Hiring Plans

Now it is time to plug the missing holes with agreement on how all of the known competency gaps will be filled. Be sure to take into account vacancies that may open when you fire people or when voluntary severance packages are offered. Hiring and developing a small reserve of A's won't hurt at all at this stage of change.

Keep It Clean

Getting rid of the resisters, the incompetents, and the perpetually skeptical once doesn't do it. You have to make sure that more don't appear. This means revised hiring and performance review standards:

- Use tough hiring standards with well-defined competencies and objective testing. (See the Key 14 chapter.)
- Weed out weak performers quickly. Two organizations I know have similar rigorous first-year review processes. One reviews at 30, 60,

90, 120, and 360 days. If, at the end of any single review, the individual is not then a B-level performer and expected to continue at that level or better, he or she is warned and, if goals are missed by the next review, terminated. The company's rigor continues with semiannual and annual reviews. This kind of scrutiny not only produces an outstanding organization but allows this company to have one of the most generous bonus and stock option systems I've ever seen. And the bonus system applies to everyone, from top to bottom.

- Use a performance appraisal system that is administered both to appraise and to judge. It should grade the entire organization on a forced curve, isolating employees who aren't contributing at expected performance levels for close scrutiny.

Watch for Closet A's

I have been continuously and happily amazed by the number of B's and C's who, challenged, became A's. In one organization that had been particularly prone to bureaucracy and throttling initiative, at least half a dozen people rated as B and C performers showed that they were really closet A's. They blossomed when they got a chance and when, finally, someone paid attention to them and spent money training them. They rose to the top. Some of their teams started pushing top management to move faster, instead of the other way around. This new monster of initiative scared the hell out of a few senior managers. But it was a wonderful surprise and dividend.

Nurture the Team

Having picked the key people to lead change, what now? Throw the job at them and see how they do? Hardly. The top team is responsible for mentoring and nurturing the change agents. They haven't figured out yet what the plan is really all about. Their reactions to being selected probably range from "Wow, sounds like a great opportunity" to nervousness and some apprehension to "Why me, God?" You have the obligation to support them to the hilt at this point and make sure that they have all the tools needed to do their job well. You should ask:

- What development does everyone need to get the job done?
- What are the particular needs of individuals we've selected?
- What needs might they have for outside help?
- What do we need to communicate to them about the change effort and their key place in it?

These issues are addressed in the Key 14 chapter ("Select, Train, and Develop for the Future—Now") and the Key 16 chapter ("Communicate to Everyone, All the Time").

Collateral Damage or Dividends?

The way you address people issues, and the timeliness with which you do so, can give you tremendous collateral dividends—or tremendous collateral damage if your effort is poorly executed.

Your selection of leverage people tells the organization immediately what you value and where you're taking the culture. If you deal effectively with the destroyers, you signal that destructive ways won't be tolerated.

You've begun to build the new culture by act and example. You'll say more with such acts than with anything you'll write, put on a plaque, or say from a bully pulpit. So be careful.

Do

- Act swiftly, matching the competencies of your managers and supervisors with the requirements of the key strategic jobs.
- Put your best A-rated supervisors and managers in the key strategic positions with the most leverage over strategic results.
- Get rid of your D's fast.

Don't

- Keep people whose performance was marginal in the past in hopes that they will do better in a different job or with a new strategy.
- Fail to give people new in their change jobs the support they need.

Key 7

Foster Creative Leadership and Mental Toughness

Principle: The single most important element in the change equation is leadership, both at the top and throughout the organization where change is needed.

Why it's important: Leaders get the tough change job done. Unled, traditional managers and followers don't.

How it's applied: The leverage leadership jobs are filled by people with the well-defined skills and competencies required by the organization's future strategy.

Expected results: Plan objectives are met. Leverage leaders build an organization that meets their high expectations so that increasingly high performance standards set in future years are achieved.

Essentials of Leadership

Are Leaders Born or Made?

Both. You can't develop a leader unless some cardinal ingredients are already there: energy level, creativity, and raw brainpower. Although those God-given advantages are essential, they are not sufficient. They need to be nourished with experiences—successes and failures while growing up—that develop confidence, communication ability, practical judgment, physical presence, and ability to work persuasively with people. But whether inherited or experiential, this set of personality traits is well in place by the time leaders enter the world of organizations.

Leadership successes sometimes come after, or maybe because of, great personal difficulties that would defeat a lesser person. If you look carefully at Abraham Lincoln's background, you'll find a man escaping from a dismal farm and father, the burden of a loved mother's death, and serious chronic depressions. He was physically and socially awkward, his manner of speaking rough. He did have some crude frontier schooling but was basically self-educated through his law studies. But trite as it may sound, he treated his many hardships as opportunities. Look a little closer and you'll discover the personal qualities that propelled him to pull himself up by his scruffy bootstraps and helped him become one of our greatest presidents. He had a warm, almost tender, and endearing personality, was a superb judge of people and genuinely fond of them, and was a consummate storyteller. He had brains and a penchant for action and was a risk taker by inclination and necessity.

How Can You Spot a Leader?

Your company's leaders will be obvious almost from the day you hire them. In fact, their leadership potential should be pretty obvious before you hire them. Their background will tell you. Leadership traits, obvious in grade school, grow in high school, often bloom in college, and then grow again, if nurtured, year after year in your company.

Once hired, leaders quickly rise to the top. They're the curious few who attract people to their views like a beacon in the fog. They're the ones who are always asked for an opinion. They stretch the boundaries to produce something elegant, beautiful, profitable, extraordinary, and beyond normal expectation. They succeed more than they fail. When they do fail, they learn from their mistakes and use that knowledge to succeed in the future. They enlist the help of others as ingeniously as did Tom Sawyer, except they're usually not duplicitous.

What Is Leadership?

By definition, a leader is the keeper of the future. What the organization will be long after this leader is gone rests in his or her hands today. Will it be an essentially healthy, vibrant entity such as Reginald Smith left to Jack Welch at General Electric or a Sargasso Sea of nightmares such as Roger Smith left to Jack Smith at General Motors?

Characteristics of Leaders

Our master strategist and keeper of the future has a number of definable characteristics. Although some of these characteristics are commonly agreed on by practitioners and scholars alike, others on the list here are compiled from my observations over the years. For your organization, you'll probably pick and choose from my list or add to it to meet your specific needs.

What to Look for in a Strategic Change Leader

Listed first are those traits that are imperative for developing and implementing strategy. If your organization is confronting strategic change without these characteristics, you haven't got a leader. You have strategic trouble. Listed next are those traits the leader must exhibit on a day-to-day basis.

Strategic Competencies

When you're picking a top-level leader to supercharge strategic change, here are the competencies—personal traits and characteristics—you should look for:

- *Vision:* Leaders have a vision for the future and the commanding direction needed today to focus and align an organization's activities and direct its resource allocation. Although the organization's vision may emerge from the collective thinking of the top team, it is usually inspired by the personal vision of the individual at the top.

- *Worldview:* Leaders scan and interpret the outside world, keeping the organization in touch, in tune, ahead of the competition, and out of harm's way. They need this broad view to feed their strategic thinking, and they don't assign a staffer to do this work for them.

- *Ability to think strategically, conceptually, and structurally:* Leaders think long-term and see many options that fit their company. They build a history of ever-escalating strategic results as they move up in the business world. They call on this experience to create the best plan and strategies when they reach the senior level.

- *Personal honesty and integrity:* Without integrity, what initially passed as leadership is soon revealed to be hollow and is despised.

- *Trustworthiness:* Leaders engender and keep people's trust. In times of strategic change, employees need to be confident that the future of the organization is in good hands and that they will always be told the truth. Without this trust, people will retreat to a place of safety—the way they used to do things—and the plan will move forward slowly or not at all.

- *Power to persuade and motivate:* Leaders have demonstrated ability to make the plan relevant to people, to rally the troops and convince them to accept the new organization, the plan, and the work methods needed to implement it.

- *Ability to communicate:* Leaders communicate the vision and strategies effectively over a long period of time. This communication is critical to motivate people to implement the plan and align their efforts with it.

• *Bias for action and change:* Leaders usually enter the business world with a well-demonstrated tendency to take action and make changes.

Leadership Traits Needed Every Day

Corporate life isn't lived totally on the brink of strategic change, but that doesn't lessen the need for leadership. These are traits that leaders need all the time:

- *Toughness and persistence:* Leaders stick to their objectives and timetable. They do the tough things such as downsizing and cutting out businesses. They don't let people talk them out of their vision, but they're flexible enough to change or bend if the situation warrants it.
- *Passion:* Leaders are passionately committed the cause, the organization, and their personal vision.
- *Confidence:* Leaders have great faith in their ability and ideas. Seldom intimidated, they relish the exchange of ideas with other people.
- *Intelligence:* Leaders are smart as hell. A Chevrolet thinker will never design a Ferrari. You might get a Ferrari look-alike (not-so-smart strategists are masters of cosmetic bodywork), but zero to sixty in twelve seconds in a cloud of dust and a rattle of bolts won't get you far.
- *Ability to involve people:* Leaders talk and listen to people, motivating, building enthusiasm, and involving the troops in developing and implementing plans. They relish challenge and debate.
- *Decisiveness:* They hesitate not.
- *Accountability:* They establish strategic and operational performance standards for the organization and hold themselves strictly accountable for the organization's results, setting the tone for rigorous accountability.
- *Process skills:* A good leader understands strategic planning, implementation, and team process skills, as well as the core business processes needed to succeed.
- *Conceptual creativity:* Leaders look at situations, see possibilities and alternatives that no one else sees, and combine them into an opportunity. They have a well-developed gut feel that points them in the right direction and makes them suspicious of wrong ones.

- *Ability to develop people:* Leaders intuitively select, empower, and develop high-leverage people.

Why You Should Be Concerned About Leadership Traits

A leadership competency list is not just something pretty to pad out a book. It's a major management tool. Leadership competencies are used to (1) select entry-level hires with leadership potential, (2) select internal personnel for leadership training and development, (3) select people for promotion to leadership positions, and (4) hire leaders from the outside, if necessary. As we'll see later, many companies tailor the lists to competencies possessed by their own successful leaders and use those lists as the basis for tailored leadership testing and development programs.

Leadership in Five Situations

Different situations call for different kinds of leadership. There are five dimensions that determine the mix of leadership skills an organization needs and a leader's effectiveness in it:

1. Your business situation
2. Your culture—present and future
3. The leader's personal style
4. The leader's situational experience
5. The leader's technical skills

Business Situation

The business situation to which the leader must respond defines which leadership characteristics are needed to solve problems. For example, the new CEO of a "bleeding-to-death" insurance company inherited a disorganized staff and a business in chaos with very little functional competence. His go-for-the-jugular personality was ideally suited for this situation. Relying little on teamwork, he immediately established a high-accountability environment to weed out poor performers and quickly assembled a staff whom he trusted. A couple of years later, after his tourniquet had done its work, the bleeding stopped. Recognizing that a stable-growth company would require a more tempered and people-oriented leader, he changed, with no small difficulty on his part, to a more effective long-range teamwork style.

Culture

A leader of change has to work effectively in the old culture while building the new. A cultural mismatch is good, to a point, when radical change is needed, but if the disconnect between the leader and the old culture is too great, neither the organization nor the leader can function.

Leaders rarely shift from industry to industry, partly because each industry requires specialized knowledge and skills, but also because the cultures are radically different. Imagine a pharmaceutical executive used to operating on large margins, with product development cycles measured in years, moving to a retail company—say, Wal-Mart or The Gap. The fast turnover, instantaneous new-product cycle, and low margins would terrorize the pharmaceutical import. If the transfer went the other way, the retail exec would be baffled by the technology cycle, befuddled by scientists and their arcane lingo, and live in perpetual fear that he must be doing something illegal to be making that much money.

Virtually all the CEOs in our survey who were successful in instituting strategic change came up through the ranks of the organization and knew the culture well. Yet they were able to keep an outside view that let them see the need for change.

Personal Style

Fortune magazine brought together the late Roberto Goizueta (Coca-Cola), a quiet but very tough, patrician Cuban, and Jack Welch (General Electric), a hockey-brawling, vociferous Irishman, for a fascinating discussion of their strategic styles. Two of the most effective strategists in America, they are acknowledged to have built more value for their stockholders in the last decade than anyone else. Yet their personal styles (not strategic approaches) were diametrically opposed.

Goizueta supplemented his retiring personality with his chief operating officer, Jack Ivestor, "Mr. Outside," who dealt with the public and the vast majority of Coke's organization. Jack Welch never heard the word *retiring* and probably doesn't supplement his personality with anyone. Different styles, equally effective, but I doubt that either could lead the other's company. Welch's abrasive personality and his penchant for high-tech, highly complicated businesses would clash resoundingly with Coca-Cola's single-product-category, low-tech, marketing-dominated atmosphere.

Situational Experience

I don't subscribe to the notion that a leader can lead anything and a manager can manage anything—at least, not without a lot of training. If you're picking someone to lead significant change, be it for a functional department or the entire company, choose someone who has done it at least once, maybe twice. For example, if you're on a board of directors that is seeking a CEO, look for someone who has successfully piloted difficult change—once as a CEO and another time as a functional vice president on the team. Asking a leader of a stable business to be responsible for change is like picking a captain of industry to command a battalion in combat. Lack of experience is probably the main reason for George Fischer's failure to move Kodak very far along the change road. He came from a very successful high-tech company with a long history of evolutionary change—exactly what Kodak does not need now.

Technical Skills

Again, I don't buy that a leader can lead anything. If you're hiring from the outside, and if you're in retail (particularly if you're in retail), hire someone from that industry. First, knowing the fundamental business allows the leader to identify and address critical issues quickly. Second, the leader speaks the organization's language, which enhances communication and respect. Third, you save time. The leader has to learn only the particulars of your company, not the entire industry. If you're promoting an inside person to head up a change effort, make sure she knows the functional area of change well. Put someone with manufacturing experience in manufacturing, marketing experience in marketing. Don't force the person to attempt to set and lead direction, learn the people, and learn the function at the same time.

Leadership and Management: Two Sides of a Coin

After the leaders create the grand design, what's left for managers to do? A lot.

About 90 percent of making strategic change happen is in the implementation. Although a handful of people developed the plan, it takes 10, 100, or 1,000 people carry it out. They have to be both led and managed.

Lower-level managers inherit the difficult leadership task of convincing 1,000 people to divert part or all of their time away from familiar turf to something that requires new skills and personal relationships. They then have the managerial tasks of setting objectives, recruiting, organizing, training, and controlling the troops. In other words, the plan creates a lot of opportunities, along with 1,000 potential managerial problems.

Management Competencies

The classic management competencies needed to implement change at any level are:

- *Planning:* Developing operating and, if relevant, strategic plans in line with the corporate plan. Setting objectives and budgets. Scheduling work and resources. Ensuring that work is aligned with the corporate plan.
- *Organizing:* Structuring the organization. Populating the organization with high performers. Administering equitable reward policies. Empowering, coaching and counseling, and developing people.
- *Controlling:* Reviewing progress and keeping the task on track. Reporting results. Holding individuals and work groups accountable for achieving their goals. Administering discipline, if needed.
- *Problem solving:* Solving the unanticipated problems that inevitably arise.
- *Team building:* Building a cohesive work team. Motivating and inspiring them to achieve their objectives.

Teams as Leaders

Can teams be "leaders"? Of course, and we'll cover this subject in detail in the Key 9 chapter, "Use Teams (Appropriately)." Suffice it to say now that teams do not supplant the outstanding individual leader. They simply make him or her more effective. For the remainder of this chapter, we'll deal with leaders as individuals and turn to the effect of "mixing" them with a team.

Getting the Right Combination of Leadership and Management at Each Level

Strategic jobs at all levels involve both leadership and management. The combination varies by position and level. As you staff your organization for change, you'll need to have the right blend of leadership and management at each of four levels:

1. Chief executive officer/chief operating officer and top management
2. Department managers reporting to senior managment
3. Leaders of program action plan teams
4. Lower-level management and work-group supervisors

Exhibits 7-1 and 7-2 show how the leadership and management skills and competencies change as you progress from one level to another. You may need to tailor this progression somewhat to meet your specific requirements.

Exhibit 7-1   Competencies by Level

		Management		
	Top	Senior*	Middle*	Lower*
STRATEGIC				
Vision	X			
Ability to think stratgically, conceptually, and structurally	X			
Conceptual creativity	X	X		
Trustworthiness	X	X	X	X
Honesty and integrity	X	X	X	X
Power to persuade and motivate	X	X	X	X
Ability to communicate	X	X	X	X
Willingness to encourage debate	X	X		
Bias for action, change, and results	X	X	X	X
OUTWARD VIEW				
Extent outward world view	X	X		
IMPLEMENTATION				
Toughness and persistence	X	X	X	X
Passion	X			
Confidence	X	X	X	X
Intelligence	X	X		
Ability to involve, empower, and develop people	X	X	X	
Decisiveness	X	X	X	X
Accountability	X	X	X	X
High standards	X	X	X	X
Process skills	X	X		

*Often have department management responsibilities

MANAGEMENT SKILLS				
Planning, budgeting, and allocating resources	X	X	X	X
Organizing—people, structure, and work flow	X	X	X	X
Controlling—scorecard, individual objectives, and budget	X	X	X	X
Problem solving	X	X	X	X
CONTENT SKILLS				
Specific technical and content experience needed by job		X	X	X

The message is twofold. First, you must match an individual's leadership qualities to the job to be done. Someone who is in over her head will be too busy trying to stay afloat to lead change. If you err on either side of the equation, put someone in a tough change job for which she is overqualified. Second, you have to train and develop people so that they can move from level to level with the skills and business perspective required. People come to your company with the potential for leadership, not with an intact set of all the skills needed in your organization. It takes considerable time to develop senior skills in even the most talented candidate for middle to upper management. If you leave leadership development to Darwinian evolution, you'll end up with your leadership roles filled by a hodgepodge of people with varying skills, cultural values, and exposure to the outside world. Selection and development of leaders are covered in the Key 14 chapter.

Top Team

Leadership Role of the Top Team During Implementation

The top team—and ultimately, the CEO—is the keeper of the 18 keys to implementation. Most important, it must pay continued attention to the following areas, making adjustments when needed.

- *Persuasion:* That the plan is right
- *Motivation:* To produce the work required
- *Communication:* Of the plan and results
- *Culture:* Modeling the new culture and monitoring the pulse of the organization to ensure that the culture is changing as desired

Exhibit 7-2   Leadership and Management

ENTRY LEVEL	LOWER MANAGEMENT	MIDDLE TO SENIOR MANAGEMENT	TOP MANAGEMENT
• Understands vision relative to job.	• Interprets functional vision. • Motivates, communicates, inspires.	• Interprets corporate vision for functions. • Functional vision • Motivates, communicates, inspires. • Some participate in corporate management.	• Vision • Communicates. • Motivates/persuades/inspires.
• Executes. • Holds self accountable.	• Executes. • Holds accountable.	• Executes. • Holds accountable.	• Holds entire organization accountable.

- **SCOPE OF JOB**
- **SCOPE, DIVERSITY OF PEOPLE**
- **SCOPE OF INSIDE/OUTSIDE WORLD VIEW**
- **SCOPE AND DEPTH OF UNDERSTANDING OF LEADERSHIP SKILLS**
- **STRATEGY, VISION, AND SUBSEQUENT EXECUTION**
- **AUTHORITY, RESPONSIBILITY, POWER, RISK**
- **VOLUME OF TRANSACTIONS AND DECISIONS**
- **DIVERSITY OF BUSINESS AND STRATEGIC SITUATIONS AND DECISIONS**
- **SCOPE OF FUNCTIONAL KNOWLEDGE**
- **INTUITIVE DECISION MAKING**

In addition, the top team is responsible for:

- Strategic thinking, including making strategic decisions and allocating resources
- The overall planning and implementation process, including annual revisions of the plan and a reexamination of strategy
- The team processes in the company, including the process used by the top team

Management Role of the Top Team During Implementation

The primary managerial responsibilities of the top team are:

- *Alignment:* Seeing that goals are passed down in the organization and that activities throughout are aligned with the corporate direction
- *Infrastructure:* Ensuring that needed support resources are available, including training, review and reward system, recruiting and selection capability, and information systems
- *Resources:* Making people, time, and money available where warranted and needed
- *Review and accountability:* Reviewing objectives at many levels to ensure that the plan is on track and holding accountable those responsible for meeting objectives
- *Organization:* Ensuring that the right people, particularly leverage leaders, are in the right place; making midcourse corrections as needed; ensuring that poor performers and resisters are removed from the organization
- *Reward:* Ensuring that the compensation system rewards strategic progress

Departments

Leadership at the Departmental Level

Leadership and strategic thinking skills are often in short supply among departmental managers, who have traditionally been picked because of their functional knowledge, with a passing nod, at best, to management skills. If you encourage a team management system at this level, department managers need not only functional expertise but also leadership and management skills, team skills, and strategic thinking abilities.

The top departmental managers are members of the top team. They will be the key keepers, teachers, and mentors of the team system at this level, responsible for leveraging the effectiveness of what were nose-to-the-grindstone functional jobs by expanding their scope and skills.

Departmental managers on the top team should exhibit all the leadership traits shown in Exhibits 7-1 and 7-2 and, hopefully, be moving toward the "full set" shown by a topflight CEO.

Leadership Roles of Department Managers

Department managers have the following leadership roles:

- Persuading, motivating, communicating, and modeling the culture—the four major top-team jobs.
- Being functional visionaries, capable of seeing what the function must become in five to ten years to be "best of class." Being able to relate the role and importance of the function to the broader corporate strategic plan and, in particular, its importance in dealing with the market and competitive trends in the outside world.
- Interpreting the outside world (outside the company and outside the department) for the department.
- Interpreting the corporate plan for the department in terms of the job that the department has to do and in a way that motivates its people to do it.
- Developing inputs on corporate and departmental strategy for corporate plan development.
- Ensuring the development of a departmental direction statement (mission, vision, business definition, values), strategies, and roles aligned with the corporate direction.
- Communicating the plan frequently, relating it to departmental activities.
- Motivating, helping set direction, expediting decisions, coaching, and counseling (this last point applies to managers who are project team sponsors).

Management Roles at the Departmental Level

Department managers also have the following traditional, day-to-day management roles to play during implementation:

- Planning, organizing, and controlling department plans and their corporate component to ensure that they meet expectations
- Ensuring that departmental activities are aligned with the corporate plan at all times
- Conducting reviews; holding people accountable

- Getting the right people in the right places; training and empowering them
- Getting rid of resisters as well as D and marginal B performers
- Intervening in team or individual performance problems or conflicts, providing coaching and counseling where needed
- Developing people and departmental skills in line with strategy for future competency needs
- Structuring the organization and its policies and processes as needed to do the job
- Coordinating interlocks and problems on major projects and resources with other departments

Program Action Plan Teams

Although the traits and responsibilities discussed in this subsection are expressed in terms of the team leader, they apply to all members of the team. A good leader will steer the team into taking collective responsibility by using consensus for decision making or rotating leadership duties.

Strategic Leadership Roles of the Program Team Leader

The program team leader's strategic leadership roles include the following:

- Persuading, motivating, communicating, and modeling the culture—the big four. Getting the team to follow his lead.
- Leading the team in developing its mission, vision, executional strategies, and action plans, which are visible and carefully tied to the corporate plan.
- Building the team into a cohesive unit.
- Stimulating strategic and conceptual thinking.
- Managing and selling upper management on the team's cause and needs.
- Making final decisions when there is no consensus.

Management Roles of the Program Team Leader

The team leader's key management roles include:

- Holding the team accountable for results
- Planning the team's work
- Learning, using, and teaching process skills

- Controlling the program to ensure that it is on time and meets its objectives
- Getting and keeping the right people with the required motivation, team, technical, and behavioral skills on or associated with the team
- Coordinating the team's efforts with other contributors outside the department
- Communicating with the top team and sponsor and other key constituencies such as functional areas providing resources or areas whose work is affected by the program
- Getting needed decisions and resources from the rest of the organization on a timely basis
- Delivering promised results
- Solving the problems that inevitably arise

Work Groups

Work groups actually produce something! They deliver the product—the tangible goods, services, process improvements, equipment, or designs required by the strategic plan.

Work groups—such as production teams, design groups, and sales districts—are integrally involved in implementing strategy. Unfortunately, both they and upper management are often unaware of their strategic importance. Typically, their scope of vision is within feet of their department on a factory floor, warehouse station, or order-entry desk.

For example, a unique and intricately shaped pair of sunglasses was the signature product in Bausch and Lomb's first women's collection. Tooling for the design was significantly behind schedule because the compound curves on the frame were considered by some very talented toolmakers almost beyond the limits of the materials in which they were working.

The result: The sunglasses were six months late. To make the season, the body of the collection had to go to market without the signature glasses featured in the company's ad. Embarrassing, and it probably wouldn't have happened had the collection been put together by a team that included representatives from key work groups such as tooling. It's often the front line of the organization that may make or break your service or product. *Stay in touch with the entire system.* Track where critical implementation actions are taking place and make sure that they're aligned in time, quality, cost, and detailed specifications.

Though limited in scope, there are leadership jobs to be done even at the work-group level.

Leadership Traits of Work Group Managers

The basic leadership traits necessary at the work-group level are:

- *Trustworthiness:* Inspires the trust of his or her employees. At this level, employees are likely to rely on their trust of their supervisor to tell them what is good and what isn't—for them and the company. Trust is essential.
- *Ability to motivate:* Inspires the team to get behind the work-group objectives and plan.
- *Team-oriented:* Builds an efficient team that can work together, improve its processes, and cross-train.
- *Ability to communicate:* Crisply and frequently articulates concepts in such a way that they are heard.
- *Ability to involve people:* Gets the commitment of those who must help the department. To the extent possible, involves the work group in setting objectives and determining ways to achieve them.
- *Accountable:* Insists on accountability for self and every team member.
- *Mental toughness:* At this level in the organization, where there is the greatest opportunity for getting off task and resisting change, work-group supervisors have to stand their ground.

Leadership Roles of Work-Group Managers

Work-group managers' leadership roles include:

- *Providing vision:* Tying the work of the group to the vision of the company and giving group members an understood and accepted vision of their own for their part in it
- *Giving input to the corporate plan:* Ensuring that the work group has input to the corporate plan through a departmental plan
- *Stimulating thinking:* Encouraging broad-scale thinking about the work group and its tasks, which can lead to significant tactical, if not long-term structural, improvements in how the work is done
- *Motivating:* Stimulating the group to achieve extraordinary results and then rewarding and publicizing those results
- *Communicating:* Communicating the corporate and department plan and their importance to the work group; ensuring that the importance of the work group's efforts is communicated up

Management Duties of Work-Group Managers

Work-group managers are the people who:

- Plan the group's work and methods
- Produce what's needed on time
- Keep the group aligned with and accountable for timing, quantity, quality, cost, and specifications of expected output
- Staff with the best skills possible for the job to be done and constantly develop those skills further
- Control the input and output of the work group to quantifiable measures where possible

When It Comes to Leadership, Should You "Build" or "Buy"?

In my experience and in the survey done for this book, most of the chief executive officers and chief operating officers who started the change process were homegrown. They had been promoted though the ranks over the years, or if theirs was a young entrepreneurial company, they were one of the key founders. Throughout this book, I occasionally mention new CEOs and the top-team members they bring in from the outside to lead critical strategic change. This chapter has emphasized the need to train and develop in-house leaders. Which is the better approach? As usual, it depends.

With the right qualifications, an insider is a safer bet for promotion to a leadership position than a new hire. Outsiders have only about a fifty-fifty chance of staying and succeeding at senior levels in an organization, so it can be a real risk to hire them. Insiders, on the other hand, know the people, the culture, and how to accomplish difficult tasks in the organization. But they must be able to separate themselves from the old culture and their old friends and be objective about the change job to be done. They must have the necessary functional and leadership characteristics, including a broad, realistic vision of the outside world. If they pass these tests, they are the best choice.

But there are times when hiring from outside makes the best sense. If the chief executive officer and chief operating officer caused the problem, the company will probably have to hire from outside since poor CEOs and COOs rarely develop good successors. If the CEO and COO have recently been promoted, the company may have to look outside to fill some other top-team positions because it now lacks the depth of talent needed. Unfortunately, too often departmental managers are immersed in the old culture, haven't been developed properly, and lack the technical and leadership skills to manage a change process. Our CEO survey showed that the percentage of top management replaced by "promoted-from-within" CEOs during the early periods of change ranged from 30 percent to 100 percent, with a median of about 65 percent. This degree of change is an unfortunate testament to the prior CEOs' lack of desire to maintain a vital culture and build a reserve of skilled leverage leaders ready to move up. Their successors aren't making that mistake.

Whenever possible, it is better to spend the time and money on growing your *own* leaders at all levels of the organization than to buy talent from outside.

Do

- Define the leadership and managerial competencies required for each level in the organization.
- Ensure that leverage jobs are filled with people who have the requisite competencies or hire candidates from outside.
- Institute a program to develop promising leaders for each next level so you have bench strength and your growth won't be restrained by limited people skills.

Don't

- Take leadership lightly. You can test for it, observe it, and develop it, so don't leave it to chance.
- Settle for people in leverage jobs with marginal leadership skills, competencies, or values, hoping that they'll grow into the jobs. They won't. Go outside.

Key 8

Remove Resistance

Principle: People who resist strategic change must be removed from leverage positions quickly. Over time, all hard-core resisters anywhere in the organization must go.

Why it's important: Resisters can cost significant time and money by slowing, damaging, or even sabotaging change efforts. They significantly lower organization morale and energy.

How it's applied: At the beginning of the change initiative, fill leverage positions with change supporters and quickly remove resisters from the top team. Identify and handle the remaining resisters in a three-part program: (1) educate and involve all, including those who initially resist, in the change program; (2) set rigorous performance objectives for all, including resisters; and (3) remove the hard-core resisters who surface as nonperformers or voluble saboteurs.

Expected results: Implementation of strategy will be faster and more efficient.

The Basics of Resistance

How Widespread Is Change Resistance Likely to Be?

Very. No subject in our survey made CEOs angrier than that of resistance. CEOs and human resources executives agreed almost unanimously that when you initiate a change program in an organization:

- About 20 to 25 percent of the people will be firmly behind you.
- About 50 to 55 percent will go along with you.
- About 25 to 30 percent will strongly resist change, mostly because they are resisters, but a small proportion because they are incompetents.

Why Do People Resist Change?

People cling to the status quo for four basic reasons:

1. Fear

- They're afraid they will lose power and position or their special niche in the organization.
- They're afraid they won't be able to meet the new and different demands of the job.
- They're afraid their job will be eliminated.

2. Lack of Information

- They don't understand the need for change, how change will specifically affect their jobs and their personal well-being, and why the change will make them better off in the future.

3. Personality Characteristics

- Almost all of us resist change to some extent. But a few people are so rigid that they find any change threatening and have great difficulty coping with it.
- Some people can't accept others' ideas. For them, it's "my way or no way."

4. Another Agenda

- People sometimes have an agenda for the business that is different from management's. A product manager or even a member of the top team, for example, may think the company should move in a different direction.
- Sometimes a personal agenda is in direct conflict with the business agenda. An officer who wants the prestige of the company plane and lavish entertaining, for example, will inevitably cross swords with a management whose agenda calls for maximum cost cutting.

Why Devote an Entire Chapter to Resisters?

Why spend so much time talking about 30 percent of the workforce? Because leaders who attempt to change and work with resisters drain their own and their company's energy on misguided attempts to convert the unconvertible or to avoid being the bad guy or gal. As we'll see later, resisters cost you a bundle at the bottom line. Worse, as more than one

CEO noted in Part I (see "What CEOs Say"), they can "take you down" by causing you to miss your objectives or by consciously poisoning your reputation with the board. It's quite a strong case for spending time on the subject and getting rid of resisters.

Types of Resisters

Overt Resisters

Overt resisters are the easy ones to identify. They openly fight direction and decisions. They are often bright, well-educated, strong-willed people. They try to get a coalition of people to follow them so it's "us" against "them." They openly criticize the senior staff and the changes management makes. They are usually beyond hope. You have to get them out of the organization as quickly as you can.

Two Resisters, Two Outcomes

George was the chief technologist, a major stockholder, and a top-team and board member of a troubled high-growth, high-tech electronics company. He was pursuing a branch of the company's technology that was a long shot but of great interest to him. When decisions were made to focus the company in a different direction for its survival, he either fought the team overtly or pretended to agree and then campaigned privately with the chairman and the board to get his way. His actions paralyzed the rest of the organization when they realized their decisions wouldn't stick when George got through with them. The company eventually replaced the chairman and spun George and his technologists off into a wholly independent company with no connection to the parent. George had his own agenda. He now gets to fund and run it. But meanwhile, the parent company lost valuable time and market position.

Sue, a talented product developer, had been working on the launch of a publisher's first multimedia product in a typical silo organization. She was very smart and showed her open contempt for the rest of the organization, particularly senior management. Buried in the organization and under weak management, she did pretty much as she pleased. As a result, her product was late because no marketing or competitive positioning work had been done.

As part of a change program, management constituted a team to move the product along. Sue couldn't work in a collaborative environment even though the others on the team had expertise she needed. She argued incessantly with the team and her colleagues about how the project should be run. She continued to make commitments outside of her area of expertise, including to outside suppliers, without seeking advice. When the publisher released the product, it discovered the full extent of the damage she had done. The company faced potential lawsuits over copyright infringements and intellectual rights to multimedia material.

Although Sue was warned by the head of the organization to change her behavior, she was retained and regrettably continued to report to a weak manager who had condoned her behavior on many previous instances. A better solution would have been to fire her or at least put her under a very strong manager where her talents could be corralled or she could be disciplined and ultimately fired if she did not meet legal and behavioral standards.

Passive Resisters

Passive resisters are the most dangerous resisters because they don't readily show themselves. Their behavior mode is to keep quiet and then follow their own agenda. Although superficially appearing to agree with the new direction, they undermine the plan through inaction or by doing things important only to them. Varieties of passive resisters include:

- *The head nodders,* who bob their heads up and down agreeably in meetings and in public but do little or nothing to push the changes forward.
- *The slackers,* who put less and less time and energy into the job.
- *The excuse makers,* who always have reasons, bordering on whining, for not getting the job done.
- *The historians,* who talk about "the way we used to do things." They circle the wagons to fend off all things new. Historians are not usually malevolent, but they just can't grasp the changes required.
- *The submarines,* who just plain hide. They try to have minimal contact with the organization.

Portrait of a Covert Resister

Sam always went along with the program. A member of the top team, he appeared agreeable to changes, rarely asked questions in meetings, and almost never challenged decisions. He participated enthusiastically in training in team principles and reengineering. Unfortunately, when he went back to his functional area, he told his people that nothing the teams did should interfere with the department's work, that the teams implementing strategy took second seat to the department priorities, and indeed, that some of the teams weren't important at all. Sam was a head nodder, apparently with the program but, sub rosa, a saboteur.

A Resisting Team

A company's senior staff members, known for their lack of cooperation with each other and silo management style, participated in the strategic planning process started by the newly promoted president. A pleasant and nonconfrontational group, they readily agreed on mutual goals. In team-building exercises, they agreed that they and their departments had deficiencies in meeting objectives, deadlines, and commitments to other departments as well as in planning, innovation, and collaboration. They agreed on action steps to achieve key strategic objectives and to increase collaboration.

And then . . . nothing changed. Deadlines went by, unmet. Objectives weren't achieved, and behavior didn't improve. Old habits were so ingrained and their egos so resistant to personal change that they couldn't adapt to the new order. After a year and a half, the president gave up on them and began replacing his entire top staff. He hired seven new top managers over a three-year period. Shortly thereafter, the company's performance started to move measurably toward meeting strategic objectives.

Cost of Resistance

It's very hard to put a number on the cost of resistance and incompetence. What is the financial impact of one marketing manager who is consistently late with her assignments because she personally considers them a waste of time? Or of a department manager who argues with every decision and directive and disparages the change program in front of his people? At the very least, the impact is negative. Even if you can't put a precise price tag on it, you know an organization can't move forward efficiently dragging that kind of baggage.

Sometimes, you can come close to pinpointing a cost. In one company, two top-team members who were overt resisters to the change effort prevented plans for market penetration from moving forward for at least one year. In the $100 million company, the value of the increased penetration, when it happened, was around $20 million. Assuming the company was a year late in starting the program, and including the loss of compounding and growth, the cost was probably $40 million over five years.

Looking at cost from a macro perspective, if you assume that 25 percent of your personnel are resisters who execute new plan tasks at half efficiency, you are going to lose 12.5 percent of your productivity—a very high cost—even if the resisters are at low levels in the organization. If they're at a high level or in areas critical to your plan's success, the cost is even greater. In addition, to make matters worse, it's the 30 percent who continually require inordinate supervisory time—sapping your efficiency and your ability to change even further.

Changing Hard-Core Resisters

Can hard-core resisters be changed? Unfortunately, the overwhelming response to that question from the CEOs and human resources vice presidents we surveyed was no. Oh, they agreed that, with work, you might get 2.5 to 5 percent of all resisters to come around. If resisters represent 25 percent of your populace, then the 5 percent of them you might convert is a very small group—1.25 percent of your total. This group has die-hard character traits or work habits that have been embedded over many years and won't budge. You can't afford to spend much time trying to change them. If they rise to the occasion, great. If not, so be it. You'll get more value from spending your time bringing the 50 percent who are at the "go-along" stage into the ranks of those "behind you."

Identifying Problem People or Areas

There are three ways to spot the people or areas that will give you trouble:

1. *Surveys:* Many organizations that undertake a change program use surveys to peg the changes needed in the culture and to establish development goals for people. These surveys can also locate individuals or organizational units where there is a morale or resistance problem. Types of surveys include:

- *Change surveys:* Organizations undergoing change often use periodic interviews and focus groups run by psychologists or consultants to probe what is and is not working in the change process. Typically, the consultant will ask whether there are functions or individuals standing in the way of progress.
- *Cultural surveys:* Cultural, attitude, and morale surveys of the organization (see the Key 10 chapter) that report results by department will often pinpoint departments where morale is significantly below the norm. This is certainly a cause for in-

vestigation and almost always reflects a problem of supervisory competence and attitude.

- *360-degree surveys:* These surveys confidentially solicit the opinions of peers, subordinates, and supervisors on an individual's performance and behaviors. They give a far more balanced view of an individual and his performance and development needs than the opinion of a single boss. The results also pinpoint people who have significant problems with attitude and resistance, giving the organization an opportunity to develop them or outplace them if they are judged to be unchangeable.

2. *Observation:* Surveys are good confirmation and verification of problems in the organization. But practically speaking, you shouldn't need surveys to identify resisters. You can uncover them by observing individuals in team meetings and casual conversations and by asking probing questions of their subordinates and peers.

3. *Performance reviews.* During performance reviews, supervisor and subordinates rate not only performance but also the extent to which the employees' behavior and competencies line up with corporate values. Resisters will inevitably have a higher view of their performance and the impact of their contributions than will their supervisors.

Dealing With Resistance

This section presents a variety of proven techniques for handling resistance.

Handling Resistance at the Top

Get resisters off the top team immediately.

You have to have your top team behind you 100 percent. They need to support the change program and have the skills to carry it out. If they don't, move quickly. As mentioned before, the CEOs in our survey replaced 30 to 100 percent of their teams. The average is about 60 percent. The root reasons are simple. The top team is often the cause of the problems in the first place. Frequently, they are set in their ways, used to dealing only with a command-and-control organization structure, and have far less energy and enthusiasm to devote to change than they had when they were climbing the organization ladder.

Quick action on deficiencies in the top team sends a strong signal about the urgency of the change program. Firing or retiring top-team members and replacing them with people who have the values and skills you need sends the message, "No second chances." On the other hand, if you signal your willingness to live with mediocrity or resistance at the top, then the organization knows you're not serious about change and it's all right for them to live with mediocrity, too.

One newly appointed Fortune 500 CEO said he got rid of top management resisters quickly because he knew they would have mounted an effort to poison his reputation with the board and ultimately get him thrown out.

That's exactly what happened to another Fortune 500 CEO who failed to act so fast. Brought in from the outside, he spent three years trying to convert key players who didn't agree with his vision and plan. The result was that company strategy was poorly executed, while the resisters poisoned the board against him. He ultimately resigned.

Handling Resistance Among Leverage People

Get your leverage leaders, managers, and team leaders right.

At the beginning of your change program, make a preemptive strike against resistance by placing only people who support the change in leverage positions. This is your first opportunity to recognize possible resisters throughout the organization and decide how to deal with them. Take the time to identify them now so you can get as many of them as possible out of the system right away.

Using Leverage People to Handle Resistance

Make it clear to your leverage people that one of their major jobs is to identify and fix resistance and competence problems early in the change program. Make it part of their performance objectives.

Use the following process:

- Set rigorous performance objectives, both job and behavioral, for resisters, just as you do for everyone else. Review them regularly and hold them accountable. Most CEOs felt that this is the most effective way of "smoking out" resisters and chronic poor performers. Many will quit because they can't handle the rigorous objectives or don't want to work that hard. Others will perform poorly, giving you a documented record to support firing.

- Identify the few highly talented resisters you most want to bring around—those you are convinced could be valuable to the organization—and assign them change tasks. You might, for example, put such a person on a project team to improve a core process. Those who are part of the solution are a lot less likely to be part of the problem. But they have to be counseled about their resistance and removed quickly if they don't come around.

   ▪ Review and counsel those who aren't performing early in the process. Try to find out why. Would training fix the problem? Could the person perform superbly in a less demanding (even lower-paying) job? Or does the person simply not care or lack the necessary smarts? You've got to determine whether these people are capable of acquiring the competencies needed for the future of the company—not just what's needed to squeak by now.

Resisters and poor performers will tell you they can and will change. It's very unlikely. Don't be surprised if their performance doesn't back up their claim. You'll have to make hard decisions about their futures in the first six to eighteen months of the change plan. Remember, it is the 75 percent who are going to make your plan work. Direct your developmental efforts toward them.

Options for Dealing With Resistance

Your options for nonperformers and hard-core resisters (shown in Exhibit 8-1) are to:

   ▪ *Retire them.* Many of them will welcome an early retirement package.
   ▪ *Downsize them.* If downsizing is a part of your plan, make sure that these people are the first to go through job elimination if the jobs they hold are eliminated or changed technically so their skills no longer apply.
   ▪ *Fire them.* Show them the door if their documented performance and behavioral problems warrant.
   ▪ *Smoke them out.* Set rigorous job and behavioral requirements and review performance frequently. This, combined with their reporting to new, tough-leverage leadership, usually causes the resisters and the underperformers to leave or ask for a severance package.
   ▪ *Place them elsewhere in the organization.* Transfers should be used only if you're convinced the involved employees will be able to do their new job well and only if you're sure they will move the change effort forward and have or will get the competencies needed for the future organization. Don't just move the problem. If you do, every manager in the organization will follow your lead. All you nice folks will just push the deadwood around. You must be rigorous in your standards.
   ▪ *Better yet, have them compete for jobs.* One of the best solutions

Exhibit 8-1   Actions to Take With Resisters

FOR THOSE WORTH SALVAGING	
Information and persuasion	Give them plenty of information about: • Changes in the outside world that require the company to change • What the company's vision, objectives, and strategies are for dealing with the outside changes • What the change program means for the individual
Involvement	Involve them in planning and implementing needed changes at some level.
Coaching and counseling	Identify any specific reasons for resistance to see whether they can be corrected.

FOR THOSE WHO CAN'T BE SALVAGED	
Options:	
Retire them.	Offer a one-time package after informing them that their future is bleak. Resisters will often welcome it.
Fire them.	Fire those whose documented job performance and behaviors are unacceptable.
Downsize them.	Provide a severance package to those whose jobs are eliminated or changed technically so that their skills no longer apply.
Smoke them out.	Set rigorous job and behavioral performance standards and review them frequently. Underperformers will often leave of their own accord.
Place them elsewhere.	Place them elsewhere in the organization where they can make a genuine contribution, and resistance should cease. But avoid the tendency to dump longtime resistant or incompetent employees in the organization.

to the internal placement problem was used by a Fortune 500 company. Displaced people had ninety days to bid on other internal jobs. They were interviewed and had to prove themselves, just as an outside hire would. (Caveat: Only qualified people went into the pool. Unqualified people and resisters need not apply.) If an internal individual was chosen, the company undertook the time and expense of any retraining needed. The organization got the clear message that the business needs of the company would prevail when picking people and that only the best, be they on the internal or external market, would be hired.

Using Severance and Early Retirement

Have severance and early retirement packages in place at the beginning of the change program.

If the terms of voluntary separation, early retirement, and involuntary separation programs are worked out and legally cleared in advance, your managers will know what tools are available to them.

Timing Your Actions Skillfully

Remove the bulk of the resisters and nonperformers at one time. The pain to the organization will be over sooner if you don't drag it out.

When do the 30 percent leave? Remove as many of the resisters and nonperformers as you can at one time within weeks or a month or two of launching the change process. Those remaining, who do not opt for retirement or severance packages, will leave within eighteen months, according to our survey, because they can't meet new performance and behavioral standards. Thus, the organization is "self-cleansing" with proper leadership and standards.

Dealing With the Go-Alongs

A major objective of the change process is to convert the 50 percent go-alongs to believers. Your strategies (shown in Exhibit 8-2) should be as follow:

- *Give them plenty of information.* Be sure they're fully informed about the need for change and the expected results of the program.
- *Involve them.* Have them participate in meaningful change work. Ensure that they understand the relationship between their work and the success of the entire change effort.

Exhibit 8-2   Actions to Take to Convert the Go-Alongs to Believers

Provide information and persuasion.	Be sure they understand the company's vision, objectives, and strategies and their meaning for individual jobs and personal growth.
Involve them.	Have them participate in meaningful change work, ensuring that they understand the relationship between their work and the success of the entire change effort.
Develop them.	Give them the training, development, and experience to meet both the organization's and their personal needs.
Praise them.	Praise them publicly for their plan contributions.

- *Develop them.* Make sure that they are part of the individual developmental process so that their growth needs and personal development wishes are addressed. *Make sure that they are developing in competency areas where they are weak. This is the surest way of bringing them on board.*
- *Praise them.* Give them kudos, publicly, when they have made substantial contributions in line with plan objectives.

Hard-core resisters, those who will always resist change, and incompetents are 25 to 30 percent of most companies' employees. Not only can they make implementation of change difficult; they can also prevent the company from meeting its goals. They have to be identified early in the

Exhibit 8-3   CEOs' Checklist: Resistance

1. ABCD your leverage and key personnel with respect to competence and resistance.
2. Prepare severance, outplacement, and retirement packages.
3. Decide on people changes during your implementation plan meeting:
   - Where your leverage managers will work
   - Who goes as a result of resistance or incompetence
4. Approve your severance and outplacement packages.
5. Make removal of poor performers and resisters part of leverage managers' performance objectives.
6. Make the first-round cuts as soon as possible after the implementation meeting.
7. Assess personnel for resistance and nonperformance at every quarterly review.

change process and removed from the organization, for as history has proved, very few will have either the capacity or the desire to change. A CEO's checklist for dealing with resisters is shown in Exhibit 8-3.

Do

- Make sure there are no resisters on your top management team or in the leverage management group. If there are, replace them immediately.
- Use your leverage managers as the primary point for identifying resisters and poor performers and dealing with them during the first year of change.
- Have well-thought-out and generous programs for dealing with those who will be pushed out: early retirement and voluntary and involuntary severance.
- Get rid of the bulk of your resisters and performance problems at one time, as early as possible during the first year of the change plan, and smoke out the rest within eighteen months.

Don't

- Get talked into believing that cleaning up and realigning the organization is unkind and that you should spend significant time and money trying to change or salvage the 30 percent. The reality is that by not dealing with the problem, you hurt the remaining 70 percent, the viability of the corporation, and your reputation.
- Relax your vigilance and lessen pressure on the organization to constantly look for and remove resisters and poor performers. Not doing this over a number of years caused the current problem. You don't want to saddle future management with a similar one.

Key 9

Use Teams (Appropriately)

Principle: Teams are by far the most effective means of implementing complex strategic programs.

Why it's important: Teams create conditions conducive to the cross-functional coordination, creativity, and commitment needed to implement complex strategic change programs.

How it's applied: Top management commits to using teams to develop strategic priority programs and manage their implementation to successful conclusion.

Expected results: Programs are executed faster, more creatively, and more thoroughly, with interfunction coordination and end results superior to those typical of a line management system.

Teams and Their Uses

Just because you bring a few good people together and assign them a task doesn't mean you've got a team. And it doesn't guarantee you the superior results promised by every book on teams you've ever read. Because it's not the label that makes the team; it's how the members work together to accomplish their task.

If team members still follow the traditional command-and-control model, they are not really a team at all. They are simply a group. Each person's primary allegiance and energy are focused on his or her particular department or business, and many key business decisions are made one-on-one between the chief operating officer and functional managers. Typically, when a group meets, it conveys information and discusses issues, but ultimately, the boss decides what to do. The decision-making power—and above all, the prime responsibility for coordinating work between functions—resides squarely with the COO.

This model worked and still works in industries and companies in which the world changes slowly and the few critical decisions necessary can all be focused at the top. It does not work in rapidly moving environments in which, to succeed, quick decisions and superb coordination between functional areas are needed for rapid implementation. It does not excel at implementing strategic change. Teams do.

Teams are temporary or permanent groups of individuals with the functional competence, interpersonal skills, and leadership abilities to work together to accomplish an important, well-defined job. They excel in managing multifunctional, cross-boundary tasks requiring coordination and the use of resources from many functional areas. There's no organization structure better equipped for strategy implementation.

To see why, let's compare a traditional line organization with a team on a number of characteristics. (For an at-a-glance comparison of teams and management groups, see Exhibit 9-1.)

The Case for Teams

Leadership

■ *In a line organization:* Leadership inevitably falls to a top manager who has so many other responsibilities that he or she doesn't have

Exhibit 9-1   Team vs. Management Group Characteristics

Dimension	Teams	Management Groups
Power and authority	Granted and earned.	Inherent in the job.
Behaviors	Team, collaborative, persuasive, consensus-driven.	Quick and more directive.
Skills	Functional and team management.	Functional and line management.
Rewards	Usually few outside the line management system.	Usually on operating results and long-term options.
Specialty	Resolving complicated multifunction issues.	Line operations that require quick decisions.
Skill balance	Correct functions and personalities assigned at start.	Whoever made it to the top.
	Some members have prior team experience, each at least one functional skill.	Each person has one or two strong functional skills, and some may have team experience.
Strategic orientation	Focused on a few aspects of plan implementation but understand relationship to overall plan.	Should be broad strategic view of inside and outside world.

the time to coordinate a complicated project well. What's called leadership is really control: "I give orders and hold meetings to check on what's been done and get information and recommendations. Then I make a decision." With the amount of rapid change in the marketplace today, an organization can't afford to concentrate decision making in a few top-level places.

■ *On a team:* The team leader is one of your most capable people who probably holds an important line job and now has the added responsibility of team leadership. It's a lot, but still not the plethora of responsibilities that one of your top executives has. The team leader has more time to spend on the project, plus he or she will be working hand in hand with capable people from a variety of functions in your organization who will share the load, bring their perspectives to the project, and participate in decision making. The work is shared, and the team's recommendations represent the thoughtful input of all the functions involved.

Coordination

■ *In a line organization:* A manager pulls various functions together during some committee or one-on-one meetings. The project has little corporate legitimacy because it's run by a single function. Cooperation from others is at best lukewarm and dependent on the personal abilities and power of the individual in charge of the project.

■ *On a team:* All of the functions involved in the project are represented on the team, which meets regularly. Through their team representatives, functions have their say, know what's going on, and have a stake in the success of the team.

Organization Learning

■ *In a line organization:* Each function does its part of the program with little interaction between functions. Results are reported to the leader.

■ *On a team:* All functional representatives work together on the team. Through their training and discussions, they learn about each other's functions and gain skills in working together effectively.

Enthusiasm for the Job

■ *In a line organization:* A top manager asks an individual to take on a task. She's glad she's been recommended, pleased to have the face time with the manager, but it's extra work, too.

■ *On a team:* There's prestige to being on a team that's doing important work, but it's still extra work. Then the team member finds he's learning a fair amount about other functions in the organization, acquiring skills in working as a team, getting exposed to the top team, and damn, it's fun to be given your head to do a job together.

Performance

▪ *In a line organization:* Who knows who did what, when, and how? Probably the top manager and maybe some department managers, but no one is keeping score, overall.

▪ *On a team:* The team and the individuals on it have performance scorecards on which they are reviewed and rewarded appropriately.

Results

▪ *In a line organization:* Decisions are as good as the person or couple of people who make them but rarely as good as those of a team. Work and results take time since everything must go up to the top and come down again. Implementation of the result usually takes longer since functions have not worked together to design a "best-for-all" answer.

▪ *On a team:* Decisions are made by the team and therefore represent the input of all the functions involved. Work is coordinated at the team level, which is time-efficient. In addition, teams develop a synergy that enables them to design and execute programs better, faster, and usually more creatively than individuals or informal committees can.

When Not to Use Teams

Teams are not for short-term or trivial projects. They're overkill for projects of a couple of months' duration and unnecessary for piddling issues. Typical functional project management is sufficient in such cases. When organizations really get gung ho about teams, there is a tendency to form a team for everything. One group self-formed a team to decide what color to paint the facility. When the CEO, a very team-oriented person, heard about it, he told them to get back to work. He was picking the color. They had more important things to do. Teams are for significant strategic issues, not minutiae.

Implementing Strategy Through Teams

In this subsection, we'll consider the four types of strategy implementation teams:

1. Top planning team
2. Departmental teams

3. Program teams
4. Special strategy project teams

Top Planning Team

The top planning team has the organization's future life in its hands and is therefore the single most important management body in the organization. It is responsible for ensuring that the strategic plan gets the desired results and that it is reexamined periodically to verify that the strategy continues to reflect the external opportunities and threats. Its duties are shown in Exhibit 9-2.

The team's membership inevitably includes the chief executive officer, chief operating officer, and their handful of direct reports. In many cases (which we encourage), the team is augmented by several lower-

Exhibit 9-2   Summary of the Top Team's Strategic Duties

Overall Objectives
- Ensure that the future of the organization conforms with or exceeds that described in the company's direction statement and measured in its strategic objectives.
- External vigilance: Look for new, fresh, and unique strategic opportunities and strategies in the marketplace by constantly interacting with customers, the marketplace, experts, and thinkers.

Key Duties
- ▼ Develop the strategic plan.
- ▼ Align the organization's work with the plan.
- ▼ Ensure that needed strategic leadership and human resources competencies are in place and being developed for the future.
- ▼ Design and maintain an accountability and reward system that aligns with objectives, pays for performance, is highly motivational, and culls poor performers.
- ▼ Review, judge, and hold accountable those executing the plan at appropriate intervals, modifying programs, resources, and funding as needed to keep on track.
- ▼ Constantly communicate the plan and ensure that every person knows his or her place in achieving it.
- ▼ Allocate resources in alignment with the plan and expected payoff, balancing short- and long-term expenditures and payoff.
- ▼ Establish and maintain a cross-functional team process to implement strategic programs effectively. Charter and staff these teams.
- ▼ Ensure that critical strategic objectives and programs that are not managed by the top team are delegated to the functional areas that will be held accountable for measurable results.

level personnel, who can make many contributions. Because of their intimate knowledge of the people in the organization, they can quickly recommend other people for teams. Because they know the informal system, they can suggest efficient ways to implement an initiative. They have a firsthand feel for the organization's "real" workload, its problems, and how high the barriers to programs and initiatives are—often a very different picture from that passed on to senior management through traditional channels. Finally, they become good communicators of the plan back to the rest of the organization.

In one planning meeting that included three lower-level members, the time needed to make decisions decreased substantially because they were quick to recommend who should implement a decision and why. In another instance, members were able to suggest new solutions to problems and volunteered to do the work or lead a team to accomplish the task. In addition, they told management point-blank that several key people and functions thought highly competent by management just weren't capable of carrying out strategic tasks.

Does the CEO still have a job? Certainly—with, thankfully, less detail work. In my experience, the CEO in a team setting can focus on seven roles:

1. Maintaining a realistic strategic perspective on the outside world
2. Stimulating creative thought on strategic alternatives
3. Decision making if the team can't reach consensus or the CEO fiercely disagrees with the team
4. Motivating the team
5. Owning the planning process
6. Managing relationships with the board and financial community
7. Developing the organization's potential top-level people

Departmental Teams

Departments such as operations can operate as a team rather than a command-and-control unit. The functional departments such as marketing, service, and operations are the most important organization units for both shaping the strategic plan and implementing it (see the Key 3 chapter, "Embed Departmental Planning," for a more detailed explanation of their role). They have all the resources—human, managerial, hard assets such as plants and laboratories, and monetary—under their control. They are on the firing line and should have the most current information on what is happening inside and/or outside the company. They, in combination with program teams that utilize their people and assets, do the actual work of plan implementation.

The strategic planning functions of departmental teams are shown in Exhibit 9-3.

Departmental team members are almost universally enthusiastic about participating in the planning process. Teamwork often comes more naturally to them than it does to people at the very top because their close day-to-day proximity requires it. Departmental personnel are delighted to have a say in the corporate plan by relaying their view of corporate priorities upstairs. Similarly, they welcome the opportunity to align their own plans with the corporate one so that they can get a fair shake when resource allocation time rolls around.

Program Teams

Program teams are cross-functional teams appointed by the top team, using departmental personnel. They are responsible for addressing priority strategic issues. Exhibit 9-4 shows the duties for which a program team is responsible.

Team leaders, sponsors, and core members of program teams are appointed between the priority-setting meeting and the resource alloca-

Exhibit 9-3   Departmental Management Team's Strategic Duties

Overall Objectives

- Participate fully in the strategic planning process by feeding both departmental ideas and issues and corporate-level ideas and issues to the top team.
- Develop a departmental plan that includes both operating (short-term) and strategic priorities, objectives, and programs.
- Execute and meet the objectives of both departmental strategic programs and those corporate programs and objectives delegated to the department.

Key Duties

- ▼ Develop a departmental strategic plan and scorecard that includes delegated corporate priorities and objectives, departmental strategic operating and infrastructure priorities and objectives, and action plans to support them.
- ▼ Keep fully up-to-date in the functional department's area of expertise through contact with other organizations, associations, and "best of class," fully understanding the linkage between the corporate strategic plan and excellence in the functional area.
- ▼ Contribute needed and agreed-upon functional human resources to corporate priority issue program teams. Oversee significant team work being accomplished in the functional area.
- ▼ Balance short- and long-term programs and activities so that both are accomplished.
- ▼ Ensure interlocks and coordination needed to achieve plans between other functions and organizations operated smoothly.

Exhibit 9-4   Strategic Program Team's Duties

PLANNING

Takes input from the top team and:
- ▼ Defines:
  - —Mission
  - —Scope of the program
  - —Objectives
  - —Strategies, programs, action plans
- ▼ Gets top team approval of direction and budget

ORGANIZATION

- ▼ Gets and organizes needed human, tangible, and monetary resources.
- ▼ Develops skills as a team through practice, self-improvement, and training.
- ▼ Ensures that the team has the best people for the job; adds and culls as needed.

EXECUTION

- ▼ Manages programs to completion.
- ▼ Delegates action and program steps where needed.
- ▼ Gets the promised results.

CONTROLS

- ▼ Self-reviews and controls in programs.
- ▼ Reviews progress with top team.
- ▼ Gives top team the bad and good news early.

SELF-DEVELOPMENT

- ▼ Learns new management techniques relevant to the team's and company's work.
- ▼ Makes contact with other organizations outside the company that can be helpful in the team's work.

AUTHORITIES

Defines authority in each of the following areas:
- ▼ Money
- ▼ Hiring, firing
- ▼ Scope of decisions

tion meeting. They develop program action plans and resource requirements for each priority strategic issue. If plans are approved, a complete team is appointed by the top team. Members work together until the project is complete, a time ranging from one year to several years.

Special Strategy Project Teams

Strategy teams with wider-ranging membership are sometimes formed to tackle a specific task and then disbanded or allowed to go dormant until needed again. While they are not in existence long enough to become a true team, properly led or facilitated, they are very effective in quickly addressing tightly defined issues. Here's an example:

Strategic Options and Scenarios. Facing a sea change in its markets and a very tumultuous decade of dealing with these changes, one Fortune 500 company formed a team of twenty—including representatives from top management, marketing, sales, finance, research and development, and human resources—to develop several scenarios of possible future events. Over the course of two months, the team isolated high-probability technological, product, competitive, pricing, distribution, and legislative events with potentially great impact on the company. It then developed several alternative strategies for dealing with these events that management could consider and act on during its strategic planning sessions. Having fulfilled its assignment, the team disbanded.

What Makes Teams Effective?

Effective teams have the following characteristics:

- *Right membership:* Members are picked because of their functional expertise and competence, not because of politics, position, or availability.
- *Chartered:* The charter (from the top team) gives the team a clear mission, job objectives, and empowerment boundaries, explicitly defining its authorities and limits on spending, hiring and firing people, making decisions, and the parts of the organization in which it is and is not free to operate.
- *Trained:* Members are thoroughly trained in team development, management, analytical and decision-making techniques, and facilitation.
- *Process- and results-oriented:* Members continuously improve

their team's processes, efficiency, and ability to work together while never forgetting that their major job is to get results.

- *Bonded:* Members are cohesive, work and play well together, and believe in the team and its cause and leadership. If anything, they are a bit chauvinistic about teams in general and theirs in particular.
- *Self-policing:* Team members are critical of their own progress and results, usually far more so than line management, because they operate with an ethic in which positive criticism is a value and not a personal assault. They police behavior of team members who are not performing, asking for the removal of those whose contributions don't meet the team's expectations.

Good team behaviors, as observed by the late Professor Douglas Mac-Gregor of MIT, include: frank, frequent, constructive criticism; a lot of pertinent discussion; members' listening to each other; disagreement and conflict over business and team process issues; a relaxed atmosphere; clear assignments; and decision making by consensus.

The Price You Have to Pay

Ten years ago, if we asked seminar participants how many used teams, a handful of hands would go up, and most of those were people using quality teams. When we ask the same question today, only a few hands *don't* go up. If we ask whether or not teams are a good idea, there is virtual unanimity that, properly used, they are. But executives also agree that teams have some downsides. Exhibit 9-5 summarizes team pros and cons reported by hundreds of company presidents who use teams.

Implementing teams takes a toll. In this subsection, we'll consider some issues you should expect to confront.

Cost

Teams cost money. I would estimate that the start-up cost of a six-person team totals eighty person-days, broken down as follows:

3–6 days:	Team training time
6–8 days:	Facilitation help from a professional facilitator
7 days:	Trainer time
30 days:	Inefficient team time while organizing

There is very little that you can do about the first three factors, other than withhold time and support—a sure way of killing the team system

Exhibit 9-5   CEOs' Views on Using Teams

PROs

- ▼ Coordination
- ▼ Commitment to outcome
- ▼ More and better ideas, creativity
- ▼ Enthusiasm and motivation
- ▼ Realism
- ▼ Increased trust in the group
- ▼ Results achieved
- ▼ Flexibility in using personnel to do multiple jobs; not for-purpose hire
- ▼ Lower cost than doing the job conventionally
- ▼ Cross-training—broadens thinking, builds strategic thinking
- ▼ New behaviors that teams and the organization have to learn

CONs

- ▼ Time
- ▼ Cost of training and time to get up and running
- ▼ New behaviors that teams and the organization have to learn
- ▼ Conflict over time splits and who's boss in team members' functional jobs

and your credibility fast. And you'll have to accept that the fourth factor is a normal part of the learning process. Almost any team is going to be inefficient at first.

Time and Loyalty Conflicts

There may be conflicts over time and personal loyalty, pitting the team members' regular job and boss against the team job and the team. Training, formation, and start-up of a project team may take 50 to 75 percent of the leader's time and 30 to 35 percent of the team members' time; thereafter, up to 20 to 25 percent sustained time will be required during full team operations. Team members may then find themselves in the unenviable position of that mythical animal the "Push Me, Pull Me," needing to negotiate a contract with both the boss and the team covering how much time will be devoted to each and what will be delivered. Typically, this issue is worked out in advance during the resource allocation meeting. If there is contract gridlock, the decision has to go to the top team. In most instances in which time conflicts are severe, line work is shifted to other employees or to temporary or borrowed help.

But if a conflict gets to this point, the problem is probably with a functional head who does not support the team system. In an egregious incident we witnessed, a senior vice president supported the project team and his team member in top-team meetings and then told her privately that the project wasn't important and not to spend much time on it. When something like this happens, you can guess that the functional head will be unsupportive of other team efforts. It begs the issue whether the person belongs in that job or in the company long-term.

The Learning Curve

Team members must learn new team management and decision-making behaviors. In the long run, this isn't really a downside, but it is painful for a lot of people. However, you shouldn't try to mitigate the pressure by allowing old behaviors to prevail. To ease their passage from old to new behaviors, give team members training in team management and facilitation and provide facilitation help. And unquestionably, put the top team through the same team formation process as the program teams—first, if possible. The top team can then start modeling correct behavior and mentor teams from a base of knowledge and understanding rather than theory.

What's in It for Team Members?

What do teams offer members to offset the pain of doing two or three jobs? A lot—for the person who likes to be challenged. The benefits include: a stimulating, important job; top-level visibility and exposure to corporate strategy; opportunities to learn new skills; interaction with colleagues and functions outside of one's own area; and possible promotion. In addition, enlightened companies reward teams on top of their regular compensation system and are looking at teams as a training ground for development of their future leaders.

Although the teams implementing strategic priority issues are the most crucial, they need the direction and support of the top team and departmental teams. Let's look at how to make all these teams effective.

Getting Started With Priority Issue Program Teams

Top-Team Preparation

Before they kick off a program of strategic change, top-team members need skills in team development, analytical techniques, and team management. At a minimum, they should receive an abridged version of the team management and facilitation training that the program teams will get. This will give them credibility within the organization and help them make better choices of team leaders and team members. It will also prepare them to manage teams better and give them techniques they can use to improve their performance in their ongoing roles.

At the same time, using a facilitator if members feel they need one, the top team should develop its strategic role in the corporation, defining:

- The top team's roles and responsibilities for developing and implementing the corporate strategic plan
- Its ongoing roles and job descriptions, including top-team members' responsibilities as managers of strategic teams
- Potential barriers to team performance and recommendations for overcoming them. Exhibit 9-6 shows the results of a survey of barriers to team effectiveness at Planar Technologies, a very successful, high-growth electronics firm.

A summary of a top team's strategic duties was shown in Exhibit 9-2.

Sponsor's Job Description

Each team needs a high-level sponsor, usually a member of the top team. This individual's role is to do all that is necessary to enhance the per-

---

Exhibit 9-6   Planar Technologies: Barriers to Team Effectiveness

WHAT MANAGEMENT IS DOING WELL

- ▼ Planned growth
- ▼ Leadership and management
- ▼ Clear relationship of department and job to plan
- ▼ Availability of training
- ▼ Motivated, aggressive, fast-moving
- ▼ Friendly, people-oriented, outgoing
- ▼ Exciting, energetic, dynamic

NEEDS WORK

- ▼ Holding people accountable
- ▼ Putting the right people in the right job

MAJOR BARRIERS

- ▼ Empowerment, accountability, and reward
- ▼ Resistance from specific individuals
- ▼ Policy and procedure barriers
- ▼ Organization structure and ability to coordinate team efforts
- ▼ Communication of plan and results throughout

---

formance of her assigned team and, through group meetings with other sponsors, ensure that the entire team system is operating smoothly.

In the first six months, a sponsor should monitor her assigned team closely to ensure that problems are fixed fast. This is accomplished by attending occasional team meetings, developing a close relationship with the team leader, and talking privately with team members from time to time.

Exhibit 9-7 provides an overview of a team sponsor's role and duties.

Program Teams

Picking the Teams

Selecting the program teams and team leaders is critical to team performance. Criteria for membership include:

- *Team members:* Although the team should represent all the major functions needed to manage a program from start to finish, only in rare cases should the core team number more than six people. Other individuals can be brought in from time to time for brief stints as their area of expertise is needed. For instance, a team with a product manager as a permanent member may bring in a market research expert for a number of meetings while it designs and executes a research program.

- *Team leaders:* Leaders must have strong functional expertise in an area important to the team. They are often from market-oriented areas such as marketing or product management—functions having relatively broad experience with most of the business functions and the outside world. Sometimes, teams are led by the area with the greatest functional job to accomplish. So in a technology-oriented program, the leader might be from engineering. Finally, team leadership can shift during the project as the focus shifts—from technology to marketing, for example.

Team leaders should have exhibited strong leadership in the past and must be respected by their peers, subordinates, and supervisors. They should be "comers" in the organization.

Requirements for Team Members

Members must have expertise in their functional area and should have a strong track record of accomplishment. They need at least acceptable skills in communication, coordination, and persuasion. They must have the respect of the organization, at least for their technical or functional expertise.

Exhibit 9-7 Overview of Team Sponsor's Role and Duties

MISSION

▼ To ensure that assigned teams are functioning at peak team performance

▼ To help a team, as an experienced internal high-level resource, meet its objectives by helping remove barriers to its work and get resources, decisions, and help that the team needs to move forward

COMMUNICATION

▼ Serves as principal liaison with and communication channel for the top team between formal team reports. Keeps both teams informed of key problems or progress.

▼ Informs team of top team discussions relevant to its area.

▼ Motivates the team by applauding progress, keeping team members informed on what is happening "upstairs," making the team's progress known to others throughout the organization.

▼ Reinforces or gives corporate perspective on important team issues to keep the team aligned with corporate direction.

RESOURCES

▼ Gets requested hard-to-acquire resources.

▼ Arbitrates disputes over time and resources with functional areas.

INTERVENTION

▼ Coaches the team leader on personnel problems and decisions.

▼ Challenges the thinking of the team and team leader as they move through the process.

▼ Suggests approaches and solutions to problems and issues.

▼ Breaks team decision deadlocks, if need be.

▼ Serves as a sounding board, if invited, for the team leader or the whole team when they are dealing with critical decisions, turning points in their projects, need to sound out top-team reaction, or in preparation for presentation to the top team.

PROCESS

▼ Attends select team meetings, at the team's invitation and with its approval, sufficient to gauge progress and identify process problems. The sponsor is not a team member and therefore only occasionally sits in on meetings as an invited observer, not as a participant.

▼ Observes competencies and values of team members for corporate development programs or to identify potential problem employees and resisters.

▼ Is member of sponsors' group charged with identifying overall process problems, personnel problems, and conflicts between functional areas servicing the teams.

ACCOUNTABILITY

▼ Provides regular verbal feedback to team leader and team on performance.

▼ Reviews and comments on team scorecard before submission to top team.

Teams as a Development Opportunity

Participation on a team is a prime opportunity for leadership development for team leaders and for the development of team and management skills for team members. It you want a team-based culture, promote team participation that way. Where possible, keep the team members' developmental objectives in mind when you make team assignments.

Getting the Teams Started

Most people who are asked to be on a team are being exposed to an entirely new management system. Chances are that their experience is in a command-and-control system that is directive and does not encourage the openness, coordination, and cooperation required of an effective team member. Or they come from a staff function in which the emphasis is on individual achievement, not group results.

It is not enough to put people together and ask them to function as a team. Unless you provide adequate training and help, you will be setting them up for frustration, slow progress, and often, failure. They need training, facilitation help, direction, and rules of operation that can enable them to become effective quickly.

Training

Once formed, the teams will require training in the following areas:

- *Team development and management:* How teams develop, how to run an effective team, communication skills, team scorecards
- *Analytical tools and techniques:* Key techniques for gathering and evaluating data
- *Facilitation:* Running meetings, managing decision making, running the entire team process
- *Project management:* Managing complex projects
- *Presentation skills:* Presenting results effectively—visually, verbally, and in writing.

Training outlines are shown in the appendix to the Key 14 chapter.

Facilitation

Make a professional facilitator, from inside or outside the organization, available to help the teams get started. Facilitators are particularly useful early in the process to demonstrate facilitation, data-gathering, and decision-making techniques to teams when they are dealing with real problems not encountered in training. Teams tend to use facilitators heavily at the beginning and sporadically later for "tune-ups" or when specific problems are encountered.

Defining the Job and Processes

The team's first responsibility is to clarify its task processes:

- *Communication:* The sponsor communicates the top team's mission and objectives to the team. The team refines them and comes back to the sponsor with a mission that it feels is appropriate.
- *Mission development:* The team develops a complete mission, vision, set of objectives, and role statement for the top team's approval. Exhibit 9-8 shows a typical team mission.
- *Operating rules:* The team develops its own operating rules— meeting rules, how it will make decisions, how often it will meet, and the separate roles assigned to members.

The major duties of a strategic program team (shown in greater detail earlier in the chapter, in Exhibit 9-4) are to:

Exhibit 9-8 Typical Program Team Mission

MISSION

To develop a system and software for measuring patient, attending physician, and staff satisfaction with the hospitals and their services

OBJECTIVES

1. Product line launched by 1/1/2000.
2. Market share three years after launch in excess of 35 percent, yielding revenue in excess of $150 million.
3. Will yield a pretax return on sales of 20 percent or more and a return on investment in excess of 35 percent in year three after launch.
4. Considered by customers "elegant" and the software of choice.

SCOPE OF PROGRAM

International market. First focus on North America. All methods of strategy— acquisition, joint venture, licensing, internal development—are open to the team.

AUTHORITIES

Initial budget for market research and to develop concept: $300,000.

Decisions the team can't make without top-team consent: hiring or firing of permanent people; proceeding beyond the concept stage without a plan and approval.

- Define its mission and objectives.
- Establish its meeting rules, rules of operation, and decision-making methods.
- Keep the top team informed and involved in major decisions.
- Obtain needed resources and people.
- Manage the job to completion.

Rules of Engagement: Keeping Decisions Moving

One of the most devastating blows to team morale is failure to get a hearing or decision from the top team. The most effective way to prevent bottlenecks like this is to establish and live by clear-cut "rules of engagement" that define when and how a team should escalate an issue or a decision request. Far from being stifling, clear rules slice through the undergrowth and facilitate getting things done fast.

The following subsections present a typical set of rules put into place by a moderate-size, hierarchical organization. Without such rules, communications up and down would be painfully slow.

Getting Quick Decisions

To get decisions from the top within forty-eight hours:

1. Attempt to get a decision, needed action, or resources through the direct efforts of the team leader and the functional team member representing the area from which you need something.
2. If the issue remains unresolved, ask your sponsor to attempt to resolve the issue with or for you.
3. If a solution still has not been found, schedule a meeting with the sponsor and chief executive officer/chief operating officer or a small group of top-team members to make a final decision. This recognizes that you probably need only these people and perhaps the functions most involved to make a decision.

Removing Blockages

To get lower-level blockages removed or obtain resources and help from other departments, you must do two things:

1. Make the team member from the relevant department responsible for getting needed help from his department, involving the team leader as needed.
2. If the problem can't be resolved, move to the second step under "Getting Quick Decisions."

Handling Problem Team Members

The sequence for dealing with problem members is as follows:

1. *Feedback from the team:* Often, a very open team will give the team member with a behavioral problem direct feedback during a meeting. This is particularly true of problems that clearly contravene the team rules, such as absences from meetings, frequent failure to complete assignments, or poor or disruptive team behavior.
2. *Leader counseling:* The team leader counsels the individual, assuming the person is worth keeping on the team. The leader must make clear what she views as the problem, why counseling is being given, and the consequences of not fixing the problem.
3. *Human resources counseling:* Sometimes, private counseling by a neutral party is necessary to get at the root of the behavior and identify possible remedies.
4. *Replacing the individual:* If the problem persists or is deemed unfixable by the team leader, the person is removed from the team.

Replacing Team Members

The steps for removing and replacing a team member who lacks the necessary competence or is resisting change are as follows:

1. The team leader gets the team sponsor's agreement that the person should be replaced.
2. The leader then explains in detail to the individual's department manager why the individual must be replaced and asks for a suitable replacement.
3. If the department manager refuses, the decision is bounced to the top team with the sponsor's support.

Remember that teams are prime vehicles for identifying and removing resisters from the system.

Managing Team Performance

Here's where we are so far: You've assigned the project teams, given them each a sponsor, and provided training in team processes. The teams have refined their mission, clarified their objectives, and agreed on their rules of engagement. They are hard at work. What now?

You should consider an audit of the team system after six months. The audit's objectives are to (1) determine what is and is not working, (2) identify actions that can remove barriers to effectiveness, and (3) pinpoint specific team or individual problems.

Audits are usually conducted by an external consultant, who polls the teams on the extent to which they are functioning effectively and interviews select team leaders, members, sponsors, and top-team members.

If team performance is poor after six months, it is time for the sponsor, leader, and perhaps an external facilitator to confront the problem.

Prescriptions for Team Performance Problems

In this subsection, we'll examine some common intrateam problems.

Failure to Gel. The individual players are good, the leadership should be good, but these people haven't become a team. Assuming that there has been adequate training and facilitation, team building may provide the solution.

Team building requires members to:

- Define how they are going to measure the team's performance and the behavioral norms (for example, completing assignments on time) for which they will be accountable.
- Measure how well they are performing against the norms.
- Agree on remedial action where performance is deficient.
- Determine how and when they will hold themselves accountable for the norms.

The team evaluates individual members the same way, assessing each person's behavior against the norms, identifying gaps, and developing solutions with that person.

In most instances, team building is a very positive experience and can elicit substantial changes in behavior over time. But it can be personally wrenching and needs to be conducted by a professional facilitator to ensure that criticisms of individuals are handled in a supportive manner.

Poor Leadership. Change the leader and make sure that you get the leadership skills right the second time.

Missing Skill(s). If key skills, such as finance and market research, are missing from a team, add the function permanently or temporarily, as needed. If a member isn't technically good at the function he represents, change the person.

Establish the rule that team member performance is managed by the team and team leader. The team member can be challenged, coached, or counseled by the team leader or the team itself. Make it easy for team leaders to approach a team member's supervisor and the team's sponsor to discuss team member performance. Allow the leader to ask for removal and replacement.

Personality Conflicts. Sometimes, key team members simply clash. Counseling by the team sponsor, individually or with the team, is in order. The penalty for their not getting along is removal of one or both from the team. In most organizations where teams are a prestige assignment, people will try to mend their ways.

Teams sometimes need intervention by a skilled psychologist or planning consultant, who interviews and counsels the team, a pair of team members in conflict, or the individual with the dysfunction. The purpose of the counseling is to determine the cause of the dysfunction and suggest a remedy.

Lack of Team and Project Management Skills. This is common and easily remedied by giving team members training in both areas.

Bad Actors. You occasionally get a disruptive, egocentric, manipulative jerk on a team. Don't worry about the bad actors. If the team members don't kill them, they'll ask for their removal quickly.

Withholding of Resources by a Functional Department. To illustrate, assume a product development team and its manufacturing member can't get a production line to run a pilot product in time. "We have a job to do," says manufacturing, "and that to is ship product. We're backlogged as hell right now." The team leader, manufacturing team representative, and top manufacturing management should be able to solve the conflict. They might recommend a third shift, outside contract pilot manufacture, research and development use of production lines during product changeover intervals, or changes to expedite the regular production schedule. But if the problem isn't resolved, it gets passed up to the top team, which must define how and when both jobs will be done and change team and functional objectives accordingly.

Resistance to Team Efforts. Sometimes, the whole organization resists helping a team. This can derive from work overload, a history of being insular and uncooperative, jealousy that a few have been singled out for an elite team assignment, or a view of the teams, realistic or not, as prima donnas.

The best tactic is to face each hub of resistance one incident at a time, appraising the functional boss and the team sponsor of the situation. If the top team is fully supporting the effort, the organization will get the message.

Expectations for Team Progress

If you are doing everything right, how rapidly should you expect teams to gel and meet their objectives?

First Year

By the end of the first year, the teams should be well trained and feeling good about process and progress. Assuming the program is a multiyear venture, there should be at least satisfactory progress versus objectives.

But most teams develop more slowly than you expect. Initial action plans almost invariably underestimate the work to be done and commit to first-year objectives that are unrealistic. Plans usually have to be changed once or twice as the team evaluates its program and its ability to manage it. The team's emotional support of the team process is a good litmus test of whether it is moving forward. Good teams feel good about themselves to the point of becoming chauvinistic. Poor teams are quick to attack the team system.

During the first year, there will probably be turf battles between some teams and functional departments, and some team members will have to be replaced.

Be patient in the first six months. Teams take time to form and solidify. They will usually come around. If they haven't gelled in nine months, there are probably serious structural problems, which the top team must diagnose and fix.

Second Year

During the second year, teams should be embedded in the culture and operating smoothly. People are seeing teams as a management tool that gets results and is here to stay. Participation in corporate teams is viewed as a desirable experience because of the strategic importance of the work, the opportunity to learn team management, the chance to be exposed to diverse functions, and above all, the interactive exposure to the top team and matters of corporate strategy.

Review and Reward

Review and reward for teams are covered in the Key 17 and Key 18 chapters, respectively.

Do

- Use cross-functional teams when you have complex strategic programs requiring fast action and cross-functional coordination.
- Establish an environment in which teams can thrive, including training, a sponsor, and rules that let teams get critical decisions made quickly.
- Use the team system as a training ground for your future leaders.
- Watch out for "teamitis"—people's tendency to form a team for everything because it's in vogue and everyone wants to get on the bandwagon. Reserve teams for critical programs requiring cross-functional action over a long period of time.

Don't

- Create teams casually. Teams represent a major new management system that takes time and effort to develop properly.
- Put in a team system if the top team isn't willing to play by the same rules and operate as a true team itself.
- Give up quickly on a team system. As with any new organization structure, it takes two to three years to function smoothly.

Key 10
Define the Future Culture

Principle: People's behavior follows their strongly held values. An organization's behavior follows, more or less, its shared values. Culture is the sum total of the organization's values.

Why it's important: If the culture and resulting behavior and work are aligned with the competitive strategies that an organization must execute to win, high performance will result. Culture is also an efficient "gating" mechanism. Much individual behavior can be guided, without supervision, because the cultural norm dictates the expected behavior—when solving a customer problem, for example.

How it's applied: Values can be taught, changed, reinforced, rewarded, and brought in with outside hires to align behavior with strategy. They are also used to identify and remove individuals who don't support the organization's effective norms.

Expected results: With good "value penetration," strategic change will accelerate far faster than with a "business-as-usual" culture.

Organizational Culture

What Is Culture?

An individual's behavior is guided by his or her cherished values. An organization's behavior demonstrates, more or less, its shared values.

Look at it this way. In the days of the cave dwellers, there was a man who hated redheads (a value). He reflexively punched out every redhead he encountered (behavior). His village was made up of people who, to a greater or lesser extent, hated redheads, too (corporate value). They spent their time plotting and executing collective war on redheads (behavior). Naturally, the villagers who really hated redheads were the top troops, generals, officers, and the general staff. Those who "sort of" believed did the logistics work. What about those who didn't actually hate redheads but only pretended to? Probably, they got found out sooner or later and were summarily dealt with. Or perhaps, over time, they began to have an influence, ameliorating the hate-redhead convictions of everyone else, and eventually changed the predominant culture of the village.

Culture, then, is the collective values and resulting behavior of all the individuals in an organization.

Why Is Culture Important?

Culture is critical because it becomes part of the embedded architecture of an organization. People bring their values to a multiplicity of decisions and interpersonal interactions. Values govern people's work ethic, influencing what they want or don't want to work on. They govern the quality of work. Values are an efficient "gating" mechanism. A single general value such as customer orientation guides strategy-aligned decisions and actions in dozens of business situations.

If values are aligned with strategy, actions throughout the organization contribute to rapid implementation of that strategy. If they are not, implementation is spotty, balky, and time-consuming.

The Ritz Carleton. The Ritz Carleton Hotel chain differentiates itself from competitors through its physical luxury, which is relatively easy to achieve with a lot of money, and its impeccable service, which is very difficult to attain. Ritz Carleton Hotels target the well-off businessperson working during the week and relaxing on weekends.

The Ritz had the luxury of starting a few years ago as a greenfield hotel chain, building the organization and culture from scratch, a far easier job than changing an inherited culture. It recruited men and women with intelligence, warmth, desire to please, a sense of humor, a strong work ethic, and the ability to engage and interact easily with guests. From their side of the counter, the employees would reflect the characteristics of the targeted customers.

The process continues. Prospective employees are trained as much in the Ritz philosophy as in how to carry a tray. During their initial two-week training program, employees are carefully evaluated; those who don't fit the Ritz's norms are weeded out. Since the average employee stays a year and a half to two years, there is ample opportunity to continue to mold the Ritz staff in the cultural direction desired through training, supervision, and coaching.

Does it work? "Certainly, sir," as Ritz employees will say two dozen times a day. For a mass-market luxury hotel, it succeeds remarkably well. Ritz service is uniformly excellent from coast to coast, so uniform that the same services are delivered the same way with the same words wherever you go. If that service is so consistent that it sometimes seems contrived, many customers find that a small price to pay for their comfort.

For better or for worse, companies get known for the values that drive them. Well-known examples include Wal-Mart for cost-consciousness, L. L. Bean for service, Corning for its focus on technology, and 3M for new products.

Where Does Culture Come From?

Cultural behaviors are driven by an individual's personally held values and beliefs. These are learned early in life from family, school, and friends and later from colleagues and supervisors in the workplace. Some values—such as honesty, work ethic, and a willingness to take risk—are bedrock and difficult to change. Others—such as manner of dealing with people, customer orientation, and collaboration—are more alterable should the situation demand.

Like any society, business organizations develop cultural norms. People in the same organization, by and large, behave the same way. Organizations hire people with the values and behaviors they want, mold those inside to the same behaviors, and isolate or expel those who don't fit. Those in power are uncomfortable with people who aren't like them. They genuinely believe, often correctly, that "this type of person is what we need to succeed." This leads to a relatively uniform culture—which, to a point, is good. You want the organization to share the core values that will make it continually competitive.

This doesn't mean there is no room in an organization for individual variations in beliefs and values. An organization filled with faceless clones who look, speak, talk, and think alike would be a dull and uncreative company indeed. Without watering down the core values, some people will reflect one or two of those values over the others. Complementing each other in the same company may be scientists who live and breathe technology and marketing people who emphasize customer orientation.

Some people will be driven by values not on the core list but not in direct conflict with core values. There will be employees, thank goodness, who act like entrepreneurs—making their own rules, building boundaries around their activities, and using unconventional ways of getting what they want. But they create, invent, and move your strategies forward. There will be artists who march to their own creative cultural drummers, bringing an enriching and often profitable repertoire of behaviors of their own to the party. They design products, packaging, and promotional materials. As long as these subcultures are productive and their "noncore" values propel the company forward, the company is richer for having them.

Values to Live By or Motherhood and Apple Pie?

We looked at dozens of corporate value statements and came up with a list of positive values by which virtually all companies profess to be guided as well as some negative values that organizations say they want to be rid of. Exhibit 10-1 contrasts these two types of values.

The stated core values of most organizations appear on the "positive" list. This begs the question: If so many companies claim to hold the same values, why are their actions often so different? The answer, of course, lies in what happens after the "values" are engraved. In the companies that treat value setting as a trendy exercise, the activity ends with the chairman's video espousing the new mission and values and the wallet cards passed out during the meeting. But many organizations convert their stated core values into specific actions that influence events in the company, the industry, and the market.

When Strategy and Culture Are Out of Sync

If your culture is out of sync with what your market or constituencies will demand in the future, you have two choices. You can do nothing, lose market share and profitability, and face a diminished future. Or you

Exhibit 10-1 Positive and Negative Cultural Values

POSITIVE VALUES	NEGATIVE VALUES
▼ Cost-oriented	▼ Indifferent
▼ Service-oriented	▼ Feels entitled to job
▼ Profit-oriented	▼ Internally focused
▼ Customer-focused	▼ Low energy
▼ Innovative	▼ "Silo" management mentality
▼ Team player	▼ Uncooperative
▼ Ethical	▼ Secretive
▼ Honest	▼ Political
▼ Confronts issues	▼ Complacent, smug, arrogant
▼ Shareholder value-oriented	▼ Not creative
▼ Open	▼ Inflexible
▼ Wants reward in proportion to contribution	▼ Putting in time
▼ Learner	▼ Not a team player
▼ High-quality-oriented	
▼ Respects the individual	

can change one or more of the values and organizational behaviors that threaten to strangle your competitive advantage.

Most organizations that we encounter need cultural change when they are significantly changing strategy—that is, when (1) they are in financial or marketplace trouble, (2) they are taking on new products or markets alien to them, (3) a competitor has changed the competitive ball game, or (4) management becomes more ambitious in its future goals.

But can you really change a culture to meet new circumstances? The answer is yes. When we talk about cultural change, we're not implying a wholesale mind makeover of a company. Nor are we talking about throwing everyone out and starting fresh with newly minted, culturally correct employees. We are talking about changing one or two driving values (in a set of probably five or six) that will bring the culture in line with the job to be done in the competitive marketplace.

People regularly change cultures. But they don't do it just by "communicating the new values to everyone." They do it by filling key positions with people who live and model the new values, demanding actions consistent with the desired culture, and providing incentives to behave in the appropriate way. As Professor Mike Beer at Harvard Business School told me, "[C]ulture is a lag variable. It's the result of a lot of tangible actions that you take in running the business, not the other way around."

Three Companies That Changed Their Culture

A Chemical Company

Exhibit 10-2 is the cultural-strategic diagram of a moderate-size specialty chemical company. You can see how much its culture was out of alignment with the dictates of the market. The new, up-from-the-ranks president faced formidable challenges. Propelled by new environmental laws, markets were rapidly changing. One-third of the company's automotive industry market was under a price attack. Internal systems provided no useful information on which to base business decisions. The company was burdened with high manufacturing costs and a molasses-like new-product development pace.

Quick, drastic change was needed. But in more than a year and a half, the new president made little progress while working with his inherited staff. He then used the cultural change tools shown in the rightmost column of Exhibit 10-2, replacing virtually his entire top team and some secondary players with people who already had the attributes listed in the "Needed Culture" column. This was the only way to achieve a culture that would foster the kind of performance required to take on marketplace demands and fix internal problems.

Exhibit 10-2   Cultural-Strategic Diagram: Chemical Company

Market Demands	Current Culture	Needed Culture	Change Tools Used
▶ New products ▶ Low cost ▶ High quality ▶ Technical service ▶ Rapid service ▶ Multiple distribution points	▶ Entitled ▶ Silo management ▶ Slow ▶ Inwardly focused ▶ Reactive ▶ Not innovative	▶ Sense of urgency ▶ Teamwork ▶ Innovative ▶ Cost focus ▶ Customer-market orientation	▶ Most of top team replaced. ▶ New incentive system installed. ▶ Select people changed at lower levels. ▶ Accountability systems installed. ▶ Strategic plan implemented.

The cultural turnaround worked. Within five years, new products were on time, top people worked as a team to solve problems, both revenue and profits increased thanks to a refocus on new markets, and customer satisfaction dramatically increased.

A Specialty Rubber Company

The new president of a specialty rubber company described some of the actions taken by his organization like this:

> For the first time, we had a strategic plan with focus. It detailed revenue, profit, new-product development, and marketing objectives and made sure that we had the organization, field sales, and production structure to meet them. From that point on, changing the culture to one that was accountable was simple. We assigned objectives to people, held them accountable in monthly review meetings (accountability by embarrassment), and rewarded them accordingly. We had the basic people and supervisory skills needed to do the job. Our people just needed direction and to be held accountable.

They also had a persistent leader, of course, who kept his eye on the ball and let no one off the hook. The company successfully retained the values of technical excellence, responsiveness to the customer, and technical service, the bedrocks of its predominantly custom-order business, while adding the values of focus and accountability.

Three years after embarking on the change plan, the company was sold for a multiple of earnings that would have been impossible prior to executing the strategic plan supported by the new cultural norm of accountability.

A Savings and Loan

A stodgy savings and loan was taken over by a bunch of young, ambitious managers from a major commercial bank at the depth of the S&L crisis. After stabilizing the institution by brutally cleaning up its loan portfolio and reducing staff to an economic level, they proceeded to build a highly profitable community bank in the middle of one of Boston's most lucrative blue-collar and middle-class markets.

The managers began with a plan. It focused on the bank's most profitable products—retail, mortgage, and consumer loans—and avoided major commitments in highly competitive, risky products like credit cards and commercial loans. Unlike many small banks, it didn't offer full service because the managers knew that most customers "shop" all of their banking services and are not loyal to a single bank. The bank built retail operations where its locations had a significant competitive advantage and closed the others. It installed new systems that improved customer service and let customers judge the performance of retail operations and other products. The bank focused on profitability, consistently performed in the top 10 percent of banks in its category nationwide, and was often number one.

All but one of the members of the top team were new at the beginning of this change process. Rather than being driven by the CEO, they were highly self-critical and self-accountable. They gave needed leadership in all areas, particularly in loan origination and management and retail operations. The CEO gave needed nudges and direction. In a very short period of time, in competitive and prosaic markets, the new management built high additional value for both the institution's shareholders and those holding stock options.

What values had to change? The new managers killed the values of entitlement and leisurely pace. They imbued the values of urgency, quality, profit orientation, and competitive spirit while retaining and emphasizing the value of customer service.

The method is familiar: Put new people in key spots; trim the organization to the size, shape, and number of people needed; develop a plan; focus on the products and services in which you have a competitive advantage; and hold people accountable. Reinforce the best values of the old culture and instill the new values needed to reach the next level of success.

Changing Your Organization's Culture

Defining the Culture You Want

How do you know what new values are needed? Your new norms come from three places: first and foremost, your competitive and external strategies; second, your internal strategies; and third, the personal choices of your owners, management, and people, which set the climate for the organization.

External Strategies. Why look externally first? Because to succeed, you must execute the detailed behaviors needed to excel in the customers' eyes far better than your competition does.

You should do a modest amount of market research—which is all it takes—to pinpoint the broad needs of your customers and the subsequent values that you must embrace to meet those needs. If you don't have a survey to guide you, you can come to an internal consensus on customer needs, what behaviors they require, and subsequent company values. You have to determine customer needs early in the planning process anyway to develop your competitive strategy.

The advantage of properly done market research is that the market-place will tell you in detail what a consumer need, such as service, means. A given value means different things to different companies and industries. Service in fast food means turnaround time, friendliness, and time of delivery of special orders. In the computer repair business, it means turnaround time, getting it fixed right the first time, friendli-ness, and availability of technicians to provide both telephone consulta-tion and on-site or carry-in service. In supermarkets, it is the number of people waiting at checkouts, speed and friendliness of the checkout clerks, the ability to get answers on location about availability of goods, and special services such as custom-prepared foods.

Through the research, the customers give you an overall value as well as the more detailed performance standards or behaviors that you will have to meet in the future to win. Such data make your values real to your employees and make it easier for them to relate their behavior and job standards to your strategic values.

Internal Strategies. In your strategic planning process, you will de-fine internal strategies needed to support external strategies and your critical success factors in the market. For example, sales and a "selling culture" are very appropriate for an insurance or securities broker. In-formation—accurate information, when and how customers want it—is an appropriate value for an insurance claims-processing department or company.

Internal Environmental Values. The organization's history and the choices made by management and employees will dictate other values, such as respect for the integrity of individuals, continuous learning, and reward based on performance. Highly personal to each company, these create the environment in which management and employees are most happy and productive. Importantly, these environmental values will be critical in attracting people with the right personality and personal char-acteristics to execute your internal and external strategies effectively.

Identifying What Needs to Change

Many companies use a psychologist to help define existing and desired internal values, point out the major differences between the two, and determine new values and behaviors that will drive strategy and can be used for measuring cultural change and individual performance during the change process. Exhibit 10-3 is an example of the values (called

Exhibit 10-3   A Not-for-Profit's Competencies

Leading Change

Setting Direction

The extent to which an individual identifies clear objectives, develops effective strategies to achieve them, and clearly communicates expectations to others.

Encouraging Innovation

The extent to which an individual fosters an environment that inspires others to seek new, creative ways to deal with business problems and is persistent in implementing changes.

Working Across Organizational Boundaries

The extent to which an individual removes obstacles and encourages others outside the unit to participate in fostering changes.

Exhibiting Teamwork

The extent to which an individual works cooperatively within and outside his or her unit, sharing resources and decision making within the team.

Resolving Complex Problems

Using General Business Tools

The extent to which an individual understands fundamental business practices and applies this knowledge when making business decisions that support the mission and strategy of the organization.

Acquiring and Interpreting Relevant Information

The extent to which an individual obtains the necessary facts, shares them with others, and distinguishes between relevant and irrelevant information.

Delivering Customer-Focused Services

The extent to which an individual recognizes key internal and external customers and is able to anticipate and respond to their needs and gain customer loyalty.

Creating a High-Performance Work Environment

Empowering Others

The extent to which an individual sets appropriate parameters to allow others to seize new opportunities, make decisions, and implement new ideas.

Developing Others

The extent to which an individual teaches, coaches, or helps others to take personal initiatives and learn from experience, and takes responsibility for his or her own growth and development.

(continued)

Exhibit 10-3   (*continued*)

Setting Realistic Performance Standards

The extent to which an individual continuously motivates others to higher, but reasonable, performance expectations, holds others and self to those expectations, and recognizes their increased success.

Respecting Others

The extent to which a person values diverse ideas and people and reinforces the self-esteem of others.

Taking Individual Accountability

Being Accountable

The extent to which an individual takes personal responsibility for leadership actions to achieve results.

Exhibiting Persistence

The extent to which an individual sustains a high level (quantity and quality) of work performance and persists to foster change in the face of adversity.

Adapting to New Situations

The extent to which an individual modifies his or her behavior and remains effective in new or changing situations.

Balancing Complex Priorities

The extent to which an individual effectively manages competing work demands and organizes work priorities to achieve his or her objectives.

Learning Continuously

The extent to which an individual learns from new experiences and pursues activities to foster his or her own growth and development.

---

competencies here) of a major not-for-profit organization compiled by a psychologist after extensive interviews with employees and consultation with management. These values will be ultimately put on performance review forms, and employees rated on them at least annually. The values are also used as a selection tool for new employees.

Using Organizational Surveys

Organization diagnostics are useful for determining the values currently driving an organization and identifying areas in which the organization's behaviors and stated values don't match. A good survey will cover:

- *Culture:* The values driving the company, such as teamwork, innovation, profit orientation, work ethic, and politics
- *Systems:* The efficiency of many systems, such as recruiting, human resources, financial-reporting, personnel development, new-product development, and service
- *Management:* Its style, the extent to which it establishes appropriate objectives, its ability to delegate, use of teamwork, planning for the future, holding people accountable, communications, leadership, and model for the development of people
- *People:* Their competence, relationships, motivation, contributions, ability to learn, and cooperativeness
- *Organization:* The effectiveness of the structure; specific departmental weak spots; the ability to coordinate across boundaries; the use of teams; and rules, regulations, and procedures that help or hinder getting work done

The results of the culture survey for an electronics materials company are shown in Exhibit 10-4. The data show an organization that is reactive, not innovative, exhibits little teamwork, and is interested only in short-term results. In a rapidly moving electronics industry, the company could not succeed for long with this profile. Management set out to change the profile, principally through downsizing changing key people.

Managing Change

You've defined the culture you want. How do you manage the change to get it? You could think of change as a chemical reaction. You can put all the proper chemicals—people, assets and resources, and money—in a vessel. Throw yourself in as a catalyst. Have someone screw down the top of the vessel and raise it to just the right temperature and pressure calculated to produce a reaction. Then hope it works. Because, in truth, cultural change is not as predictable as a chemical reaction. You can't *make* cultural change happen. You can only establish the conditions under which it can happen and keep those conditions stable until it does.

Or you could think of cultural change as something you build, patiently and persistently, using the best tools at your disposal.

Change Tools

Before we talk about the process of cultural change, it will be helpful to describe the tools available to leverage cultural values. Many of these tools, which are listed in Exhibit 10-5, are also discussed elsewhere in

(Text continues on page 248.)

Exhibit 10-4 Results of Organizational Diagnostic Survey

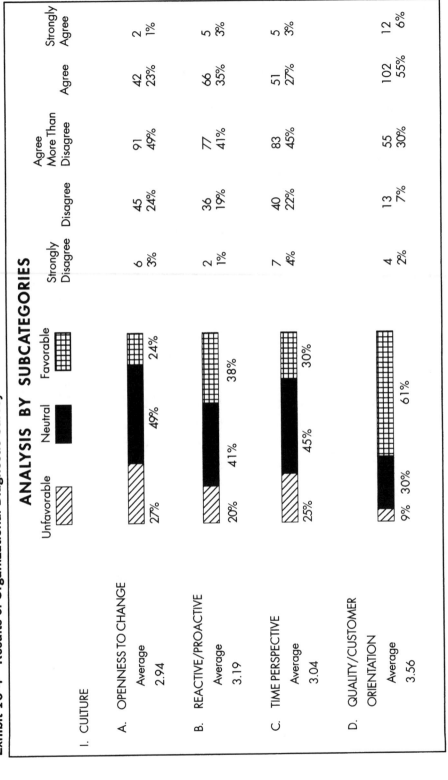

ANALYSIS BY SUBCATEGORIES

		Strongly Disagree	Disagree	Agree More Than Disagree	Agree	Strongly Agree
I. CULTURE						
A. OPENNESS TO CHANGE	Average 2.94	6 3%	45 24%	91 49%	42 23%	2 1%
B. REACTIVE/PROACTIVE	Average 3.19	2 1%	36 19%	77 41%	66 35%	5 3%
C. TIME PERSPECTIVE	Average 3.04	7 4%	40 22%	83 45%	51 27%	5 3%
D. QUALITY/CUSTOMER ORIENTATION	Average 3.56	4 2%	13 7%	55 30%	102 55%	12 6%

Legend:
Unfavorable Neutral Favorable

A. OPENNESS TO CHANGE: 27% / 49% / 24%
B. REACTIVE/PROACTIVE: 20% / 41% / 38%
C. TIME PERSPECTIVE: 25% / 45% / 30%
D. QUALITY/CUSTOMER ORIENTATION: 9% / 30% / 61%

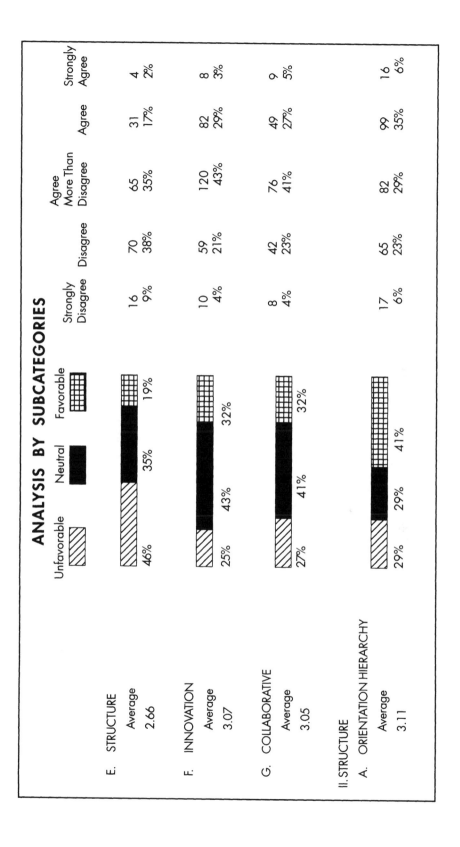

ANALYSIS BY SUBCATEGORIES

			Strongly Disagree	Disagree	Agree More Than Disagree	Agree	Strongly Agree
E. STRUCTURE	Average 2.66	Unfavorable 46% · Neutral 35% · Favorable 19%	16 9%	70 38%	65 35%	31 17%	4 2%
F. INNOVATION	Average 3.07	Unfavorable 25% · Neutral 43% · Favorable 32%	10 4%	59 21%	120 43%	82 29%	8 3%
G. COLLABORATIVE	Average 3.05	Unfavorable 27% · Neutral 41% · Favorable 32%	8 4%	42 23%	76 41%	49 27%	9 5%
II. STRUCTURE							
A. ORIENTATION HIERARCHY	Average 3.11	Unfavorable 29% · Neutral 29% · Favorable 41%	17 6%	65 23%	82 29%	99 35%	16 6%

Exhibit 10-5   Cultural Change Tools

▼ People
- Hiring those with new values
- Training those who can learn
- Getting rid of those who can't change
- Promoting performers who walk the talk

▼ Delegation of objectives

▼ Communication

▼ Measurement of cultural results

▼ Rewards and incentives for positive cultural behavior

▼ Organization forms, processes, and procedures

this book since they have multiple uses in implementing strategic change. Here we'll focus on them exclusively in terms of their relevance to culture. Pick the ones that are most applicable to your situation when you develop your implementation plan.

People

The single biggest cultural change tool is your people. Nothing else has a bigger impact or is a bigger potential hazard to your program.

Four personal attributes can support or inhibit implementation of strategy:

1. *Personal traits:* These reflect the individual's basic personality: introvert, extrovert; analytical, intuitive; nice person, jerk; articulate, thick-tongued; intelligent, not so smart; a learner and seeker of knowledge and growth, a viewer of late-night TV; collaborator, loner; ethical and honest, shady; listener, talker; arrogant, responsive to others; warm, cold; high-energy, low-energy; flexible, inflexible.

2. *Technical skills:* These include financial analysis, management of new-product development, research and development, ability to write, public speaking and communication skills, and ability to work in a team.

3. *Values:* The internal and externally oriented values necessary to drive a strategy have already been introduced.

4. *Behaviors:* These are driven, of course, by a trait or value, including the way an individual interfaces with others (a team player, a loner, and so forth), how an individual treats a customer, the way a person organizes a project for herself or for a team, how well someone works across organizational boundaries, and the extent to which she holds herself and others accountable.

As you select people to carry out your strategy, recognize that you cannot have much effect on personal traits. If a person in a key position has negative traits that will hold the change effort back, you probably can't change him. Move him.

Technical skills are often changeable over the long term. But you may need a particular skill right now. If there is a technically marginal person in a key change position, you need to judge whether her skills will suffice while she receives further training. If not, you'll have to bring in someone else.

When your goal is to change values and behaviors throughout the organization, you need to be confident that the department heads and leverage people who will spearhead the strategic change effort will demonstrate the desired behaviors right from the start. You'll have to judge from historical behavior and individual personalities whether they'll immediately accept the new values, whether information and persuasion will do the trick quickly, or whether some will be intractable and have to be moved.

To have the right people in the right place, you'll need to:

- *Pick the right leverage people.* The teams, departments, and individuals working on strategic programs should be picked as much for behaviors that match the new values as for their technical competence. These people truly are your levers and the single most important tool for change. They must be trained in the "new value set," its meaning, and how to apply it.

- *Remove people whose behavior is counter to the new culture.* Get these people out of important jobs or out of the company.

- *Promote, hire, and transfer people who fit your cultural norms into important programs.* Personnel moves should be tailored to increase the "net positive cultural quotient" of your company. All personnel moves send a powerful message to the organization. By all means, when hiring or promoting people into leverage positions, use one of the many inexpensive testing tools available to identify their values and test their probable behavior under circumstances important to your company. Testing of personnel is covered in the Key 14 chapter.

- *Set a new standard for success.* Tell the organization that those who tangibly perform and those who live the new values are those who will succeed. Make sure employees know the types of behavior that will and won't enable people to get ahead.

Delegation of Objectives

- *Use departmental plans.* Tangible objectives—such as customer service, quality levels, cost targets, or innovation goals for new products—send powerful, funded messages about the organization's values and priorities. Department managers have a golden opportunity to reinforce the value message by passing on the year's objectives to the department and individuals for execution.

■ *Focus on departmental direction statements.* Annual discussion of departmental plans provides an ideal time for the department to review its mission, vision, business definition, and values, relating them to those of the corporate plan.

Communication

■ *Communicate the new, desired values and behaviors.* This message should come from the top and be issued frequently and to everyone. Make it relevant to the strategic job. Be forceful—for example: "Speed and creativity are of the essence. Our competitors are getting twenty new products to the market in the time it take us to release ten. We won't survive long this way."

■ *Provide tangible proof of the need.* Do something dramatic—for example: "Every week, starting this week, we will have a competitor's car on the assembly line for all of you to compare with our current output. We've scored the competitor's quality and our quality. This week, the competitor has ten minor defects, and we have fifty-two defects, several of them major. If you were a consumer, which car would you buy?"

■ *Insist that managers communicate.* Make managers reporting to you responsible for getting the word down to their people on what must change. Have them relate the change to their people's jobs—for example: "This method makes sense. It lowers cost while increasing quality, two things we're emphasizing in our plan." Stress to them three or four times a week the importance of doing this.

■ *Model behaviors you want to reinforce.* Modeling, or "walking the talk," is essential. One new Fortune 500 CEO, determined to reduce the rather lavish spending of the former regime, immediately sold the company's Gulfstream IV as well as its expensive meetinghouse in an exotic location.

Measurement of Cultural Results

■ *Measure external cultural results.* You can measure the ultimate tangible result of many cultural values, such as service to the customer, responsiveness, and friendliness. Periodic customer surveys will accomplish this. Such measures can become standards of performance for some departments and individuals and subsequently reinforce the cultural message.

- *Measure the culture initially and then periodically.* Use one of the many cultural measurement and attitude survey instruments to measure your baseline performance and then subsequently measure how values and attitudes have changed. Such instruments can assess attitudes and values by individual departments, work groups, and management groups as well as by level and position in the organization. Through them, you can learn where you're doing well and where and on what dimensions work needs to be done.

- *Assess individual behaviors.* Make the value and behavioral norms part of each individual's performance appraisal, counting for a known percentage in the overall rating. When both boss and employee rate how the employee performed on each value, this provides a good opportunity to discuss examples of positive or negative behavior and offer suggestions for improvement.

There are also survey techniques such as the currently popular "360-degree" surveys, in which an individual's supervisors, subordinates, and peers all rate her on a number of performance, management, interpersonal, and cultural dimensions.

Either traditional or survey rating systems need to reinforce the positive new values and suggest how to eliminate or improve on the negative. See the Key 17 chapter for an in-depth discussion of appraisal.

- *Provide praise and feedback.* Personally praise those individuals and teams making progress. Give feedback to those who aren't, usually by reviewing their efforts, defining where they are not making tangible and/or attitudinal progress, and mutually agreeing on what they need to do differently. Give people even tougher goals.

- *Coach, counsel, and give personal attention.* Sometimes, a stalled individual or team needs some support to get on with the program. Tell people why their work is so important, remind them that they are primary change agents, and give them a pep talk. You may need to provide counseling on issues like dealing with top management, when, and how. Or they may need coaching in analytical techniques. Sometimes, they feel neglected and are just sulking a bit and want some "parental" attention.

Rewards and Incentives for Positive Cultural Behavior

- *Talk with money.* Besides tying a known percentage of each person's performance rating to values and behaviors, you'll need to make a clear connection between performance ratings and salary increases or bonus pay and promotions. In a broader sense, the entire compensation and reward system should be based on accomplishing the organization's priorities and objectives—which, in turn, are a direct reflection of values. For further discussion of rewards, see the Key 18 chapter.

■ *Go public.* Make opportunities to publicly highlight people's accomplishments and praise them for "living" the new values. At Corning, Inc., the keystone value is technical creativity. That was emphasized at an annual black-tie ceremony at which scientists who had received patents during the year went up on stage, one by one, and sold their patents for one dollar (per their contracts) to the chairman and president. In that culture—at least, figuratively—the scientist with the most patents won.

Organization Forms, Processes, and Procedures

■ *Remove organizational barriers between people who must interact.* One Fortune 500 company moved an entire division 2,000 miles to the headquarters complex to improve communication and control and to put the division near the research laboratory it was supposed to use as a resource.

■ *Modify your organization to fit your values.* If you're looking for a collaborative culture, start with cross-functional teams to integrate efforts across departments. Their advantage is that you get focused, cross-functional effort without having to dismantle your entire organization or set up an expensive new one.

■ *Remove procedural obstructions.* You can probably cut the number of steps that it takes to get approvals to hire, spend money, or approve a new-product request. I'm not suggesting abrogating responsibility, just accomplishing goals in a way that sets an environment for cultural change and doesn't frustrate those who must implement it.

■ *Use electronic means.* Use whatever form of electronic communication fits the new culture, including E-mail, interactive programs such as Lotus Notes, intranets and internal web, and teleconferencing.

The Process of Planning and Implementing Cultural Change

Illustrated in Exhibit 10-6, the process of planning and implementing cultural change includes the following steps:

1. *Develop your strategic plan.* This should include competitive, external, and internal strategies.

Exhibit 10-6   Process of Planning and Implementing Cultural Change

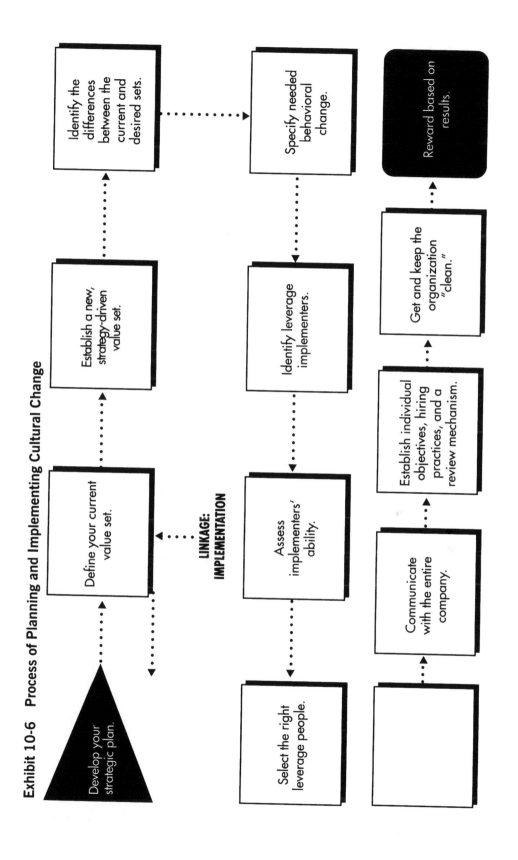

2. *Define your real current value set.* Specify what your values mean and their importance to the company's new strategy. Some of these values will have to be "unlearned" if they are detrimental to strategy.

3. *Establish a new, strategy-driven value set.* Take this from the direction statement of your strategic plan, which will be distilled by the planning process from internal and external strategies and personal desires. This set will undoubtedly include some old values as well as new ones.

4. *Identify the differences between the current and desired value sets.* Define what each value means in terms of behaviors and determine the extent to which the organization currently reflects this new value set. This is extremely important, as these behaviors will be used to establish standards for individual performance reviews.

5. *Specify needed behavioral change.* Detail how overall company behaviors must change to meet your standards in the new value set.

6. *Identify leverage implementers.* Pinpoint the people, teams, and individuals whose behavior and performance are critical to the strategic plan's success. It's from the efforts of this group that strategic change and value change will spread throughout the company.

7. *Assess implementers' ability.* Assess the ability of each person, department, and team to change, accomplish their jobs technically, and to live the new values.

8. *Select the right leverage people.* Choose those people currently living the new values—or those most capable of learning to do so. This is an absolute must for the leadership and management positions in the change process. You can live with technically excellent people who aren't "gung ho" and maybe, temporarily, with a few who will never walk the talk, but they can't be your leaders. As soon as practical, select out those who can't live the values.

9. *Communicate with the leverage group.* At this point, brief the leverage people on the importance of their jobs and the values that are needed to accomplish them, as well as the implementation tools that will be used to change or reinforce values.

Bring the leverage people into workshops to interpret the values as they relate to their strategic work, discussing, for example, the importance of speed, accuracy, friendliness, and availability of information for customer service. "Particularizing" and expanding the values' components for their jobs is exceedingly important.

They should develop a written statement of (1) how each value relates to their specific department or job, (2) their personal objectives for each value for the coming year, and (3) how, for whom, and at what pace they will introduce measurable accountabilities for values in their department. Remember, it takes four to six years in a large organization to penetrate the organizational layers and practices with new values, make people accountable, and achieve significant cultural change. The key is not an organizational pronouncement of values, it is supervisor-to-employee communication of the values relating to each individual job, the setting of employee objectives based on them, and the supervisor walking the talk for a sufficient period of time so that the organization will begin to believe in the values and that they are here to stay.

10. *Communicate with the entire company.* Communicate both the values and their relationship to the plan to the entire organization. In the Key 16 chapter, we'll talk in detail about how to do so.

11. *Establish individual objectives and a review mechanism.* Include a section rating the individual's embodiment of corporate values on the annual or semiannual performance appraisal form. (See the Key 4 chapter.)

12. *Get and keep the organization clean.* Remove the people who can't abide by the new values quickly. Ensure that hiring practices employ only those who fit the new value set. (See Keys 6, 8, and 14.)

13. *Reward based on results.* Reward individuals for both value-based behavior and tangible outcomes. (See the Key 18 chapter.)

If this seems like a lot of effort to put into something as seemingly intangible as culture, remember that virtually everything you do to stress values also has another purpose in the change process. Good leverage leadership, for example, is needed to get the tangible job done as well as support and publicize the new values. Your accountability system not only measures progress toward tangible plan objectives but also adds measurement of values and behaviors.

How Long Does It Take to Change a Culture?

There is no single and simple answer. The speed of change depends not only on the effectiveness of your change efforts but on how much the organization wants to change. Expect the process to take four to six years, paralleling the time it takes to get true structural changes in the business as a result of the strategic plan. The "gating" factors are people and plan accomplishment. Count on spending at least two to three years changing people's minds or changing the people.

Do

- Consciously define your cultural values and what they mean when turned into action.

- Ensure that your values will propel actions leading to a competitive edge for your organization in the marketplace.
- Hold your people accountable for values by measuring the extent to which they live the values and their tangible performance on business objectives that support the values.
- Go down the list of cultural change implementation tools and make sure you are using those most likely to produce the cultural changes you want.

Don't

- Simply define the values and expect communications to the troops to cause changes in behavior. It won't.
- Undertake a program of strategic and values change unless you're willing to drive values and business objectives through the departments right down to the individual.

Key 11

Allocate Resources Effectively: Putting Your Money and People Where Your Future Is

---

Principle: Where you invest your money and people determines exactly where your business will go.

Why it's important: Inadequate investment in the most important ongoing or strategic initiatives significantly hurts the short- and long-term profitability of the business. Large sums invested out of alignment with the direction statement will push the long-term business in the wrong strategic direction.

How it's applied: At an annual resource allocation meeting, funds and people are allocated between the ongoing business and strategic initiatives, based on an analysis of their potential contribution to strategic goals.

Expected results: Resources are allocated far more efficiently than by the usual budgetary processes or by funding those who shout the loudest. More money is available to spend on the future or take to the bottom line.

Resource Allocation

What Is Resource Allocation?

Your strategic resources are your dowry to trade for sustained growth and future financial success. They are those resources available after you've prudently spent what you must to keep the existing business running at its current level.

Strategic resources considered for allocation include not just dollars and leverage people but also less obvious resources such as patents, scientific knowledge, and brands. They also include products, projects, and incipient businesses strategically placed to pay off in the future if you manage them well and are lucky.

Strategic resources are also anything that can be bargained, traded, sold, or turned into cash or other assets to be used to fund more promising strategic ventures. Mature businesses, businesses and assets that might fit other companies better than yours, marginal new ventures, and any asset not precisely in line with your direction statement fall into this category. But management is frequently reluctant to tamper with assets such as these unless under extreme pressure to generate funds.

What's Strategic and What's Operational?

It is essential that the meaning of the terms *strategic* and *operational* be clear. *Strategic* deals with making the long term happen. Strategic programs and efforts are devoted to making structural changes in the business—those significant changes in products, processes, and the organization that alter the nature of the business and will deliver continuous fruits over the long term.

But you must also spend to get outstanding short-term results to make the long term viable. *Operating* or *operational* deals with what you have to do today. Operating plans, for example, plot the spending and moves needed to make this year's profit goals, launch this year's products, and carry out the myriad ongoing activities needed to reach short-term goals.

Why Are Strategic Resources So Important?

To outperform your competition, you need to spend your resources more efficiently than competitors do on strategic programs in your core competencies and in areas where you can get competitive advantages. The future of your company depends on it.

Even when companies make resource allocation an important part of strategic planning, they often deal only with the latest requests for strategic funds, leaving earlier strategic initiatives out of the process. Those earlier initiatives tend to take on a life of their own, championed by a few advocates and held sacrosanct. But programs or businesses that started as strategic can become superfluous if company direction shifts. So it's imperative that you include all strategic initiatives, new and old, in the resource allocation process, holding them up to the same scrutiny. Ask, "Are all these activities worthwhile, or do we have better strategic opportunities for some resources? Should we reallocate significant resources?"

How Can Resource Allocation Decisions Affect the Bottom Line?

Two That Did It Right

A major not-for-profit publisher did its first-ever analysis of the profitability and resource drain of each of its publication categories. Much to the company's surprise, "prestige" books by major thinkers and academicians drained editorial talent and returned so little that management cut the line back to a bare minimum, gaining significant resources for other, more important and vibrant product lines.

Similarly, a market research company examined its current and potential businesses in terms of profitability and fit with the company's criteria for future business. It found that the field market research business on which the company had been founded thirty years earlier was high-volume and low-profit with no prospects for profitable growth. The company quickly shifted substantial resources to parts of its portfolio with far more promise.

And One That Didn't

A Fortune 500 company leaped early into the market for graphic display terminals. Against the advice of internal market research people and outside experts, the company spent millions to launch its pioneering device, only to be blown out of the water when a competitor brought out a vastly superior product a few weeks later. If the company had evaluated the potential and risk of this initiative against other strategic alternatives, it might have killed the program long before incurring expensive production and market entry costs.

There's a lesson here for everyone: You need to identify, isolate, inventory, and be brutally honest about *all* your strategic initiatives during the strategic planning process.

How Efficient Can You Be?

The productivity of the strategic resources employed by companies varies considerably. My experience says that the typical, well-established company is perhaps 70 or 80 percent efficient. Work habits, work ethic, spending habits, bureaucracy, and unpressured culture all contribute to stretching out the time spent carrying out new initiatives.

How much productivity improvement is possible? CEO after CEO in our survey told us that they reduced their workforce by 30 percent or more and their capacity and efficiency went up significantly. Why? They kept their most efficient people, eliminated a lot of work that was adding little value to profits or customer satisfaction, focused their efforts on high-value-added work, and their people were working harder and longer. And of course, they were getting rewarded for the hard work.

For other evidence of how efficiency can vary from situation to situation, one need look no further than a well-run entrepreneurial company where the employees have a sense of ownership and often a lot of stock. I call the good ones 120 percent companies. The employees work 120 percent longer than most, they get 120 percent of normal results, and they want to get a zillion percent richer than most. They look upon strategic resources as their own money, time, and stock options, and they never have enough of any of them. They are focused, energized, and motivated.

How can you get entrepreneurial results? During resource allocation, decide how you're going to increase the efficiency of your spending. Your people are probably capable of working at 120 percent of their current efficiency. The resource allocation process is a good time to stretch them to that, particularly on strategic projects. Decide how much stretch to put in their objectives. Decide how tight to make their budgets. In a company that has been overspending for average results, an 80 to 90 percent budget for 120 percent results would not be unreasonable. If you put your naturally 120 percent people—and even the most somnolent of companies has some—on your most important projects, they'll get 120 to 130 percent productivity out of a 100 percent budget. For every resource request, ask whether you are getting 120 percent output for 100 percent spending. Said another way, is it a high-value-added request or just another business-as-usual spending addition? Remember, the companies that cleaned house got 115 to 130 percent results out of 100 percent resources.

In addition, your productivity has to be measurably higher than your competition's if you are to win in the long pull. You have to therefore set demanding objectives exceeding those of competition.

Objectives of the Resource Allocation Process

The objectives of resource allocation are to allocate money, people, and assets to businesses, producing:

- *Desired current results:* Profit and cash flow
- *Desired future results:* The future specified in the strategic plan's direction statement and objectives

To accomplish that, you'll need to:

- *Find cash.* Review one- and three-year profitability of existing businesses and determine the availability of cash and investable capital from them and from outside funding sources such as the capital and debt markets.

▪ *Set aside resources for the existing business.* Calculate the cash and capital needed to keep the current business healthy and growing. All other funds are available for strategic investment.

▪ *Determine the fit between new strategic initiatives and long-term direction.* To what extent will proposed new initiatives, such as priority issue programs, help fulfill the company's vision?[1]

▪ *Allocate strategic cash, capital, and human resources.* Review and allocate the long-range (three- to ten-year) profit, cash, capital, and human resources needs of strategic initiatives. (The longer time frames apply to industries like timber and aerospace that have long lead times.)

Steps in the Resource Allocation Process

In this section, we'll examine the steps in the resource allocation process, illustrated in Exhibit 11-1.

Resource Allocation Meeting Prework

Obtain Input From Corporate Priority Issues Meeting. During the first corporate planning meeting, called the priority-setting meeting, the top team decides on the following action items:

▪ Business configuration changes—any businesses or major products that will be added or dropped and the financial implications of those moves that have been calculated. By the time of the resource allocation meeting, only the surviving or new businesses are on the plate for funding, and their needs are incorporated in departmental requests or corporate strategic priority issues.

▪ Strategic priority issues.

▪ Departmental priority issues, including each department's strategic, operating, and infrastructure needs; work owed to others and work others owe to the department; the department's preliminary budget numbers; and corporate objectives that the department is expected to meet.

---

[1] It is assumed that during strategic planning, the organization did a thorough job of deciding what businesses it would and would not be in. Usually, a matrix analysis is used to decide what businesses and major product/service lines are to be grown, held, milked, or divested. Thus, by the time of the resource allocation meeting, only the surviving or new businesses are on the plate for funding, and their needs are incorporated in departmental requests or corporate priority strategic issues.

Exhibit 11-1 Resource Allocation Process

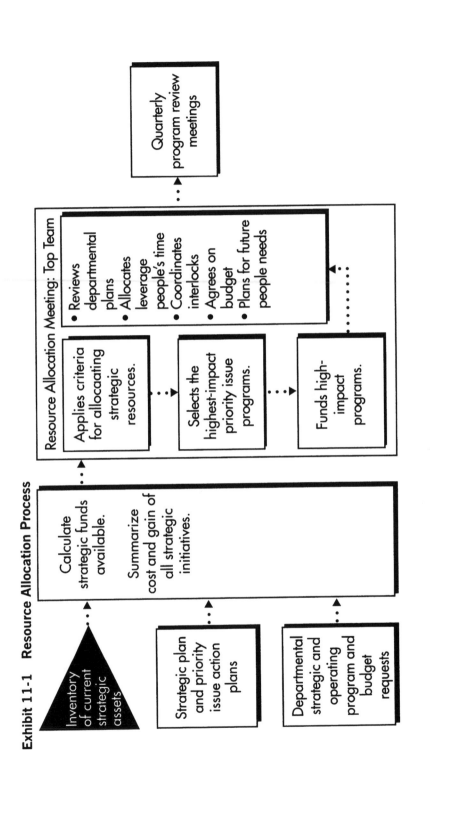

Prepare Priority Issue Action Plans. Project teams develop strategic priority issue program action plans, including resource requirements and estimated future payoff. Circulate summaries in advance of the meeting to the top team. (See the Key 2 chapter.)

Prepare Departmental Strategic and Operating Plans. Department management develops departmental strategic and operating plans with measurable objectives, resource requests, and forecast gains. (See the Key 3 chapter.)

Summarize Projected Cost and Gain. Make a summary of the resources requested, including the cost and gain of each strategic priority issue action plan, departmental strategic and operating plan, and total for the corporation. This should be done prior to the resource allocation meeting, but you can do it "on the fly" during the meeting since it is not a difficult task, and inevitably some action or departmental plans will not be available in advance.

Calculate Funds Available for Investment. The potential monies available for investment in ongoing businesses and strategic initiatives include (1) cash generated by operations, (2) new equity, (3) new debt, (4) lines of credit, and (5) disposal of existing assets and ventures. The chief financial officer usually estimates the total available over several years, deducting funds needed to keep existing businesses healthy and arriving at a residual available for new businesses. (See Exhibit 11-2.)

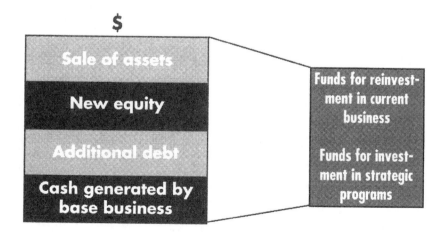

Resource Allocation Meeting, Part 1: Preliminary Allocation

Present Financial Summary. The chief financial officer briefly presents an analysis of funds available for investment and a rough assessment of how much should be made available to fund the ongoing business, new strategic priority issue initiatives, and strategic initiatives by the departments.

Review Criteria for Allocating Resources. Review the criteria for rating the future potential of strategic initiatives. Companies often add a "window in time" criterion because it has an impact on the next step—selecting priority issue programs. If there is limited time in which to respond to an opportunity—such as launching a new product before the competition introduces its product—you may decide to boost the priority of a project and fund it over candidates that rate higher on other criteria.

Tentatively Select Priority Issue Programs. Project teams present their plans. The top team then picks the programs to be funded based on decision criteria. Exhibit 11-3 suggests a process for selecting which programs to fund.

Review Departmental Plans. Examine departmental strategic, operating, and infrastructure tasks and resource requirements. All the key strategic, operating, infrastructure, and other objectives should be measurable at this time, and ballpark costs and budgets should be complete. You can use a review process similar to the one suggested for priority issue programs in Exhibit 11-3, allowing ten minutes for each presentation and fifteen minutes, maximum, for discussion after each. After all plans have been presented, the top team can discuss, approve, or deny requests or objectives, plan by plan.

Allocate Leverage People's Time. Determine where and when your key people will use their time. Identify those key people, called "leverage managers" or "leverage people," with the particular skills and managerial ability needed to accomplish priority issue and departmental program objectives. The number of leverage people is usually not large, perhaps twelve to fifteen in a moderate-size company. They are usually overloaded and in demand for a number of plan projects.

During the meeting, develop a matrix similar to the one in Exhibit 11-4 showing the project names on one axis and the names of leverage people on the other. Mark the projects for which each person is needed. Indicate where the company lacks necessary critical skills. Mark the hours of each person's time required by each strategic program. Note

Exhibit 11-3   Process for Selecting Programs to Fund

Circulate project teams' program action plans to the top team prior to the resource allocation meeting.

At resource allocation meeting:

Tape program summaries on the wall.

Give each project team ten minutes to present its priority issue plan (twenty minutes if more than one plan is under a single priority issue). After each presentation, allow fifteen minutes for top-team discussion.

After all plans are presented, give the top team time for discussion; an hour is usually enough. If desired, numerically weigh criteria for selection and score each program as a group.

Give each top-team member as much play money as is tentatively allotted to new strategic investments. Team members must vote the entire sum on proposed programs, abiding by two rules: (1) Each must fund each project fully or not at all, and (2) when his or her money is gone, it is gone.

Once funds are voted, it is usually obvious where the team thinks money should be spent. If there is disagreement on some items, discuss to consensus. As a last resort, the CEO decides.

Exhibit 11-4   People Allocation Grid: Hours of Incremental Time Requested by Project

| People | Project | | | | | | | | | | Total |
	A	B	C	D	E	F	G	H	I	J	
CGD											
AH											
MAB											
LW											
MHF											
CAF											
DD											

whether any people are underutilized, though this seldom happens—or is admitted.

Coordinate Interlocks. Departmental plans have sections for work "owed to others" and work "owed to us." Strategic priority issue programs detail "coordination requirements." Review these and tentatively agree on cross-department cooperation and coordination of work. Post these agreements; you'll confirm or modify them later in the meeting.

Resource Allocation Meeting, Part 2: Final Allocations

Adjust Funding, People, and Coordination Requirements. The entire investment picture should now be clear, so it's time for final changes and fine-tuning of the allocated resources. Note that the following three steps are interrelated, as a decision in one affects the others:

1. *Reallocate funds.* If total funds are inadequate to accomplish all the operating and strategic tasks, hard allocation decisions must be made. This will inevitably involve cutting some programs, pushing others into the future, or cutting ongoing activities to accommodate new and more fruitful pursuits.

2. *Reallocate people's time.* Propose options when leverage people don't have enough time to execute critical programs. Decide where existing talent can be used and where new people and skills must be brought in from the outside. If there is not be enough talent to complete the plan as developed, decide which of the following trade-offs to use:

- Cut projects.
- Do only part of some projects.
- Slide projects out in time.
- Cut ongoing businesses or work.
- Slide ongoing businesses or work out in time.
- Use outside resources and contractors.
- Free key people up for strategic projects by filling their regular jobs with other employees.
- Hire more people (usually the first suggestion but preferably the last resort). It may be the right decision, though, to hire for missing needed skills or to free up leverage people for more important tasks.

An open discussion of the "people" matrix with these options in mind usually leads to acceptable decisions.

3. *Reallocate cross-boundary work.* Agree on work that one department must accomplish for another during plan execution.

Pace Strategic Tasks. Review the strategic and operating jobs to be done, noting how much "stretch" is required. Is it enough? Too much?

Agree on the Budget. Tying the strategic allocations together with the departmental plans should result in a top-down budget for the coming twelve to eighteen months. Detailed allocations by line item can then be made with relative ease.

Plan Now for Future Resource Needs. There is no time like your resource allocation meeting to ask what gaps still exist in the assets and competencies needed to fulfill your vision, planned future growth, and new strategic directions.

In particular, explore the new, different, and hard-to-get resources. This is grounds for a classic now/future evaluation using some of the categories shown in Exhibit 11-5. If your needs have been covered by existing strategic plans, fine. If not, management must decide when the competency and asset gaps will be addressed.

You won't arrive at definitive answers at this meeting. You will, however, almost certainly identify areas where you want further thoughtful work done. A growing retail operation, for example, might decide to design a training and development program for select employees to build a "reserve" of potential supervisors to manage expansion smoothly.

Exhibit 11-5   Present and Future Critical Resources and Their Competencies

Categories	Now	Future
PEOPLE		
Top management		
Management		
Technical		
TECHNOLOGY		
Information		
Product		
SPACE		
Office		
Production		
Process		
TRAINING AND DEVELOPMENT		

Why the Process Is Worth the Time It Takes

The complete resource allocation meeting, if well prepared, takes about a day and a half. It might take two days if preparation is spotty and participants have to develop numbers and learn about many programs on the spot. Too much time? Not when you consider that you are agreeing on your strategic spending, your operating plan, and your budget at the same time. In truth, it is a big time-saver over traditional sequential methods. And it's time well spent when you consider the costs of allocating your resources unwisely.

Look at what can happen if resources are misallocated:

- *Lackluster bottom line:* Neither the strategic programs nor the operating units get the results they should.

- *Frustrated leverage people:* If disproportionate money, people, and attention are given to the ongoing business, it frustrates the highly talented people working on strategic programs.
- *Good people reduced to begging: Not only is it demeaning to have to beg for resources, it also slows down the job.*
- *Competitive disadvantage:* Ultimately, too little strategic spending will result in a long-term competitive disadvantage and an organization that does not fulfill its promise.

Some Final Thoughts on Resource Allocation

How the Budget Gives Teeth to Strategic Priorities

Money is power. Money gets strategic priorities addressed. If each priority issue and program is given a budget and the team assigned to that program is made accountable for spending it, you have an empowered team that:

- Answers to the top team
- Has been given a specific and measurable charter
- Has the money
- Has the people to do the job

If money for the priority issue programs is buried in someone's departmental budget or you assume you can "scrape it up" from an existing budget, then you're not really committed to the programs. Furthermore, the people who have to execute the programs become proverbial monks with their tin cups, perpetually begging for resources. It's hardly motivating.

To give teeth to your priorities, make separate budgets for the priority issue programs and put them under the control of the team or individual responsible for them.

Types of Resources That Are Usually Limited

You might think that money would be the problem, but no. In virtually every instance, it's people. Not just bodies, but people with specific skills, such as marketing, or people whose time is split between two jobs—the strategic and the operating.

You can ease these limitations with a few simple rules:

- Stretch the stretchable people in the organization, but don't break them.

- Do fewer projects and initiatives rather than more until you gauge the organization's ability to respond. This is particularly important when you are undertaking major strategic initiatives or using project teams for the first time.
- Increase people's effectiveness on strategic programs by providing:
  - —*Team training:* If people will be working in teams, this training is imperative. Don't spare the expense. (See the Key 9 chapter.)
  - —*Project management training:* Train people in project management and, if appropriate, project management software.
  - —*Initial outside help:* Use outside temps.

When Resource Allocation Is Easy

There are rare cases when resource allocation is almost a no-brainer; for example:

- *Incremental spending:* Resource allocation is usually quick and simple in small and moderate-size organizations with limited and known resources and a small number of opportunities. These opportunities are predominantly increments to their existing businesses such as product line extensions or capacity increases.
- *Focused entrepreneurs:* Resource allocation is easy in entrepreneurial companies that are strategically moving in a focused market area in which the payoff is clear and the steps toward it are obvious.
- *Companies in trouble:* In companies that are losing money, the areas in which expenses, unproductive activities, and businesses need to be cut are usually fairly obvious, although the decisions may be painful. Where to put the money to save flagging businesses is often clear as well.
- *Obvious winners:* Sometimes, the dream happens. A business opportunity so obviously fits strategy and the payoff is potentially so good that funding is a sure go.

Making Adjustments Down the Road

There is almost bound to be a need for some reallocation of resources when programs are under way. Program review meetings, which usually take place quarterly, provide regular opportunities to make changes as needed. Program leaders should come to these meetings prepared to discuss their requests for changes in direction of their programs and/or increased or decreased resource needs. The review process is covered in detail in the Key 17 chapter.

But changes in resource needs don't usually happen precisely when the quarterly review bell rings. In response to justified requests, dynamic reallocation of resources can take place anytime. The "rules of engagement" for getting key decisions made fast, covered in the Key 9 chapter, provide a very workable method for dynamic resource reallocation.

Resource Allocation in the Real World

Is resource allocation a "by-the-numbers" process? Hardly. There's too much information to process. There is a well-known Harvard Business School case describing the annual resource allocation process for a prominent Fortune 500 company. The case describes how managers from all over the world spend three days at headquarters presenting proposals to management, with resource allocation based on the potential of those proposals. It sounds smooth and virtually ideal—but somewhat sterile.

In a private conversation with the president I asked how the process really worked. He laughed and said:

> "We couldn't possibly cover all that ground thoroughly in that limited period of time. You have to know the players. If a proposal is in line with corporate direction and it's sponsored by a guy like Jim, it's an almost automatic approval. He's thorough, almost always right, and if he runs into problems, he tells us posthaste. Guys like George? Good manager but shoots from the hip. We work him over to a fare-thee-well."

So the company direction, the information presented, and the credibility of the people presenting the plans are all part of the decision-making equation.

Is It Really That Tough?

Resource allocation looks tough, complicated, and time-consuming. The first time you do it, it is. As it becomes part of your management systems and your people get used to it, it becomes much less formidable. Organizations like the process because it ultimately saves them significant time in the planning-budgeting cycle. It also ties objectives for each part of the organization to resources sufficient for their accomplishment.

Do

- Base allocation of resources on facts and your strategic plan. You're playing with the most powerful factor in your future.

- Develop an annual process that works for you and follow it year in and year out.
- Include all your resources, no matter how sacred, when you decide what you have to spend.
- Allocate and use your "leverage people" brilliantly. Do everything you can to train them and give them expert help when needed. People and their skills are the limiting factor in strategic change.
- Look ahead and ask, "What additional resources and skills supporting our new directions should we begin adding right now?"

Don't

- Let the chief executive officer and chief financial officer dictate what resources people and projects get. It leads to lousy allocations and unmotivated people.
- Separate the allocation of resources to priority issue programs from departmental plans and the ongoing (operations) budget. The result will be an incomplete picture and significant errors in allocation.

Key 12

Align Your Organization's Work With the Plan – From Top to Bottom

> **Principle:** From the top of the organization to the bottom, people's strategic and operating activities must be aligned with the plan.
>
> **Why it's important:** Nonalignment is like friction. The more the effort is out of line with the plan, the more useless heat is developed and the less energy is available to drive the organization in the right direction.
>
> **How it's applied:** Project team plans and departmental operating and strategic plans are consciously aligned with the corporate plan and tied to the corporate budget. The plans are reviewed and enforced, and achievement is rewarded.
>
> **Expected results:** Far more strategic objectives are achieved than if alignment were left to chance.

What Is Alignment?

Alignment is ensuring that all the work in the organization is in direct, measurable, and obvious support of the corporate strategy. Using the skyscraper analogy, all the load-bearing steel and supporting members (work) are bearing the stresses needed to hold the building rigid and erect and enable it to withstand the stresses of the environment. There are just enough load-bearing members to do the job, and there are no extra steel girders here and there, carrying no aligned load or stuck on for fun or decorative purposes.

Is Alignment an Implementation Tool or a Result?

If you follow the business press, you might think of alignment as a tool that you can buy in the store, turn on, and watch as it lines everyone up to march in the same direction. Not so, of course. Alignment is less something you *do* than something you *get* when you employ the other 17 implementation keys effectively. It results from the careful integration of the keys.

The implementation keys affect alignment in different ways, some immediately and some over the long term. They can be divided into three categories, reflecting the way they impact on alignment:

1. *Hard implementation keys,* which immediately cause behavior aligned with the plan
2. *Soft implementation keys,* which affect the capacity of the organization to act and also align action with direction
3. *Philosophical implementation keys,* which set general direction and provide the standards against which you test your alignment

Seventeen of the 18 keys are covered in depth in the other chapters in Part II (the 18th, of course, being alignment itself). The following subsections, which group some related keys into broader categories, summarize how the keys contribute to alignment. We'll then turn briefly to testing for alignment and maintaining alignment when strategic plans change.

Hard Keys

Hard implementation keys deal with visible and tangible commodities—money, core processes, and people. They have the most immediate effect on alignment throughout the organization. For example, money allocated to build a plant to produce a new product aligned with the company's new strategy has an immediate, aligned effect: The new plant gets built and the product introduced. The hard alignment keys are:

• *Developing accountability systems:* The top team, departments, program teams, and individuals develop objectives and action plans, then scrutinize them for alignment with the strategic plan. People charged with implementing action plans are then held accountable for aligned results.

• *Rewarding strategic results:* Money and recognition result from the achievement of aligned objectives, reinforcing aligned behavior.

■ *Changing the organization structure:* In addition to changing the structure per se, this key includes putting people with the job skills, competencies, and values that you want for the future in high-leverage positions; using creative, tough leadership; and using teams appropriately. Alignment takes place when people who are capable of interpreting corporate direction in their own plans are put into high-leverage positions. They will populate their departments with similar can-do employees.

■ *Removing resistance:* People who not only don't align their efforts with the plan but actively or passively fight alignment have to go. Alignment is easier with major resistance gone. Other employees get the message: You do what's aligned and don't fight it or you're gone.

■ *Fixing broken core processes:* Fixing core processes that are critical to delivering your market strategy by definition aligns your spending and action with the corporate direction.

■ *Allocating resources effectively:* This is a powerful tool. Money and people are allocated only to aligned actions. If the resource allocation meeting is properly run, strategic and operating funds will only be allocated to activities that are aligned with strategy or those efforts necessary to make the short term successful.

Soft Keys

Soft implementation keys have a less direct effect on alignment than do the hard ones, and their impact is likely to be long-term, not immediate. These keys include:

■ *Growing people:* Selecting, training, and developing leaders for the future has a pervasive effect on future alignment. Choose people with the values and competencies you need. Indoctrinate them in the corporate direction, your planning system and how it aligns effort, and how to link their plans to it. Ensure that they work with leaders who align their efforts. In the future, these people will become the "aligners" in the organization.

■ *Empowering execution:* When negotiating empowerment limits, ensure that alignment is a prime criterion for empowered people acting independently. Your carefully selected, trained, and empowered people can exercise their aligned skills and knowledge relatively independently throughout the organization.

Philosophical Keys

Philosophical keys are the platform and the information herald from which the future of corporation is launched. They are the hull, propulsion unit, destination map, and communication network of the ship. They can only set the stage for the use of hard and soft keys, the tiller if you will, that lead to true alignment. Like all intangibles, they have to be constantly applied to be effective and used to correct for course deviations.

- *Communicating effectively:* The strategic communication program is geared toward communicating and interpreting direction and culture and heralding good results. This reinforces what the corporation values (and doesn't). Seeing and hearing tangible accomplishments enables people to benchmark their efforts against others considered aligned and excellent helps them align their own efforts.
- *Defining the future culture:* As culture changes to increasingly reflect your new values, those values will guide action in an aligned direction.

The Direction Statement

Though the direction statement was not included as an alignment tool, it is the instrument with which the organization aligns. You developed your direction statement when you drew up your plan. Its mission, vision, business definition, and values are all yardsticks for testing the alignment of every objective and action plan. The top team must ensure that, over time, each item in the direction statement is made operational somewhere in the organization. It needs to ensure that departments develop their own direction statements, aligned with the corporate statement, to direct their own efforts.

Are You or Aren't You Aligned?

How do you know whether the work in your organization is aligned with top-level priorities and plans? Here are some ways to check:

Plan Approval and Resource Allocation. When departmental and priority issue programs are being approved and resources allocated, verify that no program leaves the meeting with an iota of misalignment.

Reviews. When you review plan execution, compare results not only to action plan objectives but also to the strategic plan yardsticks. Scrutinize any new objectives for alignment.

Systems Check. Much of the alignment that you want will take place in the bowels of the organization, where objectives will be set by lower-level departments and people who have not been party to senior-level meetings. These objectives will be set through your departmental and individual accountability systems, which must work correctly if lower-level effort is to be correctly aligned. During the first and second year of objective setting, the lower-level systems are often *not* working well. They are complicated, difficult to understand, and rely on supervisors who, irrespective of training, may have only a slightly better understanding of the system than the people with whom they are setting objectives.

It is therefore useful to check a random sample of lower-level individual objectives, tracing them up through their bosses' objectives to departmental objectives to ensure that they are aligned with the departmental plan and top corporate priorities. If they're not aligned, find out why. Chances are that (1) there is misunderstanding of the job to be done or (2) the supervisors don't understand how to set objectives and separate the strategic from the day-to-day. If there is a systemic problem—such as not enough training, fuzzy instructions, or poor communications—you can fix it and get the system fixed for the coming year.

Phone Surveys. One company uses a market research organization to call randomly selected employees in every department in the company. The researchers ask individuals about their understanding of the company direction and their role in it. The resulting data show where there is "mental" misalignment and where the company or manager has to do a better job of translating direction to the rank and file.

Alignment Meetings. If alignment was initially poor, or the coordination and alignment problem is particularly complicated, managers are often invited back to a special alignment meeting for a relook and reallocation of resources.

At this meeting, the corporate priorities are posted, and each business unit or department briefly presents its plan. Alignment of the plans with the corporate priorities is discussed, interlocking commitments are completed, and any needed resource changes are made.

To illustrate: With more than a dozen international plans to cover, a senior vice president posted the corporate priorities. He asked each of his twelve country or regional managers to present their top five priorities supporting the corporate plan and then the top five priorities of the country plan. They found significant holes in their alignment and coordination needs with other managers, involving about 20 to 25 percent of their effort. They then made the necessary corrections to alignment, coordination, and resource allocation on the spot.

How Do You Maintain Alignment When Priorities Change?

When some corporate priorities change, how do you reorient alignment to accommodate the new priorities while continuing to pursue the important older ones?

The planning and implementation system is geared to allow these changes seamlessly. You'll be able to inject changes into the plan each year, fund them, turn them into objectives and programs, and delegate them for execution while keeping older programs that are not yet complete. If your system is set up properly, the cascade of objectives, priorities, and programs down into the organization and the establishment of departmental, team, and individual objectives to support them should be well systematized.

By the time you enter phase 3 of the change process—true strategic change—your system should be working well and easily. Your people will be well versed in the complete process.

You will need to continue constant communication of the overall corporate direction and its current priorities, with particular emphasis on where the new priorities fit in the overall scheme of things set forth in the direction statement.

Do

- Recognize the importance of alignment and test for it frequently, particularly when setting objectives and reviewing results.
- Intervene with special alignment meetings or by questioning alignment at lower levels if you suspect that there is a significant alignment problem.

Don't

- Go on an "alignment" crusade. If you do your job on the implementation keys, your organization will be aligned.

Key 13
Empower Execution

Principle: Empowered teams and individuals are given as much responsibility and authority as their ability warrants and operate under a minimum of control.

Why it's important Removing constraints allows people to do their jobs better and faster. Speed is essential in staying ahead of the competition.

How it's applied: Empowerment limits are negotiated as part of team charters, departmental plans, or individual standards of performance.

Expected results: A company that shifts decision making down two or three levels responds to the environment and produces results faster than does a company in which decisions are made only at the top levels. In addition, empowered people are generally more enthusiastic about their jobs.

What Is Empowerment?

Empowerment is a popular word for a very old and important concept—defining and delegating responsibility, then holding people accountable for carrying out their responsibilities successfully. Within the business world, one frightening misconception about empowerment is that it gives people the freedom to do anything they want, any way they want, in order to get their jobs done. In that scenario, any interference by management is out of line. But that is not empowerment. It is anarchy.

Why Use Empowerment as a Management Tool?

A hierarchical company will sense a risk involved in giving increased power to individuals and teams at lower levels. What makes that risk worth taking is that, properly executed, a program to empower individuals, departments, and teams has several general benefits:

- *Fast action:* By giving people responsibility for making decisions that affect their own areas, organizations dramatically increase decision-making speed. Organizations that don't delegate decision making vertically and horizontally through the organization chart are unable to keep up with rapidly changing market conditions.

- *Superior results:* Employees and teams who have freedom to act find creative ways to meet the objectives of their strategic programs. Employees who are self-motivated produce high-quality results.

- *Self-starting teams and individuals:* Empowerment spurs employees to take initiative rather than wait to be told what to do or get permission to take the next step.

- *Happier people:* Giving people a reasonable amount of freedom creates a healthy atmosphere within the organization. People enjoy being challenged and feeling that they have more control over their own lives. Invasive controls on operations make individuals feel like cogs in a wheel rather than like productive, valued members of a team.

- *Managers who are free to concentrate on other priorities:* Empowered individuals require less attention from management. They know when they are working to their highest level of productivity and creativity and often police themselves. Top managers, freed from the drudge work of overseeing every step employees take, have more time to devote to higher priorities, such as setting policy, conducting strategic planning, . . . and golf.

- *A climate that fosters individual growth:* Empowered individuals often want to take on more responsibility. Individuals with less freedom often want to get rid of the responsibility they have.

- *Improved relationships among people:* A workplace filled with self-motivated individuals who operate freely is one in which communication problems are minimized. Empowered individuals are usually eager to be part of a team and work hard to ensure that their relationships with others are smooth. Infighting and backbiting are less frequent in an organization that adopts empowerment as a mode of operation.

For day-to-day operations, empowerment is important. For implementing strategy, it's crucial. Teams, in particular—and individuals, of course—have to be able to operate fluidly, both horizontally and vertically, to accomplish multifunction objectives. The least untoward encumbrance, such as the need for a trivial "upstairs" approval, will "lock up" an entire system of decisions and forward motion. Take another look at the team communication chart in the Key 1 chapter (Exhibit 1-7) and you will understand the concept immediately.

Succinctly put, organizations that aren't empowered learn to "look upstairs" for every decision, initiative, and strategic direction. Such organizations quickly lose their vitality and become prey for the empowered and fleet of foot.

Who Gets Empowered?

You will want to empower those directly in the strategic line of fire—program teams, departments, and individuals who are charged with executing priority issue programs and other actionables singled out for immediate action. You already have the empowerment mechanism in place—the interlocking scorecard. And job descriptions should address in what areas (spending, hiring, firing, pricing, new products) these people are empowered to do *something*. The question is, what and how much?

If you have communicated the extent of their empowerment effectively, employees should be able to answer the simple empowerment questions shown in Exhibit 13-1 without hesitation.

How Much Empowerment Is Enough?

The amount of empowerment that should be given depends on the factors shown in Exhibit 13-2, which include: (1) the risk that you're taking and the danger to the organization if the project or job performance is a failure, (2) the capability of the team or individual implementing a program or responsible for a job, and (3) the extent to which management is personally willing to "let go" of control.

Of course, empowerment will, by its nature and intent, stretch the "empowered" people, who, by necessity, must initially be high-leverage employees. We've found that the following characteristics make for an individual who accepts significant empowerment well:

- Track record of self-accountability
- Ability to get along with a wide variety of personalities
- Communication skills
- Motivation skills
- Management skills
- History of self-starting accomplishments

Exhibit 13-1   Three Simple Empowerment Questions

1   What can I do without consulting someone?
2   What can I do without consulting someone but must tell them about after the action?
3   What must I get permission to do before acting?

Exhibit 13-2   Factors Determining the Amount of Empowerment

EXTERNAL FACTORS

▼ The extent to which the market and competition require rapid decision making and response

PROJECT OR JOB FACTORS

▼ The initiative's or job's mission and objectives
▼ The risk involved in the project or job (If performance fails, how much will it cost the company?)

TEAM OR INDIVIDUAL TRAITS

▼ Technical competence
▼ Managerial ability
▼ Functional experience
▼ Quality of the individual's or team's relationship with the rest of the organization

ORGANIZATIONAL DESIRE OR INTENT

▼ The trust the organization and top team have in the individual or project team
▼ Management's willingness to "let go" and empower teams and individuals
▼ The organization's desire to develop individuals or team members
▼ The extent of management's control and oversight of empowered individuals and teams

- Ability to recover from adversity
- Ability to handle conflict
- Knowledgeable about the functional job to be done

Empowerment does not work with people who:

- Are loners
- Are self-centered
- Are highly political
- Lack functional expertise
- Are not respected by their peers
- Lack a proven record of management or being a team player
- Are abrasive or aloof
- Are uncommunicative

How Do You Design and Implement an Empowerment System?

Once you've decided to empower those responsible for implementing strategic change, you need a plan for doing that systematically. It won't work to walk into your office one day and announce that all individuals, departments, and teams will henceforth have the freedom to act independently. It will work if you think of empowerment as a management system that you must carefully plan and implement. Specific steps are outlined in Exhibit 13-3.

Armed with data on the current degree of empowerment in the organization, the top team decides its overall policy on empowerment. It follows this by establishing broad limits, somewhat like salary grades, for layers and organization units. That done, the top team establishes specific limits for strategic teams and departments, conveys them, and adjusts them, if necessary, at or after the resource allocation meeting. It is assumed that training in empowerment is done as part of the recommended training in the performance management system. (See the Key 17 chapter.) The entire empowerment process is summarized in Exhibit 13-4.

How Much Control Is Needed?

Once an empowerment program is in place, how much control should management exert over empowered individuals or teams? The top team should:

- Back away and leave individuals and teams free to succeed or make mistakes—but certainly not disastrous ones.
- Control individuals and teams through normal financial and project reviews.
- Intervene when a significant error is about to be made.
- Get involved when a learning opportunity can expand the indi-

Exhibit 13-3   Empowerment System Design and Implementation Steps

1 **Survey:** Information to aid the top team in making a policy decision on where and how empowerment should be implemented or improved comes from a survey that is part of the design of the accountability system.
2 **Policy statement:** The top team drafts a statement on empowerment during the design of the accountabilities and review system.
3 **Overall limits:** The top team establishes overall boundaries or limits on action, layer by layer, department by department.
4 **Team and department limits:** If limits on actions differ for teams or departments, the top team establishes them during the priority-setting or resource allocation meeting.
5 **Final limits:** At the resource allocation or implementation plan meeting, final agreement is reached on the degree of empowerment each department or team will have.
6 **Adjustments:** As the strategic objectives are carried out, the top team needs to adjust the amount of empowerment each department, team, and individual has.

Exhibit 13-4 Empowerment Process

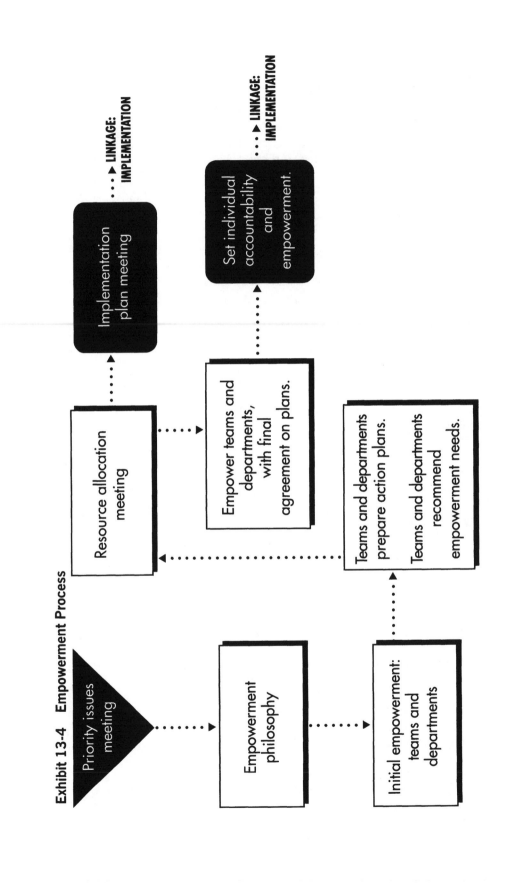

vidual's or team's capability to handle additional work without supervision and therefore increase empowerment.

- Expand the limits of empowerment on the fly as individuals or teams show they can handle broader limits.

Managers must avoid jumping in every time they feel uncomfortable about how a scenario is playing out. At the same time, the empowered individual or team must agree to bring to the attention of management any significant deviations from the plan.

■ ■ ■ ■ ■

Empowerment is a time-honored concept that fundamentally describes how much power and decision-making authority are delegated to an individual, a department, or a team. In rapidly changing environments, organizations have no choice but to empower their people. Decisions have to be made quickly. Unlike hierarchical companies, empowered organizations have a high capacity for quick response and a higher capacity for work.

Using empowerment requires more than saying "You're on your own" to individuals, teams, and departments. Empowerment is negotiated or granted to individuals, departments, or teams depending on their capacity for making and implementing effective decisions and their potential to stretch that capacity. Thus, empowerment—the lifting of limits on action—is an integral part of the organization's objective-setting and resource allocation systems.

Do

- Use the strategic change process to expand the amount of empowerment in your organization significantly.
- Make the extension of empowerment a required part of negotiating performance standards for all individuals, departments, and teams executing strategic initiatives.
- Train all empowered people to understand what empowerment means, how it applies to them, and what limits exist.
- Expand empowerment limits as individuals, departments, and teams demonstrate the ability to take on more work, responsibility, and risk.

Don't

- Unilaterally tell your organization that everyone is empowered. Not everyone will or should be.
- Forget to set limits to empowerment.
- Let the attitude of "I have the power to get my job done any way I please without intervention" prevail in your organization.

Key 14

Select, Train, and Develop for the Future – Now

Principle: The organization's people skills ultimately determine the effectiveness of strategy development, implementation, and subsequent competitive success.

Why it's important: Strategic leadership and managerial and functional skills take up to twenty years to develop internally. Developing skills to meet growing and ever-changing demands must therefore be of continuing and prime concern to senior management.

How it's applied: Use of a rigorous, continuous, and highly selective system for testing, selecting, training, and developing leaders, managers, and functional experts in the competencies needed to succeed in the long term.

Expected results: A sustainable organization with future capabilities and strategic results is far superior to competition.

Training and Development

Most organizations are using skills that got results in the past. But many of these skills will become obsolete, given the dynamic changes in the business environment and in how business is managed. Although command-and-control management systems worked well in the past, for example, more fluid systems based on teams, flat organizations, and free communication across organization boundaries will be important in the future. And although marketing was historically limited to a few well-worn channels such as face-to-face selling, electronic commerce opens up an entirely new array of marketing venues and skills needed to exploit them.

Change won't be effective without new skills in the organization.

Smart companies will begin developing these skills before they're urgently needed.

The Cost of Ignoring Training and Development

You ignore training and development at your peril. Without it, first, your people will have to learn new skills on the job, quite likely during a crisis. This invariably yields long-term inefficiency and risks significant errors since learning on the fly is usually only partial and often incorrect. Second, you may be forced to hire people from the outside to make up for skill deficiencies, an expensive and risky approach since they will be untried and unfamiliar with the ways of your organization. Third, you can stunt the growth of your company, particularly a rapidly growing entrepreneurial company, if you don't develop a depth of talent. When the chief executive officer or chief operating officer suddenly finds that the talent in the layers below is not good enough for the next expansion, the company must slow down to bring in and assimilate outside managers, professionals, and leaders.

You are far better off, in terms of both cost and future effectiveness, if you develop your talent from within. Growing their leadership talent internally is one of the reasons that great companies such as Hewlett-Packard, General Electric, Procter & Gamble, Coca-Cola, Pfizer, and a long list of others have performed superbly decade after decade, some for more than a hundred years.

Four types of training and development are needed during a strategic change process:

The Four Types of Training and Development

1. *Preplan training,* before the planning process begins. Every participant needs training in the planning process flow, the plan format, the information required, and meeting agendas. Some will require briefing in diagnostic interview skills or in facilitating departmental plans.
2. *Immediately postplan executional skills,* including process re-engineering, market research, or project management to guide the execution of the plan itself.
3. *Long-term skills,* to bolster future competencies, such as developing world-wide business or executing joint ventures and acquisitions.
4. *Leadership development,* to shape future leaders who will one day drive the organization. Your future leaders are the most crucial weapon in your competitive arsenal.

Preplan Training

Grouped by target audience, this early training should include:

- *Top team and senior management:* How to prepare for and partic-ipate in the planning process, as well as how to manage the change process, stage by stage. During this training, assignments are normally made for collection of key market, internal, and en-vironmental data.
- *Leverage managers:* Leverage managers need training in depart-mental planning and all of the postplan execution skills listed below. They also need to have special briefings on dealing with resisters and incompetents, severance and outplacement of em-ployees, and effective plan communication.
- *Planning coordinator(s):* Training in the planning process that is even more extensive than that received by planning participants. Coordinators need to be able to answer detailed questions about plan steps and help participants over the rough spots.
- *Departmental managers:* How to use the departmental planning format; how to facilitate the departmental planning process.
- *Facilitators of the planning process:* Workshop training at a mini-mum; a briefing on the common facilitation techniques needed to pull a plan together.
- *Presenters:* Training in presentation skills for anyone composing or presenting input to the plan. This is frequently a major weak-ness in organizations.

Immediately Postplan Executional Skills

All of the postplan training and development offered after plan comple-tion should support needed competencies. The following list is typical, but not every item will be relevant to every company, and each company will have other activities specific to its business:

- *Review, accountability, and reward systems:* This is a must. Be sure to include practice sessions in which participants learn how to write objectives and supervisors and employees learn how to conduct reviews.
- *Departmental planning for phase 2:* During the first year, depart-ments will most probably limit their planning to relaying their depart-mental and corporate strategic priority issues to the top team. With that done, they need training to prepare them to install a complete depart-mental strategic planning system during the second year. Training

should cover how the plan relates to plans of other departments and the corporate plan.

- *Team development and facilitation:* Most companies will use cross-functional teams to act on strategic priority issues. Teams require extensive training in developing a charter, developing rules of operation, team development, problem analysis, decision making, and using facilitation tools. The appendix to this chapter shows five courses in a typical team-training agenda.

- *Analytical tools and techniques:* Training in quality control, creativity, and analytical techniques as well as decision-making tools gives a team the instruments it needs to do a first-class job.

- *Project management:* If the change effort will involve intricate projects using a multiplicity of resources, training in formal project management techniques and appropriate software is often required.

- *Presentation skills:* People will have to communicate their results, new plans, and critical issues very efficiently—something for which few organizations are known. This training is even more important after the plan is developed than before.

- *Facilitation skills:* As teams are formed, the people who will facilitate team activity will require training. Although facilitation is perfected on the job, the basic skills need to be taught and practiced in class.

- *Team building:* Without help, even top teams don't always function well. Through team building, an intensive commitment of time and emotion, teams define how they will operate to be effective, identify where they are functioning poorly, and determine what they are going to do to improve. All team members are evaluated on their strengths and weaknesses versus the model of an effective team and decide how are they going to correct their personal deficiencies.

- *Process reengineering:* Many companies will end up reengineering core processes. This requires significant training in the reengineering process for all members of reengineering teams. Usually, the trainer is an expert consultant who pilots the teams through its first reengineering adventure.

- *Interpersonal skills:* Change situations require highly developed interpersonal skills, including communicating with people of varying abilities and styles, communicating persuasively, and resolving conflict. These skills can be taught by individual coaches or in a class/practice setting.

The appendix to this chapter shows an outline of the nine courses most frequently used immediately before strategic plan development and at the beginning of implementation: strategic planning, the change process, departmental planning, facilitation skills, presentation skills, team development and management, analytic tools and techniques, project management, and process reengineering.

Long-Term Skills

- *Content training:* Specific skills for specific jobs, which will vary significantly by company. Content training for the information systems department of a major financial institution included new advanced programming languages needed to develop the new information systems that will service the next generation of customers. In this institution, information systems is a core competency. A supermarket chain that had always been merchandising-oriented needed training in marketing, market strategy, and product category management. These new competencies were required to implement the chain's strategic objectives of protecting its mature markets, gaining market share, and expanding geographically.

Content training needs will become obvious, function by function, as departmental managers determine the skills required to carry out the plan and build new competencies to compete in the future. Human resources will use this analysis to develop an ongoing training plan and focus its recruiting plan.

- *Evergreen training:* Programs covering basic business skills in a wide number of areas. These should be compiled into a portfolio of courses and seminars from which managers can pick when they are constructing individual development plans with their people. Although many evergreen programs are taught by in-house trainers in large companies, most medium-size and small companies maintain a recommended list of courses and trainers to tap as required. See Exhibit 14-1 for a list of basic training topics offered by many companies.

Leadership Development

The Role of Succession Planning

This book is concerned with ensuring that the organization has the critical skills and leadership development necessary to implement the strategic plan. It assumes that your succession planning, however formal or informal, has identified the number, level in the organization, and core skills of leaders and senior managers needed over the next twenty to twenty-five years to propel your organization toward its vision.[1]

Building that cadre of potential leaders calls for an ongoing leadership training and development plan, incorporating the tools that follow.

---

[1] A good introduction to succession planning is William J. Rothwell, *Effective Succession Planning* (New York: AMACOM , 1994).

Exhibit 14-1   Evergreen Training

MANAGEMENT DEVELOPMENT

- ▼ Testing, interviewing, and selecting job candidates
- ▼ Managing change
- ▼ Leadership principles and development of leadership skills
- ▼ Reviewing employee performance and development plans

PERSONAL DEVELOPMENT

- ▼ Career management
- ▼ Coping with change
- ▼ Dealing with difficult people
- ▼ Telephone communication techniques
- ▼ Increasing interpersonal effectiveness
- ▼ Time management
- ▼ Stress management
- ▼ Valuing differences in people
- ▼ Writing skills

SALES TRAINING

- ▼ Basic selling skills
- ▼ Advanced selling skills
- ▼ Objection resolution and closing
- ▼ Sales management
- ▼ Negotiation skills

MANAGEMENT SKILLS

- ▼ Consultative listening, questioning, and persuasion skills
- ▼ Conflict resolution skills
- ▼ Problem-solving and decision-making skills
- ▼ Presentation skills
- ▼ Running meetings and meeting facilitation

TEAMS

- ▼ Team development and management skills
- ▼ Problem-solving and decision-making skills
- ▼ Process reengineering

TECHNICAL TRAINING

- ▼ Windows 98
- ▼ Microsoft Excel
- ▼ Microsoft Word
- ▼ FileMaker Pro

CORPORATE TRAINING

- ▼ New-employee orientation
- ▼ Performance management system
- ▼ Compensation system
- ▼ Corporate policy manual
- ▼ Strategic planning process

INDUSTRY TRAINING

- ▼ Training relative to your industry, its direction, and your business fit

EDUCATION

- ▼ A list of approved courses from local universities and training providers. The courses are usually relevant to the business. Typical courses include marketing and marketing management, leadership development, strategic planning, persuasion and communication, finance, project management, quality management, human resources management, management training, sales, and sales management.

It's a long list, and your finished plan may look like a Herculean task, but don't forget that the development effort goes on year in and year out for each person for ten to twenty years. Put into that time frame, the plan becomes reasonable.

A variety of selection tools for choosing candidates for leadership development and programs for screening outside recruits are available. The following lists include tools and programs that can be used with either external or internal candidates as well as those intended for use just with internal candidates:

For External or Internal Candidates

- *Unstructured interviews:* The objective of these interviews is to match the individual's experience, personality, and perceived leadership ability with the job. Unstructured interviews are the most often used and least effective of the selection and screening techniques because they tend to identify similarities between the interviewer and interviewee rather than probe how an individual thinks and would handle difficult situations. People selected this way often reflect the personality, style, and skills of the interviewer, sometimes the last thing that you want in a change situation. These interviews are sometimes, and not unfairly, called personality interviews.

- *Directed interviews:* These interviews consist of questions designed to assess the candidate's leadership competencies and probe how he or she has handled or would handle realistic leadership issues. If the issues are carefully thought out, directed interviews can produce good information on the individual's thinking and decision-making styles as well as some leadership traits. In addition, the questionnaire can be validated over time by comparing responses of successful leaders to those who did not attain major leadership positions. See Exhibit 14-2 for an example of a directed interview instrument.

- *Competency diagnostic:* Candidates take self-administered tests that are scored for leadership traits and compared to norms of leaders in similar businesses. Such tests can be tailored to the particular competency set of individual companies. The limitation of such tests is that the result is the self-perception of the candidate, not the perceptions of others who may have a different or more objective view.

- *Case interviews:* Trained interviewers ask candidates how they would respond to a series of progressively tougher and more complex cases. The interviewers rate the responses on leadership dimensions. The advantage of case interviews is that norms exist based on many candidates' responses and sometimes on hundreds of candidates' on-the-job performance. In addition, they reveal the individual's thinking processes and approaches to problem solving.

Exhibit 14-2   Directed Interview Instrument

DATA SUMMARY

Name of Candidate _____
Date _____

Dimension
Iniative
Assertiveness
Judgment
Planning and Organizing
Analysis
Oral Communication
Leadership
Control
Oral Presentation

INDIVIDUAL LEADERSHIP/INFLUENCING

DEFINITION
Using appropriate interpersonal styles and methods to inspire and guide individuals (direct reports, peers, and senior managers) toward goal achievement; modifying behavior to accommodate tasks, situations, and individuals involved.

KEY ACTIONS
- Use relationship skills effectively:
  - Maintain or enhance self-esteem.
  - Listen and respond with empathy.
  - Ask for help and encourage involvement.
  - Share thoughts, feelings, and rationale.
  - Provide support without removing responsibility.
- Follow logical sequence in discussions.
- Focus on the situation, not the person.
- Present suggestions or point of view in an appropriate and convincing manner.
- Anticipate reactions and have a plan to deal with them.
- Ask for and gain commitment to action.

ACTIVITY QUESTIONS/RESPONSIBILITIES
Does the incumbent in the manager job/role have to:
- Gain commitment from direct reports to try new ways of doing a job?

Oral Communication/Impact _____
_____
_____

LEADERSHIP
Utilization of appropriate interpersonal styles and methods in guiding individuals (subordinates, peers, superiors) or groups toward task accomplishment.

1. Tell me about the toughest groups you have had to get cooperation from.
   Did you have formal authority?
   What did you do?

Situation	Action	Result

2. What are some of the most difficult one-to-one meetings you have had with s

- *Style testing:* Although tests such as the Myers-Briggs personality instrument do not assess leadership or organization potential, they do assess the individual's decision-making and communication style. Sometimes, style is a major issue in mixing an individual with an established leadership team, either for fit or to balance a group that is too homogeneous. In that situation, these tests are useful.

- *Psychological testing.* These measure traits that are important to the job, such as aggression, trust, action orientation, self-initiation, and security.

- *Cognitive testing:* These tests measure math and abstract thinking skills and are useful when high intelligence and cognitive skills are required.

- *References:* If given at all, references from prior employers are always suspect.

- *Search company references, testing, and recommendations:* These can be self-serving because the search company has a strong interest in placing candidates quickly. But if the tests are good ones, and the company has a good reputation, then the information can be useful.

For Internal Candidates

- *360-degree diagnostics:* An individual's peers, subordinates, and supervisors rate her on the extent to which she exhibits leadership traits and behaviors. These diagnostics are particularly useful since they look at the person from three different levels in the organization. Questions can be tailored to specific industries, companies, and functional areas to give an even more complete picture. Many agree that 360-degree diagnostics are a potent aid in selecting people for higher positions and in plotting development programs.

  After the diagnostic is scored, individuals usually share their scores with an internal or external counselor and with their managers to get suggestions on development plans and ways to make behavioral improvements. Exhibit 14-3 shows an example of a 360-degree assessment.

- *Simulations:* Participants are given complex strategic business problems and must evaluate various situations, examine alternative solutions, and recommend action. Observers rate participants' leadership, teamwork, strategic thinking, business, and decision-making skills. This is both a training tool and a very powerful selection tool when a trained observer can see the individual interacting with others.

- *Performance records:* When all is said and done, past job and behavioral performance is one of the very best predictors of career trajectory, at least in the short to medium term. Asking probing questions of

Exhibit 14-3   Example of a 360-Degree Assessment

Developmental Feedback for Manager's QUESTIONNAIRE

This person:	To a Very Great Extent	To a Great Extent	To Some Extent	To a Slight Extent	Not At All	Does Not Apply
1 Values the contributions of all team members	⑤	④	③	②	①	(NA)
2 Accurately identifies strengths and development needs in others	⑤	④	③	②	①	(NA)
3 Readily commands attention and respect in groups	⑤	④	③	②	①	(NA)
4 Conveys clear expectations for assignments	⑤	④	③	②	①	(NA)
5 Coordinates work with other groups	⑤	④	③	②	①	(NA)
6 Translates business strategies into clear objectives and tactics	⑤	④	③	②	①	(NA)
7 Fosters the development of a common vision	⑤	④	③	②	①	(NA)
8 Takes a stand and resolves important issues	⑤	④	③	②	①	(NA)
9 Interacts with people openly and directly	⑤	④	③	②	①	(NA)

Executive Assessment REPORT OF RESULTS

PRIMARY STRENGTHS

1 You place high priority on achieving results and will act decisively in the interest of attaining your objectives. We saw evidence of this in the in-basket exercise, during which you made key decisions and created action plans that would ensure progress on all critical issues.

2 A conceptual, big-picture thinker, you prefer to focus your energies on strategic issues. You clearly relish the opportunity to conceive and implement new business ventures and to shape the direction of the organization. Your ability to see themes and trends and to develop innovative plans to address those concerns will continue to be a core asset and key to your success in taking on strategic projects.

PRIMARY DEVELOPMENT NEEDS

1 In your zeal to achieve results, you can ignore opportunities to build relationships with others. For example, in the in-basket exercise, you appeared very task-focused, neglecting to attend to the interpersonal side of issue resolution. Although you handled the tasks well, you did not attempt to foster relationships with either coworkers or customers. Tempering your drive for results and remaining sensitive to the people with whom you must interact will help you to build stronger business alliances as well as ensure that you do not alienate those whose help you will need to achieve your goals.

You need to make clear your department's role in carrying out the strategic objectives of the company. Your staff will be much more invested in the outcome of their work if they have a clear understanding of your rationale and the connection to long-term, organizational goals.

Exhibit 14-3   Example of a 360-Degree Assessment (*continued*)

Executive Assessment
REPORT OF RESULTS

DEVELOPMENTAL OVERVIEW

We enjoyed working with you during your assessment, which is aimed at understanding your strengths and development needs. Among the skills we observed, your strengths were especially notable at task completion. You demonstrated an action orientation that appropriately conveys urgency and is decisive in moving issues ahead.

Linked with that are your abilities to delegate assignments to others, to set clear expectations, and to monitor progress toward deadlines.

We also found your analytical skills to be effective and insightful regarding organizational vulnerabilities and strategic planning. Your solutions are likely to be creative, and you clearly enjoy thinking "out of the box" when making recommendations. You also enjoy team efforts, encouraging people to work together, keeping others informed about progress, and maintaining your involvement throughout a project's life cycle.

Often,
drive fo
tasks. Y
encoura
Especia
commit
the qua
you thi
articula
to them
derlying

Overall
to make
action
charact

INDIVIDUAL COACHING OBJECTIVES

ON-THE-JOB OBJECTIVES

1 Increasing interpersonal sensitivity:
  - To listen to others without interrupting
  - To show respect and appreciation of others' input through attentive active listening
  - To respond more sensitively to the needs and emotions of others
  - To become more approachable and to listen more effectively, even when highly focused on achieving an objective

2 Managing conflict:
  - To decrease your tendency to avoid or defuse interpersonal conflicts; to face conflict squarely and constructively
  - To explore and understand the reasons behind strong feelings and opinions

3 Fostering open communication:
  - To actively promote two-way communication and clear understanding
  - To convey interest in others' views and openness to alternative ways of thinking about a problem

FUNDAMENTAL SKILLS

  - Active listening skills:
    - Nonverbal attending
    - Open-ended probes
    - Paraphrasing
    - Reflective statements
  - Communication roadblocks

  - Conflict management strategies
  - Stress management techniques
  - Self-talk

  - Active listening skills
  - Constructive probing techniques
  - Accepting criticism and feedback from others

former supervisors can yield insights into an individual's positive and negative leadership behaviors.

Selecting Leaders

What Works and What Doesn't?

One of the most difficult tasks of any top manager is to select those in the lower cadres who will become the top leaders of tomorrow. It's even more difficult to select potential leaders from the outside, be they freshly minted MBAs or seasoned veterans coming in at the top-team level. People have traditionally relied on personal interviews and their "nose" to pick such people. The trouble with this method is that (1) we pick personalities that we like; (2) we're picking people similar to ourselves, which may not be what the company needs for change; and (3) leadership traits and competencies are buried too deep in the psyche to be uncovered by superficial selection methods.

Regarding effective versus ineffective ways to pick tomorrow's leaders, research has shown the following:

- *Traditional selection methods:* Time-honored methods such as interviews and references are the least effective ways to select people. The correlation of employee scores on selection tools (predictive validity) with performance was found to be as follows:

Interviews:	19%
References:	23%
Biographical data:	38%
Personality tests:	39%
Assessment centers:	43%
Cognitive tests:	53%
Work sample tests:	54%[2]

- *Group decisions:* Decisions made by groups—particularly diverse groups of subordinates, peers, and supervisors meeting together—are far better than decisions made through individual interviews (in which a single person simply interviews a candidate) and better than decisions reached through consultative selection (in which a candidate is interviewed by a number of people and the individual hiring consults a number of people before making a decision).[3]

---

[2] Mike Smith, "Calculating the Sterling Value of Selection," *Guidance and Assessment Review* 4, no 1 (February 1, 1988). Predictive validity is the percentage of variance in employee performance that is explained by differences in selection method scores.

[3] Valeri I. Sessa, Robert Kaiser, Jodi Taylor, and Richard J. Campbell, "Executive Selection: What Works and What Doesn't," unpublished working paper, Center for Leadership Studies, Greensboro, North Carolina, 1988.

■ *Job specifications and context:* The chances of making a good decision are significantly increased when the specifications for the job—traits, competencies, and the tangible job itself—are carefully articulated. In addition, the context of the job is equally important—the culture in which the individual is expected to operate and the strategic situation of the company and its industry.[4]

Unfortunately, those executives who carefully document the requirements for the job tend to use selection methods that bear little relationship to getting the information required to see whether a candidate does or does not fit the specifications.

■ *Soft skills:* Candidates who were hired and deemed "successful" obviously turned in strong performances. They also scored highest on the "soft skills"—having good relationships with subordinates, peers, and supervisors; being team players; and being generally viewed as easy to get along with. It is well documented that one of the reasons that careers derail is because an individual can't get along with people and is weak on the "soft skills." No matter the individual's functional and technical competence, the soft skills must be there or the person's career will derail. Obviously, the "soft skills" are very hard to judge in an interview.[5]

■ *Internal versus external candidates:* When a company is dealing with cultural and strategic change, a candidate hired from inside the company is more likely to be successful than one from the outside. Start-up companies are more likely to hire executives from outside the company, but those promoted from within are more likely to be successful.

Internal hires are more successful than external hires when the job requires intensive experience in a given field and someone who fits the culture, is flexible and adaptable, and has relevant job knowledge.

External hires are more successful when the hiring criterion is intelligence. When the job requires someone with specific product knowledge, ironically, the internally hired executives are not likely to be successful.[6]

The message? If you have an internal candidate who meets your qualifications, is an independent thinker and not wedded to the corporate culture, and keeps her eye on the outside world, then she will be a better choice than an outsider.

So What Do You Do?

The long and the short of it is that you are better off testing both internal and external candidates.

---

[4] Ibid.
[5] Ibid.
[6] Ibid.

Why test internal candidates whom you know so well? Well, maybe you don't know them so well in the context of the new job. With extensive testing and management development, for example, a major company like General Electric finds that only 0.5 to 2.5 percent of its entry-level employees qualify as leaders and go into its leadership development program. And few of them reach the top. They layer away in the organization as they reach the limits of their leadership competence. With those kinds of odds, it pays to test everyone so you can avoid picking a marginal individual simply because the person has performed well in the past and is well liked.

Here is a good protocol to follow:

1. *Specifications:* Write detailed specifications for the leadership job, including traits, competencies, the tangible job to be done, and the context in which the individual must be successful.

2. *Interviews:* Have candidates interviewed by a diverse group of individuals who espouse the values and culture that you want in the future, have been successful, and represent different functions and layers in the organization.

3. *Test instruments:* As we'll see shortly, there are various test instruments available that measure leadership qualities and a number of other dimensions. Use the one that suits you best. Some can only be used for internal candidates, others for both internal and external candidates. Exhibit 14-4 lists some sources of tests and testing services.

4. *Relating the selection methods to the specifications:* Make sure that the selection methods you use will address all the specifications you have so carefully crafted.

5. *Selection:* Let the interviewing group, including the hiring manager, make the decision on the individual—with access, of course, to any testing. One person with an outstanding organization has been using the following method for years: At the beginning of the selection meeting, without discussion, this person asks for a thumbs-up or thumbs-down. If the vote is unanimous, the individual is hired or not. If one or two voted against the majority, there will be a discussion to clarify their differences with the rest of the group before a final decision is made.

Development Tools

Once candidates are selected for leadership development, a variety of development tools are available. This subsection reviews these tools, and the next subsection discusses how to use them in progressive development programs for managers at different levels in the organization.

Exhibit 14-4 Sources of Tests and Testing Services

Test	Description	Instrument Name and Sources
Directed interviews	Structured questions and interview guide to probe competencies being sought.	Development Dimensions International
Business cases	Progressively difficult case studies evaluated by interviewee and scored by trained interviewers.	Potentia International
Personal style	Myers-Briggs measures personal style individual prefers for decision making and interacting with others.	Consulting Psychologists Press
Personality testing	Measures basic personality traits such as aggressiveness and initiative to match up with organization's "success" profile.	Consulting Psychologists Press
Cognitive tests	Measure basic mental skills such as math, verbal, comprehension, and spatial relationships.	NCS Assessments
Job competency tests	Individual self-rates on job competencies to be matched with desired success profile.	NCS Assessments
360-degree diagnostics	Peers, supervisors, and subordinates rate individuals on job competencies, values, and important work habits and skills.	Potentia International; Psychological Associates Center for Creative Leadership; The Applied Research Corp.
Simulations	A team works to solve a simulated strategic business problem while an observer notes team, leadership, and decision-making skills.	Center for Creative Leadership
Learning ability	Self-test of ability to learn and apply learning continuously.	Center for Creative Leadership
Leadership tests	Self- or 360-degree tests geared toward leadership competencies.	NCS Assessments

Facilitated Learning Methods

The following methods use skilled facilitators to develop and conduct the programs and assess the further development needs of participants:

- *Leadership institutes:* Institutes such as those run by large companies and public institutions such as the Center for Creative Learning offer a variety of assessment and development tools, including 360-degree assessments, business simulations, and in-box–out-box exercises in which individuals practice leadership skills and get feedback from peers and expert counselors on their leadership pluses and minuses.
- *Team building:* After the team pinpoints its strengths and weaknesses relative to corporate strategy and the competencies required to implement that strategy, it develops a list of desired behaviors for the team and a plan to correct deficiencies. Each individual is then critiqued against the desired behaviors, and corrective action is made part of the individual's development program. Team building can be a powerful developmental tool not only for identified future leaders but for the organization as a whole.
- *Coaching, counseling, and mentoring:* After an individual has completed a 360-degree assessment and committed to a development program, a counselor—usually, an external consultant—teams up with a senior-level internal mentor to guide the individual's development. The external counselor confidentially coaches the individual on his or her leadership behavior for six to twelve months after testing. The internal mentor, sometimes in combination with the external coach, gives advice and feedback on improving skills in the context of the organization.
- *Simulations:* These can deal with internal issues such as restructuring or external strategy issues. As a teaching tool, a simulation is particularly useful in helping middle managers understand the forces at work in the outside world and how they affect the organization. Canned simulations can be specially tailored to a company and its markets to teach how to gather and organize information on competition and world trends. Participants use the information gathered to generate alternate scenarios of future events and develop responses and solutions to those events. Such training may be given by individual consultants, consulting organizations, or in-house trainers in large companies.

Seminars and Classes

The following topics are usually presented in a seminar or classroom setting:

■ *Content learning:* Most leadership development programs include some training and education in specific competencies needed in the organization, usually including essential, top-level skills such as change management, strategic planning, and implementation. This training may also cover corporate strategy issues such as quality, service, innovation, marketing strategy, managing teams, and teamwork.

Other common topics include dealing with corporate stakeholders: employees, community, government—learning who they are, what issues they raise, and how to deal with them.

■ *Change management:* Many companies think it is important to give training in the change management process and leadership's role in leading and shaping it.

■ *General management/leadership skills:* These include selecting, managing, and developing people; strategic and operating planning; leadership; implementation of plans; and developing and maintaining a current and accurate view of the outside world. A variety of venues are available to give middle managers a broad-based grounding in general management, leadership, and business skills.

■ *Seminars by top management:* These sessions cover top-level and functional strategic thinking and the problems involved. Such training has multiple goals—educating employees, helping them relate their jobs to corporate strategy, and aligning their thinking and action to the strategic direction.

Action Development

The following are opportunities for a development candidate to work directly on important company issues:

■ *Special high-visibility assignments:* Included are assignments such as participation on a long-term project team to advise the top team on an important corporate strategic issue like global expansion or developing new products.

■ *Shadow cabinets or advisory boards:* These groups are informed of critical corporate issues and asked to recommend solutions to the CEO or top team as an input to those decisions. They are usually standing bodies that meet regularly, often just before monthly corporate executive committee meetings. A common tenure for an individual is two years, with half the board rotating off each year.

■ *Cross-functional assignment:* Potential leaders can significantly broaden their scope through assignments that require them to work on teams with members from a variety of functions.

Finding the Best Development Methods

The Center for Creative Leadership's research to date indicates that the developmental factors that characterize successful leaders, and their weight, are as follows:

- *The variety of experiences the person has had (40 percent):* The more cross-functional experience, the more enriching experiences outside of the organization, and the more vertical experiences within the organization the person has had, and the more people (and the more diverse the people) the person has worked with, the more likely he or she is to become a topflight leader.
- *Learning from others (20 percent):* The more the person is exposed to the leadership and managerial styles of others, and the more he or she has a chance to discuss those styles, the better.
- *Personal hardships overcome (20 percent):* People who have overcome personal hardships—business losses or failures, family difficulties, disease, or disability—have a better chance of becoming leaders than those who have not. The reason is simple: Leaders who have overcome hardships look at reverses as a learning experience, generalize from that experience, move on, and apply the principle another day to win or avoid similar difficulties.

There is no question, therefore, that action learning and those methods that get leaders actively involved with others in new, real, and important issues for the organization (1) are the most stimulating and (2) cause the most learning and development. Thus, the vote must go, for example, to participation in cross-functional teams, CEO-ordained projects, and shadow cabinets; experiences in functional areas new to the managers; simulations; and team building. This type of learning can help lessen a person's chances of derailing due to a difficulty in making strategic transitions.

The second, and very important, development activity, then, is the 360-degree assessments followed by counseling and mentoring. Not only can they help build natural skills and positive attributes, but they can also help prevent derailment due to such factors as personal and management style, inability to build a team, and interpersonal relationships.

Turning Leadership Development Into a Process and Programs

As it takes fifteen to twenty-five years to develop an individual to a point where she is a candidate for one of a company's top slots, training and development of leaders is not a haphazard matter. During that pe-riod, candidates have to be brought along carefully. Fad-of-the-year training programs now and then won't do the job.

The key principles behind a good leadership development process are as follows:

- Ultimately, it is the CEO's responsibility to oversee the program and evaluate the disposition of every candidate in the program.

- Every key manager is expected to participate in the hiring, selec-tion, and training of upwardly mobile managers, and part of his pay, bonuses, and own promotions depend on it. Some organizations won't allow an individual to be promoted until he has two potential replace-ments waiting in the wings in his department.

- The system includes a training and development protocol for each level of management.

- Potential candidates for the system are identified early in their careers and placed into tracked development.

- Leadership development subject matter as well as recruiting spec-ifications are directly tied to competencies needed in the future.

- The number of people in the leadership system is directly tied to those specified by a succession plan.

- All candidates are thoroughly reviewed annually by the CEO and the top team, their progress noted, and their development plan main-tained or changed as needed. The natural time for this review is just prior to each year's strategic planning process kickoff, when strategic resources will be assessed for the plan.

- Candidates are tracked on the dimensions of (1) background and experience, (2) performance in the current job, (3) competency pro-file—development in each of the competencies required for leadership, (4) 360-degree or other test data, (5) personal preference for future as-signments, (6) strengths, (7) development needs, (8) next developmental activities, and (9) probable ultimate position or level achievable.

- Development is a combination of (1) structured classroom work; (2) action learning—that is, learning on the job handling real and very substantive issues; (3) coaching and counseling on each person's partic-ular style and deficiencies; (4) periodic leadership-style testing to plot tangible progress and redirect development efforts; (5) education on the company's industry and strategies; and (6) exposure to, and ultimately participation in, top-level policy thinking and resolution.

Where to Find Development Skill Training

Many large companies such as Boeing and General Electric have their own development centers and staff. They put together extensive programs to instruct and evaluate the 150 to 250 top development prospects in the corporate system at any one time. Exhibit 14-5 schematically illustrates GE's Leadership Development Program. Other companies rely on university business schools to construct and deliver a program for them. Still others compile their own programs from the offerings of public sources such as consultants and training companies. Some of the many sources available for leadership training are shown in Exhibit 14-6.

Exhibit 14-5   Leadership Development Courses at General Electric

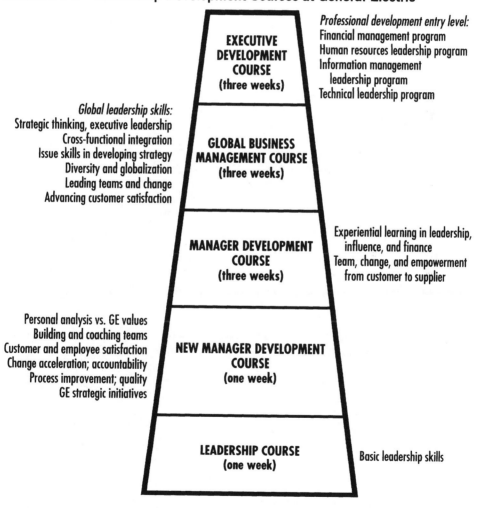

Source: Courtesy of General Electric Corporate Public Relations Department.

Exhibit 14-6   Sources of Leadership Training

FACILITATED PROGRAMS	
Leadership institutes: They offer one-week programs that train in leadership and test for leadership competencies; work on weak areas.	Center for Creative Leadership (CCL), Greensboro, N.C.
Team building: Teams define the competencies they need and those they don't have and develop action plans to fix deficiencies.	Many independent consultants
Coaching, counseling, and mentoring: An internal mentor combines with an external coach to coach the individual confidentially on improving weak skills and using strengths.	External coaches from companies such as WJM Associates (New Yrk City), and CCL
Simulations: These include custom simulations based on your business or generic simulations based on a general business model.	Custom—some independent consultants General business model—CCL
SEMINARS AND CLASSES	
Senior management and leadership courses: Emphasis is on skills needed at the top—vision, planning, people motivation and planning, dealing with the outside world, global economy, business, market and corporate strategy.	Many university courses, such as Harvard's Middle and Advanced Management course and the equivalent at Wharton, Stanford, Darden, and others (2–6 weeks) AMA's Management Course for Presidents (1 week)
Middle management courses: Focus is on planning, control, handling people, execution skills, basic marketing, and strategy.	Various universities and public training institutions
Content courses: These include areas such as sales management, marketing strategy, and programming languages.	Hundreds of vendors, from local universities and technical schools to training institutions such as the AMA, Linkage, and Forum Corporation, which offer a wide variety of public seminars
Change management	Independent consultants and universities
ACTION LEARNING	
High visibility assignments, shadow cabinets or advisory boards, and cross-functional assignments	Structured internally, often with an external consultant's help, advice, and oversight

Blocking Out a Program

Medium-size to small organizations, of course, don't have hundreds of people to assess and develop. Usually, it's a handful, maybe ten to twenty-five. And it is assumed that there are no more than four layers of management: level 1—chief executive officer/chief operating officer and vice presidents of functions (for example, vice president of manufacturing); level 2—major department managers (manager of manufacturing operations); level 3—first-line managers and supervisors (manager of engineering, shift supervisor); and level 4—entry-level personnel, managerial or not. It is also assumed that all senior managers—not just those who are candidates for the top team—would benefit from training in leadership skills. As shown in Exhibit 14-7 and detailed in Exhibit 14-8 and in the following list, there are four general levels of learning, with different objectives:

- *Level 4—company indoctrination and basic management skills:* Teaches new hires and managers the company's vision, management style, values, and core competencies, plus the basic people management framework or functional skills to allow success in an entry-level job. As in all training segments, individual traits and competencies are assessed and a development program prescribed.

- *Level 3—departmental strategy, leadership, and teams:* Teaches departmental planning and strategy, development of a basic leadership framework, and use of teams and teamwork in a cross-functional flat organization.

- *Level 2—corporate strategy and decision making:* Teaches departmental planning and strategy; decision making and control in a multi-functional environment; leadership skills; and any needed functional skills, such as industry and corporate finance.

- *Level 1—top management:* Teaches developing and implementing vision and strategy, planning and implementing change, executing plans in a complex and global environment, and leadership skills at the top.

Although each company must put together the elements that fit its needs and culture, the following pattern is typical and workable for a medium-size to small company:

Level 4 Focus: Entry-Level, First Managerial Assignment Personnel

- Help make the person successful in his or her first job.
- Teach what the company stands for, how to operate in the company, its values, how decisions are made, how work gets done.

(Text continues on page 310.)

Exhibit 14-7   Overview of Leadership Training and Development by Organization Level

Level 1: Top Team

Vision

- Vision
- Strategic alternatives
- Global thinking
- Execution in a complex environment
- Planning and managing change

Level 2: Middle to Top Management

Corporate Management Leadership

- Competitive strategy
- Leadership skills
- Developing people
- Finance
- Corporate decision making
- Vertical, horizontal, and top management relationships

Level 3: Lower to Middle Management

Leading Departments

- Basic leadership skills
- Cross-functional learning
- Teams
- Departmental strategy and planning
- Supervisory and people development skills

Level 4: Entry-Level Management

Initial Management Effectiveness

- Indoctrination into company
- Basic people management skills
- Personal skills—persuasion, motivation
- Functional skills

Exhibit 14-8 Leadership Development Program for a Medium-Size Company

Level	Objectives	Specific Topics
1. Top team or ready for top team (VP)	Vision Strategy Global thinking Execution At least one subject will be addressed through action learning and development. At least one will involve a project requiring foreign visits and negotiations.	• Strategic thinking and decision making • Global business • Leadership at the top • Succession and developing people and the organization • Customer satisfaction and quality • Innovation • Coordination and integration of the organization • Strategic options and ensuring the business's long-term future • Planning and managing continuous change • Personal skill development
2. Middle to upper management (reports to VP)	Mental transition from a lower-level manager to a senior manager Focus on: • Leadership • Developing people • Alignment of departmental with corporate plans	• Intensive leadership institute or training • Change management • Action learning tied to one of the corporate strategic priorities • Process redesign • Finance, accounting, and control • Action program involving intensive field interface with customers, vendors, and the market • Personal skill development • Developing people • 360-degree communications
3. Lower to middle management	Leadership versus management skills Strategy Broad functional exposure	• Action program involving broad internal functional exposure • Assessment of leadership skills and design of appropriate development program • Using teams and teamwork • Strategic planning and change management • Management, supervisory, and people development skills • Department plan

(continued)

Exhibit 14-8 *(continued)*

4. Entry-level management	Indoctrinate into company direction, philosophy and key decision-making methods. Begin development of basic management and leadership skills.	• Corporate plan, mission, vision, business definition, values, strategy • Economics of the company and industry • Team development and facilitation skills • Basic personal skills—persuasion, influencing, negotiation, conflict resolution, and decision making • Business analytical skills • Leadership and supervisory skills • Assessment and appropriate individual developmental plan • Basic managerial skills

- Give a basic framework for supervising people.
- Start the individual competency development process.
   —*Selection:* All entry-level personnel take the course.
   —*Content*: Company indoctrination and first job skills are presented, including:

- Senior officer coverage of corporate direction statement, strategy, and what it means for this managerial level

- Economics of the industry and the company—where and how the money is made

- Analytical and decision-making skills used in the company

- Team development and facilitation skills workshop

- Workshop on basic interpersonal skills: communication; persuasion; handling conflict; decision making; and different interpersonal styles, including testing and interpretation of each attendee's style

- Assessment of personal competencies and style and prescribed development program

- Content training for entry-level track—for example, basic leadership, management, and supervisory skills for lower-level supervisors; sales and sales management skills for sales personnel; marketing strategy for product managers

Level 3 Focus: Lower to Middle Management

- Provide a continuing pool of well-trained and experienced middle managers, some of whom will ultimately be candidates for the senior management team.

- Assess the leadership capabilities of this group.
- Give them extensive grounding in leadership skills, the development of people, and superior execution of plans.
- Give each participant a tailored plan geared to his particular needs for competency development and skill development in functional areas.
- Teach strategy of the organization and developing departmental strategic and operating plans within that context.
    —*Selection:* Participant selection is based on supervisor recommendation, performance reviews, and a 360-degree diagnostic or other instrument to evaluate values, competencies, and decision-making approach. The top team, led by the CEO, selects the final candidates.
    —*Content:* Over a five- to seven-year period, the training content for each individual includes:
- *Assessment, coaching, and counseling:* The 360-degree leadership assessment and Myers-Briggs personality instrument are used to identify leadership issues, with subsequent coaching and counseling. The 360-degree assessment is administered at least every other year.
- *General management/leadership skills.*
- *Introduction to change management.*
- *Content learning:* This is specific to the company's needs and the individual's interests.
- *Strategic exposure:* The individual participates on a cross-functional project team to resolve an important senior-level issue.
- *Functional exposure:* Participants are transferred into other functions, laterally or as a promotion, to get breadth of functional and managerial experience. As a minimum, they are given lengthy participation on a cross-functional team working on a strategic project with very high impact on the organization.
- *Developing people:* This training includes key skills in assessment, giving feedback, coaching and counseling, and forming development plans.

Level 2 Focus: Middle to Upper-Middle Management

- Provide a pool of trained middle managers, some of whom will be candidates for the senior management team while the remainder will provide increased productivity in the upper-middle range.
- Assess each senior manager's individual leadership development needs and devise a program to address them.
- Give a strategic view of the business and an understanding of the organization's strategies. Develop in these individuals a global view of markets, competition, and trends that will affect the business in the future.

- Continue assessment and development of leadership competencies.
  - —*Selection:* The people at level 2 have been selected earlier in their careers and are still considered "on track" by their supervisors and the CEO.
  - —*Content:* Developmental activities over a five- to seven-year period should include:

- *Assessment, coaching, and counseling:* A 360-degree leadership assessment and a Myers-Briggs personality instrument should be administered with counseling.

- *Team building:* This should be done with the individual's management team (direct reports).

- *Simulation:* Individuals should participate in one or more strategic simulations dealing with both internal and external issues.

- *Senior management business and decision-making skills:* Some organizations give all select senior management a broad-based grounding in general management, leadership, and business skills. These courses are particularly useful for a person who has leadership talent but whose experience has been limited to one company and one or two functional areas. The courses are literally a mini-MBA, the depth in each subject dependent on the length of the course. A variety of venues are available, from public companies, public university executive courses, and university courses tailored to each company. Such courses last from four to six weeks to a year.

- *Leadership skills:* Public leadership institutes put attendees through an intensive week of testing and learning about their leadership styles using simulations, test instruments, coaching and counseling, and peer feedback. The coaching continues for approximately six months after the session. Such institutes are very useful if internal testing and counseling are not considered sufficient.

- *Content learning:* This is specific to each individual's needs.

- *Change management process:* This includes how to plan change and execute it.

- *Strategic exposure:* Participants are made part of a shadow cabinet that is frequently asked to evaluate senior management issues for the top team and report to it before the top team makes decisions on the issues.

- *External view:* Participants are provided with action learning requiring intensive interface with external constituencies—customers, vendors, distributors, legislators, the community, shareholders, the financial community, government, and dissident groups.

Level 1: Top Management

- Expose current top managers or candidates to the skills, competencies, and responsibilities unique to the top team, chief operating officer, and chief executive officer positions.

- Provide data and observations that will help members of top management choose their successors.

—*Content:* Developmental activities should include:

- Assuring the survival and prosperity of the corporation—top-level strategic thinking, strategic alternatives, strategic decision making, vision, and development of the organization for the future

- Dealing with global businesses

- Leadership at the top—growing competencies in communication, vision, conceptual thinking, persuasion, motivation, debate, and bias for action

- Innovation

- Planning and managing continuous change

- Firsthand understanding of fundamental market strategies such as customer satisfaction, service, and quality

- Personal skill and competency development, tailored to the individual

---

Do

- Start a leadership development program with the people you have. Assess their strengths and weaknesses and design a program around their development needs and the resources noted in this chapter.
- Hire managers and potential managers who fit your potential-leader profile so you will ultimately meet your leadership needs without additional hiring or suffering significant disruptions in the business.

Don't

- Worry about cost. The cost of a program using publicly available resources is minimal compared with both the immediate benefit of increased efficiency and the ultimate success of the organization.
- Pass the responsibility and accountability for leadership development to your human resources vice president or another staff member. Those individuals can do the staff work, legwork, and paperwork and keep the process on track. But the selection and development of leaders defines the organization's future performance, and that responsibility belongs with the CEO.

Appendix: Training Course Outlines

Strategic Planning Process

▼ Why plan?
▼ Who plans?
▼ Overview of the process and handbook to be used in planning

Situation analysis—external:
  ▼ External trend analysis
  ▼ Market segment and needs analysis
  ▼ Competitive strategy
  ▼ Opportunities and threats

Situation analysis—internal:
  ▼ Core competencies
  ▼ Strengths and weaknesses
  ▼ Financial and other numerical analyses

Setting strategic priority issues

Direction statement:
  ▼ Mission
  ▼ Vision
  ▼ Business definition
  ▼ Values

Strategic objectives

Strategy summary

Action planning

Who does what in the internal process

Departmental Planning Process

▼ How it links with the corporate plan
▼ Why departments are the "big gorilla"

Market analysis:
  ▼ Market identification of both internal and external markets
  ▼ Getting information from external and internal customers
  ▼ Defining how the outside world affects you even if you don't directly interface with it
  ▼ Market segmentation

▼ Defining customer needs; your and your competitor's performance
▼ Selecting target markets and your strategy
▼ Opportunities and threats

Internal analysis:
  ▼ Evaluation of core competencies
  ▼ Numerical analyses
  ▼ Strengths and weaknesses

Priority strategic issues

Business definition:
  ▼ Mission
  ▼ Vision
  ▼ Business definition
  ▼ Values

Strategic and operating objectives

Strategy summary and corporate alignment analysis

Action planning

Change Process Training

▼ Why change is perpetual and accelerating
▼ Pressures for and against change
▼ The changes that we're making here:
  ▼ Business
  ▼ Cultural
▼ The strategic change process
▼ What happens at each stage—organization, leadership, people, tangible accomplishments?
▼ Alignment: How do changes at the top get transmitted throughout the organization?
▼ Emotional responses to change—among board members, skeptics, resisters
▼ Resisters and what to do about them
▼ Keys to changing people's feelings about change
▼ Personally coping with change

▼ Fear and anxiety
▼ Learning new skills
▼ Being a change leader instead of a follower
▼ Counseling and consulting
▼ Communications during the change process
▼ Who "wins" when the organization changes and why?

Facilitation Skills

▼ What is facilitation?
▼ Who facilitates when?
Key information-gathering skills
  ▼ Open discussion
  ▼ Brainstorming
  ▼ Round-robin
  ▼ Storyboarding
Key decision-making skills:
  ▼ Consensus
  ▼ Vote
  ▼ Assent
  ▼ Leader decision
Key analytical skills:
  ▼ Mind mapping
  ▼ Criteria weighing
  ▼ Process flowcharts
  ▼ Fishbone diagrams
  ▼ Gannt charts
  ▼ Pareto analysis
Tips for stand-up facilitators:
  ▼ Your role and participation
  ▼ Methods of recording data
  ▼ Handling difficult participants
  ▼ Handling reluctant or quiet participants
  ▼ Managing pace

Presentation Skills

Types of presentations and where and how to use them effectively:
  ▼ Informal
  ▼ Overhead
  ▼ Computer-generated

▼ Flip charts
▼ Handouts
Preparation and reading the audience:
  ▼ Large groups
  ▼ Small groups
Presentation techniques:
  ▼ Body language
  ▼ Eye contact
  ▼ Movement
  ▼ Gestures
  ▼ Emotions
  ▼ Voice variations
  ▼ Humor
  ▼ Use of objects
  ▼ Dress code and grooming
Feedback:
  ▼ Soliciting
  ▼ Clarifying
  ▼ Answering
  ▼ Confirming
  ▼ Small groups
Handling problem situations:
  ▼ Side noise and conversations
  ▼ Interruptions
  ▼ Argumentative people

Team Development and Management

▼ Why teams?
▼ What do teams do?
▼ Who should be on them?
▼ Top team's role
▼ Sponsor's role
▼ Characteristics of effective teams
▼ Stages of team development
▼ Team leadership and membership criteria
▼ Dual reporting relationships
▼ Communication and persuasion skills
▼ Effective personal behaviors for team members
▼ Typical conflicts and problems on teams
▼ Handling conflicts constructively
▼ Running effective team meetings

▼ Writing the team charter
▼ Handling paperwork and follow-up
  efficiently
▼ Processing meetings
▼ Filling out the team scorecard

Analytical Tools and Techniques

Quality control techniques:
  ▼ Data tables
  ▼ Process flowcharts
  ▼ Fishbone diagrams (cause and
    effect)
  ▼ Gannt charts
  ▼ Pareto analysis
  ▼ Scatter diagrams
  ▼ Control charts
Creativity techniques:
  ▼ Mind mapping
  ▼ Brainstorming
  ▼ Lateral thinking: De Bono's six
    hats
  ▼ Debate
Analytical techniques:
  ▼ Delphi (scenario) generations
  ▼ Criteria weighting
  ▼ Activity-based costing
  ▼ Benchmarking
  ▼ Portfolio analysis
  ▼ Value chain analysis
  ▼ Measurement of customer need
    and competitive positioning
  ▼ Customer satisfaction measure-
    ment
  ▼ Internal satisfaction measure-
    ment
  ▼ Product/customer/market/ dis-
    tribution profit measurement
Decision-making tools:
  ▼ Vote
  ▼ Consensus

Project Management

▼ What is project management?
▼ When do you use it?

▼ Cross-functional teams versus per-
  manent projects
▼ Project life cycles
▼ Project organization staffing—team
  leader and team members
▼ Project planning and tracking
▼ Project planning and control tech-
  niques:
  ▼ Scheduling and tracking
  ▼ Resource estimating
  ▼ Gannt charts
  ▼ Bar charts
  ▼ Flowcharts
  ▼ Logic diagrams
  ▼ Risk analysis
  ▼ Monte Carlo techniques
  ▼ Alternative outcome analysis
    scenarios
▼ Project financial and cost analysis
▼ Reporting

Process Reengineering Training

Principles:
  ▼ The strategic plan and core
    processes
  ▼ What is a process?
  ▼ The architecture of a business
    process
Evaluating a process:
  ▼ General process model
  ▼ Process versus functional ver-
    sus customer versus supplier
    orientation
  ▼ How to identify processes
  ▼ Defining and understanding the
    process
  ▼ Establishing the process flow
    and organization involvement
  ▼ Mapping a process
  ▼ Characteristics of a good
    process
  ▼ Measurable properties of a
    process
  ▼ Criteria for redesign prospects
  ▼ Identifying customer require-
    ments
  ▼ Value-added activities

Methodology
1　Preparation
2　Understanding
3　Direction
4　Technical redesign
5　Organization redesign
6　Implementation
7　Review

Key 15

Fix Broken Core Processes

Principle: Core processes are the most important work of the organization—producing the goods and services that meet customer needs and determining how well those needs are met.

Why it's important: The health and competitiveness of your core processes determine the extent to which customer needs are met and therefore your competitive advantage.

How it's applied: Teams redesign core processes to meet future customer needs better, produce higher-quality and lower-cost goods or services, and build in a mechanism for continuous improvement to keep the processes ahead of the competition.

Expected results: Superior long-term market position, happier customers, and higher profitability.

Process Reengineering

What Is a Core Process?

Every company has lots of processes—sequences of definable, repeatable activities that have measurable inputs and predictable, measurable outputs. Core processes, however, are the arteries of your strategy. They deliver the superior goods and services that give you a competitive advantage. They provide the cost structure that makes you profitable. If you are going to win in the marketplace, your core processes—such as new-product development, customer service, or information systems— must not only yield outputs faster and cheaper than your competition but those outputs must perform better and be of higher quality than those of your competition. By reengineering or fine-tuning your core processes, you should be able to improve market position and profitability significantly. Once reengineered, core processes must be continually improved to keep your performance ahead of the competition.

Your critical success factors in the market, including customer needs, usually drive your core processes. Rolex's critical success factors—distribution limited to expensive jewelry stores, maintenance of high prices, and image—require the company to have top-notch internal marketing processes. Hewlett-Packard's critical success factors in the printer market—technical performance, first to market, and price—mean that the company's new-product development process, marketing system, and manufacturing processes must be superior to those of the competition. Exhibit 15-1 lists the typical core processes, and Exhibit 15-2 shows the core processes for a not-for-profit organization.

Ask your people: Which departments and processes are not producing the highest value for the customer and value added for the company? Ask the customer: Where are we not meeting your needs? Where are we not consistently beating the competition's performance? Which of our departments, actions, and interfaces are not up to par?

The process value chain, pictured in Exhibit 15-3, is a good analytical tool to use during strategic planning to translate market dictates into internal processes that must be examined and may need work. This particular value chain represents a $20 million manufacturer of multiwall paper bags for the food industry. This company found that it was, at best, marginal in meeting many customer needs. Its inefficient core processes, particularly in manufacturing, not only caused ill will among some customers but were extremely costly to the company.

Although we pay most of our attention to core processes that have direct customer impact, there are customer-invisible processes—those the customer doesn't see—that are also extremely important to a company's profitability and internal efficiency. Such processes may include the purchasing and testing of procured inputs, certification and management of vendors, the order-payables/receivables cycle, even management development. These processes can drastically affect costs, quality, and the future of the company. Eventually, a company has to deal with them as well as the processes that affect customers directly.

In the 1980s and early 1990s, many people believed that reengineer-

Exhibit 15-1   Typical Core Processes

▼ Customer service and fulfillment
▼ Service or manufacturing delivery systems
▼ Strategic human resources development
▼ Information systems
▼ Fund-raising
▼ New-product and -service development
▼ Acquisitions, joint ventures, and mergers
▼ Marketing and sales
▼ Product and service distribution

Exhibit 15-2   Core Business Processes for a Not-for-Profit Organization

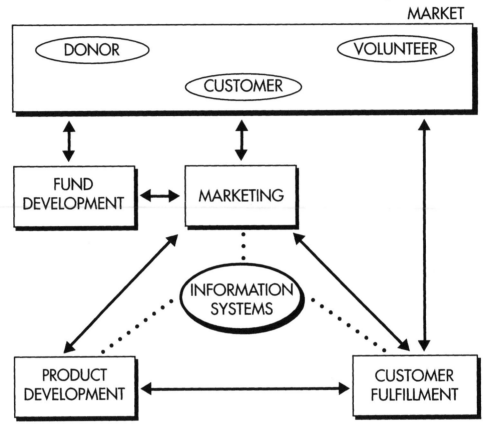

Exhibit 15-3   Process Value Chain

CUSTOMER NEEDS	CRITICAL SUCCESS FACTORS	CORE PROCESSES SERVING MARKET NEEDS	INTERNAL PROCESSES NEEDED TO MEET PROFIT GOALS
Low price	Price	Manufacturing operations	Purchasing
Exceptional quality	Delivery	Manufacturing scheduling	Vendor contributions
Rapid delivery	Quality	Order entry and customer service	
Unpredictable orders	Responsive customer service	Design and color separations	

ing was the new cure-all for ailing companies. In reality, process engineering has been around since Frederick Taylor, who, at the turn of the century, invented industrial engineering, the science of improving the efficiency of machines, people, and processes through time-and-motion studies. Industrial engineering passed through the subsequent phase of "quality processes" and evolved into reengineering, all with the intent of improving efficiency. Each metamorphosis has improved process-engineering technology; each has taken the customer more into account. The point, however, is that process reengineering is not a fad. It is one of many very effective management tools when used appropriately and not as a religious crusade.

The Role of Core Processes in Strategic Change

Because core processes are key to the organization's competitive advantage and productive ability, a high proportion of lasting change requires their redesign. During the strategic planning process, the need to change core processes is usually expressed in priority issues. In our experience, about 50 percent of all priority issues in early strategic plans address problems with core processes. Unlike one-shot fixes such as developing a single new product line or letting a large number of unproductive businesses or people go, successful core-process changes are systemic fixes that go on delivering heightened efficiency and competitive advantage day in and day out, year in and year out. Eventually, they drop off the priority issue list and become ongoing, run by a functional department or a process team. Over the years, other processes take their place on the priority issue list.

New or redesigned core processes change the way each functional area goes about its job while linking the various areas into an interdependent, measurable process. Most processes are cross-functional and cross-level, touching many parts of the organization. Because of this, reengineering must be embraced by the top team and managed by a team of your best people from a variety of functions. These team members will take back to their functional areas a mentality of process thinking and continuous improvement, which should take root and spread throughout the departments. Exhibit 15-4 shows how processes and functional areas are conceptually linked.

Is Process Reengineering Worth the Trouble It Takes?

Reengineering core processes can have immense impact on your business.

Sometimes, companies that are in serious trouble can completely

Exhibit 15-4   Process vs. Functional Area Orientation

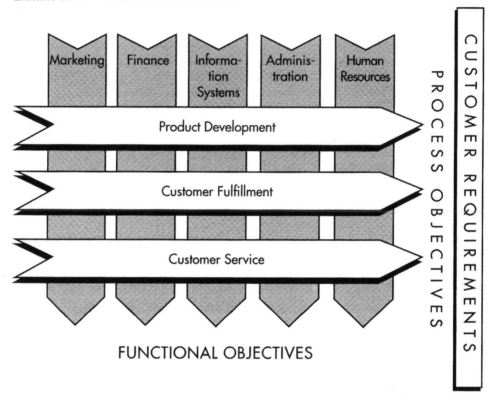

FUNCTIONAL OBJECTIVES

alter their direction by fixing broken core processes. Some benefits of process redesign are shown in Exhibit 15-5.

The paper-bag company mentioned earlier in the chapter reduced its manufacturing costs by more than one-third through process redesign, simultaneously raising its product quality. The quality improvements helped the company keep its key customers; the cost improvements brought it from the red into the black.

Exhibit 15-5   Benefits of Process Redesign

▼ Significant profit improvement
▼ Gains in market share through increased competitive advantages in product, distribution, marketing, and sales
▼ Improved customer satisfaction
▼ Improvements in internal process thinking, teamwork, and cross-functional learning and appreciation
▼ Increases in the internal sense of control, morale, and worth
▼ Measurable improvements in meeting market needs and exceeding compeptitive benchmarks
▼ Reductions in unneeded staff and increases in productivity

Wal-Mart's reengineering of its product distribution system is a much-publicized classic. Prior to reengineering, Wal-Mart, like many retailers, had merchandise delivered to regional warehouses, then redistributed to stores. Now Wal-Mart orders the bulk of its goods electronically and has each order delivered directly from the vendor to a Wal-Mart store, where it is electronically received and matched up with the purchase order. The vendor is paid electronically, then and there.

This new process has saved Wal-Mart millions of dollars in inventory costs, reduced the loss of sales due to out-of-stocks, and eliminated jobs that used to be needed to process receivables and payables. The vendors like the new process for similar reasons. It ties them more closely to Wal-Mart, helps them plan their production, and reduces both inventories and payable and receivable accounting costs. And customers are happier because the items they want are on the store shelves. All this results in a tremendous competitive advantage for Wal-Mart over its struggling competitors. From a cost and technology point of view, there was nothing preventing Kmart and Sears from installing such a process before Wal-Mart. They just didn't do it.

Why Process Reengineering Sometimes Fails

During the reengineering craze of the 1980s and early 1990s, a number of companies spent a lot of time and money reworking their core processes with little result. The reasons their reengineering efforts failed provide cautionary lessons for any company planning to use the redesign process to gain a competitive advantage. From the annals of failed efforts, here are several lists of contributing factors:

Top Management Failures

- The company wasn't committed to the project or didn't provide enough support from the top.
- The company was impatient. Reengineering takes time. Because working with teams can be time-consuming, some companies tried to move faster by making process redesign the responsibility of a single functional area. That was a mistake.
- The company lacked focus and tried to reengineer everything in sight rather than sticking to the core processes that were most important in the marketplace.
- The company lacked a sustained sense of urgency. The sense of importance and urgency has to be maintained over a considerable period of time—often, two to three years.
- The top team and sponsors did not properly manage the process.

Either they didn't consider the process important or they didn't put enough effort into learning how to manage it.

- Top management failed to offer a special incentive system for the teams. Significant monetary or psychological rewards are needed to motivate team members.
- The company suffered from cultural resistance, which the project leaders and top team failed to address. Process redesign is a change process, and there will be resistance. It has to be removed.

Redesign Team Failures

- The redesign team got buried in details, ignored the rest of the world, bogged down in trivia, and took too much time to make even minor decisions. Management, frustrated by a lack of results, killed the project rather than fixing the problem.
- The redesign team lacked good team and functional skills and was dysfunctional as a result.
- The redesign team focused narrowly on itself and the process, forgetting that the scope of the project should be broad, including both internal and external customers.
- The redesign team failed to define and quantify the desired outcome and stay focused on it.

Management Failures

- Functional managers who didn't buy into the project undermined it by pulling people away from the redesign team and forcing them to attend to departmental goals.
- Management assigned inadequate human resources to the project.
- Management failed to bring in outside help when needed. Although some large companies have the capability to go it alone, most need to bring in experts who are experienced in laying out processes and forming teams.
- Management did not publicize the "quick" wins to maintain momentum. When a process, however minor a part of the overall scheme, is fixed, management should spread the news throughout the company to reassure people that they are on the right track and are appreciated. Nothing succeeds like success.
- The redesign teams received inadequate training and support.

The Redesign Process

There are dozens of books that deal solely with process reengineering, some from a philosophical point of view, others providing the most detailed how-tos.[1] Although there are many processes, known by different labels and buzzwords, the good ones are fundamentally the same. They follow the broad outline of the typical process design project shown in Exhibit 15-6.

In its simplest terms, redesign requires the project team to tear apart a broken process and improve it or construct a new one that will meet goals defined by external performance measures. The steps in the process are preparation, understanding, direction, technical redesign, people redesign, implementation, and review. The complete process redesign is shown in Exhibit 15-7.

Defining Your Core Processes

Defining your core processes and identifying those requiring attention usually takes place during the internal and external analyses conducted the before strategic plan's priority-setting meeting. A customer survey will point out customers' wants, needs, and expectations. How well or how poorly have you been meeting these expectations? How well does the competition meet them? One way to plot this is by an importance/performance matrix, which is covered in *Team-Based Strategic Planning*.[2] This simple tool uses market research to rank the importance of customer needs and then rates your performance and that of your competitors against those needs. From this, you can see where your competitive strengths and weaknesses lie and trace back the processes that produced them. An internal audit of your strengths and weaknesses will turn up internal opinion on what needs fixing. Prior to (or during) the priority-setting meeting, you should:

1. Pinpoint your competitive advantages and trace the value chain throughout the company that supports them.
2. Identify your competitive weaknesses and the processes that are letting you down.
3. Identify the processes, such as leadership development, critical to the organization's success but transparent to the customer.
4. List your high-impact processes, the customer or internal needs that they address, the cost and potential gain of developing each,

---

[1] See Michael Hammer and James Champy, *Reengineering the Corporation* (New York: HarperCollins, 1993), which provides a broad philosophical look at reengineering and its guiding principles, with many interesting examples. Also see Dorine C. Andrews and Susan K. Stalick, *Business Reengineering: The Survival Guide* (Yourdon Press, 1994), a moderate-tech how-to-do-it guide that emphasizes the team and management aspects of reengineering.

[2] See C. Davis Fogg, *Team-Based Strategic Planning* (New York: AMACOM, 1994), pp. 105–106.

(Text continues on page 329.)

Exhibit 15-6   Seven Stages of Business Process Redesign

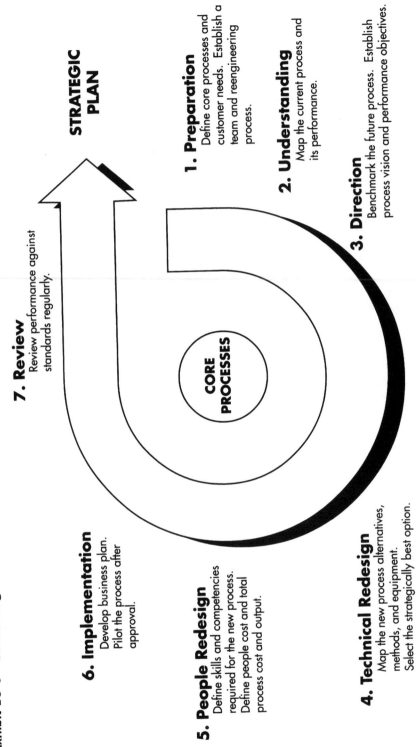

STRATEGIC PLAN

1. Preparation
Define core processes and customer needs. Establish a team and reengineering process.

2. Understanding
Map the current process and its performance.

3. Direction
Benchmark the future process. Establish process vision and performance objectives.

4. Technical Redesign
Map the new process alternatives, methods, and equipment. Select the strategically best option.

5. People Redesign
Define skills and competencies required for the new process. Define people cost and total process cost and output.

6. Implementation
Develop business plan. Pilot the process after approval.

7. Review
Review performance against standards regularly.

CORE PROCESSES

Exhibit 15-7   Core-Process Redesign

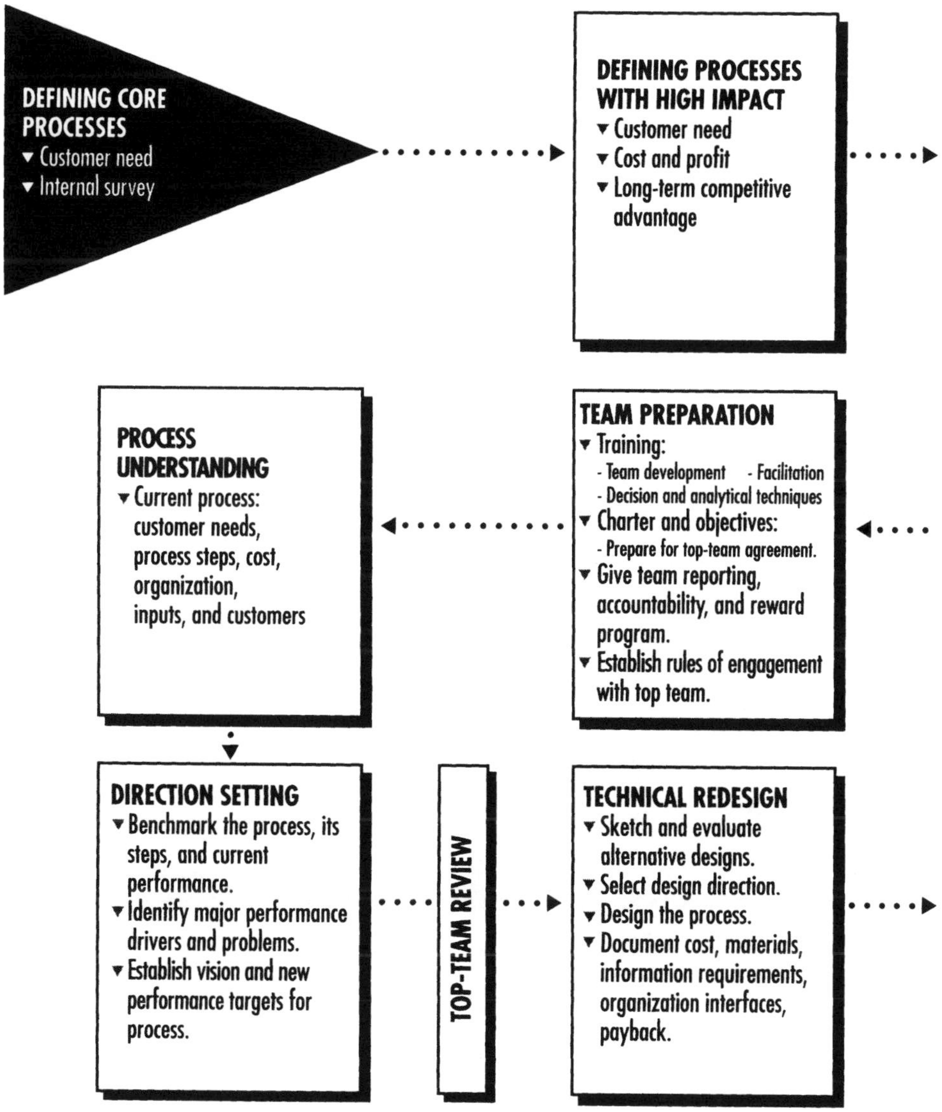

DEFINING CORE PROCESSES
▾ Customer need
▾ Internal survey

DEFINING PROCESSES WITH HIGH IMPACT
▾ Customer need
▾ Cost and profit
▾ Long-term competitive advantage

PROCESS UNDERSTANDING
▾ Current process: customer needs, process steps, cost, organization, inputs, and customers

TEAM PREPARATION
▾ Training:
  - Team development   - Facilitation
  - Decision and analytical techniques
▾ Charter and objectives:
  - Prepare for top-team agreement.
▾ Give team reporting, accountability, and reward program.
▾ Establish rules of engagement with top team.

DIRECTION SETTING
▾ Benchmark the process, its steps, and current performance.
▾ Identify major performance drivers and problems.
▾ Establish vision and new performance targets for process.

TOP-TEAM REVIEW

TECHNICAL REDESIGN
▾ Sketch and evaluate alternative designs.
▾ Select design direction.
▾ Design the process.
▾ Document cost, materials, information requirements, organization interfaces, payback.

(continued)

Exhibit 15-7 (*continued*)

STRATEGIC PLANNING PRIORITY ISSUES MEETING
▼ Make case for each process.
▼ Choose core processes for action.

ESTABLISHING TEAM FOR EACH PROCESS ISSUE
▼ Leader
▼ Team
▼ Sponsor

PROCESS SELECTION
▼ Get experts in reengineering, facilitation.
▼ Agree on process to be used.

RESOURCE ALLOCATION MEETING
▼ Make final project selections.
▼ Give teams resources, funding, human resources needed.

PEOPLE REDESIGN
▼ Process organization chart
▼ Skill, competency, and training needs
▼ Accountabilities, incentives, rewards, and career paths
▼ Management, supervision, and control

COMPLETING THE PLAN
▼ Complete business plan.
▼ Estimate final cost, timing, and payback.
▼ Prepare pilot-test program plan.
▼ Prepare full-scale implementation plan and determine timing.

TOP-TEAM REVIEW

IMPLEMENTATION
▼ Make adjustments in full-scale process.
▼ Roll out new process.

TOP-TEAM REVIEW

IMPLEMENTATION
▼ Select and train for pilot.
▼ Run pilot.
▼ Evaluate results.

and those that will give you the best long-term competitive advantage.

5. Decide on those that need immediate work to enable you to meet your strategic five- to seven-year objectives.

Priority-Setting Meeting and Establishing Teams

During your priority-setting meeting, you will review the core processes along with all of the other strategic issues that must be addressed. For each process you choose as a priority issue, you'll need to appoint a team leader, some team members, and a team sponsor from the top team. Their charge is to develop an action plan for the priority issue core process for presentation at the resource allocation meeting. For preparing action plans, see the Key 2 chapter; for resource allocation, the Key 11 chapter.

Resource Allocation Meeting

At the resource allocation meeting, the top team allocates people and money to corporate priority issue programs that pass muster for financial return and strategic importance, including the reengineering processes that make the cut.

It's imperative that the top team fully buy into the reengineering program at this point. Members of the top team and other senior functional managers will need to put in considerable time reviewing progress and dealing with redesign issues.

Selecting the Reengineering Process

If you don't have all the process-reengineering skills needed inside the organization, go outside. You'll need a reengineering expert to help design the reengineering process that will be used, train the teams, and guide them through the process as it progresses. A professional team facilitator to teach team management and help the teams when needed can also make a big difference to a redesign project. The two experts should also train team sponsors and top management in team and reengineering processes.

The reengineering program team develops process options with the help of the reengineering expert and selects the process to be used. The team develops a plan and timetable to manage it and determines and communicates the results expected in the first year. Make sure that everyone in the company knows what the redesign process is, how long it takes, and what team members will be doing. The teams will need the help of many. Unless your communication program constantly stresses the importance of their work and helps people understand what the teams are doing, it will take far longer and be far more frustrating for the teams to accomplish their task.

Determining How the Project Team and Top Team Will Work Together

Each project team and the top team need to:

1. Agree on the project team's charter and long- and short-term objectives.
2. Set a schedule for reviews and determine their content.
3. Provide a way for the project team to have immediate access to the top team when important decisions must be made.
4. Assign a sponsor for the team. (See the Key 9 chapter.)

Understanding the Existing Process

The project team is completely in charge. You're under way—hopefully, with good preparation and expert help.

The core process you are redesigning is undoubtedly made up of several parts. It is important to identify the current subprocesses, regardless of where they are carried out in the organization. You need to know how the various subprocesses relate to each other and how information and resources flow from one to another.

Before proceeding to map out a direction for the redesign project, be sure you have a clear understanding of the current process's organization, resources, use of information technology, level of performance, and strengths and weaknesses. Your understanding must be based on market-driven demands and internal efficiency needs.

Mapping out a Direction

Benchmark the major performance indicators for the process overall and its various components against the best processes in your industry and the best processes in the business world as a whole. Benchmarking allows you to identify major weaknesses and the key activities that are the true performance drivers. Some major performance drivers in the mail-order software business, for example, are the quality, courtesy, and efficiency of people taking phone orders and their speed in getting the orders from their computer terminals into the hands of shippers.

Define the vision and new performance targets for the process. For a mail-order software business, the vision for its customer fulfillment process might be: "To be the acknowledged leader in customer satisfaction in nontraditional retail. To set our customers' expectations by constantly raising our performance and the ease of doing business with us, thereby increasing their satisfaction and raising the barrier for competition.''

The new performance targets for the next three years might be as follows:

- Orders placed as late as 11:00 P.M. will arrive by 10:00 A.M. the next day.
- Cost per order—including telephone, computer interface, entry, packing, shipping, inventory cost, credit-card charges, and direct systems operation charges—will decrease 10 percent per year for at least three years.
- The customer will get a live person on the line within three rings.
- Transfers to technical service will involve no more than a one-minute wait. The hit ratio in solving the customer's problem on the spot will be 100 percent on A items, 90 percent on B items, and 75 percent on C items.
- Replacements and adjustments will be in the customer's hands by 10:00 the morning after notification.
- There will be no out-of-stocks on A items, one per hundred on B items, and two per hundred on C items.
- Customer ratings of friendliness, product knowledge, and technical service will increase from 92 to 96.

Technical Redesign

Flowchart new technical design concepts and alternatives for the process. For example, for an order fulfillment process, what type of call-routing system options are there? What type of operator stations are most effective? What information system, display of catalog information, and order-entry format make sense? What are the options for voice recognition and imaging as opposed to ''live people''? How will calls be transferred to technicians, for instance? How will the order be transmitted to a warehouse? Where should the physical goods be—in our warehouse, at the manufacturers? What will be the physical and paperwork trail for finding, picking, packing, labeling, shipping, and billing for an order?

You must then decide whether the redesign will simply improve what you have, radically alter it, or start over from scratch. It's always a good idea to define and evaluate several alternatives before picking the concept that you will design in detail.

Flowchart the process from beginning to end. For each step, what outputs and inputs are required? How will you configure functional departments or groups that will be responsible for implementing each part of the process? Define the money, technologies, equipment, physical facilities, and information systems needed to carry out each step efficiently. At the same time, determine what performance measures you will use to judge the efficiency of the overall process and that of each step. Develop a preliminary plan and timeline for technical implementation.

People Redesign

Do a complete people redesign for the process (though, in reality, this step can be accomplished in parallel with the technical redesign step). How many people are required for each part of the process? What skills must they have? How will they be supervised? Will a continuing multi-functional team oversee the entire process and its results?

Define the organization's skill, knowledge, and competency needs. Define the management structure and the system and organizational changes required.

Prepare job descriptions, pay scales, and training programs for the new process and people.

Implementation

Complete a business plan for the process, including a vision, expected financial benefit and cost, overall process design, staffing requirements, systems needs, managerial structure, and other resources required. Include a plan to test the new process before rolling it out.

After the business plan is approved, acquire the equipment, people, and systems needed to implement the process. Select and train personnel for the new process and evaluate their competencies.

Pilot the new process in a limited area. Track the process, evaluate its success, and modify it as necessary. You are now ready to implement the new process fully. Remember, though, you will need to improve the process continually through a cross-functional team.

Review

The top team reviews each step as it is completed or during a regular quarterly review before allowing the project team to proceed to the next stage of implementation. When the new process is up and running and meeting its objectives, the top team can take a hands-off approach and let a cross-functional team or designated functional area be responsible for the process. The process results are regularly reported to the top team so that intervention can take place if benchmark standards are breached.

Top Team's Roles in Process Redesign

The top team's roles in process reengineering are as follows:

- Sets direction—which processes will be reengineered, why, and the output expected from each process.
- Picks the teams and team leader.
- Educates itself sufficiently about teams and the redesign process to give teams "hands-on" help with problems.
- Approves the business plan and the budget.
- Holds regular reviews, at least quarterly.
- Is available to make key decisions within forty-eight hours if requested by a team.
- Provides counsel and support.
- Provides resources, including people, money, and approval of effort from functional departments.
- Arbitrates disputes over use of resources and departmental people and time.
- Replaces or supplements team members as needed.
- Provides recognition and financial rewards to successful teams.
- Serves as an emotional cheerleader for the program teams.

Critical Components of Successful Redesign Projects

The following are the most important components of a redesign project:

- A top-notch expert in reengineering
- A tight definition of the charter (mission, vision, end objectives, and timetable of each project) agreed on by the process team and the top team
- Teams with the right balance of team, personal, and functional skills
- Team leaders with leadership and functional skills
- Extensive training for the teams, managers of team members, top management team, and internal customers and functional areas involved in supporting the teams in the following areas:
  —Process redesign—the system to be used, what it is, who does what when to make it work

    —Team principles, team development, team management, and facilitation skills

    —Project management (possibly including scheduling and project management software if the process is complicated)

    —Presentation skills so that teams can present the projects effectively using presentation software

- A team process facilitator early in the project to get the teams started and ensure that they understand how to facilitate and later to help with the inevitable glitches
- Money and time ensured by the top team
- Involved departmental managers who will support, not fight, the team process
- A top team and chief executive officer/chief operating officer who fully support the program

---

Do

- Look at the products and services you deliver to the marketplace and determine the performance that will be dictated by the market in the future. Then determine whether your current delivery processes are capable of meeting future needs.
- Manage core-process redesign from the top. It's one of your most important change levers.
- Insist on measurable outputs and internal step-by-step process measures that are benchmarked against market demand and best of type.

Don't

- Give up or get frustrated after a brief period of time. Most important processes are complicated and take time to be reengineered to a higher level of performance.

Key 16

Communicate to Everyone, All the Time

Principle: Good communication improves both understanding of the plan and morale, and it influences behavior to align work with the plan, thereby contributing to the achievement of strategic results.

Why it's important: You need to get employees on your side. In a period of change, people are anxious and restless, and 50 percent are skeptical about the plan. If their concerns aren't answered, their anxiety and cynicism will hurt productivity, undermine commitment, and discourage others.

How it's applied: Using every available medium—personal, print, and electronic communications—the CEO spearheads a campaign to reinforce strategic priorities, tell people what's going to occur and why, and how it will affect them personally. The organization orchestrates both formal and informal opportunities for employees to share their concerns, good ideas, and feedback as the process unfolds.

Expected results: Increased employee productivity and cooperation, and alignment of employees' work with the company's change objectives.

Communication and the Strategic Change Process

For a moment, imagine yourself an employee of a company such as IBM, Sears, Apple, General Motors, or Kodak when it was on the brink of devastating upheaval: facing thousands of layoffs, the sale of businesses, the elimination of product lines, and plant closures. Besides shock and larceny, what is in the hearts and heads of employees, top to bottom, facing radical strategic change?

One bank executive, known for his superior turnaround skills and superb planning, used a survey to identify attitudes and barriers to progress when he took over a struggling bank. The survey revealed (1) a general lack of trust in top management and (2) the strong opinion that management didn't know where the company was going (which, for the prior management, was true).

The new bank president recognized that, to gain employees' respect and earn their best efforts, he would have to show them that he did, indeed, know where they were going and that his plans made competitive sense.

Why should employees, nervous about the future, trust top management? By their reckoning, it was top management that got them into trouble. If you could probe the innermost thoughts of your employees at the beginning of your change effort, you'd uncover questions like:

- What's going to happen to the company? What will be different this time?
- What's going to happen to me? I'm not very employable at 50.
- How am I going to pay the tuition bills and make the mortgage and car payments if I'm on the hit list?
- Do the "dummies" upstairs have the stuff to pull this off?
- If I'm still here, what am I going to be doing?
- What's in it for me if I do bust my butt over yet *another* transformation?
- Will there be much change after the first pass? More layoffs? More reassignments?

Those questions aren't confined to companies facing threats to their very existence. Companies that continually clean up their businesses don't have to suffer decade-long disruptions as General Motors and Kodak have done. But even the best-run companies experience periodic upheavals. In fact, the smartest ones do it more frequently but on a lesser scale and under control, responding early to market forces. Thus, we've seen General Electric divest its television business; Hewlett-Packard move into brand-new markets such as laser printers, scientific (not consumer!) calculators, and mini- and microcomputers; Emerson Electric move cost-threatened operations offshore; and Corning divest its huge medical products division and consumer products business.

Whether the change you are confronting is drastic or incremental, the people affected will have questions and concerns. To earn their support, you'll need to respond to these with direct, truthful communication.

They'll also have knowledge you need of what's happening at the front lines, what's working well and what needs fixing, and ideas on how to improve. Never underestimate the sophistication and awareness of even the lowest-level employees. Companies often pay consultants good money to tell them what employees knew all along. After a leading meatpacking company watched its market share plummet over a period of years, senior management hired a consultant to find out why. Through market research, the consultant uncovered the startling news that customer service and product innovation had become sporadic, unpredictable, and sloppy, falling way behind the competition. A simultaneous internal survey showed that lower-level employees were well aware of the problem. Top management hadn't known and hadn't asked.

What to Tell Them: Advice From an Expert

Roger D'Aprix piloted Xerox's communication program during the turbulent time when the Japanese first came ashore and entrenched themselves on Xerox's beach. He insists that good strategic communication focuses on the marketplace. It's the marketplace—products, customers, the competition, international trade and regulation—that propels change and causes pain. The marketplace is the bad guy if you're in trouble, the good guy if you find a way to perform better. Your strategic planning effort started by analyzing the marketplace and developing your response to it. What you communicate, he maintains, should have the same external focus. The following guidelines are based on his principles for market-based strategic communication:

1. *Communicate the case for change.* Explain why it's happening.
2. *Focus on market forces.* Clearly identify and communicate the market forces that the organization faces in doing business. Capture the plight of the organization to rationalize its behaviors.
3. *Develop a plan.* Formulate and communicate a responsive business plan so that frustrated people in the trenches know that the leaders grasp the problem and are moving to fix it.
4. *State consequences.* Outline the consequences of success or failure in terms your audience can identify with.
5. *Communicate frequently.* Tell the story; retell it often; and share breaking news fast.
6. *Explain people's expected role.* Tell what you expect them to do differently to help you execute the plan.

The Target Audience

The message needs to permeate the organization, but for logistical reasons, it's helpful to think of two audiences:

1. *Those who will lead the campaign:* A relatively small number of leverage leaders, managers, staff, and team leaders will lead the cam-

paign to make the strategic plan succeed. These are the people with whom the top team will interact personally and often. They, by and large, support the plan.

2. *The rest of the employees:* You'll enhance your credibility and their understanding by reaching out to the troops directly, particularly the skeptical 50 percent whom you must convert to your side. If you've done your job right with the leverage leaders, they'll become your prime conduit to the front line, serving as communicators, correspondents, and motivators during the change process.

Hallmarks of Communication

Here is where the top leadership traits—ability to communicate, persuade, motivate, and engender trust; a bias for action; and passion—enter into the picture. To support your strategic change, your communication program needs to accomplish these things:

1. *Communicate the strategic plan.* Describe the outside marketplace, where you're headed in it, the case for change, the cost of failure, the strategic priority issues, and who is primarily responsible for each.

2. *Influence achievement of needed changes as quickly as possible.* In particular, you'll need to push for the "quick wins" that demonstrate progress in the early stages of plan execution.

3. *Keep strategic priorities up front.* Keep the strategic priority issues, and why they're important, constantly in front of everyone. Tell people what they are—for example, an improvement in customer service, important because it is a high-order need and our top two competitors do a better job, which is costing us market share. Tell them what this means from the top of the company (investment in new inventory systems and electronic data interface with vendors) to the bottom (faster systems for people taking orders, increased friendliness, empowering people to go out of their way to do special things for the customer).

4. *Build and maintain a sense of high urgency.* Keep up the pressure relentlessly at all levels, constantly reminding people where you expect them to be next month, next quarter, next year; what will happen if they don't meet objectives and what the benefits will be if they do. Without urgency, there will be no change.

5. *Show your enthusiasm for the plan.* Upper management's enthusiastic endorsement of the plan inspires people to get on board.

6. *Sell the benefits.* Tell what plan accomplishment will do for employees, stockholders, and the community—the good that will be done and the bad that will be prevented.

7. *Communicate at the point of believable action.* Although top management gives the overall framework of the plan, supervisors communicate the specifics of the work to the employees who perform it. Departments are the real hubs of communication. Eighty percent of your communication effort should focus here. Employees take their cues from what they hear, face to face, from people they trust. If you've picked carefully, you have such people in leadership positions. It's their job to translate the big picture and objectives into action at the departmental level, where most of your monetary, physical, and human assets are concentrated.

8. *Communicate in a framework employees understand.* Employ words, logic, and concepts that they can use to figure out what they can do to turn the situation to their advantage. This means focusing on how jobs will change, the learning required, job security, empowerment, cross-training, and financial benefits.

9. *Maintain a constant two-way information exchange.* Information must flow between top management and those executing critical programs and objectives such as priority issue action-planning teams and leverage managers. Some of the information that needs to be exchanged is shown in Exhibit 16-1.

10. *Widely and frequently praise significant accomplishments and those responsible for them.* Give credit generously and often, no matter where the accomplishments take place.

11. *Own up to your failures, focusing on lessons learned.* You will gain credibility by being honest when you stumble, and you'll get better results next time.

Later in the chapter, we'll look at how the emphasis on each of these requirements varies depending on whether a company is facing a life-or-death situation, experiencing stable growth, or undergoing an entrepreneurial surge. We'll also see how the focus shifts during the four phases of strategic change: recognition, muddling, tangible strategic results, and continuous change.

But first, to communicate effectively, you need the right tools. The following section presents an overview of those at your disposal.

Communication Tools

To broadcast your message and listen to feedback, pick from the tools summarized in Exhibit 16-2 and detailed in this section. You may get some ideas for using these tools from Exhibit 16-3, a typical calendar of communication events for a strategic plan during the first year.

Exhibit 16-1   Information Exchanged in Strategic Communication

DOWN AND ACROSS THE ORGANIZATION

- ▼ Direction: mission/vision/values
- ▼ Focus: strategic objectives and strategic priorities
- ▼ Market conditions, our place in the market, and our outlook
- ▼ How we are performing versus the competition
- ▼ Performance versus plan objectives and priority programs
- ▼ How each functional area and level is doing its part to realize plan objectives
- ▼ Critical problems with execution inside or outside the company
- ▼ Employee's place in the plan
- ▼ Feedback on what's working and what's not
- ▼ Heroes, big accomplishments
- ▼ Small wins and gains along the way to the finish line
- ▼ Failures—why, and what was learned from them

INFORMATION FROM LEVERAGE PEOPLE UP TO THE TOP

An early-warning pipeline:
- ▼ What we see in the marketplace and the effectiveness of our efforts there
- ▼ What we really think of the change effort—what's working and what's not
- ▼ New ideas on how to address strategic priorities
- ▼ What we could do better and how; how we could fix what's not working
- ▼ People, functional areas, or policy barriers standing in the way of progress

OTHER IMPORTANT INFORMATION

From employees, focus groups, surveys, and leverage management:
- ▼ Employee satisfaction with what is being accomplished
- ▼ Employee morale
- ▼ Level and effectiveness of work at lower levels and the extent to which it is aligned with the plan
- ▼ What employees think of company, management, and supervision's handling of the plan and change process
- ▼ Confidence in the organization's ability to pull it off
- ▼ Level of resistance and cynicism at lower levels; proportion of employees in the "resister-cynic" camp
- ▼ Extent to which employees are buying into the program
- ▼ Effectiveness of the objective-setting system and pay for performance

Formal Face-to-Face Meetings

All-Hands Meetings. The CEO and president and/or senior officers make presentations to all employees and take questions. Sometimes, feedback is solicited after the meeting through small focus groups chaired by leverage managers and supervisors.

If the company is too large or geographically dispersed for a single

Exhibit 16-2 Strategic Communication Tools

OVERALL COMMUNICATION

- ▼ All-hands meetings
- ▼ Plan kickoff
- ▼ Quarterly reviews
- ▼ Special events

MAKING IT PERSONAL

- ▼ Setting departmental objectives
- ▼ Negotiating personal job responsibilities and objectives

FORMAL REVIEWS

- ▼ Monthly and quarterly top-team meetings
- ▼ Manager/supervisor monthly meetings

INFORMAL INFORMATION EXCHANGE

- ▼ President's coffees/employee roundtables
- ▼ Employee focus groups
- ▼ Casual contact
- ▼ Officer attendance at project team meetings
- ▼ Sponsor meetings with team leaders

MEDIA

- ▼ Videos
- ▼ Newsletter
- ▼ E-mail
- ▼ Intranet
- ▼ Videoconferencing

FORMAL RESEARCH

- ▼ Internal attitude surveys
- ▼ Customer panels
- ▼ Market and customer surveys

all-hands meeting, there are alternatives. You can split the company into groups, each addressed by a senior officer. For a remote operation, you may have to fall back on the local manager to conduct the meeting with videoconferencing or a satellite link, live conference call, or videotape to get a message from headquarters and then have a script for the manager to follow to relate the corporate message to the work that the department has to do. Provide an agenda that includes a discussion after the presentation where feedback is solicited so key issues can be fed back to top management.

(Text continues on page 346.)

Exhibit 16-3 Calendar of Communication Events for the First Year of a Strategic Plan

TOOL	INITIAL	1	2	3	4	5	6	7	8	9	10	11	12
								Month					
All-hands meeting	Explain plan to large groups, with small groups for questions and feedback.			Quarterly review of results			Quarterly review			Quarterly review			Review past year; plan objectives for next.
Departmental objective-setting meetings	Show how department objectives directly derive from corporate plan. Scripted.	Continued	Continued	Continued	Continued	Continued	Continued	Plan preparation and discussion of corporate priorities, where department fits				Complete departmental plan.	
Monthly and quarterly top-team meetings	Discuss plan results. Look for wins to publicize. Sponsors responsible for status report on teams.	✓	✓	✓	✓	✓	✓	✓	✓	✓	✓	✓	✓
Manager/ supervisor monthly meetings	Discuss plan relevance immediately after all-hands meeting. Provide feedback to top.	Discuss relevance of direction statement to department. Scripted.	Prepare department mission.	Discuss quarterly results of corporation versus department. Provide feedback to corporate.	Discuss corporate vision and relevance to department.	Develop department vision statement.	Discuss quarterly results of corporation versus department. Provide feedback to corporate.	Develop company business definition.	Discuss department business definition.	Discuss corporate results versus goals. Department contribution. Develop department business definition.	Discuss monthly results.	Discuss monthly results and corporate value statement.	Discuss corporate plan for coming year and where department must support. Develop departmental value statement.

TOOL	INITIAL	1	2	3	4	5	6	7	8	9	10	11	12
INFORMAL MEANS													
President's coffees or roundtables	Two groups	✓	✓	✓	✓	✓	✓	✓	✓	✓	✓	✓	✓
Employee focus groups				✓			✓				✓		
Attendance at project team meetings	CEO visit per each team	✓	✓	✓	✓	✓	✓	✓	✓	✓	✓	✓	✓
Sponsor meetings with teams and team leaders	Four sponsor visits per team outside of private meetings with team leader or members	Minimum of three public sponsor visits per team		✓	✓	✓	✓	✓	✓	✓	✓	✓	✓
Casual contact with an officer		✓	✓	✓	✓	✓	✓	✓	✓	✓	✓	✓	✓
NEWS													
Newsletter	Kickoff campaign explaining how to make direction statement relevant to everyone's job	Relevant news, wins, problems and in-depth reports on programs, people with focus on impact on customers and competitors.		✓	✓	✓	✓	✓	✓	✓	✓	✓	✓

Month

(continued)

Exhibit 16-3   (continued)

TOOL	INITIAL	1	2	3	4	5	6	7	8	9	10	11	12
E-mail bulletin	Four short inserts if there is relevant news	✓	✓	✓	✓	✓	✓	✓	✓	✓	✓	✓	✓
ELECTRONIC													
Intranet	Post latest news. Provide hot link for E-mail communication and feedback on plan.	✓	✓	✓	✓	✓	✓	✓	✓	✓	✓	✓	✓
Database	Accessible database on status of projects and due dates.	✓	✓	✓	✓	✓	✓	✓	✓	✓	✓	✓	✓
REALITY DATA													
Internal attitude surveys				Internal survey of barriers and attitudes toward first five months							Annual benchmark with results widely publicized		
Customer panels			Several panels accessible to sample of all levels in company						Several panels accessible to sample of all levels in company				
Market and customer surveys									Annual benchmark study with results given wide publicity				

TOOL	INITIAL	Month											
		1	2	3	4	5	6	7	8	9	10	11	12
EVENT					Dinner or other event honoring most promising strategic programs or achievements to date								Dinner or other event honoring most promising strategic programs or achievements to date

There are three types of all-hands meetings:

1. *Kickoff meeting,* at which the CEO and officers first lay out the plan, its priorities, and the market and competitive rationale for change
2. *Quarterly meetings* to report on the priorities, note changes in the plan and the environment, explain defeats and their causes, and applaud victories
3. *Special events* warranting explanation and celebration, such as making an acquisition or meeting a major financial or strategic milestone

Meetings to Set Departmental Objectives and Negotiate Personal Job Responsibilities and Objectives. These meetings are the direct link from the plan to where the action takes place. They are where the relationship between plan and job becomes clear and where people's concerns about their ability to achieve the objectives get addressed. These meetings are part of the departmental planning process, described in the Key 3 chapter.

Monthly and Quarterly Top-Team Meetings. Progress on priority issue programs is reviewed and critiqued, resources are allocated, team performance is reviewed, and judgments are made. Monthly meetings identify problems "by exception." Quarterly reviews are the major vehicle for judging progress, communicating progress and problems, identifying and removing barriers to success, redirecting resources, and realigning effort with the plan where indicated.

Before the top team's quarterly meeting, have your departmental managers review their department results and send them to the top team.

After each quarterly meeting, hold an all-hands meeting to inform employees of results or send a video or script to local managers to use at meetings with their people.

Monthly Manager/Supervisor Meetings. At their own monthly meeting, department managers release corporate results and briefly discuss the department's progress, focusing on contribution to corporate objectives, such as service improvement, to ensure that the department's efforts are still in alignment with the corporate direction. Managers should be trained to probe for barriers to progress and pass such observations back up to the appropriate individual or team.

These monthly meetings are an excellent time for a department leader to make sure everyone understands the company's direction and to facilitate the development of the department's own direction statement. Some organizations ask departments to allocate time at each monthly meeting to develop one element of the departmental direction statement, covering the mission at one meeting, vision at another, competitive advantage at a third, and so on. Over the course of a year, a department can develop its direction statement, aligned with the corporate one, without dedicating days to the task.

Informal Communication Methods

Formal meetings are important, but the real stuff gets aired in more relaxed, spontaneous environments. Recognizing this, many companies don't leave informal communication to chance. Instead, they set up situations that encourage frank interchange.

President's Coffees or Employee Roundtables. Many CEOs hold monthly meetings with small groups of employees from various parts of the organization. They are open, tell-me-what's-on-your-mind meetings that typically last one to two hours per group of four to six employees. Some CEOs hold one or two such sessions per month, each with different employees.

But there's an even better way. Some companies form two or three groups of employees who meet with the CEO every four to five weeks for a year, when membership changes and newly formed groups take over. Others use permanent groups, but replace half the membership each year. The advantage of this technique is continuity and depth. The group members and the CEO get to know each other well enough to get down to the nitty-gritty as they exchange information and identify change issues and solutions. Within well-understood confidentiality guidelines, the members of the group become a communication conduit from the CEO to many parts of the organization. Each group should represent a wide diversity of functional areas and jobs but be relatively uniform in level—peers or near peers, with no one reporting to another member in the group.

Employee Focus Groups. Focus groups gauge morale, test understanding of the organization's direction, and identify barriers to progress and issues specific to the various levels and functions within the organization. The best times to conduct them are at the six-month mark, giving sufficient time for plan work to start and warts to appear, and before developing the second-year plan, so you can get a head start on addressing obstacles to success. Focus groups are usually conducted by an outside consultant or neutral human resources person. In small to medium-size companies without multiple businesses, four to six groups usually suffice.

Casual Contact. Except in very small companies, top-team members don't usually hobnob with the troops around the water cooler. So even this needs to be orchestrated to some degree. Make sure the top team is out there enough to have contact, planned or unplanned, with key employees and teams. Casual meetings are a great time to ask, "How's it going?" "What's happening in the reengineering project?" "Anything standing in the way of your programs?"

Attendance at Project Team Meetings. In general, nonteam members should not attend team meetings without an invitation. These are working meetings, and the team doesn't need interruptions, the temptation to play to another audience, or strings of visiting firefighters.

But there are exceptions, although they should never occur unannounced. Arranged with the team leader's permission, a visit by the CEO or a top officer can provide a big boost to a project team. After a quick briefing on the team's business at hand, the visitor can listen for a half hour or an hour as the team conducts regular business. The CEO can motivate a team by giving positive feedback on its work and its relevance to the overall plan and offering suggestions for improvement—as long as they are not couched as orders. But feedback on changes in direction or major problems to be fixed should be channeled through the team's sponsor.

Sponsor Meetings With Teams and Team Leaders. Team sponsors need to have regular meetings with team leaders—a review once a month—plus more frequent contact as requested by either side. With the team leader's permission, sponsors should also drop in on team meetings from time to time to judge progress firsthand. At critical junctures, the team may request that the sponsor attend to serve as a sounding board.

Print Media—Traditional and New

Newsletters. These are useful for reporting on overall plan progress, focusing on progress reports from one or two project teams, heralding successes, and recognizing the people behind them. They are also a good medium for converting the plan from rhetoric to reality. We've seen excellent articles on topics like "the meaning of the mission and how it guides your own work." Some organizations have special newsletters covering the strategic planning effort; others devote a section of their company's monthly or bimonthly general newsletter to the subject.

E-Mail. This is a good way to herald major events and victories such as project completions, new techniques learned, personnel changes, and significant milestones met.

Intranet. The internal equivalent of the Internet, an intranet lets you broadcast strategic progress and the people who are contributing to it in an appealing medium that combines words, pictures, and for the most sophisticated, video. One company featured the new-product team with the prototype of a new product, and another introduced the new branch and its staff in Singapore.

Reality Checks

From time to time, you'll want to collect feedback from the outside world to identify environmental pressures and issues. Although you won't want to burden the entire organization with all the details of everything you learn, you can stimulate and direct implementation efforts by sharing select nuggets. Here are some data-collection tools and the uses to which the collected information can be put:

- *Internal attitude surveys:* Many companies conduct employee attitude surveys once a year to gauge progress on key attitudes, competencies, beliefs, and working conditions. If you do this, be sure to share the overall scorecard.

- *Customer panels:* Customers can teach you about their preferences, future wants and needs, and opinions of the company and its competition. Bring in a relatively large viewing audience of leverage people and a representative sample of all other employees to give them firsthand exposure.

- *Formal market and customer surveys:* Results from surveys of customer needs and preferences and competitors' advantages are input to market and strategic planning. Share the information with those departments it affects and the rest of the company, where appropriate to focus people on competitive strategy.

Situational Communication

In general, the same communication tools serve the same purposes in every change situation. But the emphasis varies. Let's look at communicating change in three different types of organizations: companies on the verge of failure, companies enjoying stable growth, and entrepreneurial organizations.

Company Bleeding to Death

It's a life-or-death situation. To stay alive, you need to change operating results dramatically, reduce debt, and generate cash. This usually requires fast, extreme actions—severing 30 percent or more of employees, replacing 50 to 70 percent of top management, selling some assets, and drastically paring back product/service lines.

In such a situation, the communications job is to:

1. *Tell people the game plan.* Also, make sure that supervisors link the work with the plan.

2. *Keep the heat on.* Pressure people to do the tough stuff that's been asked of them. Make it clear that this is survival, not a long-term planning exercise.

3. *Paint an honest picture.* Tell the survivors the truth about the company's prospects. If more layoffs might happen and more products might fall under the ax, tell people so. They are anxious and need to know. One psychologist who was working with a company making significant cuts put a "rumor box" in a central hall and invited everyone to contribute the best or worst rumor they'd heard. This not only provided catharsis for those inventing and spreading the rumors; it also let management respond to the most damaging and inject a little levity into the situation by sharing the funniest ones.

4. *Communicate status frequently.* Provide weekly or biweekly updates. Turnarounds move fast—up toward survival or down toward bankruptcy. The line between survival and bankruptcy may shift, week to week, depending on availability of bank loans, large customer orders or cancellations, and workforce productivity. Keep people current.

5. *Praise accomplishments.* Single out and praise positive accomplishments. These won't be plentiful at this stage, so locate as many benchmarks on the road to health as you can.

6. *Explain the negative.* If you have to get rid of people because they can't get with the program, or if a much-hyped project—such as a new-product launch—fails, make sure that the people affected know why. Actually, legitimate terminations have a salutary effect on employees—stimulating the good ones, whose judgment is usually vindicated, and jolting any remaining poor performers into action.

7. *Use private conversations effectively.* Talk with the leverage people and others who are critical to your survival, important to postsurvival recovery and growth, and could easily leave the company. Honestly and directly tell them the company plans and their place in them, and as some do, offer "golden handcuffs" to keep them on board.

Company Experiencing Stable, Planned Growth

You might expect communicating plans for growth in a company that is stable and under no threat of extinction to be the easy job. But people in this type of company may be the hardest ones to convince because they feel the least need for change. This category encompasses both of the following:

1. *The bleeder that has stabilized, has developed a longer-range plan, and is ready to move forward.* The bleeder's employees, once out of the woods, tend to heave a big sigh of relief and relax a bit. At just that moment, you've got to hit them with a new plan, new objectives, new reward systems, and new eye-opening communications.

2. *The always stable company that has decided to move forward.* Companies like this are often the toughest to jolt out of their complacency. They have been more or less successful, are frequently out of touch with the outside world, and too often have employees with bad cases of entitlement fever.

In either of these situations, the communications job is to:

1. *Blast the organization out of complacency.* Or halt its slide into relaxation after a successful turnaround. Paint reality with externally and internally generated data like customer panels, competitive positioning, and competitors' moves and internal attitude and morale data from a survey. Point out the positive outcomes possible if the company follows its plan as well as the negative probabilities if it doesn't. And keep pounding it in.

2. *Communicate the new plan.* Make sure everybody understands its objectives and priorities. Help leverage management get the doers to accept their part in it.

3. *Communicate progress versus the plan.* Early on, focus on the tough things you've already done and must continue to do in order for the company to remain successful. These include pruning back less healthy parts of the business, downsizing, and ousting noncontributors or those with old and unchangeable attitudes. They also include positive events such as adding or promoting people with new and needed skills as well as launching new products, expanding geographically, or installing new business processes. Don't let the organization catch its breath.

4. *Keep the heat on.* Maintain the sense of urgency.

5. *Focus on results delivered.* Hammer home the key result areas and measures, drawing attention to your performance on them as well as your progress on the strategic priority issues.

Entrepreneurial Company

Successful entrepreneurial companies have grown by the seat of their pants. In high-tech industries such as electronics, telecommunications, and software, the pace of the market is warp speed.

As they grow up, their strategic plans focus on several items:

- Repositioning their products and services in fast-restructuring, competitive marketplaces
- Looking for rapid growth, often with an eye toward going public
- Being opportunistic in developing new products, joint ventures, and liaisons and acquiring other companies within their competencies
- Installing objective-setting systems and budgets throughout the company and setting rigorous growth objectives
- Building infrastructure to fuel future growth (hiring critical technical people, training in new skills, developing up-to-date information and financial control systems, and finding new ways of distributing their products)

On top of their plans, entrepreneurial companies need a battle-ready infrastructure to take advantage of opportunistic growth. No matter what the base plan is, parts of that plan may change on a dime.

In a company populated by freewheeling, sometimes highly egotistical individualists, the communications job is to:

1. *Clarify the plan.* Explain its objectives and priorities, and gain its acceptance by those who must carry it out.

2. *Keep the organization focused on strategic priorities.* Maintaining a clear focus all the time is a tough job because entrepreneurs like to follow their own drummers. Remind them time and time again of the market, product, competitive focus, and strategic priority issues.

3. *Communicate progress versus plan frequently.* Take special pains to keep communications a two-way path or you may discover too late that your highly independent entrepreneurs have gone ahead and done pretty much as they pleased despite your exhortations. Put a high priority on monthly (rather than quarterly) update and communication meetings with leverage personnel and departments.

4. *Keep the heat on.* Maintain the sense of urgency. Entrepreneurs often fall in love with their product, expecting it to sell when they finally get it into the shape that satisfies them. The market doesn't work that way. Keep the heat on to meet timetables and specs. This means frequent public display of every team's and project's progress versus plan and, of course, frequent review of activities.

5. *Keep communications relatively informal.* In small companies, this is possible. In larger companies, it means communicating to smaller groups. Entrepreneurs have an inherent distrust of size; smaller-group communications will provide more opportunity for questions to be an-

swered and will net you more information and motivation than large-group sessions.

Communication Psychology and the Phases of Change

Just as the nature of the company impacts the way you communicate change, so, too, do the phases of change that were described in Part I (see "The Strategic Plan Process"). The psychology of what you need to communicate and how best to do it are different for each of the phases.

Phase 1: Elation, Shock

Your primary psychological job is to feed the fire of the shock or at least build a high level of personal discomfort. No pain, no change. In short, drive home the need for change. Paint vivid pictures of the negative market and competitive forces, bloated infrastructure and organization, low productivity, and uncompetitive businesses and don't stint on describing the painful things that have to be done to solve the problems. This is your posture for the first six to twenty-four months of a change plan, mitigated only when you begin to see results in phase 2.

Employees don't want to hear this information. They want assurances that things will be OK. Don't reassure them with smooth platitudes. Not only would it be dishonest to do so, but the impact would be all wrong. You *want* the organization to be unsettled; if it isn't, there won't be pressure to achieve your major change objectives. Emphasize that the first year's plan will only improve the situation, not solve it. It will be followed by subsequent plans that will be as tough as, or tougher than, the first one to move the company to the desired performance. Make it clear that, once that change starts, it can never stop, although it will get easier a few years down the line. Do, of course, paint a picture of the end of the rainbow, but don't overdo it.

Phase 2: Unfreezing/Muddling

By the time it's in this phase, the organization has gotten the point. People are more or less willing to change and begin to muddle through the million and one things that they must do to accomplish the plan. Although you still need an iron fist to keep up the pressure for change, you need to clothe it in a velvet glove of strong approval. Communicate the positive changes that have begun to take place and find a couple of achieving heroes to hold in front of the company. Reinforce the efforts of those who muddled into new territory and found a way to succeed.

Employees want and should get encouragement at this point. Put it in the form of praise for what they have done. The message should come through that you will give resources to those who meet your ever-increasing standards and move the plan forward. And you will applaud people who achieve legitimate milestones on the torturous road to success. But make it equally clear that you aren't anywhere near that destination. Keep the heat on.

Phase 3: Tangible Strategic Results

Applaud the results. Give the organization credit for pulling off the first plan. At the same time, make it clear that there will be a new, tougher plan and that employees' major job is to enter into a continuous cycle of learning, planning, and execution that will keep the company moving in the desired upward spiral. There are no laurels on which to rest in today's world. But you shouldn't have to keep the heat turned up too high. The organization should be confident that it can perform. People should feel motivated by pride of achievement and their capacity to accomplish more. Although a rising achievement bar will cause some discomfort, people will be unnerved by the thrill of challenge rather than the fear of failure.

Phase 4: Continuous Learning and Strategic Change

Shift your emphasis to a strong focus on the marketplace, the competition, and your major opportunities and treats. Although growth is never routine, you should be able to sustain solid growth punctuated by major new business blips that build toward the future. A good example is Hewlett-Packard's forays into scientific calculators, laser printers, and PCs overlaid on its Gibraltarlike test instrument and minicomputer business.

Your communication job doesn't change significantly, but it does get more pleasant as the focus switches to the positive. You can reduce the frequency of some communications. You may, for example, no longer need monthly reviews for some priority projects. The organization should now be driven by the challenge of overcoming hurdles and meeting objectives rather than by unsettling fear.

Your message should be one of how excellent the company is—adapting, flexible, ahead of the market, outperforming competitors and the industry. Be sure to emphasize the core competencies—things such as organization innovation, speed of response, and technical innovation—which help you keep that competitive lead.

The other constant message is, "We're not there yet." Because as long as the vision stays over the horizon, you never will be. Hit the following themes hard: (1) trends in the competitive marketplace, (2) admirable other companies and how they have stayed on top of their markets and competition, and (3) your marketplace three to five years from now—what's likely to happen and your needed response.

Do

- Ground all communication in what you're trying to achieve—the strategic objectives and priorities. They're what count.
- Remember that communication is two-way. Set up your plan so you get a lot of feedback from your employees to identify what's working and what isn't.
- Be honest and direct; no BS.
- Leverage your communications through leverage leaders and departmental managers. They're where the action is, not at the top.
- Keep the heat on. To change, the organization must be unsettled.
- Communicate and celebrate successes.
- Focus on the outside world—its events, trends, and effect on you.

Don't

- Pander to employees, telling them what a wonderful job they've done in the past and how everything is going to be great in the future—whether or not it's true.
- Overcommunicate. Stick to the essentials, making sure that what you say is pitched to your audience, received, and understood. Frontline employees don't want board-level pitches.
- Tell people no one will get laid off or "it's all over." It probably isn't and never will be.

Key 17

Review Performance

Principle: It's what you inspect that gets done, not what you expect.

Why it's important: You'll get far superior results if you inspect. People want to be looked on with favor, be complimented, be promoted, make more money, and have a feeling of self-satisfaction and self-importance. A "good" inspection gives positive feedback; a "poor" inspection, negative, sometimes painful, feedback. Pain changes behavior as much as or more than plaudits reinforce admirable work.

How it's applied: Accountability meetings are held in front of supervisors, peers, and sometimes subordinates to judge performance. Good performance is "accountability by applause"; poor performance becomes "accountability by embarrassment."

Expected results: Productivity and execution increase significantly. People who can't meet your standards wash out.

The Accounting, the Reckoning: Did We or Didn't We?

What is accountability? Simply put, accountability is being required to account for your commitments, to explain, to be judged, to be rewarded or punished.

Review or Accountability Meetings?

Make no mistake about it—you want accountability meetings. Accountability meetings make judgments. They are "Did you or didn't you?" meetings. They're where the rubber hits the road. They are where those who made promises to perform explain results and face the music, whether it's the most uplifting symphony or the most unsettling acid rock.

Accountability meetings are also where the top team, based on results achieved or changes in the inside and outside world, modifies program direction, reallocates resources, changes project personnel, and makes judgments about the capabilities of people with the purpose of speeding up plan execution and improving the effectiveness of programs. The quarterly accounting for strategic action plan results is a typical accountability meeting.

Review meetings, on the other hand, too often turn into shows in which all the players don their best tutus and dance as prettily as they can. That kind of performance just doesn't cut it at an accountability meeting. There is room for reviews whose main purpose is to convey important information and explore a subject in depth, but an accountability meeting is not that place.

Purpose of Accountability Meetings

Accountability meetings are vital interventions in the process of turning the plan into reality. Their overriding purpose is to keep the plan moving forward, which they achieve by probing for facts, motivating implementers, and making "move-forward" decisions. Their primary objectives are to:

- *Keep score:* Judge how well the people are achieving their objectives and completing their promised tasks, and then grade them.
- *Keep on track:* Ensure that you're still doing the right thing and, if not, change programs, activities, and objectives.
- *Reallocate resources:* Give the necessary resources to projects and departments in need.
- *Judge people:* Assess people's competence to carry out the job and decide on their short- and long-term deployment, particularly any C's and D's who may have surfaced.

The secondary purposes of accountability meetings are to:

- *Identify barriers:* Look for barriers to progress anywhere in the company—people, departments, policies, procedures, and resources—and find fixes.
- *Motivate:* Give people a forum and applause—loud applause—when they've earned it or an objective judgment of project shortfalls when they haven't.
- *Reinforce alignment, cooperation, and coordination:* Assure yourself that what is being accomplished is in line with corporate objectives and that coordination in all directions is adequate.

What Gets Judged

Here's the list of items to evaluate and the teams or individuals to hold accountable for them:

- *Strategic plan progress:* The extent to which the *top team* is meeting its scorecard promises and making progress toward fulfilling the key direction statement elements: mission, vision, business definition, and values. The top team or the CEO should give itself a grade that counts in team members' performance reviews and compensation.

- *Project/program team progress:* The accomplishments of the *program action plan teams* measured against objectives and promised timing.

- *Departments' achievement versus scorecard:* The accomplishments of each *department* versus the corporate strategic objectives entrusted to it and departmental strategic, operating, and infrastructure objectives. Contrary to most advice, it is most efficient for departmental management to account for departmental strategic and operating objectives at the same time.

- *Individual accomplishments:* Each employee is judged against his or her *individual scorecard,* including ongoing job objectives and individual and project team contributions, if any, to the corporate plan.

As we'll see, properly done, this assessment is not as scary as it might at first seem.

The Accountability Cycle

A typical accountability cycle parallels the planning budgeting cycle, as shown in the Key 1 chapter, Exhibit 1-2. Procedures and agendas follow for each type of accountability review. Note that the smaller and more flexible the company, the less formal and often less frequent these meetings are. Larger companies, by the nature of the beast, often have relatively rigid and somewhat ponderous structures.

Monthly Strategic and Operations Accountability Meetings

The monthly strategic and operations accountability meetings should review:

- *The financial numbers and current operating issues and problems:* The purpose is to make decisions that will achieve better future performance or get projects back on track, if necessary.

■ *Corporate strategic program action plans "by exception":* Participants focus briefly on problems that need fixing or opportunities that should be pushed or further funded. There should be no surprises here. If you established and are using good rules of engagement, problems and opportunities shouldn't have to wait for these meetings. (See the Key 9 chapter.) For example, a department with a severe sales problem isn't going to wait for a monthly review to get word to the top. Who wants to get killed for withholding material information?

Computer Reporting

A handful of companies have program teams enter their strategic project status weekly into a database so that progress can be reviewed frequently and other teams have access to interlock information. This technique is helpful when a company is just learning to be accountable and the necessity of entering progress reports into a database that anyone can access puts pressure on people to perform. It is also useful during early planning periods when plans tend to slip and in highly complex programs with many interlocks. Later, standard quarterly review with monthly exception reporting should suffice for most programs and save time.

Quarterly Strategic Accountability Meetings

At the key quarterly strategic accountability meetings, you get a relatively balanced overview of accomplishment on each of the priority issue programs. Each team submits a one- or two-page form (See Exhibit 17-1) to the top team before the review. The form states the team's original one- and three-year objectives and then reports on:

- What the team has accomplished.
- What it hasn't accomplished that it said it would.
- Key issues or problems that need resolution.
- Decisions or resources the team needs from the top team.
- Performance to numerical objectives, if relevant.

This set of topics forces teams to focus on their performance and then on issues to be resolved and decisions needed from the top team to move their programs forward.

Team leaders get half an hour to cover each priority issue and its associated action plans—ten minutes without interruption and fifteen to twenty minutes for questions and decisions from the top team. The top team sees the entire strategic program picture quickly and makes necessary decisions.

Exhibit 17-1   Quarterly Program Review Form

Quarter: _____   Program manager: _____
Program name: _____
Program description: _____
Long-term objectives: _____
Short-term objectives: _____

Program ratings—E (excellent), G (good), F (fair), or P (poor)

• Key results:

• Problems/issues to be addressed:

• Steps/objectives due but not accomplished:

• Changes in timing, objectives, resources requested:

The Numbers:	Budget	Project to Date	Forecast

Incremental
    Sales ($)
    Gross margin (%)
    Net profit
    Cash flow
    ROA
resulting from this program since yur plan was approved and you began to make changes

If hard data are not available, state what incremental returns do you think are resulting from this program? On what evidence?

What have you spent so far versus what you planned to spend?

Actual expenditures ($):_____   Planned expenditures ($): _____

($): _____

Most top-team members don't have lots of depth on most programs. But for every program, there is a sponsor and usually one or two top-team members whose functional areas are doing most of the work and who are fully familiar with it. Presumably, all top-team members have thoroughly reviewed programs in their own areas prior to the review meeting and are in a position to assure the rest of the top team that all is in order—if that is so. If not, they may recommend more extensive review at a later time if additional information is needed or critical decisions have to be made.

If the top team needs more information or a program requires critical decisions (kill a project, merge two projects, change team membership), the program goes on a "hanging issues" list. The top team will review these in depth later, when they will not hold up the entire quarterly review process.

The questions each top-team member needs to address mentally throughout these accountability sessions are shown in Exhibit 17-2.

At the meeting, followed up in writing, the top team gives each team an assessment of its performance, suggestions for improvement, and any redirection needed. Exhibit 17-3 is a good outline for written feedback to the teams.

Semiannually, the top team should meet to discuss the team process itself. Are there any process problems holding up a program, such as meeting schedules or conflicts between departmental work and team work? Are the people right? Are any high-potential people on the teams? Any losers? At the end of the year or when required by the company's personal performance review cycle, the top team should meet to give each program team a score. This score should be discussed with the

Exhibit 17-2   Questions Top-Team Members Mentally Address During Program Team Reviews

▼ Is the team really doing the job? Are the results "real"?
▼ If we're told we're on track, is there a hidden barrier to progress just around the corner? If off track, are the reasons valid or just excuses?
▼ Are the program's objectives still valid? Is it still in direct alignment with our priorities and corporate plan?
▼ Should we redirect or restructure this project in any way?
▼ Do we have the right people running it? Is our team leader as good as what we really need?
▼ Do I really have the information needed to make judgments on the team's progress and requests?
▼ Is the team process working well for this team?
▼ Does the team have the right resources and enough of them?
▼ Would the time and money be strategically better spent elsewhere?

Exhibit 17-3   Outline for Postreview Feedback to Program Teams

Accomplishment: How is the team doing versus objectives; the percentage of the program it has completed.

Timeliness: The extent to which the team is completing the program objectives on time.

Going the extra mile: The extent to which the team is exceeding expectations in accomplishment or scope of the program.

Creativity: Any use of creative methods in accomplishing the job and any creative solutions or new ideas that can be used elsewhere in the organization.

Process: How well the team is using the team process, coordinating with others, and staying in alignment.

Presentation: The team's ability to get ideas across quickly and effectively and to lead discussions to a conclusion.

Planning: How well the team plans ahead and informs the top team of what's coming.

Teamwork: The members' ability to work together as a cohesive team.

Knowledge: The team members' depth of knowledge of their subject, markets, and the business.

team as a group and integrated into the performance ratings of each individual.

The Tone and Pace of Accountability Meetings

What kind of atmosphere should you set in accountability meetings? Spanish Inquisition? Attila the Hun? Mary Poppins? Pollyanna? You have a wide range of choices. Mary Poppins comes pretty close—warm, supportive, open, direct, professional, probing, realistic, with a good sense of humor but absolutely no intentions of lowering high standards or tolerating any nonsense. And a spoonful of sugar doesn't hurt any when earned. The meeting will be short and sweet. The top team is going to ask tough questions and expect crisp answers. It will focus on a brief explanation of results and, during or after the meeting, give necessary redirection, together with a performance grade and the reasons for it.

The Informal Process

At the Top. The formal review process is bare-bones, requiring top-team members to make decisions based on a minimum of information. Top-team members supplement the *formal* review by *informally* seeking out the information they need to be comfortable making decisions.

Members of the top team who can't knowledgeably judge a program's prospects because they lack in-depth knowledge of its workings depend on someone else on the top team who has that knowledge: the sponsor or the head of the department where the bulk of the work is being done. Or they satisfy themselves on all the details in advance.

One vice president of research and development for a Fortune 500 company, a scientist, felt he couldn't get adequate information to make project judgments in short review meetings. Getting answers to his million and one questions about the organization's extensive scientific and product development projects would make the meetings inordinately long and boring to two-thirds of the group. He therefore reviewed R&D programs in considerable detail before the corporate accountability meetings, making him a source of information and judgment at the top rather than a questioner.

Team Sponsors. Sponsors, of course, should be in regular contact with the teams, helping them achieve their goals in any way possible. They are in an excellent position to assess the teams' progress and redirect them if needed before formal accountability meetings. They can also review presentations before accountability meetings, offering helpful suggestions and pointing out minefields best avoided.

Sponsors flip hats at top-team accountability meetings. They have to be supportive of their project team, but their primary role is to sit in judgment like the rest of the top team. Unlike other top-team members, they come to the meeting already knowing how well the team process is working and whether or not changes in a team are needed. The judgment they take to a top-team meeting should be agreed on or at least discussed with the project team leader or entire team first.

Department Managers. Many department managers are team sponsors. Many are on the top team. Chances are, a number of them will have project team members reporting to them who have pivotal roles in implementation. Assume, for example, that an engineer on a critical manufacturing cost reduction project reports to a department manager. The department manager will supervise the engineer's work on the implementation program just as he would for any other important project—to ensure that the engineering, subsequent equipment design, prototype manufacture, and testing are right.

He will judge the engineer's technical performance as he would that of any other engineer in his department. That judgment will get integrated into the engineer's individual performance rating, as will the performance rating for the entire project team.

Departmental Accountability Meetings

On a monthly basis in most companies, the management of each department goes over the operating numbers with the top team and discusses any particular scorecard problems in operations or strategic programs. Each quarter, however, a more extensive review is warranted for the following items from the departmental scorecard:

- Corporate priorities and objectives delegated to the department
- Departmental strategic and infrastructure priorities
- Operating issues
- Numbers
- Status of interlocks

Three-quarters of an hour is usually sufficient for each department: fifteen minutes for presentation and thirty minutes for discussion. Issues requiring in-depth discussion go on the hanging issues list. A time is set to resolve each hanging issue after the meeting.

Individual Accountability Meetings

Individuals are usually reviewed in-depth once a year—sometimes twice or more frequently if they are new to the job or company or they are on a developmental track. Both the supervisor and the subordinate complete the review format that covers the subordinate's performance on any of the individual scorecard items that are relevant. These scorecard items, which were introduced in the Key 4 chapter, include:

- Delegated corporate strategic priorities
- Departmental strategic priorities
- Departmental operating priorities
- Departmental infrastructure priorities
- Individual's ongoing job
- Team objectives
- Behaviors
- Numbers

In addition, individual accountability meetings cover:

- Values, competencies, behaviors, and job skills, with an eye to an individual development program

- The individual's future: jobs open to her, her particular desires, and training and development work needed to prepare her for a mutually agreed upon direction
- Setting objectives for the coming year

Do

- Establish an accountability (not review) system at the beginning of your change program. Make it clear that its purpose is to make judgments.
- Base the accountability system on your scorecard system.
- Put teeth in your accountability system right from the start by grading and rewarding well those who excel and by giving poor grades to those who do poorly.
- Use the accountability system to quickly smoke out and get rid of D's, marginal C's who won't make B, and all resisters.

Don't

- Let people talk you out of poor performance ratings because their job isn't "really measurable" or external conditions have changed. If, indeed, the latter happened with significant import, then there may be a cause for adjustment but usually not.

Key 18

Reward Strategic Results

Principle: Executives, teams, groups, and workers who are well rewarded for accomplishing specific, measurable tasks perform better than those who are not.

Why it's important: Money, time, and effort for developing and implementing strategy are limited. You want to apply them where you'll get the biggest bang for your buck. Often, that's on the people executing strategy.

How it's applied: Offer specific monetary and psychological rewards for accomplishing measurable strategic change tasks and for exhibiting the values and behaviors with which you want the entire organization to align.

Expected results: With appropriate awards, you can expect superior and faster strategic results, retention of superior personnel, and a rapid learning rate. Studies indicate that incentive compensation accounts for at least 25 to 30 percent of the motivation to achieve.

Compensation Systems

There is a hurricane of change brewing in compensation systems today as people discover that traditional programs don't provide adequate incentive for the achievement of strategic results. They don't motivate employees to move the corporation in the right direction or help companies hire and retain people who will lead and execute strategic change. In this chapter, we'll examine why traditional compensation fails and present new strategic compensation systems that are emerging to fill new needs.

Strategic compensation combines base pay with significant variable compensation tied to the achievement of long-term strategic objectives. It rewards future numerical results, the steps taken now to move the company toward them, and behaviors and competencies that will keep the organization strategically focused.

Most compensation systems, whether traditional or strategic, use some combination of these components:

- *Base pay:* Cash payments by the hour, week, or month for services. They are not directly related to the accomplishment of objectives unless tied to a merit pay system that gives pay increases in proportion to achievement. Merit pay increases and base pay increases upon promotion are usually modest.

- *Cash bonus:* Usually annual, but spot bonuses have their champions, too. Bonuses are paid upon attaining certain levels of organizational and/or individual achievement. Although cash bonuses often provide incentive for short-term, conservative action at the expense of the long-term, more progressive companies use them to reward actions taken now in support of accomplishing long-term goals.

- *Stock options:* Options to buy stock at a future date at a price agreed upon when the option is granted, usually the market price on that day. Options normally don't vest—become the property of the person receiving the grant—for some period of time, often three to five years after the grant. They therefore have the effect of "golden handcuffs," tying the individual to the organization. They allegedly encourage people to take riskier strategic actions in the hope of a better long-term gain on their options.

The following list offers an overview of the major forms of options used today. Each has different financial and tax advantages and disadvantages for the company and the individual. These important implications and the many variations in stock option schemes aren't examined here but are explored in most books on executive compensation.[1]

- *Stock options:* The grantee is awarded stock valued as of the date of grant. He may exercise the option (and pay the original price of the stock) as soon as it vests, sometimes within one year but usually in three, four, or five years. He is then free to do what he chooses with the stock.

- *Restricted stock options:* The grantee usually pays nothing for the shares but must hold them for a period of time and still be employed by the company before selling them. Restricted options, like performance-based shares (discussed below), sometimes require a specified level of

[1] For an explantion of the consequences of options, see Fred K. Foulkes, ed., *Executive Compensation: A Strategic Guide for the 1990s* (Cambridge: Harvard Business School Press, 1991).

future financial and strategic performance before the options may be exercised. The amount of the options are reduced or the options are lost if the performance is not achieved.

- *Stock appreciation rights:* The grantee gets the appreciation in the stock price from the time of grant until the option is exercised in exchange for the cancellation of the underlying option. The grantee pays nothing for the option.

- *Performance-based shares:* The amount of the future options depends on company performance on specific financial and strategic measures such as earnings per share or market share growth.

- *Performance units:* The unit is a dollar amount and not a share of stock. The performance unit's worth in the future when vested is contingent on achievement of specified company performance objectives.

- *Phantom stock:* Phantom, or "bookkeeping," stock is usually used in private companies where no stock is traded and the owners do not want to give up any ownership. Phantom "shares" reflect equity ownership in the company. Initial share value is calculated on the basis of the share value of equivalent publicly traded companies. Phantom share value is determined periodically by comparing the company's financial and strategic performance to the performance and stock value of a publicly traded benchmark group.

- *Time-accelerated stock plans.* In time-accelerated plans, options can be exercised and the number shares increased if performance objectives are met ahead of schedule.

Today's Norms

Although the voices championing strategic compensation are growing louder, for the last ten to fifteen years, the most typical compensation programs have looked like this:

- *The top team and senior executives* are eligible for annual cash bonuses to provide incentive for current performance and stock options to provide incentive for strategic growth.
- *Middle to lower-level managers/supervisors* are usually eligible for annual cash bonuses. A handful may be given stock options.
- *Cross-functional teams,* if given bonuses at all, get spot cash awards. Few are eligible for a cash bonus based on meeting objectives.
- *Project teams,* which are long-lived and whose members are full-time, may receive cash bonuses based on the extent to which they

meet annual objectives. Occasionally, they, too, earn spot cash awards.

- *Work teams* that are permanent and responsible for operating and improving a core process are often rewarded by gainsharing, receiving a percentage of the money that they save or the efficiencies that they achieve.

Where Today's Compensation Plans Fail

Although they may have many of the right ingredients, most compensation schemes are still heavily weighted to reward today's success, not tomorrow's. Only people at the very top get any incentive for looking beyond this year. And many companies are still saddled with compensation plans that not only don't provide an incentive for strategic action, they positively discourage it.

For the most part, today's typical compensation programs are:

- *Left over from the 1950s:* These programs originated in the good old days when, strategically, you could do little wrong. The most imaginative things these companies do are grant stock options every year or so to a few senior people and pay cash bonuses, based on annual overall operating performance, to top officers and senior managers.

- *Strictly current-numbers-oriented:* Bonuses and stock options are not tied to accomplishment of strategic actions or programs. Nor is the vesting of stock options contingent on future results, only on the passage of time. Such programs therefore do little to encourage people to devote their creative thinking, time, or efforts to programs that could reshape a company's future.

- *Still mired in "merit" pay:* For most people—even personnel assigned to strategic teams or tasks—their only hope for financial recognition lies in the onerous merit pay system. And that's a misnomer if ever there was one. Too often, almost everyone, from poor performers to outstanding achievers, gets the same increase of a few percentage points each year—hardly an amount to motivate people to stick their necks out and work on high-visibility, often risky strategic projects. No wonder people with the potential to be extraordinary get resentful and begin to ask, "Why should I work so hard if the laggards get as much as I do?" and "What am I still doing around this place?"

Although it's the people in the trenches who ultimately do the strategic work and make or break the departmental and program action plans, they seldom receive incentive compensation. We still hear people who should know better insist, "It's not necessary to give incentive compensation in our industry to attract and retain good people."

- *Blind to competencies and behaviors that drive future strategy.*

New Trends in Compensation

Happily, the norm I've just described is not the whole picture of compensation in business today. Led most visibly by young, aggressive companies in high-tech industries, organizations are seeking new ways to reward the people who are driving their futures. Although there is no pat formula and plans differ widely in their details, they share two common characteristics: They offer significant payoff for significant strategic results, and they are tied to very measurable objectives. More specifically, the following trends are emerging:

- *Pay for performance is in.* Total compensation at many levels is a combination of base pay and a bonus system that pays off if goals are met. Base pay may be market-competitive, or it may be less than competitive, attracting people willing to put some of their livelihood at risk for the opportunity to shoot for truly substantial gain.

- *Merit systems are out.* Base pay is based on the competitive market and increases only by promotion or a move into a more difficult or "learning" job—for example, a lateral move from marketing to strategic planning.

- *Objectives are both strategic and operational.* Rewards for both are tied to measurable standards of accomplishment.

- *Multiple plans are common.* One size doesn't fit all when the aim is to reward performance where it is delivered and can be measured. That requires many different plans to provide incentive for people at all levels and functions to accomplish targeted strategic and operational tasks. One large bank has thirty different compensation plans.

- *Incentives are in "line of sight."* When pay is directly linked to scorecards, employees can see that it is a direct result of specific actions they take or outcomes they impact. With incentives in their line of sight, employees can not only predict what their rewards will be, they can influence them.

- *Systems are flexible.* They allow for frequent adjustment in response to changes in the strategic plan or external competitive circumstances. They also allow for "spot" bonuses outside the normal system to reward extraordinary achievements.

- *Incentive pay goes broader and deeper into the organization.* It reaches cross-functional teams and lower-level departments and individuals. Eligibility is determined by the strategic job to be done, not by level or tenure.

- *The tougher and riskier the job the greater the incentive.*

- *Behaviors and values count heavily.* They are being measured, are part of the performance management system, and are often the basis for up to 15 percent of bonus pay.

Why Incentive Compensation Works

CEOs whom we surveyed placed incentive compensation at the top of their list of factors making their change program successful. Several CEOs replied "money" when we asked them to name the most important motivational and accountability tool. Studies have confirmed that significant incentive compensation, both short- and long-term, motivates performance. People will stretch hard to attain incentive payments that are significantly above ordinary compensation.

Besides putting a roof over our head and food on the table, money buys toys and, perhaps even more important, status. With a sports car in our garage and a swimming pool in our backyard, our prestige in the neighborhood rises; we become the "Jonses." And both on the job and in society, money is how we keep score. High pay at work means our job must be important; bringing it home convinces us of our own success.

Of course, using money as an incentive isn't new. What is new is using it to encourage participation in projects whose payoff for the company is a few years down the road.

Strategic compensation is tied to results from priority issue action plans and corporate and departmental strategic initiatives, which take time to show tangible results. It is paid out when the objectives or important intermediate steps are achieved. Strategic compensation is ultimately tied to strategic objectives such as market share and customer satisfaction. Of course, it has to be combined with compensation that also provides an incentive for operating performance. The purpose of a strategic compensation plan is to establish a very careful balance between motivating ordinary operating performance and pushing strategic initiatives.

Exhibit 18-1 illustrates the line of sight between Empire Realty/ Strategic Plan direction statement (see Exhibit 3-4), several employees, their scorecard, and their incentive system.

Designing a Strategic Compensation System

Who Gets Strategic Compensation

To design a strategic compensation system, you'll need to identify every leverage manager, team, and individual as well as every functional de-

Exhibit 18-1   Line of Sight Among Empire Electric Employees: Their Scorecard and Their Incentive System

	Chief Executive Officer	Vice President of Development	Vice President of Leasing	Director of Information Systems
Direction statement elements	• Increase shareholder value • Exceptionally profitable • EPS of $7.20 by 2002 • 16% return on investment	• Reach $10 billion in assets and 3.5 million sq. ft. in 1999 • Return on investment of 16% • Superior site selection • Impeccable execution	• Highest return to our stockholders • High tenant satisfaction levels • Strong tenant relationships	• Impeccable execution of development processes • Properties open on time • Properties meet or exceed tenant expectations • Best core competency of asset management in industry • Standard
Allocation of bonus*	C BU I 100% 0 0	C BU I 30% 50% 20%	C BU I 30% 50% 20%	C BU I 30% 0 70%

Performance standards weight**	• 75% earnings per share
	• 25% total shareholder return
		• 50% dollar amount of transactions
		• 50% return on investment
			• 25% core portfolio occupancy
			• 25% acquisition property occupancy
			• 25% development property occupancy
			• 25% tenant relationships
				• 25% maintenance
				• 25% development of long-term information systems plan
				• Implementation improvements
				  – Project A = 25%
				  – Project B = 25%

*C = corporate; BU = business unit; I = individual

**Weight for corporate performance for CEO, business unit for vice president, development and leasing, individual for information systems partment with strategic tasks to perform and develop the system around the strategic job to be done by each. This typically includes:

- The top team
- Functional departments or strategic business units
- Strategic priority issue program teams
- Select individuals
- Core process teams
- Permanent project teams

Exhibit 18-2 shows some guidelines for compensating these people.

Criteria for a Strategic Compensation Plan

When you build a strategic compensation plan, keep the following guidelines in mind:

- *Base compensation on your scorecard system.* Your scorecards reflect the short- and long-term performance measures you felt were most important and the performance expected from each organization unit, individual, or team. If an objective is worth putting on a scorecard, it is worth basing compensation on it. Therefore, link incentive payments directly to the scorecards, including behaviors and competencies, so there is no question about how success is measured.

- *Align your compensation plan with the strategic plan.* Your strategic compensation plan should reflect your strategic plan's programs and its key objectives and values. Be scrupulous about not letting it spill over and reward worthy-sounding but unaligned and unmeasured actions and objectives.

- *Separate strategic compensation from compensation for ongoing business results.* Both base pay and incentive compensation may have strategic and operating components. Don't let the division between strategic and operating get fuzzy for either type of reward.

- *Keep an appropriate balance between the two.* The ratio between rewards for strategic tasks and rewards for ongoing tasks should reflect the split between strategic and operating work done by the recipient.

- *Make payout large enough to motivate.* Set award levels and frequency high enough compared to base salary to provide significant motivation to achieve outstanding, not just acceptable, results on strategic tasks.

- *Hit all strategic leverage points.* Give strategic compensation wherever strategic action exists in the organization, irrespective of organization level or type of unit.

Exhibit 18-2 Who Gets Strategic Compensation

	Basis for Strategic Compensation	Typical Method
Top team	Achievement of strategic numbers, short-term departmental strategic tasks, strategic priority issues, benchmarks, corporatewide behaviors	Annual cash bonus partially based on strategic factors and operating results
	Long-term strategic results and behaviors	Stock options
Departmental vice presidents, middle to upper management	As for the top team plus achievement of all their specific departmental objectives	As for the top team
Lower-level management and supervisors	Achievement of program objectives and benchmarks	Cash bonus based on scorecard plus stock options for selected individuals
Strategic priority issue teams	Achievement of program objectives or benchmarks; behaviors	Cash bonus based on measurable results and spot awards
Individuals	Achievement of major strategic objectives or benchmarks; behaviors	Cash bonus based on measurable results and spot awards in cash or stock options
Lower-level process teams running and improving core processes	Gainsharing or awards based on improved process performance; behaviors	Cash bonus based on measurable process improvement and spot awards
Long-term, full-time project teams	Achievement of program objectives or benchmarks; behaviors	Cash bonus based on annual objectives and spot awards

- *Make the compensation program logical and equitable.* It should be viewed as both generous and fair by most employees, particularly those not eligible for strategic compensation. Those contributing only to ongoing results—securing the company's present so that there can be a future—should also get incentives that reward their proportionate contribution to a short- and long-term profit. Strive for some, but not perfect, equity between strategic and operating incentives.

- *Provide rewards for extraordinary actions and results.* Reward specific extraordinary strategic actions or accomplishments by teams or individuals outside of the regular compensation system. A Fortune 500 company gave one young woman, employed for only a year at a level where there usually was no or little incentive pay, an unprecedented amount of stock and a cash bonus. Her supervisors said she did two years' work in one year, was well liked and motivated people, and was clearly on the fast track—and the company wanted her to know that.

- *Keep it flexible.* Strategic objectives can change quickly to reflect changes in the outside world or progress toward goals. Be sure you can adjust the compensation plan accordingly.

- *Keep momentum going.* Pace rewards so that they maintain momentum in strategic task achievement throughout the organization.

- *Scale payout for varying degrees of achievement of objectives.*

- *Think retention and hiring.* Ask yourself the question your leverage people and potential recruits will ask themselves: "Can I get a better deal elsewhere?"

- *Make the plan clear and understandable to your employees:* Your strategic compensation system must provide line of sight between payout and objectives.

- *Reward program accomplishments as well as current numbers.* Steps in a strategic program that are accomplished and reflect in a scorecard and that will pay off in profits three years from now can be as more important than immediate financial results and should be treated and compensated as such.

- *Assess it as an investment.* The financial returns of your strategic programs/actions should ultimately far outweigh the cost of the incentives.

Typical Incentive Plans

Typical short-term focused incentive plans, called common plans here, are shown in Exhibits 18-3 through 18-9 and explained below. The purpose of the exhibits is to illustrate the structure of the plans. The num-

Exhibit 18-3 CEO's Traditional and Strategic Compensation Plans

CASH	CEO Ordinary	CEO Strategic
BONUS SCOREBOARD	Based on current financial performance	• Current corporate financial results • Strategic numbers • Strategic program results • Other CEO scorecard measures, including personal objectives
BASE	Competitive	Market competitive
OPTIONS	Unrestricted options granted each year equal to approximately 3/4 salary. Vest 1/3 in each of years 3, 4, 5.	One large grant every 3-5 years equal to 4-5x current salary. Vests in 1/3 increments in years 3, 4, 5. One-half unrestricted options. One-half restricted exercise is based on accomplishment of strategic objectives.
% one-year compensation based on: • strategic measures • current financial performance	0 100%	60 40
% long-term (5-year) compensation based on: • strategic results • financial results	100%	70 30

bers, ratios, and strategic factors on which incentives are based will vary substantially by industry, company, and the company's financial and strategic condition.

Basic Top Management Incentive Plan

The CEO

Let's start with the basics. The left-hand side of Exhibit 18-3 depicts the structure of the most common long-term incentive plan for a CEO. It has the following features:

■ *Base salary:* This is based on competitive companies and the industry and reflects the individual's skill and what it took to get him or takes to keep him.

■ *Cash bonus:* A potential cash bonus from 100 to 200 percent of the CEO's base salary is based on annual results, which are only a small portion of the top-team scorecard. The bonus kicks in at about 85 to 90 percent of targeted financial performance; the CEO is paid 25 or 30 percent of the bonus pool for hitting the target and the entire bonus for hitting 200 percent of target.[2]

■ *Options:* Options are given each year, and vest—that is, the grantee is free to dispose of them as she sees fit—in three to five years, with a ten-year limit. The options are unrestricted: Once granted, there are no performance or other restrictions on their sale other than the grantee's remaining with the company. Option amounts granted are competitive industry practice and figured according to one of several accepted formulas. Here, each year's options are expected to be worth 75 to 125 percent of base salary at the exercise date.

So what's wrong with this picture? Nothing as far as the executive is concerned. He can pay a lot of attention to the short term, make a lot of money, not screw the company up, and make even more money on the options if the stock market goes up.

Unfortunately, the scheme as painted does little to encourage the CEO to continually shape and reshape the company for the future.

We can change that with a few strokes of the pen. The weights of the scorecard can be changed to fit the particular circumstances of the organization each year and with each grant of stock options. And of course, the operating portion of the scorecard increases as you go to lower levels, where, for many positions, operating responsibilities predominate. The right-hand side of Exhibit 18-3 shows a hypothetical, truly strategic, pay system for the CEO, based on the top-team scorecard, weighted as shown in Exhibit 18-4. The following subsections examine the similarities and differences.

Operating Bonus (40 Percent of Potential Bonus). Our CEO can still make the same annual bonus. Note, however, that the bonus is divided into seven parts, weighted as shown on the scorecard. Traditional financial performance and achievement of the operating objectives on his scorecard receive a 30 percent weight. Ten percent is dependent on how, collectively, the functional areas performed in meeting their objectives. This is important to some companies for two reasons. First, they have significant work to do in bolstering current and future performance. Sec-

[2] Foulkes, *Executive Compensation.*

Exhibit 18-4   Top-Team Scorecard Weighted

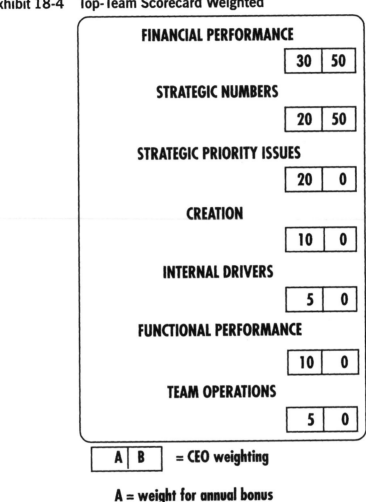

	A	B	= CEO weighting

A = weight for annual bonus
B = weight for restricted stock options

ond, as a peer group, paying a bonus on each other's performance provides a strong incentive to coordinate their efforts and achieve.

Strategic Bonus (60 Percent). Twenty percent of the CEO's bonus under this scheme is based on how well the company meets scorecard strategic performance measures—service, quality, employee satisfaction and behavioral ratings, market share, and innovation indices. Another 20 percent is based on how well the program teams are meeting the company's strategic priority issue program objectives from the corporate scorecard. Remember, these programs—such as quality improvement, geographic expansion, or external growth—will structurally and permanently change the company's future. And of course, it may be years before the impact is seen at the bottom line. Thus, the CEO (and the top team) are being given an incentive to see that these "steps along the way" are carefully taken and executed.

Ten percent each is allocated to creation and team operations. There is probably a program, such as development of new technologies, in the creation section of the scorecard. The team operations are still a major scorecard area, indicating that the kinks aren't worked out of the system, and there are still no critical programs addressing internal drivers that warrant scorecard weight at this point.

While 100 percent of the CEO's one-year bonus under an ordinary compensation scheme is based on current results, a truly strategic scheme places 60 percent or more of the annual bonus on achievement of strategic objectives and programs and only 40 percent on operating goals. This is as it should be for the person whose primary responsibility is to direct and ensure the future of the organization.

Options. Instead of options' being given every year, a much larger block of options is given every five years and an amount of stock whose value could far exceed the "normal" plan. They vest, one-third each, in years three, four, and five. However, half the options are contingent, with their vesting based on hitting minimum, well-understood, and measurable financial and strategic performance measures, such as earnings per share, return on investment, earnings growth, share of market, and strategic indices in service, quality, innovation, and employee satisfaction. The remainder of the options are unrestricted: Once granted, there are no performance or other restrictions on their sale other than the grantee's remaining with the company.

If the performance levels aren't achieved in the targeted year, the executive keeps the unrestricted options but loses the restricted ones. If the performance levels are achieved prior to the targeted year, the vesting is moved forward and the stock received "early."

The bottom line for the CEO is 70 percent of total long-term compensation and is based on strategic performance that includes the portion of annual bonuses awarded for strategic progress and the gains on *restricted* stock options.

Figure 18-5 illustrates how a strategic compensation scheme can double a CEO's compensation over five years if his strategies lead to performance superior to that of his company's peers. This is not unreasonable, if indeed conservative, based on our experience with underperforming public companies who have strategically focused their efforts.

Caveat. So there are the basics. I must say, however, that I never found two plans alike and that incentive compensation is one of the

Exhibit 18-5   Strategic Compensation Plans for Executives Reporting to Top-Team Members

	Year One*	Cumulative Year Five
Ordinary Compensation Scheme		
• Bonus	$100	500
• Options exercised, net value	0	145
• Total		$645
CEO Strategic Compensation Scheme		
• Bonus	$100	500
• Options exercised, net value	0	800
• Total		$1,300

* $ '000

Percentages assume that the company's stock will appreciate by 10 percent per year for five years without strategic compensation and 20 percent per year with strategic compensation combined with a good strategic and implementation plan. Strategic compensation equals stock appreciation plus the total of annual bonuses allocated to strategic objectives. While these numbers are not based on an objective survey, the author's experience has been that the stock performance of strategically managed companies far exceeds that of comparable benchmark companies. An obviously unrealistically low CEO salary level of $100,000 per year, without increases, was picked to simplify calculation and understanding of the example. An average cash bonus of $100,000 based on meeting plan targets was assumed.

most controversial and complicated fields of endeavor. Sometimes, the plan depends more on the penchant of the CEO and the board than it does on any professionally proven scheme. Other times, a unique plan that would drive a compensation expert nuts really works. The bottom line is that the basics as outlined are workable and there are a thousand variations on this theme, depending on what behaviors you want to encourage and how generous you want to be. Because compensation has pervasive effects on motivation and retention and because every compensation scheme has tax repercussions for the company and individual, you should have an expert review your scheme. You can have a first-rate compensation consulting organization look over your shoulder for about $35,000 or do a complete plan for about $150,000. Needless to say, there are independent consultants who would likely charge less.

Other Members of the Top Team

Now let's turn to the chief operating officer and the vice presidents reporting to the COO who are members of the top management team. If the business is truly being run as a team, the group would have the same or similar scoreboard as that of the CEO, shown in the right-hand side of Exhibit 18-6. The exceptions are that both will have slightly more short-term emphasis in their objectives, particularly the COO and his direct reports. In the example I've given, the COO would have a maximum bonus of 150 percent of salary and other contingent payments scaled down proportionately. The other top-team members would have a bonus percentage of perhaps 100 percent. Under a more traditional system, the vice presidents would have a departmental scorecard similar to that noted below for departmental managers.

Exhibit 18-6   Compensation Scheme for Other Officers and Managers

Cash	COO Ordinary	COO Strategic
BONUS SCOREBOARD	Based on current financial performance	• Current corporate financial results • Strategic numbers • Strategic program results • Other CEO scorecard measures, including personal objectives
BASE	Competitive	Market competitive
OPTIONS	Unrestricted options granted each year equal to approximately 3/4 salary. Vest 1/3 in each of years 3, 4, 5.	One large group every 3-5 years equal to 4-5x current salary. Vests in 1/3 increments in years 3, 4, 5. Unrestricted options given on time basis, restricted options based on strategic performance.
Percentage of one-year compensation based on: • strategic measures • current financial performance	0 100	50 50
Percentage of long-term (5-year) compensation based on: • strategic results • financial results	100%	60 40

Executives Reporting to Top-Team Members

Executives reporting to top team members and ofter called directors, are usually responsible for one or more important functional areas. Again, the bonus and salary would be appropriately scaled down, with a bonus percentage of perhaps 80 percent. Their scorecard measures, as shown in Exhibit 18-6, would change. Short-term bonus would be based principally on the individual's ongoing job objectives, behaviors, and values. The other short-term bonus items—delegated corporate strategic priorities, departmental strategic priorities, and team objectives—depend on whether the department is involved in those areas. In Exhibit 18-7, it is assumed that the department is predominantly involved in short-term departmental areas.

Bonus levels vary substantially by industry. We saw CEO bonuses ranging from 50 percent up to 400 percent, with bonuses for subordinates scaled down according to industry practice.

Other Lower-Level Managerial Personnel

Lower-level managers and supervisors, as shown in Exhibit 18-9, concentrate heavily on execution of their departmental and individual objectives and are rewarded only by annual bonuses. How far down do you take bonuses and/or options? As far as you want. Some Fortune 500 companies give them to every managerial and professional employee, and that is an ideal goal. You should at least have the vice presidents reporting to the chief operating officer/chief executive officer and the next layer down on a bonus/option scheme, as well as all leverage managers throughout the corporation, irrespective of level. The bonus percentages and option amounts will scale down proportionately, of course.

Teams

Program Teams. Program teams should be able to earn a bonus of up to 20 percent of their collective salaries each year for the life of their program, with the bonus being tied directly to their measurable objectives and milestones. The payments are staggered so that the last payment is made one year after the program has ended based on the performance in that last year. Usually, the team leader receives a higher bonus than other team members. One or two team members whose time and efforts were extraordinary are also above the average, with the remainder splitting the pie equally. A good case can be made for awarding

Exhibit 18-7   Developing a Strategic Compensation System

Cash	VICE PRESIDENTS REPORTING TO CHIEF OPERATING OFFICER Ordinary	VICE PRESIDENTS REPORTING TO CHIEF OPERATING OFFICER Strategic
BONUS SCOREBOARD	Based on current financial performance	• Current corporate financial results • Strategic numbers • Strategic program results • Own departmental scorecard results, including personal objectives
BASE	Market competitive	Market competitive
OPTIONS	Unrestricted options granted each year equal to approximately 3/4 salary. Vest 1/3 in each of years 3, 4, 5.	One large amount every 3-5 years equal to 4-5x current salary. Vests in 1/3 increments in years 3, 4, 5. Unrestricted options given on time basis, restricted options based on strategic performance.
Percentage of one-year compensation based on: • strategic measures • current financial performance	 0 100%	 50% 50%
Percentage of long-term (5-year) compensation based on: • strategic results • financial results	 0 100%	 60% 40%

the team leader the bonus that the top team feels she should receive and then asking the team to allocate the rest.

Project Teams. The basis for their bonus is the same as for the program teams.

Core Process Teams. The basis for their bonus is the same as for the program teams until the objectives of the process redesign are met. They

Exhibit 18-8   Reward Suggestions

Cash	FUNCTIONAL DIRECTORS Ordinary	FUNCTIONAL DIRECTORS Strategic
BONUS SCOREBOARD	Based on weighted departmental scorecard	• Current corporate financial results • Departmental scorecard strategic results • Other departmental scorecard results • Personal objective results
BASE	Market competitive	Market competitive
OPTIONS	Unrestricted options granted each year equal to approximately 3/4 salary. Vest 1/3 in each of years 3, 4, 5.	One large amount every 3-5 years equal to 4-5x current salary. Vests in 1/3 increments in years 3, 4, 5. Unrestricted options given on time basis, restricted options based on strategic performance.
Percentage of one-year compensation based on: • Strategic measures • Current financial and short-term performance	Some Most	Depends on function
Percentage of long-term (5-year) compensation based on: • Strategic results • Financial results	Some Most	Depends on function

then switch over to a "gainsharing" formula if the process will be run by a team.[3]

Variations on a Theme

Not all situations are equal. Neither are all strategic compensation schemes. We see four basic strategic situations, in which the compensa-

---

[3] For a comprehensive look at team pay, see Steven E. Gross, *Compensation for Teams* (New York: AMACOM, 1995).

Exhibit 18-9 Sample Ordinary and Strategic Compensation Systems

Cash	LOWER-LEVEL Ordinary	LOWER-LEVEL Strategic
BONUS SCOREBOARD	Based on departmental or individual scorecard	• Current corporate financial results • Departmental scorecard results • Individual scorecard results, including personal objectives
BASE	Market competitive	Market competitive
OPTIONS	No options	Options to selective "leverage" personnel
Percentage of one-year compensation based on: • Strategic measures • Current financial and short-term performance	Some Most	Some Most
Percentage of long-term (5-year) compensation based on: • Strategic results • Financial and short-term results	Some Most	Some Most

tion schemes follow or deviate from the "norm" described in the preceding section:

1. *Bleeding company:* Losing substantial money and cash. In danger of going under.
2. *Stabilizing company that's planning for growth or experiencing initial growth:* Out of trouble. Financially on firmer ground, ready to begin planning for some growth and changes in the base business.

3. *Stable and growing company:* Stable over a long period of time with the resources to grow beyond its current modest rate.
4. *High-growth company in high-growth market:* Generally entrepreneurial with many opportunities, reasonably well funded, and using planning to focus its efforts.

What follows are variations from the norm. You can't lift one of these schemes from the pages of this book and install it. Each company needs to tailor the elements to its particular business, financial situation, and culture.

Bleeding Company

Company Situation. The company is at breakeven or losing money. Cash flow may be positive, but there is very little surplus. The company has viable products, services, and strategic competencies, but they are below competitive standards. The company is losing market share.

Job to Be Done. Stabilize the company financially. If cash flow is negative, aim at reversing that fast. Reorganize the balance sheet to minimize debt, sell off expendable assets, prune unprofitable products and services, and pare all costs to the bone. Then remove unproductive people, keeping only those who will be future high performers, hold the keys to the company's competitive competencies, or are needed to generate cash flow now. All of this has to be done without cutting muscle— key people, core competencies, and customer and supplier loyalty and goodwill.

Incentive Compensation. Target those people and organization units critical to survival. These will be the people working on key objectives: to increase revenue and gross profit, reduce costs on all fronts (including people cuts), trim product lines, improve cash management, increase production efficiency, and instill new values. Go through the organization chart and determine where the work is being done that will contribute most to achieving objectives. Certainly you'll include the top team, functional department heads and other key managers or supervisors reporting to the department heads, plus strategic program teams and teams working on cleaning up core processes.

Types of Incentives. Base salary plus cash bonus based on one-year results on very specific measures: cash, profitability, market performance, personnel count, and behaviors. Measures should be based on external best-of-class performance benchmarks. Using external benchmarks has two advantages. First, it tells the organization that the benchmarks are neither arbitrary nor unrealistic, and if the company is to become achieving, it will ultimately have to match what the competition is doing. Second, it prevents an underachieving company from setting lackluster objectives that may feel like a stretch for this company but fall way behind the competition.

Sales incentives will probably be based on revenue and gross profit as well as profitability increases. Cash bonuses for cross-functional teams in critical areas should be based on specific team results versus objectives. Team participants eligible for individual bonuses don't participate in team bonuses.

Bleeding companies may or may not offer stock options. If not, they are promised when the company is stabilized. This latter approach will further increase the incentive to get the company stabilized because employees will want to get options at the lowest possible price.

A regional bank, in the throes of a turnaround and led by a new chairman, changed the company's compensation system substantially. The chairman expanded incentive compensation to more than sixty people who would have strong influence on the turnaround. The annual cash payout was based on behavioral objectives as well as progress in meeting benchmark goals for becoming financially sound and building an infrastructure that could move the company forward.

After three years, when the bank was stabilized, he changed the objectives and the compensation system. The new objectives called for performance that matched that of industry leaders. The new compensation program, designed to encourage people to "think like a stockholder," combined competitive base salary with cash bonuses based on each year's results and long-term options. Individuals could take their bonus money and purchase long-term options, which the company matched one for one. The change in the bonus system refocused the organization on growth goals. Over five years, the company's stock price grew 14.5 times.

Stabilizing Company That's Planning for Growth or Experiencing Initial Growth

Company Situation. The company is experiencing a stable financial situation with sufficient access to cash to begin to grow. Its structure is sound. There is no excess overhead. Unproductive people and assets are gone.

Job to Be Done. Plan for future growth and begin to execute the plan.

Incentive Compensation. Target people in those functions critical to strategic growth, which means expanding the list included in the "bleeding" stage to all leverage managers and others with strong influence on growth—for example, marketing and technology.

Types of Incentives. This follows the "normal" case described in the preceding section. Stock options come back on the menu or at least more of them than in the bleeding case. Incentive compensation spreads to more people. The levels that can be earned go up somewhat. The basis on which incentives are paid shifts from "today," such as cash, to a combination of annual financial performance and long-term strategic performance, to the extent that it has been defined.

Spreading Ownership. Many companies feel it motivates employees for everyone in the company to own stock and make it easy to do so. One Fortune 500 company, having just emerged from a restructuring and regained market momentum, gave every employee one hundred shares of stock. The CEO wanted everyone to be an owner and to feel and act that way. He said that employee surprise, positive reaction, and pride in the company were palpable—and phenomenal. This is a wonderfully motivating and aligning way to get people to pull behind you when they've lived through the tough stuff and are now being asked to make the company's new direction work.

Another company allowed all employees to use up to 10 percent of their salary each year to purchase stock at 85 percent of the year's low price. Another company allowed its executives to purchase shares up to the full amount of their cash bonuses and then matched the shares one for one.

Stable and Growing Company

Company Situation. The company is stable and financially sound, often in a mature market, and is seeking ways to grow revenue and profitability. Many such companies have become lethargic and overweight, and their competencies are getting a bit ragged.

Job to Be Done. Clean the ship and mount a thrust forward. Usually, this requires a combination of cutting costs, pruning unprofitable products, and removing excess or unproductive people while developing and executing a strategic plan to put the company on a growth path.

Incentive Compensation. This case, too, now follows the normal model. The plan might be expanded to include a few more people and the amounts increased for cash bonuses and stock options if the company can afford it and deems it motivational.

A large superregional bank, revitalized and growing, offers top-level personnel a 50 percent cash bonus if goals are met each year. Every five years, they get stock grants, which vest in fifteen years. Middle levels in the bank can earn incentives of 15 to 30 percent. Individuals or groups in specific important jobs can earn 15 to 35 percent of their base each year for meeting their individual objectives. Although these bonus level are less than those for service and high-tech industries, they are quite good for a mature consolidation industry such as banking.

High-Growth Company in a High-Growth Market

Company Situation. The company is reasonably stable financially with sufficient access to capital to grow. Its market position is good, as are its products and services, but it may be a bit haphazardly organized. It is focused more on growth and getting the job done than on production or managerial efficiency.

Job to Be Done. Penetrate and lock in desirable market niches before anyone else does. The company must get out of peripheral products and niches, keep key people (like programmers and scientists) from leaving, get the company in the hands of "professional" management, and install solid information and control systems. Managers want to make a ton of money, because that's what they're all there for, and go public, if they haven't already, at the right time.

Incentive Compensation. Target people in functions and jobs critical to strategic growth.

Types of Incentives. To provide an incentive for long-term growth and put golden handcuffs on key staff, give substantial but infrequent blocks of stock options that don't vest for five to seven years. Reward short-term performance with cash incentives similar to those described in the preceding subsections for stabilizing companies and stable, growing companies.

Give incentive pay for high performance on very specific short- and long-term measures. Appropriate short-term measures include revenue, profitability, market performance, growth, and behaviors. Long-term payout may be based on strategic measures such as customer satisfaction, quality, market share, and product/service innovation.

Key cross-functional strategic teams get moderate cash bonuses based on specific team results versus objectives. Team bonuses do not go to team participants who are eligible for individual bonuses.

Who's Included. The incentives go to all the leverage people, including managers and individual contributors—that is, those with the clout to grow the company plus a few of the "supporting cast" considered critical. The list probably includes the top team, functional department heads, some lower-level functional people, strategic project teams, and work teams that are carrying out strategic process improvement.

Amount of Bonus. Growth companies are shy of cash. Salaries for entrepreneurial organizations are usually market-par or below-par, whereas incentive pay systems tend to have unique structures and to be lavish. One very successful health-care company pays top management a 100 to 400 percent cash bonus above salary annually, depending on the extent to which the company meets short-term goals. Percentages are lower but nonetheless lavish for management below the top team, with bonuses of 10 to 20 percent at the lowest supervisory levels, which don't receive bonuses at all in most organizations. Options in rapidly growing high-risk companies can also be lavish. In this particular health-care organization, even nurses supervising individual facilities have become millionaires.

A company in the property management business internationally pays out 35 percent of its pretax profit in bonuses that extend down to relatively low-level city managers. Even lower-level managers get options, and if the company beats its earnings-per-share objective by two cents at a given time, the options vest in two years instead of four. In addition, this company puts 10 percent of its after-tax profits into a profit-sharing plan for employees.

In each of these cases, the companies are highly decentralized and need to motivate relatively independent employees at all levels. Each looks for aggressive recruits, hires only the best, and quickly washes out those who don't measure up. Each company puts a high premium on training, and each is very successful.

The Acid Tests

Do you have the right plan or not? Taken from the list of strategic compensation plan criteria presented earlier in the chapter, here are the key tests:

■ *Does your plan motivate?* It will if the objectives are "stretch" but attainable and the amounts potentially substantial. In cash, anything below 10 to 20 percent for lower-level people and 50 to 60 percent for senior people won't noticeably change performance. If you are to get and keep the best people, the potential payoff has to be at least as good as, if not better than, that of competitors in your industry and labor market.

- *Is it worth it?* Calculate your five-year upside, probable, and downside results and factor in the cost of your incentive system. Are the potential gains far more than you're paying out? There are no guidelines here, but the most that I have seen incentive plans dilute pretax profits is 35 percent.

- *Does it retain the best people?* Is it is good enough to retain your very best people? It should be good enough to attract the very best recruits as well.

- *Is it flexible?* Can you change it quickly if the marketplace changes? Can you give spot cash or stock to someone who has done something exceptional? Can you provide incentives for one department that beats to a different drummer—for example, research and development or product development—on a basis different from the incentives used for the business side of the company?

- *Does it balance the short- and long-term?* Unless your company is bleeding to death, your compensation plan should encourage people to work on strategic programs as well as on producing the short-term earnings and cash you need to stay alive.

How to Put Together a Plan

The flowchart in Exhibit 18-10 outlines the general steps for putting a compensation plan together. But first, find a good compensation consulting organization. Compensation methods, accounting, and tax laws can be complicated and require expert advice. Then be prepared to:

1. *Develop a policy statement for your new compensation system.* Cover your business mission (return to profitability and position the company for growth), the key objectives (cash flow and profit), the philosophy of the compensation scheme (motivate short-term profitability without cutting muscle), and the use of cash bonuses at all leverage points to reward measurable performance in the direction of current objectives.

2. *Review strategic plan actionables.* Review the actionables and the plans they have spawned: priority issue programs, strategic objectives, and departmental plans. Your compensation plan—particularly, incentive compensation—must support these initiatives.

3. *Identify the organization units where the actionables will be accomplished.* Examine an organization chart to be sure you have identified all the departments, teams, and individuals with direct influence over your key tasks and objectives.

Exhibit 18-10 Developing a Strategic Compensation System

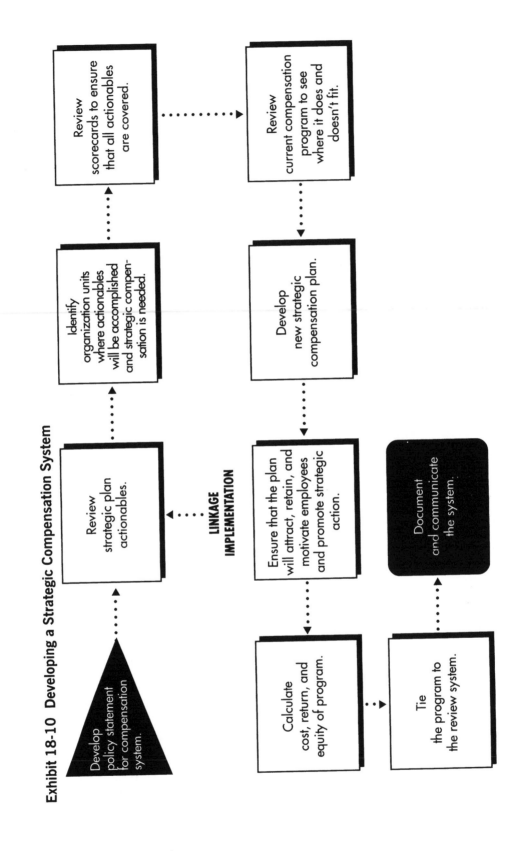

4. *Review the scorecards for the units where the action will take place.* Make sure they have an appropriate balance among strategic, operating, and behavioral objectives.

5. *Review your current compensation program.* Determine where it supports your new objectives and where it does not.

6. *Develop your new strategic compensation plan.* Base it on your new scorecards, confirming that it supports your desired balance among strategic, operating, and behavioral tasks and objectives.

7. *Verify that the plan will motivate.* Apply the probable payout to the scorecards for high-leverage departments, teams, and individuals to make sure that it is enough to motivate. Remember, at lower levels, 20 percent of base salary is very motivational; at middle levels, 20 to 30 percent; but at senior levels, 50 to 60 percent is the threshold.

8. *Calculate the cost, return, and equity of the program.* Make sure that you can afford your program by calculating its cost at maximum, median, and low payout. Compare organization units that are on incentive pay with those that aren't to ensure that you have not set up pay inequities that could cause significant motivational problems.

9. *Confirm that it's aligned with your review system.* Make sure the objectives on the scorecards are weighted to produce an overall payout that rewards only desired performance and behavior. Assume, for example, that you develop a system that provides your top team with bonuses of 40 percent of base pay based on corporate performance. Even if the organization meets the target, you need to be able to reduce the payout for an individual who does not meet several important individual goals.

10. *Document and communicate the system.* This must be done both in writing and verbally. The details of compensation systems can soon be forgotten, so a written communication is important. But the only way to make the program truly meaningful is to have supervisors explain it to employees using their actual scorecards.

Other Rewards

Of course, there are rewards other than money, and they should be used to the hilt. They can play a major role in delivering messages and motivating people. Take advantage of them to:

- Make people feel good about their achievements and about the organization, motivating them to even greater accomplishment.
- Set examples for others.
- Celebrate behaviors that exemplify the culture you want.

- Maintain and increase strategic momentum by showcasing excellence and creating competition.

Developing a Program

Although it doesn't need to be carved in stone, a recognition program deserves some organization. Here's one approach:

1. Think out in advance the goals and behaviors you want to support and the kinds of rewards you're willing to offer. Communicate these to the organization.
2. Put together a team representing a cross section of the organization to help develop the reward criteria and put their seal of approval on the program.
3. Ensure that everyone who meets the criteria is eligible to earn a reward.
4. Determine the mechanism for identifying eligible people.
5. Select one person, probably in human resources, to be the focal point for administering the program: keeping award materials, serving as the contact for those wanting to make an award, and doing the legwork to make the more complicated awards happen.

Events That Warrant Recognition and Reward

What should you recognize with a nonmonetary reward?[4] Here are some suggestions:

Best Achievement. This award recognizes, annually, the best strategic achievements from all fronts within the corporation. These might include the successful completion of priority issue programs, meeting strategic objectives, or the most inventive solution to a strategic problem. "Best Achievement" awards warrant a large public celebratory forum such as a dinner or a major meeting at which you set aside time to honor the recipients.

One major supermarket holds an annual two-day conference for its marketing and product management group. The conference features first-class speakers on topical subjects as well as entertainment. The highlight, however, is the singling out of the product managers whose strategic programs (1) had the greatest profit impact on the company, (2) were the most creative, and (3) were the most promising in meeting the

---

[4] A comprehensive list of potential rewards and how to put together a reward program is contained in a brief and excellent book: Donna Deeprose, *How to Recognize and Reward Employees* (New York: AMACOM, 1994).

company's objectives. The reward for the highest-impact program was a trip for two to Hawaii for a week.

Major Milepost. Successfully reaching a major milepost in a strategic program or in meeting strategic objectives merits widespread recognition. The achievement can be showcased at a quarterly all-hands meeting at which the chief operating officer and chief executive officer review strategic progress. It's a good idea to invite the successful team or individual to give a brief description of the accomplishment. An inexpensive gift—like a shirt or hat with a logo or message—serves as reminder of both the achievement and the moment of fame.

Of course, the event should get widespread recognition in the strategic newsletter, on the intranet, and via E-mail.

Quick Wins. Everyone agrees that quick wins early in a program are important and should be widely publicized. What warrants quick-win recognition? Here are some examples: A team expedites customer order entry before the reengineering program is far along; a sales rep brings home the first account in a new, strategically important distribution channel.

How might you reward such a team or individual? First, broadcast the accomplishment through the normal company communication channels. Then personalize the recognition by direct contact. A senior officer could attend a team meeting to congratulate the team and give each member a tangible quick-win token such as a coffee mug or paperweight. The sales rep could be invited to lunch by a "heavy" and given the same tokens of esteem.

Observed Behavior. When individuals or teams exhibit, way beyond the norm, the cultural behaviors you are trying to imbue in the organization, they deserve showcasing. For example, if creativity and innovation are values, make a big deal of it when a product development team shows extraordinary ability to come up with ideas and put them into effect. Highlight the team's accomplishments through the usual communication media, arrange lunch with the president, and present a tangible token to take home or display in the office.

Substantial Gifts. There are times when an achievement is so outstanding that a substantial gift award is warranted if cash is not appropriate. As one wag put it, make sure that the award passes the VCR test: If it doesn't cost at least as much as a topflight VCR, it will be considered cheap.

Exhibit 18-11   Reward Suggestions

MAJOR AWARDS
- ▼ Cash
- ▼ Trips
- ▼ Highlighting achievements in major company meetings

POWER AWARDS
- ▼ Lunch or dinner with the CEO/COO or senior officer
- ▼ Opportunity to present story to top management

MEDIA SHOWCASING
- ▼ Achievements featured via E-mail, in newsletter, or on intranet

HANDOUTS
- ▼ Coffee mugs
- ▼ Golf shirts
- ▼ Hats
- ▼ Desk paperweights
- ▼ Plaques

PERSONAL TOUCH
- ▼ Handwritten note
- ▼ Telephone call
- ▼ Pat on the back in person
- ▼ Mentioning achievement in front of others

GIFTS
- ▼ Dinner for two
- ▼ Candy, flowers, cigars, books, gourmet food
- ▼ Wine
- ▼ Theater, sporting event, music event tickets
- ▼ Gift related to individual's hobby
- ▼ Gift certificates to neat stores

Casual Programs

Do you need a highly orchestrated program to use nonmonetary rewards successfully? I don't think so. I think that the top team can, with an arsenal of tools, hand out recognition as it sees fit. For an individual or a team, there is nothing like receiving the personal recognition of a senior officer: a handwritten note, an invitation to lunch, a visit to tell them how well they're doing. These rewards aren't programmed, should come from the heart, and are highly motivational.

The only caveat is that spontaneous recognition has to be distributed equitably, lest it appear arbitrary or smacking of favoritism. If, for example, you take a program action plan team to dinner to celebrate an outstanding achievement, you'd better do the same for the next team that pulls off a notable feat. If you don't, you'll demoralize not only the second team but everyone who hears what happened.

■ ■ ■ ■ ■

Exhibit 18-11 is a brief shopping list of rewards that you can use spontaneously or as part of a formal program should you choose to mount one. Donna Deeprose's *How to Recognize and Reward Employees* and Joan P. Klubnik's *Rewarding and Recognizing Employees* have hundreds more suggestions from which to choose.[5]

Do

- Base both your short-term bonus compensation and a healthy portion of your long-term compensation on your interlocking scorecards. If an objective is worth putting on the scorecard, you should attach money to the resulting score.
- Make your system truly pay for performance. In the long run, you not only get superior performance, but you weed out the nonperformers, whose compensation will suffer.

Don't

- Go it alone in devising your compensation system. Use an in-house or hired expert, because you need to be certain that you're more than competitive and also because the tax implications of different schemes vary and can be costly to you and your employees.
- Forget nonmonetary rewards. You can get a big bang for very few bucks.

---

[5] Ibid; Joan P. Klubnik, *Rewarding and Recognizing Employees* (Chicago: Irwin, 1995).

PART *III*

Putting It All Together

The Implementation Process

Principle: Strategic plan implementation is most effective when all the implementation keys are in place and ready to go when the strategic plan is completed.

Why it's important: All the keys align the organization's actions with the plan, establish strong accountability, and reward success. Any late or missing pieces dilute these imperative components of strategic change.

How it's applied: Begin work on long-lead-time implementation keys when strategic planning starts. Phase in work on other keys so that an implementation plan meeting can be held within four to six weeks of strategic plan completion. Final implementation plans are agreed on at this meeting, and strategic and implementation plans are kicked off.

Expected results: With the implementation keys in place, you can expect quick movement through phase 1 of change (recognition of the need) into the second phase (muddling and unfreezing), where the real change begins. Introducing the interlinked implementation keys at one time has maximum motivational and emotional impact on the organization. The resulting actions—particularly, quick removal of problem people and other barriers—will accelerate implementation.

Strategic and Implementation Planning

We've examined each of the keys to implementation separately. Now the question is, how do you put them together in a process that works in concert with your strategic plan?

The implementation plan should be developed as an integral part of the strategic planning effort for two reasons:

1. It takes advantage of the valuable thinking that goes on during planning. If you wait, this thinking will be partly lost when the time finally comes to turn strategy into actions.
2. If you have a strategic plan but no corresponding process to implement it, you'll probably fall back on the same tools you used with only modest success in the past. Unfortunately, many organizations develop a plan and then expect to pull off significant change using antiquated compensation, communication, and accountability systems, managed by people with the same competencies they had twenty years ago. It won't work.

Look at it this way. The strategic plan is a beautiful twelve-meter America's Cup hull; the implementation plan is the sails and the crew. One doesn't get very far without the other.

Take the time to develop a complete strategic and implementation package. Doing them together may add eight to ten weeks to your planning effort. But it's worth it. You'll have a plan you can implement instead of a two-month "wonder plan" that ends up unimplemented in everyone's drawer. We've seen too many situations in which people complained that planning and the plan were no good, when the plan may have been excellent, but the implementation and leadership to implement it were at fault.

Parallel Development

The accompanying exhibit shows the entire strategic and implementation planning process, with implementation planning conducted, as it should be, in parallel with strategic planning. The dark blocks are part of a standard strategic planning process. The medium-shade blocks are part of the recommended strategic planning process and a necessity in the implementation planning process. The lower blocks are solely implementation planning steps. I'll assume that you are familiar with the standard strategic planning process (the dark boxes) and describe the implementation sequences.

A "first" strategic plan, a ground-up effort starting with extensive market analysis and strategy development, normally takes three to five months to develop.[1] Integrating implementation planning will extend the time to five to seven months.

[1] The complete strategic planning process is explained in C Davis Fogg, *Team-Based Strategic Planning* (New York: AMACOM, 1994).

Strategic and Implementation Planning Process

Situation Analysis
- 7-factor analysis
- Market segmentation
- Competitive strategy
- Industry analysis
- Internal analysis
- Core process evaluation
- Financial, numerical analysis
- Barrier audit

Departmental Planning
- Corporate priority issues
- Departmental priority issues
- Strategic priority issues
- Operating priority issues
- Infrastructure priority issues

Priority Issues Meeting
- Corporate/competitive strategy
- Start direction statement
- Corporate priority issues
- Departmental direction and priority issues
- Start corporate objectives
- Accountability system design
- Progress report—compensation system
- Results barrier audit

Resource Allocation Meeting
- Complete direction statement
- Corporate priority funding
- Approve departmental plans/funding
- Corporate strategic objectives
- New organization structure
- Leverage leaders
- Leader competencies
- Progress report on compensation

Implementation Plan Meeting
- Organization structure
- People
- Leadership
- Accountability
- Reward
- Resisters
- Communications
- Severance and outplacement
- Training and development
- Testing programs

Budget

Final Version
- Departmental plans
- Priority issue action plans
- Corporate objectives

Individual Accountability

Departments
- Complete strategic and ongoing business plans.

Strategic Priority Issue Teams
- Develop corporate program action plans.

Individuals
- Define their part of departmental plans and corporate teams.

Design communication plan.

Design leadership plan.

Develop training plan.

Define values, competencies, culture.

Analyze/plan organization structure and people needs.

Design reward system.

Design accountability and review system; run trial.

Implement communication plan.

Implement people structure and rewards plan.

Implement leadership plan.

Implement training plan.

IMPLEMENT

REVIEW

SYSTEMS

Organizing to Develop the Plans

The Strategic Plan

Developing the strategic plan alone usually involves the following groups:

- *Marketing team:* This team or individual performs the external analysis, market segmentation, and competitive analysis and recommends the company's strategic alternatives and ultimate competitive strategy.
- *Financial team:* This team does the "numbers" work, including financial forecasts and financial evaluation of any designated products, markets, customers, or core processes.
- *Functional departments:* They prepare their input for the corporate plan and develop their own departmental strategic and operating priorities.
- *Top team:* Its members prepare their own private view of the organization's priority issues.
- *Priority issue program teams:* These teams flesh out the action steps for the approved strategic priority issues and implement the program.

The Implementation Plan

Developing the implementation plan involves adding the following teams or individuals, who are responsible for putting together their assigned plans and for seeing that the plans are effectively executed and adjusted as needed over the first few years of strategic change:

- *Organization team,* which takes responsibility for (1) defining corporate values and culture, (2) defining job competencies for key positions, (3) defining the new organization structure and staffing needs, (4) preparing the leverage leadership plan, (5) removing resisters, and (6) performing a barrier audit
- *Accountability team,* which takes responsibility for developing (1) the accountability system, (2) the reward system, and (3) severance and outplacement packages
- *Communication person or team,* often a team of two—the CEO and a marketing person—who put together the initial and annual communication and feedback plan
- *Training person or team,* which pulls together and sources all the training that will be needed both during the preplanning stage and after the plan kickoff

How many people does it take to develop the implementation plan? That depends on the size of the company and the use of outside talent. The bulk of the implementation tasks fall into the human resources functional area. Small to medium-size companies—say up to $200 million—usually don't have lots of time and staff, particularly in the human resources area, to spare for implementation teams. In addition, the amount of work to be done—interviews, for example—is less in small companies than in big ones. Small companies therefore often assign one person as the "team leader" and supplement that individual with a consultant from the outside who can do most of the legwork for him or her. Larger companies with significant marketing and human resources staffs can do the bulk of the work internally.

The following subsections present the steps in developing the implementation plan, linked to development of the strategic plan. Implementation planning steps that require strategy inputs before they can be completed are time-phased appropriately. The timing of the implementation teams' tasks (that is, who does what, when) is shown in the accompanying exhibit.

Step 1: Prior to the Start of Planning

Training Team

The team or individual handling training develops or sources training in the strategic planning process and departmental planning so that all who will be involved are adequately trained in the process and their part in it.

Step 2: From Situation Analysis to the Priority Issues Meeting

Strategic planning starts with a situation analysis and departmental planning. At the same time, the organization team begins the following three implementation tasks, which have long lead times:

Organization Team

1. *Defining values:* The organization team defines the future values that should drive the company's culture and will be central to the direction statement. It conducts interviews with select members of the organization and perhaps uses an organization cultural and strategic survey to identify current values and new values perceived to be needed. Members of the organization team can work with the marketing team developing competitive strategy to identify the values that will be needed to compete in the future external environment and to pinpoint those held by best-of-class companies and competitors. The resulting value set and

(Text continues on page 408.)

Timing of Implementation Teams' Tasks

	Month		Priority Issues Meeting	Month		Resource Allocation Meeting	Month		Imple-mentation Meeting
	1	2		3	4		5	6	
Organization									
1. Define corporate values and culture.	●		⊗						
2. Define job competencies for key positions.		●				⊗			
3. Define new organization structure and key staffing needs.				●		⊗			
4. Plan for leverage leaders in new organization.				●		⊗			
5. Remove resisters.									
6. Barrier audit.	●		⊗	●					⊗
Accountability									
1. Develop the accountability system.									
a. Overall system design	●		⊗						
b. Complete system			●						⊗
2. Develop the compensation and reward system.									
a. Progress report		●				⊗			
b. Final recommendation						●			⊗
3. Establish severance and outplacement packages.	●								⊗

	Month		Priority Issues Meeting	Month		Resource Allocation Meeting	Month		Imple-mentation Meeting
	1	2		3	4		5	6	
Communication									
1. Develop initial and annual communication and feedback plan							●		⊗
Training									
1. Training and development programs				●					⊗
2. Leadership training and development programs (with organization teams)				●					⊗
3. Testing programs for new hires, internal promotion and leadership, and professional development.				●					⊗

tight definitions of each value are presented for discussion at the priority-setting meeting during the discussion of the direction statement.

2. *Identifying job competencies:* The organization team determines
for the organization overall and for at least three leadership levels—
senior, middle, and lower—the future job competencies that will lead
to success. It describes the behaviors that must result from these competencies to spell success for your company. This involves interviewing
individuals at the three leadership levels, preferably including both
those who have excelled and those who haven't, and identifying the
handful of competencies that drive success. Talking to other companies
with competency programs at this point is very fruitful. Assessing competencies needed in light of proposed competitive strategies is a must.
Once the competencies are selected, the behaviors that must result from
the competencies are carefully described. These competencies will be
used to judge the progress and potential of existing employees, design
individual employee development programs, select new employees,
and help determine the form and staffing of the organization structure.
The competencies will be discussed and agreed on at the resource allocation meeting.

3. *Performing a barrier audit:* The organization team holds focus
groups and conducts individual interviews to identify organizational
impediments to change, such as policies, procedures, and decision-
making methods. Some of these interviews have to be held after the
priority issues meeting, so the team can ask, "Given our new strategy,
what impediments do you see?" Although any group could conduct
these interviews, it makes sense for the organization team to handle this
task—first, because the team will be interfacing with a large number of
employees in its competencies survey and the addition of a few more
questions is only a slight burden and, second, because the answers will
be important in designing the organization and its "lubricants," one of
this team's later tasks. The barriers will be presented at the priority issues meeting.

Accountability Team

Accountability system: The team can begin to design the accountability system at the beginning of the planning process. The scope of the
design should embrace the top team, departments, program teams, and
individuals. The effectiveness of the existing accountability system is
examined. A sampling of employees, departmental personnel, and the
top management team are interviewed to find out (1) for what they as
individuals and, where relevant, as an organization unit are actually
held accountable, (2) how and when they are held accountable, (3) the

type of system that makes sense for them, and (4) where accountability works (and why) and where it breaks down (and why).

The process itself—with formats for and examples of scorecards, objective-setting procedures, job descriptions, review formats, and a training course—can be designed and then discussed at the priority-setting meeting. At that meeting, the remaining information needed to complete the process is presented: (1) the final set of corporate values and (2) the key result areas (KRAs) and measures that will be used for the overall business, departments, and program teams.

Step 3: Priority Issues Meeting

The following implementation items get added to the normal agenda, shown in the accompanying exhibit:

- *Barrier audit results:* The results are discussed before strengths and weaknesses as an input to the SWOTs (corporate strengths, weaknesses, opportunities, and threats) and priority issues sections.
- *Definition of values and key job competencies:* These are discussed and used as an input for choosing corporate values.
- *Accountability system:* A flowchart of the entire system and the elements to be included at each level—top team, departments, program teams, and individuals—is discussed. Agreement is reached on: (1) scorecards for each level, (2) KRAs and measures and values mandated by the top team for each level, and (3) the annual accountability cycle.

Step 4: Between the Priority Issues Meeting and the Resource Allocation Meeting

Organization Team

- *Organization structure:* Now that the corporate strategy has been agreed on during the priority issues meeting, the organization team (1)

Priority Issues Meeting Agenda

- ▼ Corporate/competitive strategy
- ▼ Agreement on direction statement elements
- ▼ Corporate strategic priority issues
- ▼ Approval of department strategic and operating priority issue
- ▼ Corporate objectives started
- ▼ Discussion of barriers audit results
- ▼ Review of progress on accountability system design
- ▼ Compensation system progress report

---

develops alternative structures to implement the strategy based on the strategy, the new work to be done, and the new competencies needed to accomplish the new work and (2) recommends a structure.

■ *Leadership competencies:* The team assigns future competencies to each leverage leadership position on the new organization chart. It *ABCD*s each leader/manager in the company who is a possible candidate for a leverage position. The assessment includes prior performance, consultation with current and prior supervisors, and 360-degree testing specifically for this purpose. The outcome focuses heavily on the extent to which each candidate possesses or can quickly develop the competencies required by the new job.

The assessment is particularly critical in two areas. First, is the person exceptionally strong in the primary leadership competencies needed to lead strategic change? The individual should be strong in *all* the strategic and managerial traits for his level in the company. He must be particularly well developed in trustworthiness, integrity, honesty, power to persuade and motivate, bias for action, toughness and persistence, accountability, and high standards. Without reasonably well developed traits in these areas, an individual will fail as a change agent in a leverage position. Second, will the person be an enthusiastic supporter of the change plan? There is no room for skeptics or unbelievers or resisters in leverage positions. The organization team then recommends who should occupy leverage positions in the new structure and, if outside hires will be necessary, what their qualifications should be.

The preceding activities continue until the implementation meeting, at which they are presented and discussed.

■ *Leadership development:* The organization team works with the training and development team to define the leadership testing and development program.

■ *Resisters:* Although not a primary assignment at this point, the organization team should ask managers and interviewees about people and functions in the organization who are resisting the change effort or are likely to do so. Probable resisters and their disposition will be discussed at the implementation meeting.

Accountability Team

Reward system: The accountability team starts work on the new reward system now that the key elements driving it have been determined—the organization's vision and strategic objectives, the industry and businesses it will be in, its grand strategies from internal development through acquisition, the key result areas and measures at key levels in the organization, the corporate values, and key job competencies. The team can, should it choose, start work before this point, looking at other companies' reward systems and getting comparative studies of compensation systems in the industries in which the company participates or intends to participate.

Training and Development Team

- *Training:* The team starts developing indoctrination training based on the strategy and direction statement. It starts sourcing immediately postplan training, such as leverage manager training, team development, and process reengineering based on priority issues and corporate strategy. It also starts work on evergreen training.

- *Development:* The training team starts defining leadership training and development techniques now that strategy, values, and needed job skills and competencies are known. It works with the organization team on this task.

- *Testing and screening:* The team begins work on testing and screening instruments for hiring, promotion, and internal management and leadership development programs.

Step 5: Resource Allocation Meeting

The following items are added to the normal resource allocation meeting agenda, shown in the accompanying exhibit:

- *Organization structure:* The organization team makes its recommendations. Should the organization structure be changed? To what and why? When?
- *Leadership:* Leaders and managers are given ABCD ratings using the organization team's conclusions as a base. Decisions are made regarding who the leverage managers will be in the new structure and what will happen with the remaining, nonleverage individuals (grow their skills? terminate them?).
- *Reward:* A status update on the development of the reward system is presented. No decisions are scheduled at this point.

Resource Allocation Meeting Agenda

▼ Complete corporate direction statement
▼ Corporate priority issue selection and resource allocation
▼ Departmental plan approval and resource allocation
▼ Corporate strategic objectives
▼ Leader competencies
▼ ABCD leaders/managers
▼ Leverage leader selection
▼ Update on compensation and reward system

Step 6: Between the Resource Allocation Meeting and the Implementation Plan Meeting

Organization Team

■ *Leadership plan:* The organization team works with the training team to develop a leadership succession schedule, testing, and a training and development process for managers and leaders.

■ *Resisters and C and D players:* The organization team gives top management a framework for identifying resisters and C and D players in the organization, pointing out that if these individuals are identified and dealt with during round one of layoffs, the organization will move forward more efficiently.

Accountability Team

■ *Reward system:* The accountability team completes the compensation and reward system based on corporate strategy, organization structure, and industry norms.

■ *Severance:* The team develops severance packages for (1) voluntary early retirement, (2) involuntary early retirement, and (3) outplacement options.

Training and Development

■ *Training:* The training and development team completes the schedule of postplanning training needed to directly support the plan as well as the schedule and sourcing of evergreen training. It recommends professional (for example, finance, marketing, technical management) development programs and sources.

The team also outlines in detail the amount of training that people in general categories of jobs—clerical, executive assistant, sales rep, computer technician, supervisor—should get each year and what a progressive training program might look like over the years for several typical career paths outside of management and leadership.

■ *Leadership development:* The training and development team works with the organization team to complete the leadership selection, training, and development program.

Communication Team

■ *Initial announcement:* The communication team or person prepares scripts and players involved in the initial announcement of the plan. This includes describing how the script will be cascaded down throughout the organization by supervisors to make the plan relevant to each organization unit and providing mechanisms for feedback from employees on the initial communication.

- *Continuing communication:* The team prepares the communication plan for the year.

- *Good news plan:* The team prepares communication methods to get the good news out when plan benchmarks are made and early wins happen, working in conjunction with the rewards team, which coordinates appropriate rewards.

- *Bad news plan:* The team prepares communications to be used when the first wave of layoffs takes place and if major plan objectives are thwarted or delayed.

Step 7: Implementation Plan Meeting

The accompanying exhibit shows the agenda for the implementation plan meeting. This meeting is not part of the standard strategic planning process, so all the topics are new.

After the Implementation Plan Meeting

After the implementation plan meeting, begin immediately to:

- Communicate the plan and what it means for the company's ability to compete in the outside world. Announce the direction statement, its meaning, and how, if followed, it will make the company and its people a world-class organization. Hit vision, values, and strategy hard. Announce supporting actions: (1) any changes in the organization structure and key players, (2) the new compensation system, (3) the new accountability system, and (4) the new training system.

- Communicate what's in it for employees. Point out the difference between people benefits in world-class, highly competitive companies and average-performing companies in base compensation, extra compensation, perks, atmosphere, physical surroundings, training and development, and benefits and retirement plans. Emphasize that all is earned, not given.

Implementation Plan Meeting Agenda

▼ Compensation and reward system
▼ Resisters or C's and D's to be dealt with immediately
▼ Severance and retirement packages
▼ Training, testing, and leadership development program
▼ Communication program

- Train employees in the new accountability, compensation, and reward systems.

- Kick off the setting of individual accountabilities.

- Make any planned personnel, product line, staff function, or business-unit cuts immediately.

During the First Year

During the plan's first year, struggle aside, there will be signal events. Poor performers and resisters will be separated. Poor-value-added products, functions, and people will go. New people will join the organization to fill key gaps. Parts of the organization will get energized by achieving early wins on strategic programs or in the course of ordinary business. You will find some outstanding performers you never knew you had. Some people considered outstanding in the past will fall on their faces. Best of all, if you've planned well, you will have met or come close to meeting most of your operating and strategic objectives and weathered the turmoil of the first stage of taking the company apart and putting it back together again.

It's absolutely vital to keep the pressure on and to keep the bar high. Set and maintain the highest standards. Make sure that the early wins happen. Don't back off the game plan, no matter how hard people try to persuade you to do so. It is critical that people see progress, not just paper plans and dislocation of people. Keep communication levels exceptionally high and communication channels open in both directions.

The Second Year

Developing the second plan, after twelve to eighteen months, is not difficult. First, all of the hard analytical work was done for the first-year plan. Unless conditions in the outside world have changed drastically, you don't need more analytical work. Second, the second-year plan is a continuation and an update of the first because it is very unlikely that your priority strategic issues have changed. What will change is what you do about them given your progress in resolving them during the first year.

For the second-year strategic plan, ask: What has changed in the outside world and inside environment? How does it affect our objectives and priority issues? Then revise your priority issue programs to reflect progress in the last year and agree on objectives and action steps for the coming year. If there is a new priority issue for some reason, develop a plan for it and get on with it. For the implementation plan, review the effectiveness of each part of the plan—training, development, reward, leadership, and communication—and fine-tune it.

The accompanying flowcharts show a typical second-year planning process.

Some Final Thoughts on Implementation Planning

Small Companies and Big Ones

Obviously, the implementation plan seems like an overwhelming burden, and indeed, it is not easy and takes time to accomplish. Small to medium-size companies have neither the time nor the internal resources to accomplish everything necessary in a short period of time. They're not gargantuan organizations like Microsoft or Hewlett-Packard, which have an abundance of such resources in-house.

Here are two pieces of advice. First, use outside resources to help you do a good deal of the implementation planning. When you really think about it, on a cost versus long-range benefit basis, they're dirt cheap. Second, lengthen the planning process. There is nothing that says that your first plan must be finished on a given date to fit into your budget cycle or by the end of the year when the board wants it. Don't lengthen it so much, however, that you lose momentum.

The Role of Human Resources

It should come as no surprise that virtually all the keys to implementation:

- Are within the traditional bailiwick of human resources
- Are not one-time events but involve processes such as compensation, accountability, development of leaders, and team management that must constantly be maintained and updated
- Focus on putting the right people in the right places, motivating them, maintaining and upgrading skills, and providing leadership

This, of course, underscores the importance of the human resources function, whose strategic role in change is noted in the accompanying exhibit. It behooves those organizations that intend to lead in continuous change to hire the very best human resources talent, whether it's a single individual, outside resources, or a large internal staff. Indeed, in some organizations, the administrative and facilitation responsibility for strategic planning is placed human resources because it (1) is a proc-

(Text continues on page 418.)

Process Overview for Second and Subsequent Years

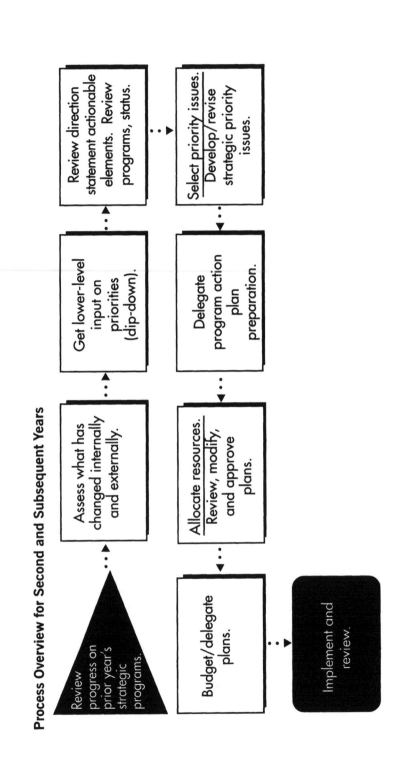

Detailed Second-Year Planning Process

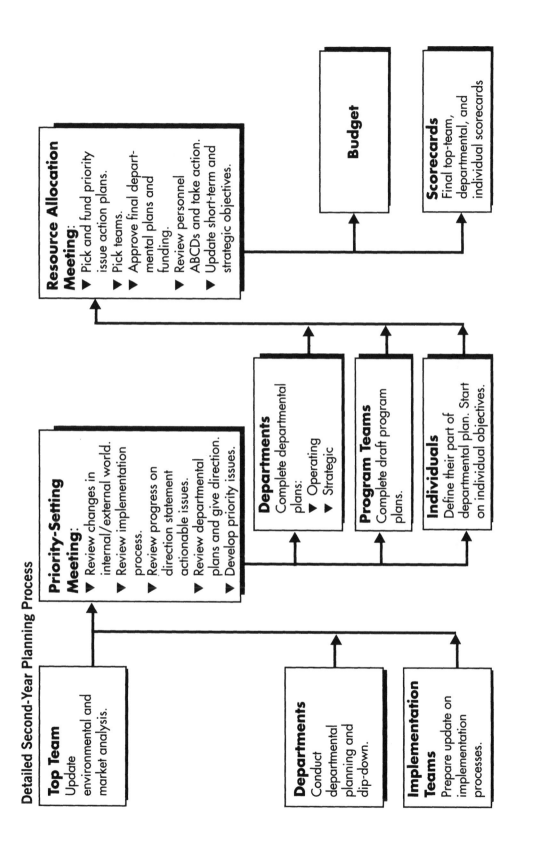

Top Team
Update environmental and market analysis.

Priority-Setting Meeting:
▶ Review changes in internal/external world.
▶ Review implementation process.
▶ Review progress on direction statement actionable issues.
▶ Review departmental plans and give direction.
▶ Develop priority issues.

Departments
Conduct departmental planning and dip-down.

Implementation Teams
Prepare update on implementation processes.

Departments
Complete departmental plans:
▶ Operating
▶ Strategic

Program Teams
Complete draft program plans.

Individuals
Define their part of departmental plan. Start on individual objectives.

Resource Allocation Meeting:
▶ Pick and fund priority issue action plans.
▶ Pick teams.
▶ Approve final departmental plans and funding.
▶ Review personnel ABCDs and take action.
▶ Update short-term and strategic objectives.

Budget

Scorecards
Final top-team, departmental, and individual scorecards.

Role of Human Resources in Change

▼ Internal diagnosis
▼ Individual and organizational testing and assessment
▼ Leadership development
▼ Strategic compensation design and implementation
▼ Leverage skills assessment
▼ Strategic long-term skills and gap evaluation
▼ Strategic succession planning
▼ Recruiting
▼ Skills training
▼ Education
▼ Strategic planning
▼ Plan implementation
▼ Accountability system design and implementation
▼ Interventions
▼ Training, facilitating, and preparing teams
▼ General sounding board/lubricant for all
▼ Strategic plan progress communication programs

ess of the type that that function is used to maintaining, (2) is heavily dependent on people's cooperation and inputs, and (3) ultimately leads to the human resourcesdriven implementation processes.

What You Get Out of It

What do you get out of a complex and difficult process of planning and implementation? I would like to own stock in every company that we've helped with strategic planning. Those that are public have performed exceptionally well compared to their peers and the marketplace. They had leadership, made up their minds to change, developed a strategic plan for direction, and then toughed it out during the implementation process. We don't take credit for their success. Their leadership, people, and the focus provided by good strategic and implementation planning made it happen.

> ### *Do*
>
> ▪ Conduct strategic planning and implementation planning in parallel, no matter how painful it is the first year.
> ▪ Use internal teams to install and drive strategic programs in (1) organization structure, (2) accountability, (3) compensation and reward, (4) training and development, and (5) communication.
> ▪ Bring in outsiders if you don't have internal expertise in or-

ganization or compensation. The benefits far outweigh the costs.

- Spend as much time during the first year of implementation worrying about how the processes, systems, organization structure, and leadership are working as you do thinking about bottom-line results. If the former are right, results will follow.

Don't

- Omit any of the 18 keys to implementation. Every CEO we talked to reinforced this conclusion. All eventually must be used, and they are more powerful used quickly in concert rather than serially over time.
- Back off from implementing the entire system as soon as possible. If your staff screams about time and timing and you think there is genuine justification for the noise, present the job to be done and let them establish timing that you and they can live with.
- Back off from confronting organization structure, leadership, and disposition of people—particularly, resisters and poor producers—right off the bat. This is absolutely essential to change.
- Back off your standards or your program. Many will try to talk you out of them. Don't back off.

Index

32710150R00249

Made in the USA
Middletown, DE
14 June 2016